Handbook of Cost Accounting Theory and Techniques

Handbook of Cost Accounting Theory and Techniques

Ahmed Belkaoui

Q

Quorum Books
New York · Westport, Connecticut · London

Library of Congress Cataloging-in-Publication Data

Belkaoui, Ahmed, 1943-
  Handbook of cost accounting theory and techniques / Ahmed
Belkaoui.
      p. cm.
  Includes index.
  ISBN 0-89930-583-0 (alk. paper)
  1. Cost accounting. I. Title.
HF5686.C8B355 1991
657'.42—dc20
90-45142

British Library Cataloguing in Publication Data is available.

Library of Congress Catalog Card Number: 90-45142
ISBN: 0-89930-583-0

First published in 1991

Quorum Books, 88 Post Road West, Westport, CT 06881
An imprint of Greenwood Publishing Group, Inc.

Printed in the United States of America

The paper used in this book complies with the
Permanent Paper Standard issued by the National
Information Standards Organization (Z39.48-1984).

10 9 8 7 6 5 4 3 2 1

To Hedi and Janice

D' indigène à immigrant, rien n' a changé, et tout a changé

Contents

Tables and Figures

Tables

Figures

Preface

In writing the *Handbook of Cost Accounting Theory and Techniques,* my goal was to create an accounting text that would combine cost accounting theory and techniques with theories and techniques from other related disciplines on the basis of their usefulness to cost accounting decisions.

The book is intended to meet the needs of both practitioners and business students by providing a thorough exposure to both the traditional and the new dimensions of cost accounting. I believe that this book defines an expanded scope and new boundaries of cost accounting by presenting a multidimensional framework for the discipline.

First, the fields of cost accounting, economics, behavioral sciences, operations research, statistics, and mathematics provide the tools as well as the concepts necessary for the classification, accumulation, and reporting of relevant data for internal decision making as well as the tools and concepts for the interpretation and evaluation of resulting decisions. This approach reflects the state of the art in cost accounting as a discipline involved with the choice of the best decision on the basis of the best available information.

Second, the standard cost accounting techniques are complemented by other possible approaches to problems. The organization of the material is intended to stress not only the descriptive but also the normative solutions to cost accounting problems, giving to cost accounting the status of a legitimate multidisciplinary line of inquiry.

Finally, the book covers the cost accounting techniques as they affect (1) the planning and control of routine and nonroutine decisions and (2) inventory valuation and income determination. In addition to the conventional accounting techniques, this book covers the major developments that characterize the new manufacturing accounting. These developments include the following:

1. Behavioral, organizational, and decisional foundations (see chapter 1).

2. Economic model of cost, labor as a fixed cost, long-term variable costs, and fixed costs (see chapter 2).

3. A thorough coverage of variance analysis.

4. A presentation of flexible manufacturing systems (see chapter 14).

5. A presentation of accounting for quality costs (see chapter 15).

6. A thorough presentation of variance proration in a case involving beginning inventories (see chapter 16).

7. Pricing and product profitability analysis (see chapter 17).

8. Behavioral considerations in cost allocation (see chapter 18).

No book can be written without the help of numerous individuals and organizations. A special note of appreciation is extended to my teaching and research assistants, Pamela Mathew, Kelly Karabatsos, Liz Ramilis, Arun Hariharan, and Jyh-herng Hsieh, for their cheerful and intelligent assistance. Finally to Hedi and Janice, thanks for making every moment a treasure.

The Conceptual Foundations of Cost Accounting

Accountants today occupy many of the top positions in their firms. Their role of decision maker affects every facet of the organization, whether the organization is a proprietorship, partnership, or profit or nonprofit corporation. In response to the expanding role of accountants, *cost accounting* (also called management accounting) is becoming increasingly multidimensional. It rests not only on accounting but also on organizational, behavioral, decisional, and other foundations.[1] An understanding of these foundations is necessary to an understanding of the accountants' new role.

This chapter examines the conceptual foundations of cost accounting. In doing so, it illustrates the multidimensional scope of cost accounting and establishes a frame of reference for the entire text.

Upon completion of this chapter, you should be able to do the following:

1. Differentiate between the various classes of accounting, define cost accounting, and identify the concepts and qualitative characteristics of information that form the emerging cost accounting conceptual framework.
2. Identify the elements of the organizational structure that may affect the ways cost accounting will be exercised: the organizational chart, the line and staff relationships, and the role of the controller in the organization.
3. Identify five theories of motivation and their implications for cost accounting: need theory, two-factor theory, value/expectancy theory, achievement theory, and inequity theory.
4. Identify the conceptual frameworks for viewing decisions and decision systems proposed in the cost accounting and information systems literature.

1.1 THE ACCOUNTING FOUNDATIONS

1.1.1 Classes of Accounting

Cost accounting is traditionally and justifiably considered a unique and distinct accounting function, different from the other main accounting function, financial accounting. An understanding of the many facets of accounting will clarify the scope of cost accounting.

Accounting is a process of identifying, measuring, recording, classifying, interpreting, and communicating economic information to facilitate decision making by its users. Information is produced and disseminated for two distinct but closely related purposes: (1) reporting to those outside the organization who have a legitimate interest in its affairs (financial accounting, tax accounting, and auditing) and (2) making decisions within the organization (internal or cost accounting).

Financial accounting strives to provide necessary and specific information to external users. Its main tasks involve recording, classifying, and communicating the transactions of an entity by issuing periodic financial statements (usually annually or quarterly, but sometimes monthly). These statements include the balance sheet as an expression of the firm's financial position, the income statement as an expression of the firm's financial performance, and the statement of changes in financial position as an expression of the firm's financial conduct. Financial accounting must operate within set boundaries and must strictly adhere to generally accepted accounting principles (GAAP).

Tax accounting supplies necessary information to both top management and the Internal Revenue Service. It determines the tax liability of the firm on an annual and quarterly basis. The information is conveyed in federal forms 1040 and 1120. Tax accounting rests on rules governed by the Internal Revenue Code in the United States and on Revenue Canada in Canada.

Auditing provides information to top management and the public, mainly through opinions on the conformity, fairness, and consistency of the firm's financial statements. The expression of opinion, referred to as the *attest function of the auditor,* reports that the financial statements are "fairly presented, in conformity with generally accepted accounting principles, applied on a consistent basis." The auditor's opinion is prepared annually in accordance with generally accepted auditing standards.

Cost accounting strives to provide pertinent information to the firm's managers. It is charged with the following tasks:

1. Preparation and execution of plans and budgets, defined as *planning*.
2. Cost accumulation to determine inventories and cost of goods sold, defined as *product-costing*.
3. Income determination and reporting, a subset of *financial accounting* or *external reporting*.
4. Preparation of performance reports to assist in the control of operations, defined as *control*.
5. Preparation of information for short- and long-term decisions. Various questions must be considered when examining routine decision problems: What is the decision to be made? What is the best rule for making the decision? What information is required in

making the decision? How accurate must that information be? How frequently should the information be supplied? What is the most logical source for generating the information? How can the information best be obtained and transmitted to the user?

6. *Feedback* of information on performance to subordinates and superiors.

Each of these cost accounting tasks is essential to managerial processes. Planning is achieved through the preparation of plans and budgets, coordinating through cost accumulation and periodic reporting, and controlling through the preparation of performance reports and the comparison of budgeted and actual results. The deviations of actual results from budgets are called *variances*. They are used by managers when relying on *management by exception*, which is the technique of focusing on deviations that need to be controlled and ignoring areas that seem to be running smoothly. The implementation of these tasks requires the design of a cost accounting system to supply relevant and timely information for both routine and nonrecurring decisions.

In assessing the appropriateness of a cost accounting system for a routine decision area, the following deficiencies are common:

1. *Overinformation,* where too much information is supplied to the user.
2. *Underinformation,* where there is a lack of adequate information to make an appropriate decision.
3. *Untimely information,* where the information comes too late for the user to benefit.

Each of these deficiencies must be corrected in the design of a cost accounting system.

1.1.2 Toward a Cost Accounting Conceptual Framework

In contrast to financial accounting, which rests on techniques conforming to generally accepted accounting principles, cost accounting relies on techniques from various disciplines and is not governed by generally accepted accounting principles. The Committee on Management Accounting of the American Accounting Association (AAA) developed a definition of *management (cost) accounting:*

The application of appropriate techniques and concepts in processing the historical and projected economic data of an entity to assist management in establishing plans for reasonable economic objectives and in the making of rational decisions with a view toward achieving these objectives. It includes the methods and concepts necessary for effective planning, for choosing among alternative business actions, and for control through the evaluation and interpretation of performance. Its study involves consideration of ways in which accounting information may be accumulated, synthesized, analyzed, and presented in relation to specific problems, decisions, and day-to-day tasks of business management.[2]

These techniques may be drawn from such fields as accounting, mathematics, sociology, psychology, and economics. A conceptual framework is necessary within which qualitative characteristics of information can guide the development of cost accounting techniques. These techniques will then be considered good not only because they are used in practice but also because they are based on accepted concepts and qualitative characteristics of information—they conform to a cost accounting conceptual framework.

Cost Accounting Concepts

An accepted, exhaustive list of cost accounting concepts does not yet exist. However, the 1972 American Accounting Association Committee on Courses in Managerial Accounting identifies measurement, communication, information, system, planning, feedback, control, and cost behavior as the cost accounting concepts that represent a necessary, if not a minimum, foundation for a cost accounting conceptual framework.[3]

Applied to accounting, *measurement* is defined as "an assignment of numbers to an entity's past, present or future economic phenomena on the basis of past and present observation and according to rules."[4] This concept is essential to cost accounting.

Communication is also essential in cost accounting to allow movement from measurement to information. As defined by Shannon and Weaver, communication encompasses "the procedures by means of which one mechanism affects another mechanism."[5]

Data upon which action is based are *information*. The term refers to those data that reduce the user's uncertainty.

A *system* is an entity consisting of two or more interacting components, or subsystems, intended to achieve a goal. Cost accounting is generally a subsystem of the accounting information system, which is itself a subsystem of the total management information system within the organization.

Planning refers to the management function of setting objectives, establishing policies, and choosing means of accomplishment. It may occur at different levels in the organization, from strategic to operational, and may have behavioral implications.

Feedback is the output of a process that returns to become an input to initiate control. It is basically a revision of the planning process to accommodate new environmental events.

Control refers to the monitoring and evaluation of performance to determine the degree to which actions conform to plans. Ideally, planning precedes control, which is followed by a feedback corrective action or a feedforward preventive action.

A cost results from the use of an asset for production. The identification, classification, and estimation of costs—the study of *cost behavior*—are essential to any evaluation of alternative courses of action.

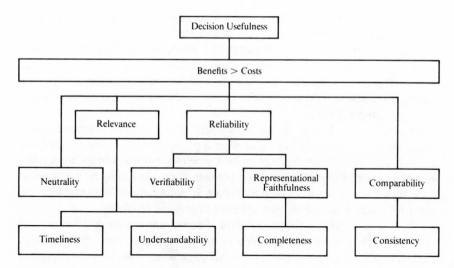

Figure 1.1
A Hierarchy of Qualitative Characteristics

Qualitative Characteristics of Cost Accounting Information

To be useful, a cost accounting report must meet certain qualitative criteria. These criteria are intended to guide the cost accountant to produce the "best," or most useful, information for managers.

The Financial Accounting Standards Board (FASB), a standard-setting body for financial accounting, has proposed certain criteria for selecting and evaluating financial reports, including decision usefulness, benefits over cost, relevance, reliability, neutrality, verifiability, representational faithfulness, comparability, timeliness, understandability, completeness, and consistency.[6] As shown in Figure 1.1, these criteria may be organized as a hierarchy of informational qualities.

Most cost accounting is concerned to some degree with decision making, so *decision usefulness* becomes the overriding criterion for choosing between cost accounting alternatives. The type of information chosen is the one which, subject to any cost considerations, appears to be the most useful for decision making.

Cost accounting information, like any other commodity, will be sought if the benefits to be derived from the information exceed its costs. Thus, before preparing and disseminating the cost accounting information, the *benefit and cost* of providing the information must be compared.

Relevance has been appropriately defined as follows: "For information to meet the standard of relevance, it must bear upon or be usefully associated with the action it is designed to facilitate or the result it is desired to produce. This requires that either the information or the act of communicating it exert influence . . . on the designated actions."[7] Relevance therefore refers to the information's ability to influence the managers' decisions by changing or confirming their expectations about the result or consequences of actions or events. There can be degrees of relevance. The relevance of particular information will vary among users and will depend on their needs and the particular contexts in which the decisions are made.

Reliability refers to that "quality which permits users of data to depend upon it with confidence as representative of what it proposes to represent."[8] Thus, the reliability of information depends on its degree of faithfulness in the representation of an event. Reliability will differ between users, depending on the extent of their knowledge of the rules used to prepare the information. Similarly, different users may seek information with different degrees of reliability.

The absence of bias in the presentation of accounting reports or information is *neutrality*. Thus, neutral information is free from bias toward attaining some desired result or inducing a particular mode of behavior. This is not to imply that the preparers of information do not have a purpose in mind when preparing the reports; it only means that the purpose should not influence a predetermined result. Notice that neutrality is in conflict with one of the concepts of cost accounting, namely, the feedback concept. It may be argued that cost accounting reports are intended to report on managerial performance and influence behavior and hence cannot be neutral.

Verifiability is "that attribute . . . which allows qualified individuals working independently of one another to develop essentially similar measures or conclusions from an examination of the same evidence, data, or records."[9] It implies consensus and absence of measurer bias. Verifiable information can be substantially reproduced by independent measurers using the same measurement methods. Notice that verifiability refers only to the correctness of the resulting information, not to the appropriateness of the measurement method used.

Representational faithfulness and completeness refer to the correspondence between the accounting data and the events those data are supposed to represent. If the measure portrays what it is supposed to represent, it is considered free of measurement and measurer bias.

Comparability describes the use of the same methods by different firms, and *consistency* describes the use of the same method over time by a given firm. Both qualitative characteristics are more important for financial accounting information than for cost accounting information.

Timeliness refers to the availability of data when they are needed or soon enough after the reported events. A trade-off is necessary between timeliness and precision.

The clarity of the information and ease of grasp by the users are its *understandability*. The preparer's level of understanding is generally different from the user's. Thus, efforts should be made by the preparer to increase the understandability of accounting information, in both form and content, to increase its usefulness to the user.

1.2 THE ORGANIZATIONAL FOUNDATIONS

1.2.1 Organizational Structure

Cost accounting rests not only on accounting but also on organizational foundations. It is this formal organizational structure that management often seeks to change to improve the organization's functioning. In turn, elements of the organizational structure may affect cost accounting—its techniques, approaches, and role in the firm. The strongest influences on cost accounting are the organizational chart, the line and staff relationships, and the role of the controller in the organization.

The organizational chart reflects the pyramidal system of relationships of an organization's staff. The chart results from deliberate, conscious planning of the areas of responsibility, specialization, and authority for each member of the organization. As shown in Figure 1.2, each vertical level in the hierarchy depicts different levels of authority. Each horizontal dimension is differentiated by specialization. This process is *departmentalization;* employees are grouped into organizational units on the basis of similar skills and specialization. A firm may departmentalize horizontally by function, by location, by process, and by product. *Vertical differentiation* by authority and responsibility and *horizontal differentiation* through departmentalization lead to the creation of separate organizational units and necessitate provision for periodic planning and control. This need is met by the cost accounting system.

As shown in Figure 1.2, the lines connecting the organization units may imply either line or staff relationships. *Line authority* implies a basic relationship as defined by the chain of command. It is exerted downward by a superior over subordinates. *Staff authority* implies that part of the managerial task, of an advisory nature, has been assigned by an executive to someone outside the chain of command. *Functional authority* implies a basic relationship of command laterally and downward.

The authority relationships between the staff member and employees of the line at the same or lower levels may be one of four types: staff advice, compulsory advice, concurring authority, or limited company authority.

The concepts of line and staff influence cost accounting in the following ways. First, cost accounting is supportive by nature, providing services and assistance to other units in the organization. It is basically a staff function. Second, as a staff member, the cost accountant's authority may range from purely advisory to limited authority. Third, because of its great need for the cost accountant's specialized knowledge, the organization will likely position this person rather

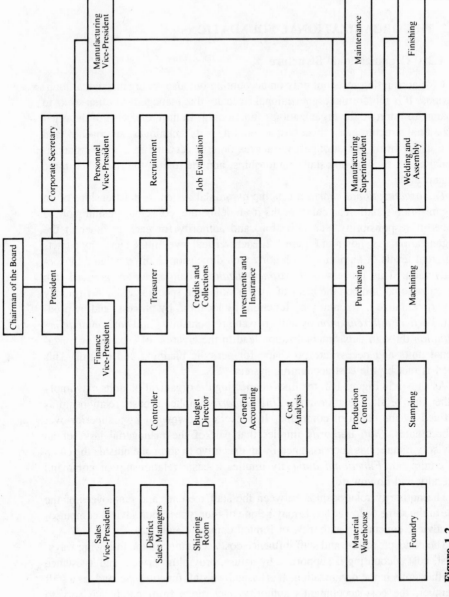

Figure 1.2
Organizational Chart of a Manufacturing Company

high in the organization. In any case, cost accounting is a *decision support system*.

1.2.2 Controllership

The manager in charge of the accounting department is known as the *controller*. A staff member of the top management team, the controller also has a line relationship within the department. The immediate supervisor is generally the vice-president in charge of finance. As a staff person, the controller advises management in the areas of corporate reporting, planning, and control. The following are the controller's main activities:

1. Responsibility for the supervision of all facets of financial accounting leading to the publication of the annual reports.
2. Coordination of all the activities leading to the establishment of the master budget and long-term plan of the firm.
3. Maintenance of a system of control through proper circulation of performance reports.
4. Playing an essential part in the proper collection, dispersion, and channeling of pertinent and timely information as a designer and activator of the basic organizational communications system, the electronic data processing system.

As business entities increase in size and complexity, as the use of planning and control techniques grows, and as most accounting attains a multidimensional scope, the importance of the controller in the organization also increases. The corporate controller has moved to center stage as the chief accounting executive.

As companies expand their operations, the duties and responsibilities of the accounting department increase, as does the size of the controller's staff. What may result is a flat organization, in which all subordinates report directly to the controller. Such a structure in the controller's department may benefit downward and upward communication between the controller and subordinates. Accuracy of upward and downward communication can increase because fewer people are in the vertical chain. This reduces the likelihood of perceptual error. Communication speed can increase. Finally, the controller can initiate more direct control communication and is able to obtain firsthand information about the department performance.

The flat organizational structure may also create downward and upward communication problems. There may be increased competition for the controller's time. Too much information may obscure the pertinent information. The controller may be unable to initiate timely control communication. These negative effects, however, may be reduced by the appointment of a staff assistant for the controller. This will make it easier for the controller to adopt a democratic rather than an autocratic approach to management.

The types of functions and responsibilities assigned to the controller are generally different from those assigned to the *treasurer*. To avoid the confusion and distinguish between the controller and treasurer functions, the Financial Executives Institute presented the following as job responsibilities for each area:

Controllership Functions	Treasurership Functions
1. Planning and control	1. Provision of capital
2. Reporting and interpreting	2. Investor relations
3. Evaluating and consulting	3. Short-term financing
4. Tax administration	4. Bank and custody
5. Government reporting	5. Credits and collections
6. Protection of assets	6. Investments
7. Economic appraisal	7. Insurance

The primary objective of the treasurer, then, is to deal with the financing function, whereas the primary objective of the controller is to deal with the information system. Note that cost accounting is essential to the implementation of the controller's first three functions.

The controller and the head of accounting for planning and control are involved in three major tasks: scorekeeping, attention directing, and problem solving.[10] Notice that the role of these people goes beyond scorekeeping.

1.3 THE BEHAVIORAL FOUNDATIONS

Cost accounting should be built on behavioral foundations. Its explicit aim is to positively affect the behavior of individuals. To accomplish this, cost accounting must be adapted to the different characteristics shaping the "cognitive makeup" of individuals within an organization and affecting their motivation to perform. The identification of the factors and situations that may influence employees' actions allows the cost accountant to adapt the services to the realities of human behavior.

The literature on motivation identifies five theories of motivation: need theory, two-factor theory, value/expectancy theory, achievement theory, and inequity theory. Each either identifies the factors within the individual and the environment that activate high performance or attempts to explain and describe how behavior is activated, what directs it, and how it is controlled and stopped. Each of these theories of motivation has distinct implications for cost accounting.

1.3.1 Need Theory

Originally advanced by psychologist Abraham Maslow, need theory holds that people are motivated to satisfy a hierarchy of needs. These needs are as follows (in ascending order of priority):

1. *The physiological needs:* food, shelter, warmth, and other bodily wants.

2. *The safety needs:* security and protection.

3. *The need for love and belongingness:* desire to both give and receive love and friendship.

4. *The need for esteem:* self-respect and the respect of others.

5. *The self-actualization need:* achieving one's full potential.[11]

People strive to satisfy these needs in sequential fashion, starting with the physiological needs and ending with the self-actualization need. What this implies for cost accounting is that assuming individuals in the organization are well remunerated, the emphasis should be on the introduction of cost accounting techniques in general and control techniques in particular that are consistent with the satisfaction of higher-level needs.

1.3.2 Two-Factor Theory

In a series of studies, Herzberg and his associates developed the "motivation hygiene" theory.[12] They found two factors affecting a job situation, which they labeled *satisfiers and dissatisfiers.* The satisfiers were related to the nature of the work itself and to rewards that flowed directly from the performance of that work. The satisfiers were (1) perceived opportunity for achievement on the job, (2) recognition, (3) a sense of performing interesting and important work, (4) responsibility, and (5) advancement. The dissatisfiers were related to the context rather than the content of the job. They were concerned with (1) company policies that foster ineffectiveness, (2) incompetent supervision, (3) interpersonal relations, (4) working conditions, (5) salaries, (6) status, and (7) job security.

The implications of Herzberg's theory for cost accounting are twofold: First, to contribute to employee motivation, cost accounting techniques should focus on better measurement and reporting of achievement, recognition, work, responsibility, and advancement. Second, given that the key to motivation is to make jobs more meaningful, cost accounting should focus on job enrichment. Managers effect job enrichment by designing tasks that create positive feelings about the job and by building in the opportunity for personal achievement, recognition, challenge, and growth.

1.3.3 Value/Expectancy Theory

Value/expectancy theory attempts to explain and describe how behavior is initiated, maintained, and terminated. Originally developed by Lewin,[13] and later specifically applied to work motivation by Vroom,[14] the basic tenet of the theory is that an individual chooses his or her behavior on the basis of (1) expectations that the behavior will result in a specific outcome and (2) the sum of the valences (that is, personal usefulness or rewards derived from the outcome).

House's formula for the value/expectancy model can be expressed as follows:[15]

$$M = IV_b + P_1 \left(IV_a + \sum_{i=1}^{n} P_{2i}EV_i \right)$$

$$i = 1, 2, \ldots, n$$

where

M = Motivation to work

IV_a = Intrinsic valence associated with successful performance of the task

IV_b = Intrinsic valence associated with goal-directed behavior

EV_i = Extrinsic valences associated with i^{th} extrinsic reward contingent on accomplishment of the work goal (a given level of specified performance)

P_1 = The expectancy that goal-directed behavior will accomplish the work goal; the measure's range is $(-1, +1)$

P_{2i} = The expectancy that work goal accomplishment will lead to the ith extrinsic reward; the measure's range is $(-1, +1)$.

This formula shows some of the implications of expectancy theory for cost accounting. Appropriate cost accounting techniques may be chosen to affect the independent variables of this model in the following ways:

1. By determining what extrinsic rewards (EV_i) follow work goal accomplishment.
2. By increasing through timely reports the individual's expectancy (P_{2i}) that work goal accomplishment leads to extrinsic rewards.
3. By increasing the intrinsic valence associated with work goal accomplishment (IV_a) through giving the individual a greater role in goal setting and task directing.
4. By recognizing and supporting the individual's effort, thereby influencing P_1.
5. By increasing the net intrinsic valences associated with goal-directed behavior (IV_b).

1.3.4 Achievement Theory

The concept of achievement motive, first introduced by McClelland and Atkinson, is based on the desire of people to be challenged, to be innovative, and to adopt an "achievement-oriented behavior" directed toward meeting a standard of excellence. The achievement-oriented individual assumes responsibility for individual achievement, seeks challenging tasks, and takes calculated risks commensurate with the probabilities of success. Therefore, such a person "will take small risks for tasks serving as stepping stones for future rewards, take intermediate risks for tasks offering opportunities for achievement, and will attempt to find situations falling somewhere between the two extremes, providing the highest probability of success, and hence maximizing his sense of personal achievement."[16] For cost accounting, this theory implies (1) the necessity of constructing ways to develop the achievement motive at all managerial levels and (2) the need to introduce cost accounting techniques and to report cost accounting information that encourages and facilitates the performance of high achievers.

1.3.5 Inequity Theory

Walster and her colleagues and Adams say that individuals in a relationship have two motives: to maximize their own gains and to maintain equity in the relationship.[17] Inequity results when the rewards from a relationship are not proportional to what a person has put in. Inequity theory is based on the premise that when individuals compare their own situations with others' situations and feel they are rewarded too much or too little for their contributions, they experience increased tension and strive to reduce it.

The inequity theory suggests, then, that the employee must see rewards as fair or equitable. An appeal to equity norms can reduce conflict. Cost accounting can restore equity by insuring correct and accurate measurement and reporting of performance and the corresponding rewards. To avoid creating feelings of inequity, the methods of measuring performance and rewards should be made public to the employees.

1.4 THE DECISIONAL FOUNDATIONS

Cost accounting attempts to facilitate and support an organization's decision making. To accomplish this fundamental objective in the most appropriate areas, the cost accountant should be aware of the kinds and levels of decisions involved. Several conceptual frameworks proposed in the cost accounting and information systems literature provide a good basis for viewing the types of decisions and decision systems, the types of information needed, and the role of cost accounting.

1.4.1 Anthony's Framework

Although it is a typology of managerial activities, Anthony's framework may also be conceived as a hierarchy of decision systems—*strategic planning, management control,* and *operational control.*[18] Each requires different planning and control systems.

Strategic planning involves determining the objectives of the organization; the changes in these objectives; the resources used to attain the objectives; and the policies that govern the acquisition, use, and disposition of the resources. The strategic planner's main concern is the relationship between the organization and its environment, a concern expressed in the formulation of a long-range plan.

Strategic planning formerly was the responsibility of senior managers and analysts, who approached problems on an ad hoc basis as the need for a solution arose. However, strategic planning is fast becoming an accepted, necessary, and separate management process advocated by most management consulting firms. For example, Arthur D. Little developed Strategy Center Profile techniques for integrating business planning with corporate planning as well as the "alternate futures" concepts. Boston Consulting Group advocates the experience curve, the concept of correlating relative market share with production costs, and the growth-share matrix. McKinsey and Co. developed the "shop-light" matrix with General Electric. Finally, the Strategic Planning Institute developed an expected business performance data base—Profit Impact of Marketing Strategy (PIMS)— for businesses with different characteristics.

Management control is the process by which managers insure that resources are obtained and used effectively and efficiently in the accomplishment of the organization's objectives. Managerial activities within the framework established by strategic planning sometimes require subjective interpretations and involve personal interactions. Management control involves both top management and the middle managers, who approach problems using a definite pattern and time-table to insure efficient and effective results.

Operational control insures that specific tasks or transactions are carried out effectively and efficiently. It is governed by rules and procedures derived from management control that often are expressed in terms of a mathematical model.

Anthony recognizes that the boundaries between the three decision categories often are not clear. The categories are useful, however, for the analysis of managerial activities and their information requirements. The decision categories form a continuum and require different information, summarized in Table 1.1.

Anthony's framework is simple, and it facilitates communications between individuals in the organization by categorizing different types of decisions and their information requirements. For cost accounting the framework implies a tailoring of the data to the context and category of the particular decision. It also calls for different approaches in the areas of strategic planning, management control, and operational control.

1.4.2 Simon's Framework

Like Anthony's framework, Simon's framework presents a taxonomy of decisions.[19] However, while Anthony's framework focuses on the decision making activity, Simon's framework focuses on problem solving by individuals, regardless of their position within an organization.

Simon maintains that all problem solving can be broken down into three distinct phases: intelligence, design, and choice. *Intelligence* consists of survey-ing the environment for situations that demand decisions. It implies an identifica-tion of one or more problems, the collection of information, and the establish-ment of goals and evaluative criteria. *Design* involves delineating and analyzing various courses of action to solve the problems identified in the intelligence

Table 1.1
Information Requirements by Decision Category

Information Attribute	Strategic Planning	Management Control	Operational Control
Source	Externally Generated	Mostly Internally Generated	Internally Generated
Accuracy	Accurate in Magnitude Only	Accurate within Decision Bounds	Very Accurate
Scope	Summary Data	Moderately Detailed Data	Detailed Data
Frequency	Periodically Reported	Regularly Reported	Frequently Reported
Time Span	Long Range	Medium Range	Short Range
Organization	Loose	Structured	Highly Structured
Type of Information	Qualitative	Mixed	Quantitative
Age of Information	Old	Mixed	Current
Characteristic	Unique to Problem	Exception Reporting	Repetitive
Nature	Relates to Establishment of Broad Policies	Relates to the Achievement of Organizational Objectives	Relates to a Specific Task

phase. An enumeration and combination of feasible alternatives and their evaluation are based on the criteria established in the intelligence phase. Finally, *choice* involves choosing the best alternative. Although not mentioned by Simon, decision making involves a fourth phase, *implementation,* designed to insure proper execution of choice.

Simon's framework distinguishes between *programmed* and *nonprogrammed decisions:*

Decisions are programmed to the extent that they are repetitive and routine, to the extent that a definite procedure has been worked out for handling them so that they don't have to be treated de novo each time they occur. Decisions are nonprogrammed to the extent that they are novel, unstructured, and consequential. There is no cut-and-dried method of handling the problem because it hasn't arisen before, or because its precise nature and structure are elusive or complex, or because it is so important that it deserves a custom-tailored treatment. . . . By nonprogrammed I mean a response where the system has no specific procedure to deal with situations like the one at hand, but must fall back on whatever general capacity it has for intelligent, adaptive, problem-oriented action.[20]

Because they are repetitive and routine, programmed decisions require little time in the design phase. Nonprogrammed decisions require much more time. The terms *structured* and *unstructured* are used for *programmed* and *nonprogrammed* to imply less dependence on the computer and more on the basic character of the problem solving activity in question. The two classifications advanced by Simon may be viewed as polarities in a continuum of decision making activity. For example, semistructured decisions may be those for which one or two of the intelligence, design, and choice phases are unstructured.

That decisions may fall on a continuum from structured to unstructured has implications for cost accounting. Structured decisions are solvable by analytic techniques, while unstructured decisions generally are not. The analytic techniques required for structured decisions may be based either on clerical routine and habit or formalized techniques from operations research and electronic data processing. The decision techniques required for unstructured decisions may be based either on intuition and judgment or heuristic techniques. While the role of cost accounting for structured decisions is obviously one of providing and assisting in the use of fixed routines, its role is not obvious in unstructured decisions, where the user of accounting information may rely more on decision style, intuition, or heuristic techniques.

1.4.3 Gorry–Scott-Morton Framework

Anthony's framework is based on the purpose of the decision making activity, while Simon's framework is based on the methods or techniques of problem solving. The Gorry–Scott-Morton framework combines both in a matrix that classifies decisions on both a structured-to-unstructured dimension and on an operational-to-strategic dimension.[21] Table 1.2 shows an expanded example of

Table 1.2
An Expanded Example of the Gorry–Scott-Morton Framework

	Operational Control	Management Control	Strategic Planning
Structured	Accounts Receivable	Budgeting	Tanker Fleet Mix
	Order Entry	Short-Term Forecasting	Warehouse and Plant Location
	Inventory Reordering	Engineered Costs	
		Linear Programming for Manufacturing	
Semistructured	Inventory Control	Variance Analysis	Mergers and Acquisitions
	Production Scheduling	Overall Budget	Capital Acquisition Analysis
	Bond Trading	Budget Preparation	New Product Planning
Unstructured	Cash Management	Hiring Personnel	R&D Planning
	PERT Cost Systems	Sales and Production	

the matrix obtained from the synthesis provided by Gorry and Scott-Morton. The implications for cost accounting from both the Anthony and Simon frameworks apply also to the Gorry–Scott-Morton framework. The synthesis, however, has additional implications.

First, because different information requirements and methods of data collection are required for the three decision categories borrowed from Simon, there may be three types of decisions:

1. Decisions for which adequate models are available or can be constructed and from which optimal solutions can be derived. In such cases, the decision process itself should be incorporated into the information system, thereby converting it to a control system.

2. Decisions for which adequate models can be constructed but from which optimal solutions cannot be extracted. Here heuristic procedures should be provided.

3. Decisions for which adequate models cannot be constructed. Research is required here to determine the relevant information. If decision making cannot be delayed, then judgment must be used to guess what information is relevant.[22]

The second implication of the Gorry–Scott-Morton framework is that different organizational structures, different managerial skills and talents, and different numbers of managers may be required for each decision category. The decision process, the implementation process, and the level of analytic sophistication will differ among the three decision categories and call for different organizational structures:

On strategic problems, a task force reporting to the user and virtually independent of the computer group may make sense. The important issues are problem definition and problem structure; the implementation and computer issues are relatively simple by comparison. In management control, the single user, although still dominant in his application, has problems of interfacing with other users. An organizational design that encourages cross-functional (marketing, production, distribution, etc.) cooperation is probably desirable. In operational control, the organizational design should include the user as a major influence, but he will have to be balanced with operational systems experts, and the whole group can quite possibly stay within functional boundaries.[23]

A final implication is that model requirements may differ in the three areas, given the differences in information requirements, frequency of decision in each area, and their relative magnitude. The operational control system calls for frequent decisions, so the models for these decisions must be efficient in running time, have ready access to current data, and be easily changed. In contrast, the models in strategic planning, and to a lesser extent management control, are infrequent, individual, and dependent on the managers involved.

Because cost accounting is a decision support system, it requires people with different skills and attitudes, different technologies, different models, and different processes to accommodate structured and unstructured decisions on one hand

and strategic planning, management control, and operational control on the other.

1.5 CONCLUSION

To meet the diverse needs of today's managers, cost (or management) accounting has evolved into a multidimensional area of inquiry resting on accounting, organizational, behavioral, and decisional foundations.

The accounting foundations consist of cost accounting concepts to guide the development of cost accounting techniques. The cost accounting concepts alleged to represent a necessary, if not a minimum, foundation for cost accounting's theoretical structure include measurement, communication, information, system, planning, feedback, control, and cost behavior.

The organizational foundations include the elements of the organizational structure that shape the techniques, approaches, and role of cost accounting in the firm: the organizational chart, the line and staff relationships, and the role of the controller in the organization.

The behavioral foundations of cost accounting include the motivation theories identifying the factors and situations that may influence and coordinate employees' actions. The main theories are the need theory, the two-factor theory, the value/expectancy theory, the achievement theory, and the inequity theory.

The decisional foundations of cost accounting are the different conceptual frameworks for viewing types of decisions and decision systems in an organization: Anthony's framework, Simon's framework, and the Gorry–Scott-Morton framework.

NOTES

1. Ahmed Belkaoui, *The Conceptual Foundations of Management Accounting* (Reading, Mass.: Addison-Wesley, 1980), 1–4.

2. American Accounting Association, Committee on Management Accounting, "Report of the Committee on Management Accounting." *Accounting Review* (April 1959): 210.

3. American Accounting Association, Committee on Course in Managerial Accounting, "Report of the Committee on Courses in Managerial Accounting." *Accounting Review* 47 supp. (1972): 7–8.

4. American Accounting Association, Committee on Foundations of Accounting Measurement, "Report of the Committee on Foundations of Accounting Measurement." *Accounting Review* 46 supp. (1971): 3.

5. Claude E. Shannon and Warren Weaver, *The Mathematical Theory of Communication* (Urbana: University of Illinois Press, 1949), 95.

6. Financial Accounting Standards Board, Exposure Draft, "Qualitative Characteristics: Criteria for Selecting and Evaluating Financial Accounting and Reporting Policies" (Stamford, Conn.: FASB, 1979).

7. American Accounting Association, *A Statement of Basic Accounting Theory* (Evanston, Ill.: AAA, 1966), 9.

8. American Accounting Association, Committee on Concepts and Standards for External Financial Reports, *Statement of Accounting Theory and Theory Acceptance* (Sarasota, Fla.: AAA, 1977), 16.

9. American Accounting Association, *A Statement of Basic Accounting Theory,* 10.

10. H. A. Simon, G. Kozmetsky, and G. Tyndall, *Centralization vs. Decentralization in Organizing the Controller's Department* (New York: Controllership Foundation, Inc., 1972).

11. Abraham Maslow, "A Theory of Human Motivation." *Psychological Review* 50 (1943): 370–396.

12. F. Herzberg, B. Maumer, and B. Snyderman, *The Motivation to Work,* 2d ed. (New York: Wiley, 1959).

13. K. Lewin, *Field Theory and Social Sciences* (New York: Harper & Bros., 1951).

14. V. H. Vroom, *Work and Motivation* (New York: Wiley, 1964).

15. R. J. House, "A Path-Goal Theory of Leader Effectiveness." *Administrative Science Quarterly* (September 1971): 321–338.

16. D. C. McClelland, *Personality* (New York: William Sloan, 1951); McClelland, *The Achieving Society* (Princeton, N.J.: Van Nostrand, 1961); and J. W. Atkinson, "Toward Experimental Analysis of Human Motivation in Terms of Motives, Expectancies, and Incentives," in *Motives in Fantasy, Action and Society,* ed. J. W. Atkinson (Princeton, N.J.: Van Nostrand, 1958).

17. E. Walster, E. Berscheid, and G. W. Walster, "New Directions in Equity Research." *Journal of Personality and Social Psychology* 25 (1973): 151–176; and J. S. Adams, "Toward an Understanding of Inequity." *Journal of Abnormal and Social Psychology* 22 (1965): 422–426.

18. R. N. Anthony, *Planning and Control Systems: A Framework for Analysis* (Cambridge, Mass.: Harvard University Graduate School of Business Administration Studies in Management Control, 1965).

19. H. A. Simon, *The New Science of Management Decision* (New York: Harper & Row, 1960).

20. Ibid., p. 69.

21. G. A. Gorry and N. S. Scott-Morton, "A Framework for Management Information Systems." *Sloan Management Review* (Fall 1971): 55–70.

22. R. L. Ackoff, "Management Misinformation Systems." *Management Science* (December 1967).

23. Gorry and Scott-Morton, "A Framework," 68.

SELECTED READINGS

Ackoff, R. L. "Management Misinformation Systems." *Management Science* (December 1967): 147–156.

American Accounting Association, Committee on Courses in Managerial Accounting. "Report of the Committee on Courses in Managerial Accounting." *Accounting Review* 47 supp. (1972): 1–14.

American Accounting Association, Committee on Internal Measurement and Reporting. "Report of the Committee on Internal Measurement and Reporting, 1972." *Accounting Review* 48 supp. (1973): 209–242.

Anthony, R. N. *Planning and Control Systems: A Framework for Analysis.* Cambridge, Mass.: Harvard University Graduate School of Business Administration Studies in Management Control, 1965.

Belkaoui, Ahmed. *The Conceptual Foundations of Management Accounting*. Reading, Mass.: Addison-Wesley, 1980.

Benston, G. J. "The Role of the Firm's Accounting System for Motivation." *Accounting Review* (April 1963): 347–354.

Caplan, E. H. *Management Accounting and Behavioral Science*. Reading, Mass.: Addison-Wesley, 1971.

Chatfield, Michael. "The Origins of Cost Accounting." *Management Accounting* (June 1971): 11–20.

Collins, F. "Management Accounting and Motivation: The Relationship." *Management Accounting* (March 1979): 22–26.

Donbrovski, Willis J. "Management Accounting: A Frame of Reference." *Management Accounting* (August 1965): 20–25.

Donnelly, Robert N. "The Controller's Role in Corporate Planning." *Management Accounting* (September 1981): 13–26.

Earnest, Kenneth R., "Applying Motivational Theory in Management Accounting," *Management Accounting* (December 1979): 441–444.

Elnicki, Richard A., "The Genesis of Management Accounting," *Management Accounting* (April 1971): 30–36.

Fertakis, John P., "Toward a Systems-Oriented Concept of Controllership," *Management Accounting* (December 1968): 20–26.

Francia, Arthur J.; Grossman, Steven D.; and Strawser, Robert H., "The Attitudes of Management Accountants," *Management Accounting* (November 1978): 35–40.

Fourke, D. V., "The Emerging Controllership," *Cost and Management* (November–December 1970): 20–25.

Giacomino, Don E., "University Controllers: Are They Management Accountants?" *Management Accounting* (June 1980): 32–35.

Gibson, J. L., "Accounting in the Decision Making Process: Some Empirical Evidence," *Accounting Review* (July 1963): 492–500.

Giesler, Conrad, "Compensating Sales Reps," *Management Accounting* (April 1980): 34–36.

Goodman, Sam R., and Reece, James S., *Controller's Handbook* (Homewood, Ill.: Dow Jones-Irwin, 1978).

Grinnell, Jacques D., and Kochanek, Richard F., "Capabilities and Role of the Contemporary Management Accountant," *Cost and Management* (July–August 1976): 40–43.

Hale, Jack A., and Ryan, Larry J., "Decision Science and the Management Accountant," *Management Accounting* (January 1979): 42–45.

Hayes, David, "The Contingency Theory of Managerial Accounting," *Accounting Review* (January 1977): 22–39.

Hernandez, William H., "Is the Controller an Endangered Species?" *Management Accounting* (August 1978): 48–52.

Horngren, C. T., "Choosing Accounting Practices for Reporting to Management," *NAA Bulletin,* (September 1962): 3–15.

Imhoff, Eugene A. Jr., "Management Accounting Techniques: A Survey," *Management Accounting* (November 1978): 41–45.

Janell, Paul A., and Kinnemen, Raymond M., "Portrait of the Divisional Controller," *Management Accounting* (June 1980): 15–19, 24.

Johnson, Eugene A., "The Controllership Function," *Management Accounting* (March 1972): 13–20.

Keller, Wayne I., "The Link between Accounting and Management," *Management Accounting* (June 1969): 13–16.

Killough, Larry N., "Does Management Accounting Have a Theoretical Structure?" *Management Accounting* (April 1972): 13–19.

Kotchian, A. C., "A President's View of the Chief Financial Officer," *Financial Executive* (May 1978): 18–24.

Krogstad, J. L., and Harris, J. K., "The CMA Examination: A Content Analysis," *Management Accounting* (October 1974): 21–23.

Lewis, Eldon C., "Successful Interface between Accounting and Management," *Management Accounting* (March 1969): 12–16.

Livingstone, Leslie, ed., *Management Accounting: The Behavioral Foundations* (Columbus, Ohio: Grid, 1975).

Madden, D. L., "The CMA Examination: A Step toward Professionalism," *Management Accounting* (October 1974): 17–20.

"MAP Committee Promulgates Definition of Management Accounting," *Management Accounting* (January 1981): 58–60.

Meagher, Gary N., "Motivating Accountants," *Management Accounting* (March 1979): 27–30.

Moller, George, "The Financial Executive: His Role in Over-all Company Planning," *Controller* (January 1968): 17–18, 22.

Murray, Daniel R., "How Management Accountants Can Make a Manufacturing Control System Effective," *Management Accounting* (July 1981): 25–31.

Plummer, George F., "The Financial Executive: His Role in the Corporate Organization," *Controller* (January 1962): 16, 34.

Sauer, John R., "Psychology and Accounting: The Odd Couple?" *Management Accounting* (August 1980): 14–17.

Seed, Allen H. III, "Strategic Planning: The Cutting Edge of Management Accounting," *Management Accounting* (May 1980): 10–16.

Shenkir, William G.; Welsch, Glenn A.; and Bear, James A. Jr., "Thomas Jefferson: Management Accountant," *Journal of Accountancy* (April 1972): 12–14.

Simon, H. A., *The New Science of Management Decision* (New York: Harper & Row, 1960).

Van Zante, Neal R., "Educating Management Accountants: What Do CMAs Think?" *Management Accounting* (August 1980): 18–21.

Young, W. M. Jr., "The Challenge of Change: How NAA Is Meeting It," *Management Accounting* (January 1980): 52–57.

Cost Theory, Classification, and Accounting

> The general idea of cost covers a number of different meanings. . . . A great deal of controversy [exists] as to whether certain items are properly costs at all. Most of this controversy will disappear if we carry our study far enough to recognize that there are different kinds of problems for which we need information about costs, and the particular information we need differs from one problem to another.[1]

A firm's production activities center around the relationships between two decision variables: inputs and outputs. The transformation of inputs, or scarce resources, into outputs, or goods and services, creates a cost to the firm. The concept of cost is complex, with differing scopes and classification schemes in response to the different needs of economics, accounting, finance, engineering, and law.

This chapter will evaluate the theoretical foundations, the terminology, and the treatment of cost in cost accounting, taking into account implications from these other disciplines.

Upon completion of this chapter, you should be able to do the following:

1. Differentiate between the economic and accounting theories of cost and between the notions of *asset, cost, expense,* and *loss.*

2. Identify the cost classification scheme for a particular decision and/or information need. Costs may be classified according to a natural classification, the time when computed, the degree of averaging, the behavior in relation to the volume of activity, the management function, the ease of traceability, the degree of control, the timing of charges against revenues, the relation to managerial policies, and the relation to decisions to be made.

3. Identify the cost classification on financial statements, the cost accounting cycle, and the possible format and content of the manufacturing and income statements of a manufacturing concern.

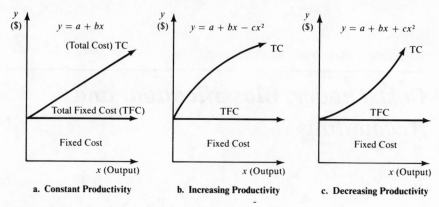

Figure 2.1
Three Kinds of Short-Run Cost Functions

2.1 COST THEORY

2.1.1 The Economic Theory of Cost

The economic theory of cost deals with the relationship between input and output. Letting x be the input and y the output, the most general statement of the cost function of a firm is $(x_1 + x_2 + \ldots + x_n) - (y_1 + y_2 + \ldots + y_n) = 0$. In other words, inputs equal outputs. Although the level of the cost curve will be affected by different factors such as prices, lot size, plant utilization, etc., the theoretical approach is to assume first that these factors are constant and second that a unique functional relationship exists between total cost and output.

The curvature of the cost curve will depend on the nature of the underlying production function. Thus, as depicted by Figure 2.1, the total cost curve is linear in the case of constant productivity and parabolic with increasing or decreasing productivity. Figure 2.1a shows that an assumption of constant productivity implies that for each additional unit of input there is a constant additional amount of output and cost. The assumption of increasing return in Figure 2.1b implies that each additional unit of input adds more additional output and leads to less cost per unit of output. In Figure 2.1c, each additional unit of input adds less to total output, resulting in higher cost per unit. However, given the changing nature of production over time, three phases of returns—constant, increasing, and decreasing—may lead to the total cost function as depicted in Figure 2.2. Point Q_2 is the point of diminishing returns; Q_3 is the point of absolute diminishing returns.

2.1.2 The Accounting Theory of Cost

The term *cost* has different meanings to accountants, economists, engineers, and others facing managerial problems.

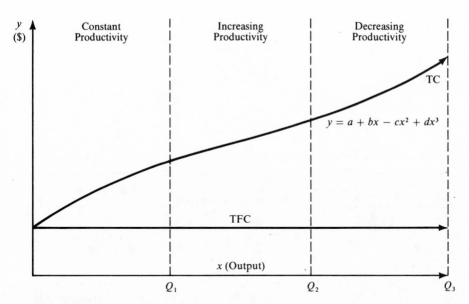

Figure 2.2
Conventional Short-Run Total Cost Function

In a cost accounting context, cost corresponds to a sacrifice resulting from the use of assets. A basic distinction should be made between unexpired cost (asset) and expired cost (cost), as well as between cost and expense. Cost results from the use of assets toward the creation of revenues, and as long as the assets are idle no cost is created. Cost also must be distinguished from the term *expense*.

Four case analyses of costs, as depicted in Figure 2.3, may help avoid confusion between cost, expense, loss, and asset.

Case 1 The acquisition of resources with potential benefits results in the creation of *assets* or *unexpired costs*.

Case 2 The use of the assets in the manufacturing process results in the *cost* of a product. The eventual selling of the product transforms this cost into an *expense* to be matched with sales.

Case 3 The use of the assets in the selling and administrative processes results in an *expense* to be matched with sales.

Case 4 The failure to use the assets in the manufacturing, selling, or administrative process and a misuse of the assets result in a *loss*.

Thus, events in manufacturing occur in the following sequence: (1) acquisition creates an *asset*, (2) manufacturing creates a *cost* of a product or activity, (3) expiration of allocation creates an *expense*, and (4) misuse creates a *loss*.

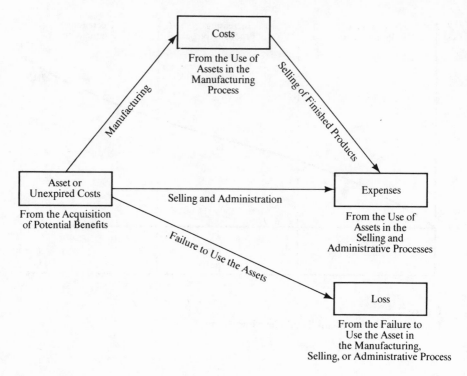

Figure 2.3
Asset-Expense-Loss Differences

2.2 COST CLASSIFICATION SCHEMES

Once identified, costs must be accumulated then classified to help decision making.

The accumulation of cost—the collection of cost in a systematic way—is accomplished by a *cost accumulation system*. The main objective of cost accumulation in most cost accounting systems is to determine the cost of a product or *product costing* for inventory valuation and income determination. Other purposes for cost accumulation do exist as the firm faces different decisions and different organizational problems. For each of these decisions and/or organizational problems, cost must be accumulated and classified. This crucial task of cost classification is accomplished on the basis of a *cost objective,* or an activity for which a cost is desired. A synonym is *cost object.* In other words, the decision or organization problem calls for the determination of the cost of something. That something is the cost objective or cost object.

Decision usefulness generally governs the choice of a cost objective. At one time, most cost accounting systems emphasized one single cost objective, namely, product costing for inventory valuation and income determination. Because of the expanding and complex needs of modern organizations, however, many cost objectives are now considered pertinent in managerial decision making. This has generated new ways of classifying costs:

- A natural classification
- Time when computed
- Behavior in relation to the volume of activity
- Management function
- Ease of traceability
- Degree of control
- Timing of charges against revenues
- Relation to managerial policies

Because decision making emphasizes the proper classification of costs, each of these classifications is examined next.

2.2.1 Natural Classification

The natural classification refers to the basic "physical" aspects of cost. Hence, the accountant classifies costs as either direct labor, direct material, or manufacturing overhead.

Direct material refers to all materials that become an integral part of a finished product. In general, the ease of traceability of a material product is the determinant for its classification as a direct material. For example, wood is the direct material in a piece of wooden furniture. Materials that are not significant on a per-unit basis are *indirect materials;* glue, nails, rivets, and screws are examples.

Direct labor is the labor expended directly upon the direct material. It constitutes, then, the labor easily traceable to a finished product. For example, the wages of the production line workers constitute direct labor. *Indirect labor* cannot easily be identified with a finished product; examples include the wages of supervisors, janitors, and inspectors.

Manufacturing overhead (also called *factory overhead*) refers to all costs necessary for the manufacturing and operation of a product except direct labor and direct material. It consists of the costs of indirect material; indirect labor; and all other manufacturing costs that cannot easily be traced to a specific product, including plant depreciation, machinery and equipment depreciation, rent, insurance, taxes, maintenance, power, heat, light, supplies, small tools. Manufacturing overhead may also be labeled as *indirect manufacturing costs, factory burden,* and *manufacturing expenses.* Manufacturing overhead is generally subclassified in the following two categories:

1. *Variable factory overhead* to include the part of factory overhead that varies proportionally to the level of activity. It includes such indirect material as power and supplies and most indirect labor.

2. *Fixed factory overhead* to include the part of factory overhead that remains fixed for a given level of activity called the *relevant range*. It includes such accounts as rent, insurance, depreciation, property taxes, and supervisory labor.

Direct labor combined with direct material generally is referred to as *prime cost*. Direct labor and manufacturing overhead are what converts the direct material into a finished product. Thus, direct labor combined with manufacturing overhead is *conversion cost*.

Idle time, overtime premiums, and payroll fringe benefits in labor are not easily classified. Idle time represents wages paid for unproductive time caused by machine breakdowns, material shortages, and any work stoppage. For example, if a press operator earning $5 per hour of straight time has worked thirty-five hours and was idle five hours because of material shortages, the earnings would be computed as follows:

Direct labor ($5 × 35 hours)	$175
Idle time (manufacturing overhead) ($5 × 5 hours)	25
Total earnings	$200

Overtime premium represents the cost of direct labor and indirect labor due for time beyond the straight time of the regular workday (as specified in some labor union contracts) or time over the forty-hour workweek. Overtime premium is considered indirect labor unless caused by a specific job. Thus, a job worked on during the overtime period is not attributed the overtime premium that applies to all the jobs of the period. For example, if a press operator worked forty hours at $5 per hour and ten overtime hours at an additional $3 per overtime hour, the earnings would be computed as follows:

Direct labor ($5 × 50 hours)	$250
Overtime premium ($3 × 10 hours)	30
Total earnings	$280

Finally, payroll fringe benefits include various employment-related costs such as contributions to Social Security, employee insurance programs, life insurance, hospitalization plans, pension plans, and annuity and retirement plans. These costs are classified as direct labor, indirect labor, or partly direct labor and partly indirect labor. It varies from one company to another.

2.2.2 Time When Computed

Costs may be classified as historical or budgeted according to the time when they are computed.

Historical costs are past costs valued at the acquisition costs of the asset. Conventional financial accounting records assets on the books at their acquisition or historical cost. Historical costs have the basic advantage of conforming to generally accepted accounting principles and so are presumed to be objective, verifiable, and free from bias.

Budgeted or standard costs express the future trend of historical costs and result from prediction models. Useful for planning and control, budgeted costs set yardsticks for future performance. They depend, however on the accuracy of the estimation techniques used for their derivation. There are three basic approaches to their estimation: (1) qualitative judgments, (2) quantitative models, considering external variables, and (3) time series quantitative models. The cost estimation problem is fully investigated in chapter 3.

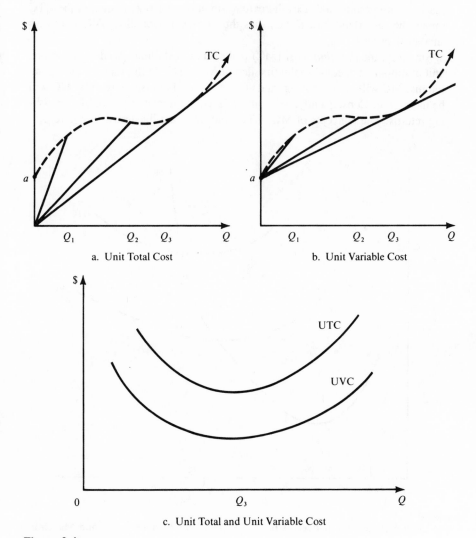

Figure 2.4
Derivation of Unit Cost Curves

2.2.3 Degree of Averaging

Costs may be classified as total, unit (average), or marginal. A *total cost* (TC) encompasses the total level of activity. A *unit cost* (UC) is related to a single unit of activity, so UC is simply TC divided by the total level of activity. Figure 2.4 illustrates the derivation of UC. The unit total cost (UTC) is equal to the slope of the line passing through the origin and tangent to the curve (Figure 2.4a), and the unit variable cost (UVC) is equal to a similar tangent line starting at the fixed cost level (Figure 2.4b). These slopes decrease up to the point of absolute diminishing returns and increase thereafter. As illustrated in Figure 2.4c, the UTC falls, reaches a minimum, and rises thereafter. Similarly, the UVC, equal to the UTC minus the unit fixed cost (UFC), has the same behavior. So, UVC is always smaller than UTC.

Similarly, the *marginal cost* (MC) is the additional outlay needed to add one unit of output. It is equal to the first derivative of TC. At the stage of increasing returns, MC will be decreasing, and at the stage of diminishing returns, MC will be increasing. Consequently, MC will be at a minimum at the point of diminishing returns. The concepts of MC, UTC, and UVC are illustrated in Figure 2.5.

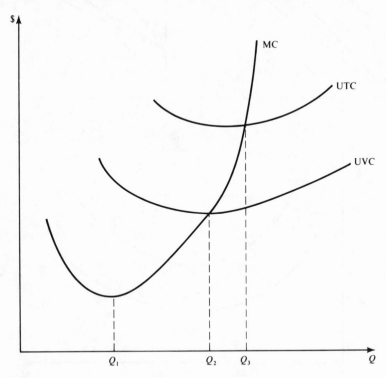

Figure 2.5
Graphic Relationship between Unit Total Cost, Unit Variable Cost, and Marginal Cost

When UTC and UVC are falling, UTC and UVC are equal to MC, and when UTC and UVC are rising, UTC and UVC are equal to MC. Consequently, MC = UVC at the minimum unit variable cost, and MC = UTC at the minimum total cost.

Since these costs are depicted in terms of their relation to output, the concept of *elasticity* may be used to measure the sensitivity between cost and output. In the following equation, the *elasticity,* e, of total cost measures the percentage change in TC created by a small change in output, X:

$$e_{TC} = \frac{\frac{\Delta TC}{TC}}{\frac{\Delta X}{X}} = \frac{X \Delta TC}{TC \Delta X}.$$

Given that MC = $\Delta TC/\Delta X$ and UC = TC/X, this formula could be expressed as follows:

$$e_{TC} = \frac{\frac{\Delta TC}{\Delta X}}{\frac{TC}{X}} = \frac{MC}{UC}.$$

In other words, the elasticity of total cost is equal to the ratio of marginal cost to average total cost. These cost relationships are illustrated in Figure 2.6, and Table 2.1 shows their derivation.

2.2.4 Behavior in Relation to the Volume of Activity

Costs may also be classified in terms of their behavior in relation to the volume of activity. Thus, costs may be strictly variable, strictly fixed, semivariable, or semifixed.

Strictly Variable Costs

Strictly variable costs vary directly and in proportion to the volume of activity. They may be expressed as y = bx, where y = total variable costs, x = level of activity, and b = unit variable cost.

Consequently, the total variable cost, y, is equal to zero when x = 0. Assuming constant productivity, the total variable costs are linear, and the unit variable cost (b = y/x) is fixed. The slope of the cost line is b; it is equal to $(y_2 - y_1)/(x_2 - x_1)$. Figure 2.7 illustrates the strictly variable cost.

Examples of strictly variable costs are direct material and direct labor, which occur in the manufacturing of any product. The amount of direct material and/or direct labor fluctuates in direct proportion to the operating volume or level of activity. Suppose, for example, that a firm pays salespeople solely on commission. As the volume of sales increases, the commissions will increase propor-

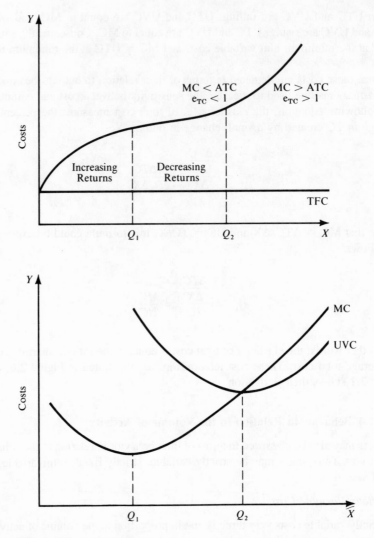

Figure 2.6
Behavior of Cost Elasticity

tionally. Thus, the commissions are a variable cost arising from sales. If the firm pays as commission 10 percent of its dollar sales, the total commission paid for three months is as follows:

Month	Sales in Dollars	Commission Paid
1	$ 1,000	$ 100
2	20,000	2,000
3	30,000	3,000

Table 2.1
Derivation of Cost Schedules

Level of Activity (1)	Total Cost (2)	Total Fixed Cost (3)	Total Variable Cost (4)	Unit Total Cost (5)	Unit Variable Cost (6)	Unit Fixed Cost (7)	Marginal Cost (8)	Cost Elasticity (9)
X	TC	TFC	TVC = (2) − (3)	(2)/(1) = UTC	(4)/(1) = UVC	(3)/(1) = UFC	Δ(2)/Δ(1) = MC	(8)/(5) = CE
0	$ 200	$200	$ 0	—	—	—	—	—
10	300	200	100	$30.0	$10	$20.0	$10	0.33
20	380	200	180	19.0	9	10.0	8	0.44
30	440	200	240	14.6	8	6.6	6	0.41
50	500	200	300	10.0	6	4.0	3	0.30
100	700	200	500	7.0	5	2.0	4	0.57
150	1200	200	1000	8.0	6.7	1.3	10	1.20
200	2200	200	2000	11.0	10	1.0	20	1.80

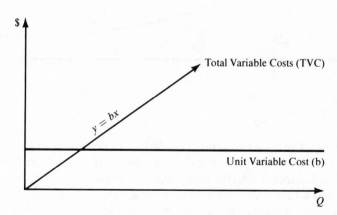

Figure 2.7
Total Strictly Variable Costs

Notice that the total commission paid (total variable cost) varies proportionally to the volume of activity as expressed by the sales dollars, while the commission rate (unit variable cost) is fixed.

Strictly Fixed Costs

Strictly fixed costs, or strictly total fixed costs (TFC), do not vary with the level of activity; however, unit fixed costs (UFC) do vary with the level of activity, as shown in Figure 2.8. TFC may be expressed as $y = M$, where y = total fixed costs and M = lump sum. Similarly, UFC = $y/x = M/x$. Therefore, UFC decreases proportionally with the level of activity.

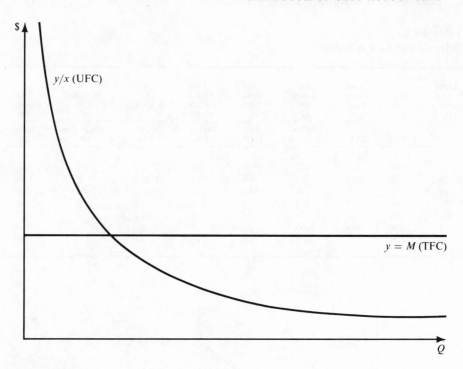

Figure 2.8
Fixed Cost Curves

The concept of total fixed costs as independent of changes in the volume of activity includes two basic assumptions: the time period and the *relevant range* of activity. In other words, the accountant may conceive of a relevant range of activity and a time period for which the total fixed cost concept is definable. Property taxes, depreciation expense, insurance expense, and time and motion studies are examples of fixed costs. To illustrate, assume that a plant is leased for $10,000 per month. The lease cost is a *capacity cost:* it is necessary to provide or maintain the current operating capacity.

Suppose, however, that the use of the capacity varies each month. For output levels of 1,000, 5,000, and 10,000 units, the average fixed cost (UFC) will be as follows:

Month	Total Rental Cost	Level of Activity	Average Fixed Cost
1	$10,000	1,000 units	$10
2	$10,000	5,000 units	$ 2
3	$10,000	10,000 units	$ 1

The capacity costs may be further classified. The *standby costs* are those capacity costs that would be incurred even if the productive facilities closed down. They are fixed whether or not work is performed. The *enabling costs* are those capacity costs that would not be incurred in a shutdown.

Semivariable Costs

Semivariable costs include both a fixed and a variable component. They may be linear, quadratic, or cubic.

If the total cost of the fixed and variable quantities is denoted by y, then $y = a + bx$ represents a *linear cost function*. The equation's mathematical properties are as follows:

$$\text{Total fixed costs (TFC)} = a.$$

$$\text{Unit cost (UTC)} = \frac{y}{x} = \frac{a}{x} + b.$$

$$\text{Unit variable cost (UVC)} = b = \text{constant}.$$

$$\text{Marginal cost (MC)} = \frac{\Delta y}{\Delta x} = \text{constant}.$$

$$\text{Elasticity } (e_{\text{TC}}) = \frac{b}{\dfrac{a}{x} + b}.$$

Figure 2.9 illustrates the linear total cost function curve and its properties. The relevant range dichotomizes the semivariable costs into fixed and variable components.

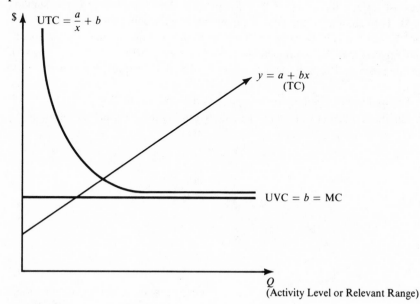

Figure 2.9
Linear Total Cost Function Curve

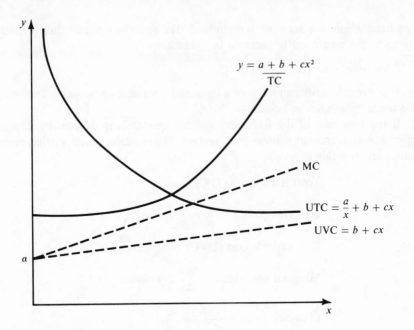

Figure 2.10
Quadratic Cost Curve Properties

The cost of equipment maintenance and repairs is semivariable. One part of the cost varies with the use of the equipment, and another part represents standby costs. For example, if the cost of repairs and maintenance amounts to $1,000 a month plus a repair charge of $20 per hour, the cost of equipment maintenance and repairs may be expressed as $y = \$1,000 + \$20x$, where y = cost of maintenance and repairs, and x = level of activity expressed in direct labor hours.

The *quadratic cost function* is represented by the equation $y = a + bx + cx^2$. Its distinct mathematical properties, shown in Figure 2.10, are as follows:

$$UTC = \frac{y}{x} = \frac{a}{x} + b + cx.$$

$$MC = \frac{\Delta y}{\Delta x} = b + 2cx.$$

$$e_{TC} = \frac{b + 2cx}{\dfrac{a}{x} + b + cx}.$$

With increasing productivity, the following equation represents the quadratic cost curve: $y = a + bx - cx^2$. Its mathematical properties are as follows:

$$UTC = \frac{y}{x} = \frac{a}{x} + b - cx.$$

$$MC = \frac{y}{x} = b - 2cx.$$

$$e_{TC} = \frac{b - 2cx}{\frac{a}{x} + b - cx}.$$

The *cubic cost function* is expressed by the now familiar equation $y = a + bx - cx^2 + dx^3$ shown in Figure 2.2. Its mathematical properties are as follows:

$$UTC = \frac{y}{x} = \frac{a}{x} + \frac{b}{x} - cx + dx^2.$$

$$MC = \frac{\Delta y}{\Delta x} = b - 2cx + 3dx^2.$$

$$e_{TC} = \frac{b - 2cx + 3dx^2}{\frac{a}{x} + \frac{b}{x} - cx + dx^2}.$$

Table 2.2 summarizes the properties of all the semivariable cost functions in a theoretical example. In practice, however, the task of classifying the semivariable costs as linear, quadratic, or cubic is very difficult. One popular simplification is to assume the cost behavior pattern to be linear rather than quadratic or cubic.

Table 2.2
Properties of Semivariable Cost Functions

Nature of the Equation	Form of the Equation	Total Fixed Costs	Total Variable Costs	Marginal Cost
Linear	$y = 5 + 2x$	5	$2x$	2
Quadratic I	$y = 5 + 2x + 3x^2$	5	$2x + 3x^2$	$2 + 6x$
Quadratic II	$y = 5 + 2x - 3x^2$	5	$2x - 3x^2$	$2 - 6x$
Cubic	$y = 5 + 2x - 3x^2 + 6x^3$	5	$2x - 3x^2 + 6x^3$	$2 - 6x + 18x^2$

This approach is not without limitations. First, the linear approximation may oversimplify the true relationship between costs and the activity level and thus may lead to incorrect decisions or evaluations. Second, the conditions necessary for simple linearity may be difficult to achieve in cases such as the following:

1. The raw material goes through various physical processes before becoming a finished product.
2. The cost of acquiring each input is a function of the amount purchased. It could be an exponential increasing function (in the case of scarce resources) or a decreasing function of the amount purchased (when quantity discounts apply).
3. Other intervening variables exist to affect the relationship between costs and the activity level.[2]

Semifixed Costs

Semifixed or step costs are fixed for a given level of activity and eventually increase by a constant amount at some critical points (see Figure 2.11). This level of activity must be large enough to avoid confusion with the strictly fixed cost.

The salary of the basic supervisory staff rises in steps. Assume that the supervisory staff can inspect 1,000 units a day. The addition of personnel for any activity level above 1,000 units raises the cost of supervision to a higher plateau.

In practice, the discontinuity of the stepped costs may be ignored to facilitate decision making. If the activity increments are relatively small, the semifixed cost may be approximated by a strictly variable cost. Economists favor this alternative. If the increments are relatively large, each increment may be considered a relevant range of activity and the semifixed cost approximated by a strictly fixed cost. Executives and accountants prefer this treatment.

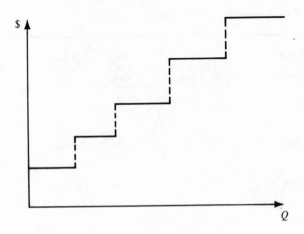

Figure 2.11
Semifixed Cost

For practical purposes, the only measure of activity level used in this chapter has been the number of units produced. Other indexes of volume that may be used when classifying costs in terms of their behavioral patterns include direct labor hours, machine hours, materials quantity, and direct labor cost. Accounting criteria for choosing the activity index for allocation will be presented in chapters 17 and 18. A major criterion is the possibility of measuring the organization's overall efficiency. Because such a *macro-activity index* should lead to motivational behavioral patterns, its potential for socially beneficial results must be considered.

2.2.5 Management Function

This classification differs whether the going concern is associated with manufacturing or merchandising. *Manufacturing* involves the transformation of materials into finished goods through the use of labor and overhead. *Merchandising* involves the *selling* of goods without a change to their basic form.

Both going concerns, manufacturing and merchandising, also include two other functions—selling and administration. These two management functions create two new cost classifications: (1) *selling overhead* and (2) *administrative overhead*.

Selling overhead includes the cost incurred after the manufacturing process to facilitate the sale of goods or services. It encompasses all expenses necessary for the transition of the product from the manufacturer to the immediate buyer. Administrative overhead includes all the expenses necessary for the maintenance of an efficient management administration.

2.2.6 Ease of Traceability

Costs are classified on the basis of traceability relative to an object of costing, such as a product line. A *direct cost* is easily identified and traceable to an object of costing. The prime cost and some overhead are usually directly traceable to a product, department, or segment of the firm. A cost that cannot be identified and traced to one segment of a firm is an *indirect cost* and is usually associated with several segments of the firm. Therefore, the salary of a given worker may be a direct charge to a department but an indirect charge to a product.

The distinction between direct and indirect costs facilitates decisions in areas such as product line and pricing policy. Table 2.3 shows the distinction between direct and indirect costs and between variable and fixed costs for a given product line (product X). Notice that even a fixed cost may be either direct or indirect in terms of its association with an object of costing.

Organizations also use the direct and indirect costs concept in performance evaluation, pricing, and resource allocation. In general, the degree of traceability of cost rests on the delimitation of responsibility in *cost centers*, units that control the incurrence of cost rather than sales. The whole corporation may be perceived

Table 2.3
Product Line Income Statement (Product X)

Sales		$10,000
Minus Direct Costs		
Direct Variable Costs	$1,000	
Direct Fixed Costs	2,000	3,000
Equals Excess of Sales over Direct Costs		$ 7,000
Minus Indirect Costs		
Indirect Variable Costs	$2,000	
Indirect Fixed Costs	3,000	5,000
Equals Product X's Net Income		$ 2,000

as a cost center, or all other segments of the firm—divisions, departments, branches, shops, and machines—may be cost centers. The total configuration of cost centers within the organization determines the traceability of costs. In general, direct costs are incurred within and for the cost center, while indirect costs are external to the center and can be identified with it only through allocation.

Direct costs may also be classified as *common* or *joint costs* if used by more than one costing unit. The common or joint costs refer to services provided to more than one costing object, and as such ought to be allocated on an objective basis. Joint or common costs arise when one input goes into a process yielding several outputs. They refer to services required for the production of different outputs. The cost allocation problem is investigated in chapters 17 and 18.

2.2.7 Degree of Control

Classifying costs as either *controllable* or *noncontrollable* assigns responsibility and provides a basis for cost control. A cost is called controllable by a given entity if it is under that entity's direct influence. A controllable cost's source of incurrence and responsibility are known. Consequently, the classification of a cost as controllable or noncontrollable depends on the following time period and point-of-reference assumptions: (1) for any given organization, there is always in the organizational hierarchy an individual with the power to authorize a given cost, and (2) the longer the time span, the more controllable a given cost will become. In the long run, someone in the organization can be held responsible for the ultimate decision concerning the incurrence of any cost. Note that an organization must objectively justify the assignment of controllability of a given cost to avoid a negative effect on morale. This implies that for any given responsibility center some unallocated costs should be listed separately and identified as uncontrollable.

A few fallacies concerning controllability should be recognized:

1. All variable costs are controllable, and all fixed costs are noncontrollable.
2. All direct costs are controllable, and all indirect costs are noncontrollable.
3. All long-run costs are controllable, and all short-run costs are noncontrollable.

In other words, controllability should not be confused with ease of traceability, cost behavior, and time.

2.2.8 Timing of Charges against Revenues

The classification of costs according to the timing of charges against revenues depends on whether the costs are considered *product* or *period costs*. Product costs—unexpired or *inventoriable costs*—relate to the products on hand, either unsold finished goods or semifinished goods. They are inventoried and carried forward as assets until the goods to which they relate are sold; then they are matched against sales. Period costs—expenses or losses—are costs that are associated with the revenues of the current period. They are not assigned directly to the products on hand because they do not represent value added to any specific product.

The classification as product or period costs varies between merchandising accounting and manufacturing accounting, as shown in Figure 2.12. In merchandising accounting, the purchase costs of inventory are product costs, while the selling and administrative overhead are period costs. In manufacturing accounting, the manufacturing costs are product costs, while the selling and administrative overhead are period costs.

2.2.9 Relation to Managerial Policies

Fixed or capacity costs are fixed for various reasons and can be divided into two categories: *committed* or *discretionary costs*.

The committed fixed costs are those fixed, unavoidable costs necessary for maintaining a basic organization and a productive capacity. Their incurrence continues even if the volume of activity is zero. Examples of committed costs are depreciation, property taxes, rent, insurance, and so on.

The discretionary, managed, engineered, or programmed fixed costs reflect a given management policy or philosophy. Because management initiates and can change discretionary costs, they are often the first costs examined in the introduction of a cost reduction program or a new managerial policy.

The distinction between discretionary and committed fixed costs may be useful for a decision concerning the elimination of a segment of the firm. For

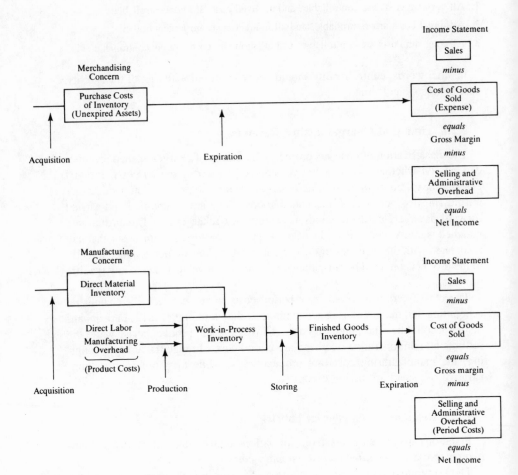

Figure 2.12
Distinctions between Product and Period Costs

Table 2.4
Taxonomy of Costs

A. Manufacturing Costs
1. Prime Costs
1.1. Direct Material
1.2. Direct Labor
2. Variable Manufacturing Overhead
2.1. Indirect Material
2.2. Indirect Labor
2.3. Others (Overtime, Idle Time, Payroll Fringe Costs, and So Forth)
3. Fixed Manufacturing Overhead
3.1. Fixed Discretionary Manufacturing Overhead
3.2. Fixed Committed Manufacturing Overhead

B. Selling Costs
1. Variable Selling Overhead
2. Fixed Selling Overhead
2.1. Fixed Discretionary Selling Overhead
2.2. Fixed Committed Selling Overhead

C. Administrative Costs
1. Variable Administrative Overhead
2. Fixed Administrative Overhead
2.1. Fixed Discretionary Administrative Overhead
2.2. Fixed Committed Administrative Overhead

---

such decisions, the variable costs obviously must be examined. The relevance of the fixed costs will depend on the following scheme:

	Separable	**Joint**
Discretionary	Relevant	Not relevant
Committed	Not relevant	Not relevant

In other words, for the short-run decision affecting a segment of a firm, only the variable costs and the *separable* discretionary costs are relevant. However, in the long-term decision, all costs are discretionary and hence relevant.

The taxonomy of costs shown in Table 2.4 summarizes most of the cost classification schemes discussed so far.

2.3 MANUFACTURING ACCOUNTING

2.3.1 Cost Classification on Financial Statements

The basic difference between manufacturing and merchandising accounting stems from the fact that a merchant buys and sells merchandise in a finished state, whereas the manufacturer transforms different inputs into a final output to be sold. Therefore, both the balance sheets and income statements of merchandisers and manufacturers will differ in format and content.

The inventory accounts in the balance sheets of the merchandising and manufacturing concerns differ. While the merchandising concern has only one inventory account, which is the merchandise inventory account, the manufacturing concern has three inventory accounts, each of which reflects a stage in the production process as follows:

1. *Direct-Materials Inventory,* which represents the inventory on hand and available for use in the production process.
2. *Work-in-Process Inventory,* also labeled as *Work-in-Progress* or *Goods-in-Process,* which represents the production in process awaiting full completion. The costs included in the account are the product costs of direct materials, direct labor, and manufacturing overhead.
3. *Finished-Goods Inventory,* which represents the completed units awaiting potential sales to customers.

The balance sheet content and format, consequently, will be different for the current asset section:

Current Asset Section of Balance Sheet

Manufacturer			Merchandiser	
Cash		$ 5,000	Cash	$ 5,000
Receivables		5,000	Receivables	5,000
Finished Goods	$10,000		Merchandise Inventory	29,000
Work-in-Process	5,000		Other Current Assets	6,000
Direct Material	4,000		Total Current Assets	$45,000
Total Inventory		19,000		
Other Current Assets		1,000		
Total Current Assets		$30,000		

For a merchandising firm, the cost of goods sold eventually comprises the purchase costs of goods, including freight in, that have been purchased and sold. For a manufacturer, the manufacturing cost of goods sold comprises a proportion of the three major elements of costs: direct labor, direct material, and manufacturing overhead. The computation of the manufacturing cost of goods sold will be examined in the next section.

2.3.2 Cost Accounting Cycle

The accounting system used by a manufacturer may be either the so-called *general accounting system* or a *cost accounting system.*

The general accounting system is a non-cost system. It uses *periodic* physical inventories for raw materials, goods-in-process, and finished goods that do not require a day-to-day recording of inventory changes. A periodic inventory system determines the costs of goods sold by adding the period manufacturing costs to beginning inventory (obtained by physical count) and subtracting the ending inventory (obtained by physical count). This system is used mainly by drugstores, grocery stores, and others specializing in the sale of low-priced items.

A cost accounting system uses a *perpetual* inventory system of accounting for goods on hand and sold. Such a system determines the costs of goods sold during a period, as well as the ending inventory, from the accounting records without a physical inventory. This system facilitates management control and the preparation of interim financial statements. In a cost accounting system, the orderly sequence of bookkeeping is as follows:

1. Assets become costs.
2. Costs become goods-in-process.
3. Goods-in-process are completed and transferred to the Finished Goods Inventory account as *cost of goods manufactured*.

Table 2.5 depicts a simple cost accounting system for a manufacturing concern. The entries in the accounts are keyed to the following explanations:

1. The purchase of raw materials is debited to the Raw Materials Inventory account. A corresponding entry is made either to Cash or to Accounts Payable (if purchased on credit).
2. The direct material used in production is debited to the Work-in-Process Inventory, and the indirect material is debited to the Manufacturing Overhead account.
3. The cost of direct labor previously debited to the Payroll account is debited to Work-in-Process Inventory, while the indirect labor is debited to the Manufacturing Overhead account.
4. The charges for factory overhead services are debited to the Manufacturing Overhead account.
5. A proportion of Manufacturing Overhead is "applied" to Work-in-Process Inventory on the basis of an overhead rate.
6. The cost of goods completed is transferred as a debit to the Finished Goods Inventory.
7. The cost of goods sold is transferred to the income statement as a period expense to be matched with the period revenues.
8. Selling and administrative overhead are transferred to the income statement as a period expense.
9. Finally, the net operating income is computed.

Step 6 leads to the production of a *manufacturing statement*, also labeled *Statements of Costs of Goods Manufactured*, as illustrated in Table 2.6; and step 9 leads to an *earnings statement*, as illustrated in Table 2.7. This earnings statement uses a multiple-step format that presents various levels of earnings

Table 2.5
A Cost Accounting System for a Manufacturing Concern

Raw Materials Inventory	
Beginning Inventory	(2a) Direct Raw Material Used in Production
(1) Purchase of Raw Materials	(2b) Indirect Raw Material Used in Production
Ending Inventory	

Payroll	
(3) Wages Incurred	(3a) Direct Labor Used
	(3b) Indirect Labor Used

Manufacturing Overhead	
(2b) Indirect Material	(5) Applied Overhead
(3b) Indirect Labor	
(4) Overhead Services	

Work-in-Process Inventory	
Beginning Inventory	(6) Cost of Goods Manufactured and
(2a) Direct Raw Material Used	Transferred
(3a) Direct Labor Used	
(5) Applied Overhead	
Ending Inventory	

Cost of Goods Sold	Finished Goods Inventory	
(7) Cost of Goods Sold	Beginning Inventory	(7) Cost of Goods Sold
	(6) Cost of Goods Manufactured and Transferred	

while offering more disclosure of both irregular items and items not related to the enterprise's main activities.

Note that the manufacturing statement is used to compute the cost of goods manufactured. To compute the cost of goods manufactured the following format is used:

	1. Direct materials
Add	2. Direct labor
Add	3. *Manufacturing overhead*
Equals	4. Total manufacturing cost
Add	5. *Work-in-process, beginning inventory*
Equals	6. Total work-in-process during the period (available for production)
Deduct	7. *Work-in-process, ending inventory*
Equals	8. Cost of goods manufactured.

Table 2.6
ABEL Manufacturing Company, Ltd., Manufacturing Statement for the Year Ended December 31, 19X6

Raw Materials			
Raw Materials Inventory, Jan. 1, 19X6		$15,000	
Raw Materials Purchased	$30,000		
Freight on Raw Materials Purchased	2,000		
Delivered Cost of Raw Materials Purchased		32,000	
Raw Materials Available for Use		$47,000	
Raw Materials Inventory, Dec. 31, 19X6		22,000	
Raw Materials Used			$25,000
Direct Labor			$50,000
Factory Overhead Costs			
Indirect Labor		$ 1,500	
Indirect Material		1,000	
Power		1,000	
Repairs and Maintenance		1,000	
Factory Taxes		500	
Supervision		1,500	
Factory Insurance Expired		200	
Small Tools Written Off		200	
Depreciation of Equipment		800	
Depreciation of Building		1,800	
Total Factory Overhead Costs			$ 9,500
Total Manufacturing Costs			$84,500
Add: Goods-in-Process Inventory, Jan. 1, 19X6			11,500
Total Goods-in-Process during the Year			$96,000
Deduct: Goods-in-Process Inventory, Dec. 31, 19X6			36,000
Cost of Goods Manufactured and Transferred			$60,000

Note that the earnings statement is used to determine the earnings of the period as well as the cost of goods sold. To obtain the cost of goods sold the following format is used:

1. Finished goods, beginning inventory

Add 2. *Cost of goods manufactured* (see manufacturing statement)

Table 2.7
ABEL Manufacturing Company, Ltd., Earnings Statement for the Year Ended December 31, 19X6

Net Sales			$300,000
Cost of Goods Sold			
Finished Goods Inventory, Jan. 1, 19X6		$20,000	
Cost of Goods Manufactured		60,000	
Goods Available for Sale		$80,000	
Finished Goods Inventory, Dec. 31, 19X6		15,000	
Cost of Goods Sold			65,000
Gross Profit			$235,000
Operating Expenses			
Administrative and General Expenses			
Office Salaries Expense	$22,500		
Miscellaneous General Expense	6,500		
Bad Debts Expense	3,500		
Depreciation Expense, Office Equipment	5,250		
Office Supplies Expense	7,250		
Total Administrative and General Expenses		$45,000	
Selling Expenses			
Sales Salaries Expense	$11,500		
Advertising Expense	2,500		
Delivery Wages Expense	6,500		
Shipping Supplies Expense	2,500		
Delivery Equipment Insurance Expense	7,500		
Depreciation Expense, Delivery Equipment	5,500		
Total Selling Expenses		36,000	
Total Operating Expenses			$ 81,000
Operating Earnings			$154,000
Nonoperating (Irregular) Income			
Earnings from Joint Venture of Limited Duration		$100,000	
Interest Income		50,000	
Gain on Sale of Assets		60,000	
Total			$210,000
Nonoperating (Irregular) Expenses			
Research and Development		30,000	
Cost of Discontinuing Product Line		20,000	
Foreign Currency Translation Loss		54,000	
Total			$204,000
Earnings before Interest and Taxation			$160,000
Financial Expense			
Mortgage Interest Expense		4,000	
Long-Term Debt Expense		10,000	
Other		16,000	
Total			$ 30,000
Income Taxes			$ 60,000
Net Earnings			$ 70,000
Net Earnings per Share (10,000 Shares Outstanding)			$7.00

Equals   3. *Finished goods available for sale*
Less   4. *Finished goods, ending inventory*
Equals   5. Cost of goods sold during the period.

2.4 CONCLUSION

Management accounting attempts to provide necessary information for all the normative decision models of its many internal users. Consequently, there are several concepts of costs, which differ depending on managerial uses and viewpoints. The particular object of costing justifies a cost's classification. Although the object of costing may differ between such groups as accountants, economists, and engineers, all view cost as a "sacrifice" and associate cost with decision alternatives, an activity, or an action. Staubus states:

Costing is the process of determining the cost of doing something, e.g., the cost of manufacturing an article, rendering a service, or performing a function. The article manufactured, service rendered, or function performed is known as the object of costing. . . . Objects of costing are always activities. We want to know the cost of doing something. We may, however, find ourselves speaking of the cost of a product as an abbreviation for the cost of acquiring or manufacturing the product.[3]

NOTES

1. J. Maurice Clark, *Studies in the Economics of Overhead Costs* (Chicago: University of Chicago Press, 1923), 35.
2. P. S. Singh and G. L. Chapman, "Is Linear Approximation Good Enough?" *Management Accounting* (January 1978): 53–55.
3. George J. Staubus, *Activity Costing and Input-Output Accounting* (Homewood, Ill.: Irwin, 1971), 1.

SELECTED READINGS

American Accounting Association, Committee on Cost Concepts and Standards, "Report of the Committee on Cost Concepts and Standards." *Accounting Review* (January 1952): 174–180.

American Accounting Association, 1955 Committee on Cost Concepts Underlying Reports for Management Purposes, "Tentative Statements of Costs Underlying Reports for Management Purposes." *Accounting Review* (April 1956): 182–183.

Anthony, Robert N. "Cost Concepts for Control." *Accounting Review* (April 1957): 229–234.

Bedford, Norton M. "The Nature of Business Costs: General Concepts." *Accounting Review* (January 1957): 18–24. Reprinted in H. Anton and P. Firmin. *Contemporary Issues in Cost Accounting*. Boston: Houghton Mifflin, 1966, 21–30.

Bisgay, Louis. "Report on Fiscal and Variable Expense Research." *Management Accounting* (June 1980): 43–50.

Clark, J. Maurice. *Studies in the Economics of Overhead Costs*. Chicago: University of Chicago Press, 1923, chaps. 3 and 9.

Connolly, H. Andrew. "Planning a New Cost System: The 'Unfreezing' Stage." *Management Accounting* (November 1979): 19–24.

Demski, J. S., G. A. Feltham, C. T. Horngren, and R. K. Jaedicke. *A Conceptual Approach to Cost Determination.* Iowa City: Iowa State Press, 1980.

Dickey, R. I., ed. *Accountants' Cost Handbook.* New York: Ronald Press, 1960, secs. 1 and 2.

Haseman, Wilber E., "An Interpretive Framework of Cost." *Accounting Review* (October 1968): 738–752.

Hazelton, W. A., "How to Cost Labor Settlements," *Management Accounting* (May 1979): 19–23.

Herman, Michael P., "Uniform Cost Accounting Standards: Are They Necessary?" *Management Accounting* (April 1972): 15–19.

Horngren, Charles T., "Choosing Accounting Practices for Reporting to Management," *NAA Bulletin* (September 1962): 3–15.

Leininger, Wayne, "Opportunity Costs: Some Definitions and Examples," *Accounting Review* (January 1977): 248–251.

McRae, T. W., "Opportunity and Incremental Cost: An Attempt to Define in System Terms," *Accounting Review* (April 1970): 315–321.

Nestor, Joseph, "How Cost Accountants Can Improve Public Housing Programs," *Management Accounting* (October 1979): 40–42.

Rayburn, Gayle L., "Marketing Costs: Accountants to the Rescue," *Management Accounting* (January 1981): 37–41.

Shillinglaw, Gordon, "The Concept of Attributable Cost," *Journal of Accounting Research* (Spring 1963): 73–85.

Spencer, Milton H.; Seo, K. K.; and Simkin, Mark G., *Managerial Economics: Text, Problems and Short Cases,* 4th ed. (Homewood, Ill.: Irwin, 1975).

"The Uses and Classifications of Costs," *Research Series No. 7,* reprinted in *NAA Bulletin* (May 1946): 10–13.

Wallace, Edward L., "Some Comments on the Statement of Planning Costs," *Accounting Review* (July 1957): 448–466.

Wallace, Witt, "Work Measurement of Indirect Labor," *Management Accounting* (November 1971): 31–34.

Cost Estimation Techniques: Fundamentals

Man who relies only on the seat-of-his-pants to predict the future may soon lose his shirt.[1]

Most cost accounting decisions depend on the reliability of the information produced by the accounting system. This information consists of *anticipated* data on different alternatives. In response to these information needs, business forecasting has developed as an integral part of the cost accounting discipline. Because business forecasting emphasizes cost reduction and control, *cost estimation* is at its center. A knowledge of future costs and the behavior of costs over time may be useful for a *structural analysis* of costs, which determines the structural relationships between costs and the factors most likely to affect them; *budget forecasting* of costs, which builds on the structural relationships to extrapolate the behavior of costs in the future; and *cost control,* which compares the actual behavior of costs with the predetermined costs.

The forecasting activities, therefore, consist of three temporally interrelated phases:

1. A *structural phase* to determine the independent variables affecting the behavior of costs (or cost estimation)
2. A *prediction phase* to forecast the future behavior of costs based on the results of the structural analysis (or cost prediction)
3. A *control phase* to evaluate the reliability of the prediction phase.

The success of these phases depends on the definition of an adequate theoretical or other relationship between costs and other variables, and on the choice of an estimation technique. This chapter will evaluate each of these problems.

3.1 STRUCTURE OF THE COST ESTIMATION MODEL

A cost estimation model relates to a set of structures that are defined by relationships between economic variables. Each structure is defined by a set of equations according to which of the following types of relationship exists:

1. Definitions or identities which need no further proof for their existence, e.g., Sales Revenue = Price × Quantity Sold.
2. Technological relationships determined by the "state of the arts" as may be given, e.g., Output = F (Labor, Capital).
3. Institutional or historical relations, which are incorporated by virtue of belonging to the given society, e.g., Sales Tax Revenue = Tax Rate × Volume of Sales, where the tax rate is determined by the appropriate governmental institution.
4. Behavioral relationships, which describe how particular variables in the economic behavior of an individual or a group respond to changes in other variables, e.g., Aggregate Consumption = F (Aggregate Income).[2]

A structure based on any of these relationships will be specified by the dependent variable, or costs, and the independent variables. The structure or set of relationships determines the functional relationship of the model. These relationships may take the following forms, resulting in different equations:

1. A positive linear relationship between costs and one independent variable may be expressed as $y = a + bx$, where, for example, a is the total fixed cost, b the unit variable cost, and x the total level of activity.
2. A strictly linear relationship between costs and one independent variable may be expressed as $y = bx$, with $a = 0$ and $b = dy/dx > 0$.
3. The polynomial model $y = a + bx + cx^2$ depicts a relationship between costs and output with *decreasing* productivity.
4. The polynomial model $y = a + bx - cx^2$ depicts a relationship between costs and output with *increasing* productivity.
5. The total long-run cost of a firm may be depicted as $y = a + bx + cx^2 + dx^3$.
6. Other forms of curves may be transformed into straight lines by the use of transformations:

$$\text{Log } y = a + bx \text{ becomes } Z = a + bx \text{ if Log } y = Z.$$

$$y = a + \text{Log} \times \text{ becomes } y = a + bw \text{ if Log } X = w.$$

$$y = ax^b \text{ becomes Log } y = \text{Log } a + b \text{ Log } X.$$

$$y = \frac{1}{a + bx} \text{ becomes } Z = a + bx \text{ if } Z = 1/y.$$

$$= a + b\frac{1}{x} \text{ becomes } y = a + bw \text{ if } w = 1/x.$$

The transformations do not change the fundamental properties of the relationships of the variables.

These equations imply a perfect relationship between the variations of the dependent and independent variables. Most of the time, however, some variations remain unexplained. Consequently, the structural relationship will be as follows:

$$y = f(x, \mu)$$

where μ is a symbolic variable representing the random variations. It is called the *disturbance term*, the error term, or the stochastic term.

3.2 COST ESTIMATION TECHNIQUES

The accountant faced with the choice of cost estimation techniques needs selection criteria. One obvious criterion is the *predictive ability* of the model. Another may be that the improvement in the quality of the decision must exceed the cost of obtaining the information. In other words, the choice of a cost estimation technique must involve a *cost benefit analysis*.

There are two main estimation techniques: *intuitive* or *judgmental forecasting* and *quantitative forecasting*.

The judgmental method is based on the collection of experiences, opinions, and feelings about the subject which may be translated into a considered judgment or a prediction. Examples of this approach are opinion polls, panels of experts, and the more refined delphi method. Statisticians and psychologists have criticized the judgmental method, and it may be impractical, unappealing, and cumbersome when applied to cost estimation.

The quantitative method is based on a model representing the real-life situation involving the cost object. This model may be either statistical (least squares method) or nonstatistical, and the following discussion reflects this dichotomy in cost estimation techniques.

The nonstatistical techniques identified in the literature and in practice as particularly useful to the cost estimation problem are the *engineering method,* the *accounts method,* the *high-low method,* and the *visual curve fitting method.*

3.3 ENGINEERING METHOD

The engineering approach to estimation bases its results on the input-output relationships implied by the production function. For every output mix, the engineering specifications, or input mix, indicate the particular mix of material, labor, and capital equipment. Consequently, given a study of the input mix—the physical relationships between quantities of inputs and each unit of output (what the economist calls the "production function")—the total cost of material and labor may be estimated.

For example, suppose a given product, alpha, uses material, labor, and capital equipment. The production function or input mix specifies that two pounds of material are needed for each unit of output. A time and motion study (or any other engineering study) shows that three hours of direct labor are needed for the completion of a unit of output. The estimated price of material is $5 per pound, and the wage rate is $4 per hour. On the basis of this information derived from the engineering study, the total prime cost (TPC) per unit of output will be TPC = (2 pounds × $5) + (3 hours × $4) = $22. The input mix and output mix derived from engineering studies are used to estimate the total prime cost used in future periods for prediction.

Engineering methods can also be used to predict overhead costs. For example, plant design work requires estimates of overhead costs using engineering principles.

The engineering method, although fairly accurate, presents some serious problems:

1. The final cost of any product should include a fair share of the overhead costs. These are, by definition, indirect costs to the final product, so they cannot be linked directly to an individual product and estimated by an engineering study. The engineering method is generally useful for the estimation of the prime costs of the product and may ignore secondary relationships between the inputs and outputs. The method is most applicable when the direct costs make up a large proportion of total costs and when the input mix is fairly stable over time.

2. The material and labor estimates made by the engineering method are ideal estimates: They do not take into account possible material waste and labor inefficiency. The total prime cost estimated by the engineering method, to be more accurate, should include additional allowances for material wastes and labor inefficiency.

3. The engineering method implicitly assumes that the actual input and/or output mixes are optimal mixes. The method ignores other possible input or output mixes which may be more beneficial to the firm in terms of cost reduction, better product quality, imposed productivity, and even improved morale.

4. The engineering method may be costly to use.

The engineering method, therefore, is most useful with the concurrent use of other estimation techniques. An NAA report describes its use as follows:

The industrial engineering approach to determination of how costs should vary with volume proceeds by a systematic study of materials, labor, services, and facilities needed at varying volumes. The aim is to find the best way to obtain the desired production. These studies generally make use of past experience, but it is used as a guide or as check upon the results obtained the desired production. These studies generally make use of past experience, but it is used as a guide or as a check upon the results obtained by direct study of the production methods and facilities. Where no past experience is available, as with a new product, plant, or method, this approach can be applied to estimate the changes in cost that will accompany changes in volume.[3]

Table 3.1
NANEX, Inc.: Total Costs for Department X

Account	Total	Variable	Fixed
Direct Labor	$ 5,000	$ 5,000	
Direct Material	10,000	10,000	
Indirect Labor	5,000	5,000	
Indirect Material	12,000	12,000	
Depreciation	2,000		$ 2,000
Power	3,000	3,000	
Maintenance	5,000		5,000
Selling Overhead	10,000		10,000
Miscellaneous Items	3,000		3,000
		$35,000	$20,000
Volume of Activity	5,000 units		

3.4 ACCOUNTS METHOD

The accounts method relies on the existence of past accounting records and the expert judgment of the cost accountant. The steps in applying the method are as follows:

1. The cost accountant classifies the total cost at a given level of activity (for example, x_0) into either a fixed or a variable category on the basis of past experience and knowledge.
2. The variable category total is an estimation of the total variable costs (for example, $\sum_i VC_i$), and the fixed category total is an estimation of the total fixed costs (for example, $\sum_i FC_i$).
3. The unit variable cost (b) is computed as follows:

$$b = \left(\sum_i VC_i \right)/x_0 .$$

4. The total fixed cost (a) is equal to $\sum_i FC_i$.
5. The total cost equation (TC) is expressed as follows:

$$TC = a + bx$$

or

$$TC = \sum_i FC_i + \left[\left(\sum_i VC_i \right)/x_0 \right] x.$$

To illustrate, suppose that the cost accountant of NANEX, Inc., classified total costs at an output of 5,000 units, as shown in Table 3.1. Based on the accounts method, the cost equation would be:

$$TC = \$20,000 + \frac{\$35,000}{5,000} x$$

$$= \$20,000 + \$7x.$$

The accounts method, although expedient and rather inexpensive, suffers from serious drawbacks:

1. It relies heavily on the intuitive judgment of the cost analyst. The reliability of the estimates is difficult to evaluate, and another cost accountant is very likely to come up with different classifications.
2. The classification of costs as either fixed or variable is at best restrictive, if not unrealistic. Assuming linearity, costs may be fixed, variable, or semivariable; the semivariable category, ignored in the accounts method, is most suitable to most overhead items. If semivariable costs are classified as either fixed or variable, the unit variable cost and total fixed costs could be overestimated or underestimated.
3. The accounts method depends heavily on the financial accounting and recording system. For example, the recording of a transaction into given accounts may influence the classification of the accounts as variable or fixed, which will affect the resulting unit variable cost and total fixed costs.

In conclusion, although the accounts method is inexpensive and expedient, it should be used with caution and when only crude approximations of cost behavior are needed.

Table 3.2
JABEX, Inc.: Total Labor Hours and Production Costs for 19X9

Month (t)	Labor Hours (x)	Total Production Costs (y)
January	2	7
February	1	5
March	3	10
April	4	12
May	2	8
June	3	11
July	5	13
August	6	15
September	2	9
October	4	10
November	5	11
December	3	9
$n = 12$	$40 = \Sigma x$	$120 = \Sigma y$

To illustrate the application of the following methods for the estimation of the structural relationships of a mixed cost, one theoretical problem will be used. Assume that JABEX, Inc., which manufactures and sells widgets, wants to estimate its production costs. The labor hours and production costs for the 12 months of 19X9 are shown in Table 3.2 and plotted in Figure 3.1. The problem is to estimate the semivariable equation $y = a + bx$, where y = total cost of production, a = total fixed costs, b = unit variable cost, and x = level of activity.

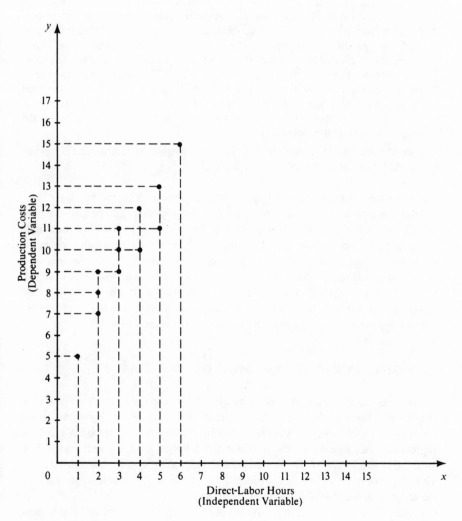

Figure 3.1
JABEX, Inc.: Plotting of Direct-Labor Hours and Production Costs

3.5 HIGH-LOW METHOD

The high-low method is an estimation technique which relies on the relationship between the highest and lowest observed values of costs. The steps in this method are as follows:

1. The highest and lowest levels of costs are determined. In our example, the lowest level of activity is one unit with $5 in production cost, and the highest level of activity is six units with $15 in production cost.

2. If the two extreme observations identified in step 1 are assumed to be representative of the cost relationships, then the parameters of the equation line that connects them may be determined as follows. The unit variable cost will be the slope of the equation line and, consequently, will be equal to the difference between the highest and lowest values of cost divided by the differences in the corresponding values of the dependent variable: b = unit variable cost = ($15 − 5)/(6 − 1) = $2. The total fixed cost will be the intersection of the equation line with the y-axis. Consequently, it may be computed on the basis of either an equation based on the lowest observation, $5 = a + $2 × 1, or an equation based on the highest observation, $15 = a + $2 × 6. In either case, the total fixed cost (a) is equal to $3.

3. It may be concluded that the basis of the high-low method, the equation line estimating the production costs of JABEX, Inc., is $y = $3 + $2x$.

The cost line resulting from the high-low technique is depicted in Figure 3.2.

Like the accounts method, the high-low method may be inexpensive and expedient. However, it relies heavily on the observation of the two extremes and, consequently, may ignore the information included in the remaining observations. Furthermore, the high and the low cost values are, by definition, extreme situations which might reflect more an abnormal than normal cost situation. The reliability of the method depends on how representative the high and low cost values are. Therefore, the high-low method should only be used when crude, general approximations rather than precise estimates are needed.

3.6 VISUAL CURVE FITTING METHOD

The visual curve fitting method is an estimating technique which relies on the general trend of the plotted points on a *scattergraph,* or *scatter diagram.* When the total costs observed at various levels of activity are plotted on a graph, a regression line, passing by the maximum number of plotted points and in line with the general trend of the plotted points, is fitted by simple visual inspection. The slope of such a line is considered to be the unit variable cost, and the intercept with the y-axis is the total fixed cost.

Figure 3.3 presents a scattergraph for the JABEX, Inc., problem. The regression line strikes the y-axis at $5.30, which represents the total fixed cost. This *arbitrary* trend line is also drawn through points x = 2, y = $8, and x = 5, y =

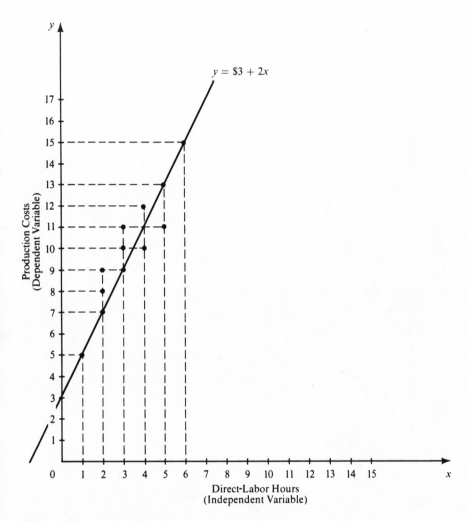

Figure 3.2
JABEX, Inc.: Cost Line Resulting from the High-Low Method

$13. The unit variable cost is ($13 − $8)/(5 − 2) = 1.66, and the equation line is
y = $5.30 + 1.66x.

The visual curve fitting method has serious limitations. To be useful, the
scattergraph and regression line must be drawn by a very experienced cost
analyst. A knowledge of extraordinary events leading to adjustment of the cost
behavior (strikes, natural disasters, wars, and so forth) is necessary to insure the
accuracy of the regression line. The regression line obtained through the visual
curve fitting method is subjective: *Using the same data, another cost accountant
is likely to draw a different line.*

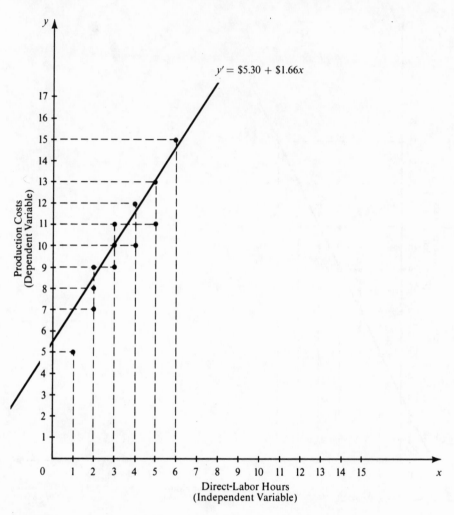

Figure 3.3
JABEX, Inc.: Scatter Diagram

3.7 SIMPLE REGRESSION METHOD

The simple regression method measures the average amount of change in the dependent variable of costs that is related to unit change in one independent variable (labor hours in our example). Assuming for the time being that the assumptions of regression analysis have been met, the method applied to our example yields the following cost equation:

$$y' = \$4.45 + \$1.66x$$

where y' is the estimated production costs for any amount of labor hours used (x). The equation also yielded a \$4.45 constant or intercept term and a slope coefficient of \$1.66.

The cost equation obtained using the simple regression method is shown in Figure 3.4.

The cost equation y' = \$4.45 + \$1.66(10 labor hours) = \$21.05.

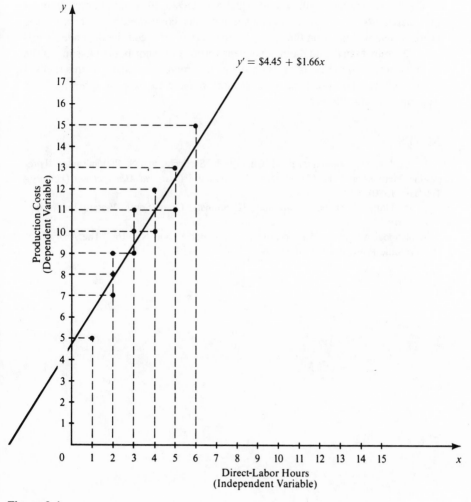

Figure 3.4
JABEX, Inc.: Computation for Simple Regression Method

3.8 CONCLUSION

It is interesting to note at this point the different equations obtained by using the high-low method, the visual curve fitting method, and the simple regression method:

1. $Y' = \$4.45 + \$1.66x$ for the simple regression method
2. $Y' = \$3 + \$2x$ for the high-low method
3. $Y' = \$5.30 + \$1.66x$ for the visual curve fitting method.

The use of any one of these cost equations leads to the estimation of different budgeted costs. The cost accountant is naturally concerned because he or she needs to use the equation that provides the best fit between the dependent variable of product costs and the independent variable of labor hours. Assuming the benefits outweigh the costs of using the simple regression analysis, this method should be used because it provides a more reliable fit than the other methods examined in this chapter.

NOTES

1. Attributed to Confucius. K. H. Chan, F. L. Sbrocchi, and N. R. VanZante, "Forecasting Methods and the Management Accountant." *Cost and Management* (January–February 1980): 44.

2. M. Dutta, *Econometric Methods* (Cincinnati, Ohio: South-Western Publishing, 1975), 10.

3. National Association of Accountants, Research Report No. 16, "The Analysis of Cost-Volume-Profit Relationships" (New York: NAA, 1965), 17.

4

Cost-Volume-Profit Analysis

Cost-volume-profit analysis involves an examination of cost and revenue behavioral patterns and their relationships with profit. The analysis separates costs into fixed and variable components and determines the level of activity where costs and revenues are in equilibrium. The cost-volume-profit analysis is a normative model for understanding the relationships between the cost, revenue, and profit structures of a firm. It is a key factor in all decisions based on selling prices, variable costs, and fixed costs. Acquisitions, resource utilization and disposition, product mix determination, product pricing, and even fixed assets acquisitions are decisions in which an understanding of cost-volume-profit relationships may avoid undesirable results.

This chapter first covers the accounting approach to breakeven analysis. The cost-volume-profit analysis, or breakeven analysis, is a useful managerial decision making tool that can be adapted to specific situations by relaxing any of the limiting and typical assumptions of the conventional breakeven analysis.

4.1 ACCOUNTING APPROACH TO BREAKEVEN ANALYSIS

The cost accountant uses the cost-volume-profit analysis, commonly known as *breakeven analysis,* to compute the volume or level of activity for which the profit generated is zero and beyond which any increase in production will lead to a positive result, or profit. The *breakeven point* corresponds to the volume of activity at which total revenue equals total costs.

4.1.1 Breakeven Formulae

In algebraic terms, profit or loss may be given by

$$\mu = Pq - (F + Vq)$$

where

μ = profit before income taxes

P = unit selling price

q = sales volume in units

F = total fixed costs

V = unit variable cost.

The breakeven point at which sales equal total costs and profit equals zero may be found as follows: $Pq^* - (F + Vq^*) = 0$, where $q^* =$ breakeven volume. Consequently, we may write

$$q^* = \frac{F}{P - V}$$

where $P - V = $ *contribution margin per unit*. Therefore, the breakeven point equals the ratio of total fixed costs (F) divided by the contribution margin per unit $(P - V)$.

To convert q^* to dollar terms, multiply both sides of the q^* formula by P as follows:

$$Y = Pq^* = \frac{PF}{P - V}$$

or

$$Y = \frac{F}{1 - \dfrac{V}{P}}$$

where

Y = breakeven sales

$1 - \dfrac{V}{P} = $ contribution margin ratio.

The last formula expresses the breakeven sales or breakeven point in dollars. It equals the ratio of the fixed costs (F) divided by the contribution margin ratio, also referred to as the variable profit ratio,

$$\left(1 - \frac{V}{P} \right).$$

To illustrate, consider the following example. Clara Smith plans to open a frozen yogurt business. She determined the following revenue and expense relationships:

	Dollars	Percent
Sales Price per Cup of Yogurt	.50	100
Variable Expense per Cup	.30	60
Monthly Fixed Expenses		
Rent	1,000	
Wages for Two Employees	1,500	
Payroll Fringe Costs	500	
Liability Insurance	50	
Other Fixed Costs	6,450	
Electricity	500	
	10,000	

The breakeven analysis proceeds as follows:

1. The unit contribution margin, or excess of unit sales price over unit variable cost:

$$P - V = \$.50 - \$.30 = \$.20.$$

2. The breakeven point in terms of units sold:

$$q^* = \frac{\$10,000}{\$.20} = 50,000 \text{ cups per month.}$$

3. The contribution margin ratio, or variable profit ratio:

$$1 - \frac{V}{P} = 1 - \frac{\$.30}{\$.50} = 40\%.$$

4. The breakeven sales:

$$y = \frac{\$10,000}{0.40} = \$25,000$$

or $y = Pq^* = \$.50 \times 50,000 \text{ cups} = \$25,000.$

4.1.2 Breakeven Charts

The profit structure of a company may be portrayed in a simple *breakeven chart* depicting the interactions between the cost and revenue structures. Figure 4.1 is a breakeven chart showing the relationship between sales volume as an independent variable and total costs as a dependent variable. The main breakeven point is the intersection between the total revenues line and the total cost line. The area between the total revenues line and the total cost line at a volume below the breakeven point represents the loss area. The corresponding area above the breakeven point represents the profit area. Whereas Figure 4.1 presents the breakeven chart in total dollars, Figure 4.2 presents it in average dollars.

Another approach to graphic cost-volume-profit analysis is shown in Figure 4.3. Known as the *profit graph approach,* it portrays the relationships between profit as a dependent variable and sales volume, or dollar sales, as an indepen-

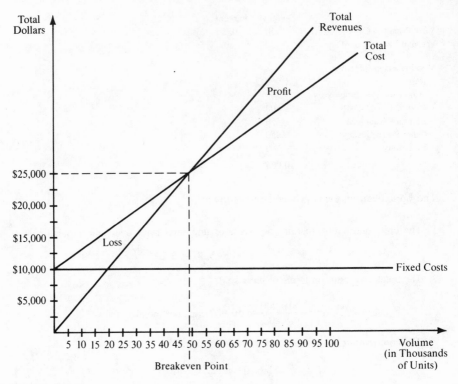

Figure 4.1
Smith Company: Breakeven Point in Total Dollars

dent variable. Where the profit line crosses the sales volume axis is the breakeven point.

4.1.3 Limiting Assumptions of Breakeven Analysis

The user of breakeven analysis must be aware of the limiting assumptions or simplifications of the model:

1. Expenses may be dichotomized into variable and fixed categories.
2. The behavior of revenues and expenses is accurately portrayed and is linear. This is possible when (1) unit selling price will not change with volume (for example, the firm does not adopt any discriminatory pricing); (2) unit variable cost will not change with volume; and (3) some costs are fixed for a given period and over a particular level of activity (the relevant range).
3. The difference between beginning and ending inventory is insignificant.
4. A single product is produced.
5. The situation is deterministic, and the values are known with certainty.

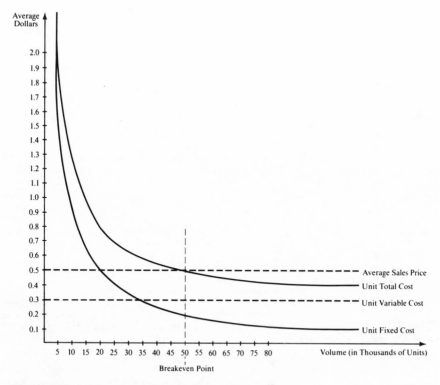

Figure 4.2
Smith Company: Breakeven Point in Average Dollars

6. The analysis is intended to satisfice rather than optimize a profit motive.

7. The cost of capital is absent in the analysis.

8. The implications of the elasticity of the product and demand are not included in the analysis.

These assumptions or simplifications implied in the accountant's model are justified if they are assumed to lead to the same or better decisions than might be provided by more realistic, complex, and costly models. The sections that follow present extensions to the accountant's breakeven analysis on the basis of the relaxing of some of these assumptions. The added benefits and better decision making are assumed to outweigh the additional costs of these more complex models.

4.2 USEFULNESS OF THE ACCOUNTING APPROACH

A knowledge of the breakeven structure, the proposed changes in revenue, and the operating characteristics of a firm permits the identification of areas of cost,

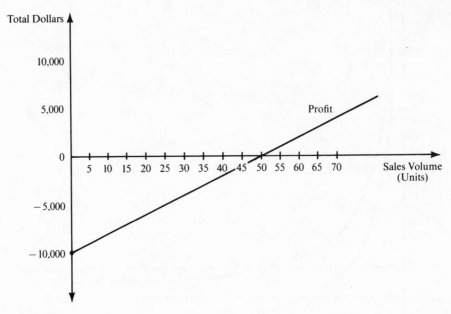

Figure 4.3
Smith Company: Profit Graph

revenue, and profit fluctuations, as well as evaluation of the breakeven area. In other words, an analysis of the changes in each of the parameters and variables of the breakeven formulae allows assessment of the significance of possible estimation errors in the breakeven point. Each possible change may also be identified with a managerial problem. The sections that follow discuss these problems.

4.2.1 Change in the Unit Selling Price

An increase in the selling price will raise the contribution margin and, consequently, decrease the breakeven volume. To illustrate, suppose that Smith decides to decrease the selling price from $.50 to $.40, and all other variables remain unchanged. What is the monthly breakeven point in number of cups? In dollar sales?

These questions can be answered by turning to breakeven formulae for q^* and y:

$$q^* = \frac{\$10,000}{\$.40 - \$.30} = 100,000 \text{ cups per month,}$$

and $y = 100,000$ cups $\times$ $.40 = $40,000, or

$$y = \frac{\$10,000}{1 - \dfrac{\$.30}{\$.40}} = \$40,000.$$

4.2.2 Change in the Unit Variable Cost

An increase in the unit variable cost leads to a decline in the unit contribution margin and an increase in the breakeven volume. Similarly, a decrease in the unit variable cost will decrease the breakeven volume.

To illustrate, suppose that Smith decides to pay the manager $.10 per cup as a commission, and the other variables remain unchanged. What is the monthly breakeven point in number of cups? In dollar sales? The question can be answered by turning again to breakeven formulae for q* and y:

$$q^* = \frac{\$10,000}{\$.50 - \$.40} = 100,000 \text{ cups per month,}$$

and $y = 100,000$ cups $\times$ $.50 = $50,000, or

$$y = \frac{\$10,000}{1 - \dfrac{\$.40}{\$.50}} = \$50,000.$$

4.2.3 Change in the Total Fixed Costs

An increase in the total fixed costs will result in an increase in the breakeven volume. Similarly, a decrease in the total fixed costs will result in a decrease in the breakeven volume.

To illustrate, suppose Smith's rent was tripled and she wanted to determine the breakeven point in terms of cups and dollar sales. The breakeven formulae are again used to solve the problem:

$$q^* = \frac{\$10,000 + \$2,000}{\$.50 - \$.30} = 60,000 \text{ cups per months,}$$

and $y = 60,000$ cups $\times$ $.50 = $30,000, or

$$y = \frac{\$12,000}{1 - \dfrac{\$.30}{\$.50}} = \$30,000.$$

4.2.4 Target Sales for a Given Target Profit

The breakeven formulae can be adapted to determine the sales volume necessary to achieve a desired net income. The conventional formula for computing a profit before taxes (μ) is as follows:

$$\mu = Pq - (Vq + F).$$

To solve for the volume q necessary to achieve μ, the formula may be rearranged as follows:

$$q = \frac{F + \mu}{P - V}.$$

In other words, the sales volume necessary for a desired net income before taxes equals the ratio of fixed costs plus the desired net income before taxes divided by the contribution margin per unit.

To find the sales dollars needed to achieve the desired net income before taxes, adjust the formula for the sales volume as follows:[1]

$$y = \frac{F + \mu}{1 - \dfrac{V}{P}}.$$

The sales dollars necessary for a desired net income before taxes equals the ratio of the fixed costs plus the desired net income before taxes divided by the contribution margin ratio.

Given a tax rate equal to t, formulae for both q and y can be adjusted to determine the sales volume or sales dollars necessary to achieve an after-tax profit Z. The formulae are rearranged as follows:

$$q = \frac{F + \dfrac{Z}{1 - t}}{P - V}$$

and

$$y = \frac{F + \dfrac{Z}{1 - t}}{1 - \dfrac{V}{P}}.$$

To illustrate, what sales must Smith try to achieve to obtain a net income after taxes of $20,000 if the tax rate is 50 percent? The formula for the sales volume necessary to achieve a given profit yields:

$$y = \frac{\$10,000 + \dfrac{\$20,000}{1 - \$.50}}{1 - \dfrac{\$.30}{\$.50}} = \$125,000.$$

4.2.5 Operating Profit at a Given Sales Volume

Given that the operating profit before taxes at the breakeven volume equals zero, the operating profit for any given sales volume greater than the breakeven volume equals the profit realized by the additional volume beyond the breakeven volume.

Consequently, the operating profit for any given sales volume q', given a breakeven volume of q^*, equals $(q' - q^*)(P - V)$. In other words, it equals the difference between the volume of sales desired and the breakeven volume, multiplied by the contribution margin per unit.

You will recall that Smith Company's breakeven volume was found to equal 50,000 cups. Smith now wants to find the profit before taxes associated with sales volumes of 60,000 cups, 70,000 cups, and 80,000 cups. Operating profit for 60,000 cups sold = $(60,000 - 50,000)(\$.50 - \$.30) = \$2,000$. Operating profit for 70,000 cups sold = $(70,000 - 50,000)(\$.50 - \$.30) = \$4,000$. Operating profit for 80,000 cups sold = $(80,000 - 50,000)(\$.50 - \$.30) = \$6,000$.

4.2.6 Effects of Multiple Changes

If the interaction of volume, selling price, variable costs, and fixed costs are taken into account, the breakeven formulae can be adapted to reflect the simultaneous changes in all relevant variables. For example, assume that Smith is considering the impact of different changes on her original estimates. She believes that a decrease of 20 percent per unit in the selling price may lead to a 30-percent increase in the sales volume. She also believes that an improvement in production techniques would lead to a decrease of 90 percent per unit in the unit variable cost and an increase of $46,500 per year in the fixed costs. What level of sales dollars must Smith achieve to attain an after-tax net income of $18,000 if the current tax rate is still 50 percent?

All these changes may be shown in one formula, as follows:

$$q = \frac{F + \Delta F \pm \dfrac{Z}{(1 - t)}}{1 - \dfrac{V \pm \Delta V}{P \pm \Delta P}}$$

where Δ stands for changes. This is calculated as follows:

$$q = \frac{\$10,000 + \$46,500 + \dfrac{\$18,000}{(1 - \$.50)}}{1 - \dfrac{\$.30(1 - \$.90)}{\$.50(1 - \$.20)}} = \$100,000.$$

4.3 OTHER COST-VOLUME-PROFIT RELATIONSHIPS

4.3.1 Margin of Safety

In addition to predicting the impact of changes in relevant variables, as discussed in the preceding section, breakeven analysis can provide additional insight into a firm's planning and control processes by furnishing information such as the *margin of safety* and the *margin of safety ratio*. The margin of safety is given sales less breakeven sales. The margin of safety ratio is the margin of safety expressed as a percentage of sales:

$$\text{Margin of safety} = \text{Given sales figure} - \text{Breakeven sales.}$$

$$\text{Margin of safety ratio} = \frac{\text{Given sales figure} - \text{Breakeven sales}}{\text{Given sales figure}}.$$

From the data in section 4.1.1 and with sales equaling \$50,000, the margin of safety and the margin of safety ratio are as follows:

$$\text{Margin of safety} = \$50,000 - \$25,000 = \$25,000.$$

$$\text{Margin of safety ratio} = \frac{\$50,000 - \$25,000}{\$50,000} = 50\%.$$

In other words, sales have to decrease by more than 50 percent before the company suffers a loss. The margin of safety is, therefore, a tool to be used to point out the existence of a problem.

The margin of safety for a single product firm can also be expressed in terms of unit of product by dividing the margin of safety by the unit selling price.

4.3.2 Contribution Margin Ratio

The *contribution margin ratio,* also known as the *profit-volume* ratio, is equal to the contribution margin per unit divided by the unit selling price:

$$\text{Contribution margin ratio} = \frac{\text{Contribution margin per unit}}{\text{Unit selling price}}.$$

In section 4.1.1, the contribution margin ratio is equal to 40 percent. This indicates that, for each dollar increase in sales, total contribution margin will increase by 40 cents ($1 sales × a contribution margin ratio of 40%). Assuming no changes to fixed costs, profit will also increase by 40 cents.

This provides a useful rule of thumb: *Assuming no change in fixed costs, the change in net income resulting from a change in sales is obtained by simply applying the contribution margin ratio to the dollar change in sales.*

4.3.3 Operating Leverage

Operating leverage is a measure of the extent to which fixed costs are used in a firm. High fixed costs and low variable cost per unit characterize companies with a high operating leverage. Low fixed costs and high variable cost per unit characterize companies with a low operating leverage.

The degree of operating leverage is measured as follows:

$$\text{Degree of operating leverage} = \frac{\text{Contribution margin}}{\text{Net income}}.$$

Returning to the example in section 4.1.1 and assuming a level of sales equal to 60,000 cups, the profit will be equal to:

$$r = [(\$0.50 - \$.30) \times 60,000] - \$10,000 = \$2,000.$$

Therefore, the degree of operating leverage corresponding to the sales of

$$60,000 \text{ cups is equal to } \frac{\$12,000}{\$2,000} = 6.$$

The degree of operating leverage of "6" indicates at the given level of sales of 60,000 cups how a percentage change in sales volume will affect profit.

For example, for a 10-percent increase in sales, the percentage increase in net income is equal to:

Increase in net income = Percentage increase in sales × degree of operating leverage (10% × 6) = 60%.

Therefore, a 10-percent increase in sales from 60,000 to 66,000 cups will cause the net income to increase from $2,000 to $3,200. To verify: The profit resulting from a 10-percent increase in sales is [($.50 - $0.30)(66,000 cups)] - $10,000 = $3,200.

The largest degree of operating leverage is not the breakeven point. As sales and profit rise above the breakeven point, the degree of operating leverage decreases. This is shown in the following calculations based on the example in section 4.1.1.

Sales in Units	50,000 cups	55,000 cups	60,000 cups	70,000 cups
Sales in $	$25,000	$27,500	$30,000	$35,000
Less Variable Expenses	$15,000	$16,500	$18,000	$21,000
Contribution Margin	$10,000	$11,000	$12,000	$14,000
Less Fixed Expenses	$10,000	$10,000	$10,000	$10,000
Net Income	$ 0	$ 1,000	$ 2,000	$ 4,000
Degree of operating leverage	∞	11	6	3.5

Notice that closer to the breakeven point, as in the case of sales equal to 55,000 cups, a small increase in sales will result in a sizeable increase in profit. Hence, a 10-percent increase in sales will result in a 110-percent increase in profit (10% × 11). At that level, the additional sales effect exercised by management will be very rewarding in terms of a very high increase in profits.

4.3.4 Cash Breakeven Point

Management may be more interested in the impact of volume activity on cash or working capital than on accrual profits. One request may be to determine the "cash breakeven point." In that case, the cash breakeven point is found as follows:

$$\text{Cash BEP} = \frac{\text{Fixed costs} - \text{Noncash fixed costs}}{\text{Cash contribution margin per unit}}.$$

Using the example from section 4.1.1 and assuming a $4,000 depreciation as the only noncash fixed costs, the breakeven point is found as follows:

$$\text{Cash BEP} = \frac{\$10,000 - \$4,000}{\$.50 - \$0.20} = 20,000 \text{ cups per month.}$$

The formula for cash BEP presented, although widely accepted, results in an upward biased output estimate. This bias results from ignoring the true savings due to the deductibility of noncash expenses.

The cash breakeven point assuming tax recovery is found as follows:

$$\text{Cash BEP} = \frac{\text{Fixed costs} - \dfrac{\text{Noncash fixed costs}}{(1 - \text{tax rate})}}{\text{Cash contribution margin per unit}}.$$

Returning to the same example as before and assuming a 50-percent tax rate, the cash BEP is found as follows:

$$\text{Cash BEP} = \frac{\$10,000 - \dfrac{\$4,000}{(1 - 0.50)}}{\$0.50 - \$0.20} = 6,666.6 \text{ cups per month.}$$

4.4 BREAKEVEN ANALYSIS FOR THE MULTIPRODUCT FIRM

4.4.1 In the Absence of Constraints

The previous analysis assumed a single-product firm; however, most manufacturers make more than one product. Each of the products has its own contribution margin and any changes in one product's contribution margin will affect the total contribution margin. To assess the impact of the product mix on the overall profit rates, a knowledge of the breakeven point for the product mix is useful.

For a single-product firm, the contribution margin ratio may be expressed as

$$\frac{P - V}{P}.$$

Given the existence of a sales mix, the contribution margin ratio for a multiproduct firm will be equal to a weighted summation of the individual contribution margin ratios. If n is the number of products included in the product mix, the overall contribution margin ratio is given by

$$\sum_{i=1}^{n} [q_i(P_i - V_i)] / \sum_{i=n}^{n} P_i q_i,$$

where

n = number of different products $(i = 1, \ldots, n)$

q_i = estimated sales volume for the ith product

P_i = unit selling price for the ith product

V_i = unit variable cost for the ith product.

Thus, the breakeven sales for a multiproduct firm are given by

$$\text{Breakeven sales} = \frac{\text{Fixed cost}}{\text{Overall contribution margin}}$$

$$= \frac{F}{\sum_{i=1}^{n} [q_i(P_i - V_i)] / \sum_{i=1}^{n} P_i q_i}.$$

To illustrate the above formulae, consider the following information on a three-product firm:

Product	Alpha	Beta	Gamma
Sales (units)	6,000	5,000	4,000
Unit selling price	$5	$6	$15
Unit variable cost	$3	$2	$ 8
Fixed expenses: $30,000.			

The overall contribution margin ratio is equal to:

$$\frac{6,000(\$5 - \$3) + 5,000(\$6 - \$2) + 4,000(\$15 - \$8)}{(6,000 \times \$5) + (5,000 \times \$6) + (4,000 \times \$15)} = \frac{60,000}{120,000} = 50\%.$$

$$\text{BE sales} = \frac{\$30,000}{50\%} = \$60,000.$$

If the sales mix changes, then the breakeven point will also change. For example, if the rate changes from the profitable line (which has a 50-percent overall contribution margin ratio) to a less profitable line (which has only a 30-percent contribution margin ratio), the breakeven sales will be equal to

$$\frac{\$30,000}{30\%} = \$100,000.$$

This multiple product breakeven analysis does not allow for the inclusion of resource constraints. Since a firm's product mix decision generally is constrained by the limiting supply of diverse resources, an adequate framework for product mix decisions must consider the impact of these limiting factors. A linear programming solution is needed, as will be shown in chapter 5.

4.4.2 Product Mix Decisions with One Resource Constraint

Every company has at least one limiting factor, and its optimal use is an important consideration in product mix decisions. The firm's objective is to secure maximum profit, which depends on achieving the highest contribution margin per unit of the limiting factor. When a firm has one resource constraint, the optimal product mix may be derived as follows:

1. Determine the contribution margin per unit of output.
2. Calculate the contribution per unit of the constraining factor by dividing the contribution margin per unit of output by the number of units of the constraining factor required for each unit of output.
3. Rank the products on the basis of the size of their contribution margin per unit of the constraining factor.

Table 4.1
Contribution Margin per Hour

Product	Contribution Margin per Unit	Labor Hours per Unit	Contribution Margin per Labor Hour	Ranking
A	$15	5	$3	4
B	$12	3	$4	3
C	$14	2	$7	1
D	$15	3	$5	2

This procedure establishes the preferred order in which products should be manufactured. For example, assume that plant hours is the factor constraining the volume of production at the XYZ Company. The contribution margin per hour is computed as shown in Table 4.1. To maximize the contribution to profit per unit of the constraining factor, the XYZ Company should produce its products in the following order of priority: C, D, B, and finally A.

Assume that the labor hour capacity is limited to 47,000 hours per month, and the following monthly sales estimates are provided:

Product	Monthly Sales Estimates	Hours Required
A	5,000	25,000
B	2,000	6,000
C	4,000	8,000
D	6,000	18,000
	17,000	57,000

The optimal plant capacity can be computed as shown in Table 4.2, which takes into account both the preference order established by the ranking of the contribu-

Table 4.2
Allocations of Capacity on the Basis of the Contribution Margin per Unit

Product	Contribution Margin per Unit	Labor Hours per Unit	Monthly Sales	Total Hours	Contribution Margin
C	$14	2	4,000	8,000	$ 56,000
D	$15	3	6,000	18,000	90,000
B	$12	3	2,000	6,000	24,000
A	$15	5	3,000	15,000	45,000
			Total Supply of Labor Needed	47,000	
			Total Contribution Margin		$215,000
			− Total Fixed Costs (Given)		$115,000
			Total Profit per Month		$100,000

tion margin per hour and the limited supply of hours. This analysis assumes that the firm elects to produce only 3,000 units of A at a time, when sales of A could be 5,000 units.

CONCLUSIONS

Breakeven analysis is a useful cost accounting technique for situations that involve the relationships of profits, revenues and costs. The accounting approach to breakeven analysis can be supplemented to (1) examine sensitivity analysis and (2) examine and assess product mix decisions.

NOTE

1. The profit formula (μ) may be rearranged to solve for other variables. To solve for P:

$$P = V + \frac{F + \mu}{q} .$$

To solve for V:

$$V = P - \frac{F + \mu}{q} .$$

To solve for F:

$$F = q(P - V) - \mu.$$

SELECTED READINGS

Connie, Thomas E., Jr. "A Pedagogical Note on Cash Break-Even Analysis." *Journal of Business Finance and Accounting* (August 1987): 437–441.

Dow, Alice S., and Orace Johnson. "The Break-Even Point Concept: Its Development and Expanding Applications." *Management Accounting* (February 1969): 29–32.

Hartl, Robert J. "The Linear Total Revenue Curve in Cost-Volume-Profit Analysis." *Management Accounting* (March 1975): 49–52.

Richardson, A. W. "Some Extensions with the Application of Cost-Volume-Profit Analysis." *Cost and Management* (September–October 1978): 30–35.

5

Divisionalization and Performance Measurement

The effective planning and control of an organization must be guided by a reporting system or *responsibility accounting system,* that allows the optimal association of variances and such responsibility centers as *cost centers, profit centers,* and/or *investment centers.* The number of types of responsibility centers depends on the organizational structure used to accomplish corporate objectives.

Two types of organizational design are in general use: the *centralized functional form* and the *decentralized divisional form.* In response to the uncertainty created by technology and environment, most complex organizations decentralize (in other words, segment the organization into parts). Consequently, the growth of corporations and their need for a decentralization of operations has created the need for appropriate performance evaluation and transfer pricing.

This chapter introduces responsibility accounting, types of organizational design, and performance evaluation methods.

5.1 AREAS OF RESPONSIBILITY

Areas of responsibility such as cost centers, profit centers, and investment centers are important to the efficient functioning of a responsibility accounting system. Consequently, the nature of responsibility accounting will be addressed first.

5.1.1 Responsibility Accounting

Responsibility accounting is a technique used within the total system of an organization for classifying and reporting in accordance with managerial responsibilities. It is based on a system for reporting revenue and cost information to the manager responsible for the revenue-causing and/or cost-incurring function. A responsibility accounting system is a reporting system designed to control expenditures by directly relating the reporting of controllable expenditures to the individuals in the company organization who are responsible for their control.[1]

Central to responsibility accounting is the assignment of responsibility and authority: first, in conformity with the relationships defined by the organizational structure and second, for each activity in terms of expenses, income, capital expenditures, asset investment, and other criteria. Under the responsibility accounting system, information on the results of each activity is reported on the basis of where the results were incurred and who has responsibility for them.

The responsibility accounting system has the following characteristics:

1. The areas of responsibility are defined in conformity with the decision centers resulting from the organizational structure.

2. Items and responsibility are assigned to managers so that they are only charged with the items over which they can exercise a significant degree of direct control.

3. The information of significance to each area of responsibility is highlighted in the performance reports.

4. Heads of responsibility units participate in the preparation of their budgets. They must feel that the budget is their budget rather than some unrealistic and unworkable budget forced upon them.[2]

Thus, the most useful distinction in a responsibility accounting system is between controllable and uncontrollable costs for each responsibility center. Suggested guidelines for making this distinction follow:

1. A person who has authority over both the acquisition and the use of a service should be charged with the cost of such services.

2. A person who can significantly influence the amount of a cost through his or her own action may be charged with such costs.

3. Even a person who cannot significantly influence the amount of a cost through direct action may be charged with such costs when management wishes this person to influence those responsible.

To design a responsibility accounting system, management may have to rely on the formal organizational system, charts, and manuals to identify responsibility centers and to determine the decision and resources controllable by each center.[3] For example, according to Prince:

The business organization under scrutiny contains a clearly defined organization chart with well established lines of authority for the conduct of the organization. Following these lines of authority the supervisory and administrative functions for the various groups of operations must be delegated to the various supervisory personnel. Concurrent with this delegation of responsibility . . . there is an accountability which flows in the reverse order . . . [and later] since the organization chart is the backbone of a responsibility accounting system.[4]

The backbone of any company's responsibility accounting system is the organizational chart of the company. Figure 5.1 illustrates a simple organizational

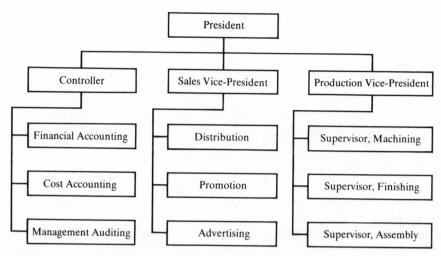

Figure 5.1
XYZ Company: Simplified Organizational Chart

chart of the XYZ Company, which indirectly portrays the different levels of responsibility in the company. For example, each of the supervisors is responsible to the production department vice-president. The production vice-president, sales vice-president, and controller are responsible to the president.

The responsibility accounting system is based on a set of reports to the areas of responsibility as defined by the organizational chart. Hence, each area of responsibility identified in Figure 5.1 will be the subject of a regular performance report outlining the nature of the difference between the actual and planned performance for a given control period. The information included in the performance report of a given level of responsibility is included in the reports of all the higher levels of responsibility. Examples of performance reports are shown in Table 5.1. The flow of responsibility starts with the assembly supervisor and goes to the production vice-president and the president. The information is sequentially integrated and can be traced from one report to another. The assembly supervisor reports only the $50,000 under his or her direct control. This amount figures in the production vice-president's report, given that the supervisor is under the vice-president's jurisdiction. The production vice-president reports a total of $150,000 under direct control. This amount figures in the president's report, given that the production vice-president is under the president's jurisdiction.

The success of the responsibility accounting system depends on at least the following factors:

1. The system should emphasize exceptions or deviations and avoid unnecessary, voluminous reports on uncontrollable or immaterial variances. This factor is known as *management by exception*.

2. A necessary condition for the implementation of a responsibility accounting system is the creation of well-defined areas of responsibility, which can take the form of a cost center, a profit center, or an investment center.

3. Managers must be familiar with the reporting system concept and be trained to understand and use its results.

4. The reports must be prepared on a timely basis.

5. The general content and details of the reports must be relevant to the manager's responsibility and authority. A full knowledge of an individual's controllable costs was found to be positively correlated with the relevance of budgets, with positive attitudes toward budgets, and with a high level of cost consciousness.[5]

Table 5.1
Responsibility Accounting Monthly Reports for the Assembly Supervisor, the Production Vice-President, and the President for the XYZ Company

President's Performance Report

	Amount		Variance Favorable (Unfavorable)	
	This Month	**Year to Date**	**This Month**	**Year to Date**
President's Office	$300,000	$ 870,000	$ 26,000	$ 52,000
Controller	200,000	610,000	(12,000)	11,000
Production Vice-President →	150,000	445,000	16,000	2,000
Sales Vice-President	100,000	290,000	4,000	13,000
Total Controllable Costs	$750,000	$2,215,000	$ 34,000	$ 78,000

Production Vice-President's Performance Report

	Amount		Variance Favorable (Unfavorable)	
Machining Department	$ 40,000	$ 115,000	$ (4,150)	$(13,120)
Finishing Department	60,000	185,000	20,630	27,280
Assembly Department →	50,000	145,000	(480)	(12,160)
Total Controllable Costs →	$150,000	$ 445,000	$ 16,000	$ 2,000

Assembly Supervisor's Performance Report

	Amount		Variance Favorable (Unfavorable)	
Direct Material	$ 20,000	$ 72,000	$ 1,800	$ (210)
Direct Labor	10,000	26,000	400	(2,975)
Manufacturing Overhead	20,000	47,000	(1,720)	(8,975)
Total Controllable Costs →	$ 50,000	$ 145,000	$ 480	$ (12,160)

6. The reports should focus on controllable items requiring management attention, including evidence of good, improving, or bad performance. The inclusion of non-controllable items in performance reports was found to produce unfavorable ratings for those reports, whereas favorable ratings occur when reports clearly establish an individual's responsibility.[6]

5.1.2 Cost Centers, Profit Centers, and Investment Centers

Cost centers, profit centers, and investment centers differ in terms of the nature of responsibility they assume.

Cost Center

A cost center is the smallest segment of activity or area of responsibility for which costs can be accumulated. Responsibility in a cost center is restricted to cost. For planning purposes, the budget estimates are cost estimates; for control purposes, performance evaluation is guided by a cost variance equal to the difference between the actual and budgeted costs for a given period. In general, cost centers are associated with the segments of the firm that provide tangible or intangible services to line departments. For example, cost centers may include departments providing services such as legal advice and accounting, personnel, and data processing services. Cost centers may also be found in producing or line departments. Where a production process requires different types of machines and operations, cost centers are created to enhance the accumulation of costs by operation.

The method of evaluating the performance of a cost center can result in dysfunctional behavior. For example, a cost center manager may feel that to insure a budgeted amount in successive years similar to the present's, the present budget allowances should be spent. The manager may be inclined to authorize unnecessary expenditures at the end of the year to insure that "nothing is left in the budget." To minimize and/or prevent such a situation, a company should identify and assign costs so that managers are motivated to act in a way beneficial to the firm. The American Accounting Association Committee on Cost Concepts and Standards gave the following advice:

The basis of measurement used in providing cost data for control is often a matter of management discretion and an important consideration in motivation. Different bases may significantly affect the way in which different individuals are motivated. For this reason, the basis of measurement selected should be consistent with the type of motivation desired. For example, different types of motivation may result when maintenance costs are charged to a responsibility center on the basis of: 1) a rate per maintenance labor hour, 2) a rate per job, or 3) a single amount per month.[7]

Profit Center

A profit center is a segment of activity or area of responsibility for which both revenues and costs are accumulated. The manager holds responsibility for both revenues and expenses. For planning purposes, the budget estimates are both revenue and cost estimates. For control purposes, performance evaluation is guided by both a revenue variance and a cost variance. In short, the objective function of a profit center's manager is to maximize the center's profit.

Although the profit center concept is vital to the implementation of *decentralization,* it can be also used in firms with *centralization.* In other words, the profit center concept leads essentially to a divisionalized firm, but not necessarily to a decentralized firm. As we will see later, decentralization implies the relative freedom to make decisions.

Investment Center

An investment center is a segment of activity or area held responsible for both profits and investment. For planning purposes, the budget estimate is a measure of the rate of *return on investment* (ROI) estimate. For control purposes, performance evaluation is guided by an ROI variance. In short, the objective function of an investment center is to maximize the center's ROI. The merits of the ROI measure and the possible problems associated with such a measure will be illustrated later in this chapter.

5.2 TYPES OF ORGANIZATIONAL DESIGN

To insure the implementation of responsibility accounting, responsibility centers and authority should be well defined. That is, the design of a formal organizational structure must contribute to the attainment of corporate objectives. Such design must take into account four process criteria and a design criterion.[8]

5.2.1 Process Criteria

The process criteria necessary in the design of a formal organizational structure include the following:

1. *Steady state efficiency* is achieved when the unit cost of output is minimized for a given level of activity. This involves analyzing such factors as economies of scale, of skills, and of overhead.

2. *Operating responsiveness* measures an organization's ability to make efficient changes in its production level in response to environmental changes. It involves inventory control and access to all information.

3. *Strategic responsiveness* measures an organization's ability to make efficient changes in the nature of its production process in response to environmental changes. It involves a possible expense for technological and market-related changes.

4. *Structural responsiveness* measures the ability of a firm to design and implement new structures when the first three criteria cannot be met.

Each of these criteria should be applied toward the evaluation of an organizational design's potential success in meeting the objectives of the firm.

5.2.2 Structural Design

The criteria just described can be met by at least two possible types of organizational designs: the centralized functional form and the decentralized divisional form.[9]

Centralized Functional Form

The centralized functional form consists primarily of a departmentalization by function. In a manufacturing firm, such functions include production, finance, sales, accounting, personnel, purchasing, research and development, and so forth. Such a design is justifiable in terms of steady-state efficiency by allowing for economies of scale, of overhead, and of skills. It results, however, in relatively low strategic and structural responsiveness.

Decentralized Divisional Form

The decentralized divisional form consists primarily of a series of organizational units, or divisions, responsible for a specific product market under the direction of a manager having strategic and operating decision prerogatives. This form achieves steady-state efficiency and operating responsiveness, because departmentalization by function is used within each division. This design is justifiable mainly in terms of strategic and structural responsiveness. Since World War II, the decentralized divisional form has become the most frequent in large firms. It is accomplished most often through either a departmentalization by location (geographical diversification) or a departmentalization by product.

The simplified organizational charts in Figure 5.2 illustrate the difference between a centralized and a decentralized company producing two products (X and Y). In the centralized concern, the production, marketing, personnel, and purchasing activities fall under the supervision and responsibility of a production, marketing, personnel, and purchasing vice-president, respectively. In other words, the concern is departmentalized by function. In the decentralized concern, each of the products X and Y are produced and managed in a separate division.

5.2.3 Decentralization through Divisionalization

Nature of Decentralization

The diversification of the types of activities of many business entities has led to the realization that centralized control and coordinating mechanisms at corporate headquarters are not always in the best interests of the firm as a whole. A brief look at some types of organizational growth will show the necessity and main reasons for decentralizing the decision making process.

The first type of organizational growth arises through the creation of new product lines. A second type arises from *vertical mergers* and consolidations in which firms involved in different stages of production of the same product are

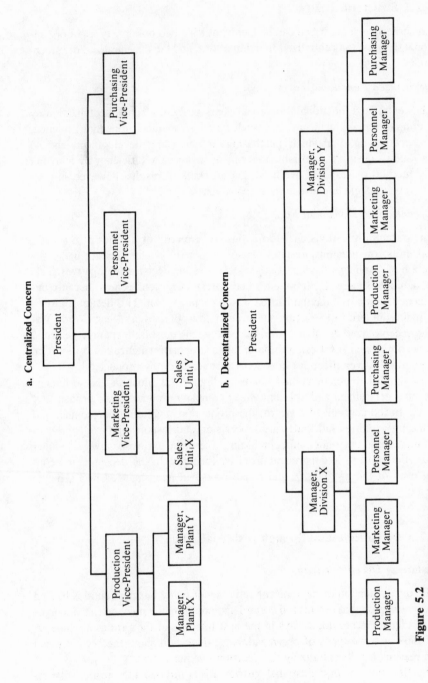

**Figure 5.2
Types of Organizational Designs**

combined. As a result, the new, merged corporation achieves greater control over its production, purchasing, and distribution processes. Examples of this growth type can be found in the automative and petroleum industries. Another type of growth, the *horizontal merger,* involves the merger of firms in the same line of business. This eliminates duplicate facilities and allows the establishment of auxiliary divisions that provide commonly needed goods or services to other subunits in the organization. The last major growth type is the *conglomeration,* where firms of unrelated lines of business are combined. Interdependencies among the subunits are usually minimal. Practical factors, including lower taxes, lower transportation costs, and the increased security of belonging to a large organization, lead to the creation of conglomerates.

These types of organizational growth require the creation of decentralized organizational structures. Ideally, management will choose the degree of decentralization that will achieve corporate goals. Decentralization should not be confused with divisionalization, which is a major organizational device for decentralization, although it does not indicate to what degree. Decentralization is essentially the freedom to make decisions.

Benefits and Costs of Decentralization

Numerous arguments have been advanced in the literature in support of decentralization:

1. The modern, integrated, multiple-product firm will function best if it is made into a miniature of the competitive free enterprise system.[10]
2. Divisional managers may be more motivated, resulting in better decisions and greater efficiency. David Solomons summarizes the benefits as follows:

First, decentralized decision making is likely to result in better decisions because the people who make them are closer to the scene of action and have a smaller area of responsibility to worry about. Second, greater efficiency results from the sense the divisional managers have that they are running "their" businesses. In motivating these managers, divisional profit plays an important part. Third, giving a person responsibility for running a division is perhaps the best way of providing preparation for a top management role at the corporate level.[11]

3. The division manager is in a better position to process information concerning resource allocation.[12]
4. The division manager is in a better position to process and transmit information in general. This information economics advantage is reflected in the following two early observations:

Given realistic limits on human planning capacity, *The decentralized system will work better than the centralized.*[13]

[Decentralization] is advantageous in economizing on the transmission of information. In particular, the detailed technical knowledge of the process need not be transmitted to a central office but can be retained in the department. We may regard it as close to an impossibility for individuals in close contact with the productive process to transmit their information in all its details to another office. This proposition, long recognized in practice, is the basis of the management literature on the questions of centralization and decentralization.[14]

5. The division manager's nearness to the marketplace provides relevant information regarding changes in the prices of output and input.[15]
6. Size and diversity of modern corporations and the promotion of morale (because of the decision making autonomy of managers) support the concept of decentralization.[16]
7. Decentralization represents a response to two major sources of uncertainty for a complex organization: its technology and its environment.

The costs associated with decentralization are also important.

1. Incongruence between the divisional goal and the corporate goal can result.
2. Decentralization can lead to dysfunctional decision making and, consequently, to *suboptimization* (that is, a decision that increases current divisional profit but limits the company profit as a whole).
3. Higher interdependence between the divisions will make every decision beneficial to one unit and harmful to another (and perhaps to the organization as a whole).

It can be concluded that decentralization is likely to be most beneficial and least costly when the organizational units are fairly independent.

Decentralization: Differentiation, Integration, and Accounting

The decentralization of an organization not only creates some independent subunits, but induces different behavioral patterns in the organizational members in terms of mental processes, working styles, decision criteria, and perceptions of reality.[17] To avoid suboptimization and insure that the efforts of all the subunits (now appropriately differentiated) contribute to the overall organizational goal, an integration process is required.

P. R. Lawrence and J. W. Lorsch showed empirically that successful firms are those that have achieved the right trade-off between integration and differentiation.[18] Some integrating mechanisms have been suggested by J. R. Galbraith:

Rules, routines, and standardization

Organizational hierarchy

Planning

Direct contact

Liaison roles

Temporary committees (task forces or teams)

Integrators (personnel specializing in the role of coordinating intersubunit activities)

Integrating departments (departments of integrators)

Matrix organization (an organization that is completely committed to joint problem solving and *shared* responsibility).[19]

The accounting system in a complex organization can be designed to achieve the trade-off between differentiation and integration. The differentiation can be achieved by an appropriate number of cost, profit, and investment centers equal to the number of differentiated units. Integration can be achieved by implementing some of the mechanisms suggested by Galbraith or by an adequate control system designed to (1) provide yardsticks for divisional performance measurements and (2) contribute to intrafirm company transfer pricings.

Three criteria are helpful for designing or judging a particular accounting control system in a decentralized setting: goal congruence, performance evaluation, and autonomy.[20] Goal congruence focuses on harmonizing the objectives of the managers with the objectives of the organization as a whole. Performance evaluation is needed to make predictions for future decisions, to appraise the abilities of the managers, and to assess the profitability of the capital invested in an organizational subunit as an economic investment. In other words, the divisional performance measures and the transfer prices must facilitate the profitability evaluation of the divisions of a firm. Finally, a preservation of the autonomy of each decentralized entity is necessary for a decentralized organization. In other words, the divisional performance measures and the transfer prices that create corporate as well as divisional profit maximization must at the same time preserve the operational autonomy of the division as a profit center.

5.3 APPRAISING DIVISIONAL PERFORMANCE

Investment centers can be evaluated using either an ROI or a residual income measure.

5.3.1 Rate of Return on Investment

Rather than using absolute dollar profits as a test of divisional profit, most financial control systems emphasize the use of a relationship of profit to invested capital. This relationship, usually expressed by the ROI, has received wide market acceptance.[21]

E. I. du Pont de Nemours and Company is generally credited with the development of the ROI concept. Alfred P. Sloan, Jr., evaluated the principle of ROI as follows:

I am not going to say that the rate of return is a magic word for every occasion in business. There are times when you have to spend money just to stay in business, regardless of the visible rate of return. Competition is the final price determinant and competitive prices may result in profits which force you to accept a rate of return less than you hoped for, or for that matter to accept temporary losses. And, in times of inflation, the rate-of-return concept comes up against the problem of assets undervalued in terms of replacement. Nevertheless, no other financial principle with which I am acquainted serves better than rate of return as an objective aid to business management.[22]

Measurement of Rate of Return on Investment

The ROI is found simply by dividing the net income by the amount of investment. It relates the profit to invested capital, both of which are important areas of management responsibility. The rationale lies in the belief that there is an optimal investment level in each asset leading to an optimal profit level. The ROI is the product of two components: *profit margin* and *investment turnover*. The profit margin equals net income divided by sales and indicates the segment's ability to transform sales into profit. The investment turnover equals sales divided by invested capital. Thus, the ROI can be expressed as follows:

$$\text{ROI} = \frac{\text{Net income}}{\text{Invested capital}} = \frac{\text{Sales}}{\text{Invested capital}} \times \frac{\text{Net income}}{\text{Sales}}.$$

This formula shows that the ROI can be increased by either an increase in the profit margin or the investment turnover, and it can be decreased by either a decrease in the profit margin or the investment turnover.

To illustrate, assume that a division desires a 25-percent return on invested capital. The present performance of the division is as follows:

$$\frac{\text{Sales}}{\text{Invested capital}} \times \frac{\text{Net income}}{\text{Sales}} = \text{ROI}$$

or

$$\frac{\$200}{\$100} \times \frac{\$20}{\$200} = 20\%.$$

Two alternatives are possible to improve the ROI up to 25 percent:

1. A \$5 decrease in expenses would increase net income to \$25 such that

$$\text{ROI} = \frac{\$200}{\$100} \times \frac{\$25}{\$200} = 25\%.$$

2. A \$20 decrease in inventories would decrease invested capital to \$80 such that

$$\text{ROI} = \frac{\$200}{\$80} \times \frac{\$20}{\$200} = 25\%.$$

These are not the only alternatives. Figure 5.3 shows the factors that can affect the final ROI outcome.

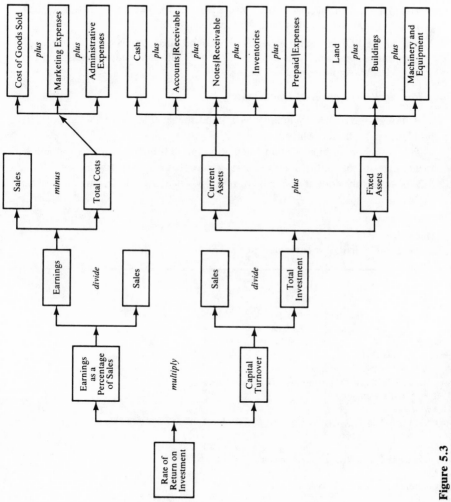

Figure 5.3
Relationship of Factors Influencing the Rate of Return on Investment

The advantages of using the ROI to measure divisional performance include the following:

1. The ROI is a composite measuring tool that combines both net income and investment features. It is useful for a comparison among the divisions of a given firm as well as for a comparison of divisional performance with that of companies in similar industries.
2. Use of the ROI encourages an effective use of resources and could serve as a corporate budgeting tool and aid in making short- and long-range plans.
3. Use of the ROI may have a positive behavioral effect on managers by creating a competitive spirit and by motivating increases in efficiency, effectiveness, and congruency with corporate goals.

Rate of Return on Investment Issues

Although the ROI may qualify as a good management tool, some potential problems must be recognized.

The net income figure used in calculating the ROI may require certain adjustments that do not conform with generally accepted accounting principles. Table 5.2 illustrates the format and content of a divisional income statement. Distinc-

Table 5.2
Format and Content of a Divisional Income Statement

Revenues		X
External Sales	X	
Internal Sales (Transfer Price Equal to Market Value)	X	
Internal Sales (Transfer Price Different from Market Value)	X	
Minus		
Variable costs		X
Variable Cost of Goods Sold	X	
Variable Selling and Administrative Divisional Expenses	X	
Total Contribution Margin		X
Add (Deduct)		
Fixed Costs Allocated to Other Divisions for Transfers Made at Other than Market Value	X	
Deduct		
Controllable Discretionary and Committed Fixed Costs	X	
Equals		
Controllable Operating Income		X
Deduct		
Uncontrollable Fixed Costs	X	
Operating Income before Taxes		X
Income Taxes	X	
Net Income (after Taxes)		X

Source: David Solomons, *Divisional Performance—Measurement and Control* (New York: Financial Executives Research Foundation. 1965). p. 82. Adapted by permission.

tions are made between sales to outside customers and sales to other divisions, between controllable and uncontrollable costs, and between variable and fixed costs. This format allows the possibility of distinguishing between the performance of the manager and the performance of the division. Two rates of return can be computed—the controllable ROI and the net ROI—as follows:

Controllable ROI = Controllable income ÷ Controllable capital investment.

Net ROI = Net income after taxes ÷ Total capital investment.

Another problem with the ROI is that the investment figure used in calculating the ROI may lead to an "unrealistic" ROI. Hence, the most obvious figure is the net book value of assets, which is the original cost minus depreciation to date.[23] Such a measure has inherent weaknesses. For example, it enables divisions with older assets to earn a higher rate of return than divisions with new assets, given the low book value resulting from greater depreciation charges.

Several solutions can overcome this limitation of the ROI method:

1. Gross book value can be used. However, this approach still enables a divisional manager to increase the ROI by scrapping nonprofitable assets that may be detrimental to the company.
2. Four nonhistorical cost valuation methods can be used: the *economic value* or *capitalized value*, the *replacement cost*, the *net realizable value*, and the *general price level adjusted historical cost*.[24] The first three methods approximate the current value, whereas the last merely adjusts historical cost. The replacement cost represents the amount of cash or other consideration that would be required to obtain the same asset or its equivalent. The net realizable value represents the amount of cash for which an asset can be sold. The capitalized value refers to the present value of net cash flows expected to be received from the use of the asset. The three current values are relevant to different types of decisions. For example, a disposal, continuance, or expansion program would entail the following alternatives:

	Alternatives		
	Disposal (Sell)	**Continuance (Hold)**	**Expansion (Buy)**
Decisions	Capitalized Value *versus* Net Realizable Value	Capitalized Value *versus* Net Realizable Value	Capitalized Value *versus* Replacement Cost

Although the capitalized value appears to be dominant, it is a subjective value based on the present value of expected cash flows. Replacement cost and net realizable value may be more available and constitute a better alternative to historical cost.

3. The use of an *increasing-charge depreciation* will lead to a lower income related to the investment base. Such depreciation called either compound *interest depreciation* or *annuity depreciation* allows consistency between the use of the discounted cash flow method for capital budgeting and the use of accrual accounting rate of return for performance evaluation. The compound interest depreciation is computed in such a

manner that the year-to-year accounting rate of return on the beginning investment is equal to the internal rate of return on the investment. If the cash inflows, generated by the investment each year, are equal, the depreciation is called annuity depreciation.

Therefore, compound interest depreciation is based on the financial concept that depreciation represents the return on investment. Suppose a company is considering buying an asset with a two-year life and no salvage value. If the cost of the asset is estimated to be $8,680 and the yearly cash flow to be $5,000, the ROI using a discounted cash flow method can be obtained by solving the following equation for r:

$$\$8,680 = \sum_{t=1}^{2} \frac{\$5,000}{(1 + r)^t} \; .$$

$$r = 10\% \; .$$

Given the knowledge of the ROI, compound interest depreciation assumes a capital recovery factor. Table 5.3 presents the results of compound interest depreciation, showing each cash payment to be equal to the interest on investment plus principal. Table 5.4 shows the superiority of sinking-fund depreciation with the income statement and the ROI computations using constant, increasing, or decreasing depreciation.

The compound interest depreciation method results in a stable, constant ROI figure as compared with the fluctuating results obtained by the straight-line and accelerated methods. Therefore, compound interest depreciation is preferred by many companies to measure divisional profitability.

An appropriate allocation of assets to divisions makes the ROI more meaningful and contributes to goal congruence. Such allocation differs from one company to another, given that some companies elect to centralize certain activities and decentralize others. For instance, in most decentralized companies the home office centralizes cash management, billing, or receivable collections.

Table 5.3
Example of Sinking-Fund Depreciation

Year	Initial Investment (a)	Cash Earnings (b)	Return of 10% (c = 10%a)	Depreciation (d = b − c)	Unrecovered Investment (e = a − d)
0					$8,680
1	$8,680	$5,000	$868.0	$4,132.0	$4,548
2	4,548	5,000	454.8	4,545.2	2.8[a]

[a] Due to rounding.

Table 5.4
Depreciation Methods and Rate of Return Computations

	Straight-Line		Accelerated Depreciation		Sinking-Fund Depreciation	
			Methods of Depreciation			
Year	1	2	1	2	1	2
Cash Earnings	$5,000	$5,000	$5,000	$5,000	$5,000	$5,000.0
Depreciation	4,340[a]	4,340[a]	5,786[b]	2,893[b]	4,132[c]	4,545.2[c]
Net Income	$ 660	$ 660	$ (786)	$2,107	$ 868	$ 454.8
Investment Base	$8,680	$4,340	$8,680	$2,894	$8,680	$4,548.0
Rate of Return on Investment	7.6%	15.2%	−9%	72%	10%	10%

[a] $8,680 ÷ 2 = $4,340.
[b] $8,680 × 2/3 = $5,786. $8680 × 1/3 = $2,983.
[c] See Table 13.3 for results.

As a general rule, the basis of allocation of assets to divisions should be *controllability*. That is, the amount of assets controllable by any given segment in its managerial activities should be the amount allocated to that segment in the computation of the rate of return on divisional investment.

To summarize, the ROI limitations can be corrected if the investment base is a current value net of depreciation and if a sinking-fund depreciation method is used.

5.3.2 Residual Income

Developed in the 1950s by General Electric Company, the concept of *residual income* to measure divisional performance is defined operationally as divisional income in excess of a prescribed interest on investment. This concept directs the manager toward the maximization of income above a charge for assets used. The interest rate used corresponds conceptually to the firm's cost of capital. For example, if a divisional income were $50,000 for a budgeted investment of $200,000 and a cost of capital of 10 percent, the residual income would be computed as follows:

Divisional net income	$50,000
Minus	
Imputed interest at 10 percent of assets	20,000
Equals	
Residual income	$30,000

There are two advantages to the residual income method for divisional performance evaluation:

1. The method enables the division to continue to expand as long as it meets the cost of capital requirement. For the previous example, the cost of capital was 10 percent, whereas the ROI was 25 percent ($50,000 ÷ $200,000). In other words, using the ROI of 25 percent as an investment criterion would eliminate projects whose returns might exceed the cost of capital and, consequently, would eliminate projects acceptable from the point of view of the corporation as a whole.

2. The method requires setting a rate of return target for every type of asset, regardless of the division's profitability. The end result is a yardstick for comparisons between divisions. However, the adequate determination of the cost of capital and/or the rate of return of individual assets is a possible problem.

5.4 EMERGING ISSUES IN PERFORMANCE MEASUREMENT

The success of the firm's activities rests not only on achieving a desired level of profitability but also on meeting new critical factors of the new manufacturing environment. These factors include a good record on quality, a minimization or elimination of inventories, an increase in manufacturing flexibility, and the provision of an excellent service to customers. In response to the concerns a different kind of performance measurement is required, including a greater focus on global rather than departmental performance measures, a greater reliance on nonfinancial measures, a throughput in the new manufacturing account, a classification of costs as value added or nonvalue added, and production control by observation rather than by accounting report.[25] Each of these data issues are examined in the following sections.

5.4.1 Use of Global Evaluation Techniques

Although the measurement of departmental performance is still part of the control process, the focus in the new manufacturing strategy is to emphasize plant-wide performance. Measures that focus on the flexibility and performance of all departments include cycle time/amount of throughput, setup times by product, and downtime (other than setup).[26]

The degree of automation, also, dictates a shift from an emphasis on an individual performance to an emphasis on group performance. Witness the following comment:

In an automated manufacturing process as well, the whole system is so integrated and controlled by computers that individuals' performance would be confined to following the preprogrammed flow of the process. The system's productivity would be affected very little by the varying degrees of individual employees' ability, once the employees acquire the proficiency needed to operate in that setting.[27]

5.4.2 Greater Reliance on Nonfinancial Measures

ROI and residual income capture important aspects of performance, but they are not sufficient since other aspects must be accounted for if a firm has adopted the basic goal of providing the best product at the best price. Exchange of critical factors that must be measured at every level of activity include cost, quality, delivery, and people.[28] Performance measurement in these critical aspects of the new multifaceted firms must be derived by its management accounting and control system. For example, the criteria for evaluating management accounting and control systems in an advanced manufacturing environment are as follows:

• Rapid feedback
• Sensitivity to profit contribution of various activities and products
• Flexible and migratory measurement systems
• Holistic product costing and control measures
• Identification, measurement, and elimination of nonvalue-added costs
• Focus on variance reduction in such areas as quality, cycle time, and product complexity (e.g., total parts)
• Reclassification of costs based on assignability and value-adding characteristics
• Enhanced traceability of costs to specific products and processed to decrease allocations and their distortions.[29]

A second example is provided by Harley Davidson's adoption of the following ten measurements to assess manufacturing effectiveness:

1. Schedule attainment
2. Manning requirements
3. Conversion costs
4. Overtime requirements as a measure of flexibility
5. Inventory levels
6. Material cost variance
7. Scrap and rework
8. Manufacturing cycle time as a measure of flexibility
9. Quality level
10. Productivity improvement.[30]

These measures are deemed more appropriate for inclusion in a cost management system within a JIT (Just-in-Time) environment than the traditional measures of direct labor efficiency, direct labor utilization, direct labor productivity, and machine utilization.

5.4.3 Throughput in the New Manufacturing Accounting

The new manufacturing accounting puts a heavy emphasis in throughput, a measure of how many good units are produced during a particular period. It can be calculated by dividing the good units produced by the total time or by multiplying the three components of throughput: productive capacity, productive processing time, and yield. The three components of throughput have been defined by Cheatham as follows:

1. *Productive capacity* is the maximum a particular manufacturing cell or segment can produce given the technology in place. It is measured by dividing total units processed by the processing time.
2. *Productive processing time* shows how much time is spent on activities that add value to the product. It is computed by dividing processing time by the total time the product spends in a particular segment of the factory.
3. *Yield* shows the percentage of good units. It is determined by dividing the good units produced in a particular time period by the total units started during the period.[31]

Based on these definitions, Cheatham offers two formulae:

1. Good units produced per period = productive capacity × productive processing time × yield.
2. Good units/total time = (total units/processing time) × (processing time/total time) × (good units/total units).[32]

5.4.4 Classification of Costs as Value Added or Nonvalue Added

A new feature of performance measurement is the separation of value-added costs from nonvalue-added costs. A nonvalue-added cost is any cost that results from an activity or procedure that does not add a value to the product or to the firm. The desired goal is to minimize the value added costs subject to the quality level sought by the firm and to eliminate nonvalue-added costs. For example, consider the following general steps that constitute the lead time associated with manufacturing a salable product:

- *Process Time* is the amount of time that a product is actually being worked on.
- *Inspection Time* is the amount of time spent either assuring that the product is of high quality or actually spent reworking the product to an acceptable quality level.
- *Move Time* is the time spent moving the product from one location to another.

- *Queue Time* is the amount of time the product waits before being processed, moved, or inspected, or whatever.

- *Storage Time* is the amount of time a product spent in stock before further processing or shipment.[33]

Within a JIT philosophy, only process time adds value to the product. Given that process time generally amounts to 10 percent of the lead time, 90 percent of the lead time adds costs but no value to the product.[34]

5.4.5 Use of Observation in Operational Control

Without discounting the importance of accounting reports in the area of performance measurement and reporting, the reports should be supplemented and sometimes replaced by observation. Ortman and Buehlmann cite the example of the immediate observation of a production problem with material and assembly "because they cause bottlenecks, which occur because there is no inventory to 'cushion' errors."[35]

5.5 CONCLUSION

Firms have adopted the multidivisional form because of its association with better profitability and internal control. Performance evaluation in this new type of organization remains a complex issue. The literature must examine some of the operational and strategic issues that arise from the implementation of a multidivisional structure.

NOTES

1. John A. Higgins, "Responsibility Accounting." *Arthur Anderson Chronicle* (April 1952): 1.
2. Ibid.
3. J. Pick, "Is Responsibility Accounting Irresponsible?" *New York Certified Public Accountant* (July 1971): 487–494.
4. T. Prince, *Information Systems for Management Planning and Control* (Homewood, Ill.: Irwin, 1970), 15.
5. C. H. Hofstede, *The Game of Budget Control* (Assen, The Netherlands: Royal Van Gorcum, 1968), 2.
6. D. Cook, "The Psychological Impact of Certain Aspects of Performance Reports." *NAA Bulletin* (July 1968): 26–34; and Graeme M. McNally, "Responsibility Accounting and Organizational Control: Some Perspectives and Prospects." *Journal of Business Finance and Accounting* (Summer 1980): 167.
7. American Accounting Association, Committee on Cost Concepts and Standards, "Report of the Committee on Cost Concepts and Standards." *Accounting Review* (April 1956): 189.

8. H. I. Ansoff and R. G. Brandenburg, " A Language for Organizational Design: Parts 1 and 2." *Management Science* 17 (1971): 705–731.

9. Ansoff and Brandenburg considered two other possible designs, namely, the adaptive design and the innovative design. However, these designs are more applicable to program and project development than to a corporate firm.

10. Joel Dean, "Decentralization and Intracompany Pricing." *Harvard Business Review* (July–August 1955): 65–74.

11. David Solomons, "Divisional Reports," in *Handbook of Cost Accounting,* ed. S. Davidson and R. L. Weil (New York: McGraw-Hill, 1978), 44–49.

12. Nicholas Dopuch and D. F. Drake, "Accounting Implications of a Mathematical Programming Approach to the Transfer Price Problem." *Journal of Accounting Research* (Spring 1964): 10–21.

13. J. G. March and H. A. Simon, *Organizations* (New York: Wiley, 1958).

14. K. J. Arrow, "Optimization, Decentralization, and Internal Pricing in Business Firms," in *Contributions to Scientific Management* (1959), 9–18.

15. Joshua Ronen and George McKinney III, "Transfer Pricing for Divisional Autonomy." *Journal of Accounting Research* (Spring 1970): 99–112.

16. J. T. Godfrey, "Short Run Planning in a Decentralized Firm." *Accounting Review* (April 1971): 286–297.

17. D. J. H. Watson and J. V. Baumler, "Transfer Pricing: A Behavioral Context." *Accounting Review* (July 1975): 467.

18. P. R. Lawrence and J. W. Lorsch, *Organization and Its Environment* (Homewood, Ill.: Irwin, 1967), 13.

19. J. R. Galbraith, "Organization Design: An Information Processing View," in *Organizational Planning: Cases and Concepts,* ed. J. W. Lorsch and P. R. Lawrence (Georgetown, Ontario: Irwin Dorsey, 1972), 20.

20. Ronen and McKinney, "Transfer Pricing," 99–112.

21. In a survey of 3,525 companies, John J. Mauriel and Robert N. Anthony found that 92.36 percent of responding firms who had investment centers used ROI as a measure of performance. See John J. Mauriel and Robert N. Anthony, "Misevaluation of Investment Center Performance." *Harvard Business Review* (March–April 1966): 101.

22. Alfred P. Sloan, Jr., *My Years with General Motors* (Garden City, N.Y.: Doubleday, 1964), 140.

23. The Mauriel and Anthony study showed that of the companies using ROI, 78 percent used net book value. Mauriel and Anthony, " Misevaluation of Investment Center Performance."

24. Ahmed Belkaoui, *Accounting Theory* (New York: Harcourt Brace Jovanovich, 1980), chaps. 5–7.

25. Richard Ortman and David Buehlmann, "Supplementing Cost Accounting Courses in Response to the Changing Business Environment." *Issues in Accounting Education* 4, no. 1 (Spring 1989): 172.

26. Ibid, 174.

27. John Y. Lee, *Managerial Accounting Changes for the 1990s* (Reading, Mass: Addison-Wesley, 1987), 70.

28. C. J. McNain and William Mosconi, "Measuring Performance in an Advanced Manufacturing Environment." *Management Accounting* (July 1987): 28–31.

29. Ibid. 25.

30. Robert D. Macllhattan, "The JIT Philosophy." *Management Accounting* (September 1987): 25.

31. C. Cheatham, "Measuring and Improving Throughput." *The Journal of Accountancy* (March 1990): 89–91.

32. Ibid, 90.

33. Macllhattan, "The JIT Philosophy," 20.

34. Ibid. 21.

35. Ortman and Buehlmann, "Supplementing Cost Accounting Courses," 174.

SELECTED READINGS

Ansoff, H. I., and R. G. Brandenburg. "A Language for Organizational Design: Parts 1 and 2." *Management Science* 17(1971): 705–731.

Arrow, K. J., "Optimization, Decentralization, and Internal Pricing in Business Firms." In *Contributions to Scientific Management* (Calif.: 1959), 9–18.

Belkaoui, Ahmed. *Accounting Theory* (New York: Harcourt Brace Jovanovich, 1980), chaps. 5–7.

Cook, D. "The Psychological Impact of Certain Aspects of Performance Reports." *NAA Bulletin* (July 1968): 26–34.

Dean, Joel. "Decentralization and Intracompany Pricing." *Harvard Business Review* (July–August 1955): 65–74.

Godfrey, J. T. "Short Run Planning in a Decentralized Firm." *Accounting Review* (April 1971): 286–297.

Higgins, John A. "Responsibility Accounting." *Arthur Anderson Chronicle* (April 1952): 1.

Hofstede, C. H. *The Game of Budget Control* (Assen, The Netherlands: Royal Van Gorcum, 1968), 2.

March, J. G. and H. A. Simon. *Organizations* (New York: Wiley, 1958).

Ortman, Richard, and David Buehlmann. "Supplementing Cost Accounting Courses in Response to the Changing Business Environment." *Issues in Accounting Education* 4, no. 1. Spring 1989): 172.

6

Transfer Pricing

Decentralization calls for the creation of separate segments or divisions. These separate units may and most often elect to exchange goods and services for a price. That price is called the *transfer price*. It is an important factor because it affects the selling division and the costs of the buying division as well as the profits of both divisions. Recall that the measures used to evaluate the performance of divisions, like the ROI or the residual income, are dependent on the profits of the divisions. Therefore, the transfer price by its effects on the profit of the division may be used to lower or raise ROI or the residual income. As a result, corporate management pays close attention to transfer price as it may become an effective management tool for motivating the divisions and contribute to the overall smooth running of the decentralizing process. Notice that the transfer does not affect the firm's income, but it may affect the behavior of the divisions because the performance evaluation of these divisions may depend on the transfer price agreed upon.

6.1 NATURE OF TRANSFER PRICING

Transfer pricing is, therefore, a major issue confronting decentralized organizations that expect division managers to operate their divisions as a semi-autonomous business. These organizations face the problem of what price to charge for goods and services sold by one organizational unit to another in the same company. This situation prevails within vertically integrated organizations, where transactions often occur between the company's profit centers. When goods and services are transferred between divisions, the revenue of the supplying unit becomes the cost of the purchasing unit. These intracompany charges ultimately will be reflected in the profit and loss statements of the respective divisions. Since divisional performance is evaluated by a profit-based criterion such as ROI or residual income, the profit center managers will attempt to maximize their own center's profit. A conflict occurs when improved divisional performance is achieved at the expense of overall company profits.

In theory, to optimize an organization's profits, the transfer price should be selected so that it motivates and guides managers to choose their inputs and outputs in coordination with the other subunits. Ideally, any intracompany pricing method should be consistent with the goals of maximizing both company and divisional profits: *Transfer pricing should insure goal congruence between units.*

Because of the potential conflicts that can arise in transfer price determination, three primary objectives can be used to establish a proper transfer price:

1. The first objective of a transfer pricing system is to *assist top management in evaluating and guiding divisional performance* by providing adequate information on divisional revenues and expenses.
2. The second objective is to *help the division manager in running the division.*
3. The third objective is to *insure divisional autonomy* and allow each profit center to act as an independent agent.

In theory, the design of a transfer pricing scheme ultimately must point each division manager toward top management's goals. The scheme must reward divisional external economies and prevent and penalize diseconomies. Furthermore, a firm's transfer pricing divisions must acknowledge domestic and foreign legal and tax requirements, as well as antitrust and financial reporting constraints.

Developing a set of transfer pricing rules that can integrate the complex dimensions of an organization, insure divisional autonomy, and at the same time achieve overall corporate goals is a very difficult task. Consequently, a transfer pricing system must be developed with an awareness of these difficulties.

The main positive characteristics of a transfer pricing system include insuring goal congruence, being fair to all concerned parties, and minimizing conflicts between divisions. Some corporations set guidelines to insure an effective pricing system.

Basically, a transfer price is the price agreed upon between two divisions, a selling division I and a buying division II, for a product or service A supplied by the selling to the buying division. The buying division uses the product or service for further processing toward a final product B. The product A is termed an

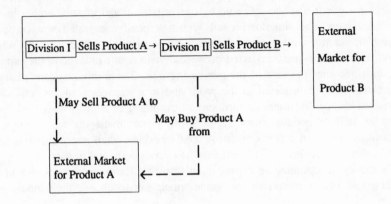

intermediate product and product B may be either another intermediate product, if it is sold to another division, or a final product of the firm, if it is sold to an external market. In most situations, the buying division II may have the option of buying the product A from an external market rather than internally from division I, and the selling division may have the option of selling outside. If the firm is perfectly decentralized, the option of buying and selling outside is available to both divisions.

Three fundamental transfer pricing methods are used:

1. Market-based transfer prices
2. Cost-based transfer prices
3. Negotiated prices.

6.2 EXAMPLE OF TRANSFER PRICING

Backwoods Lumber is a decentralized company with three divisions operating as profit centers:

1. The Raw Lumber Division manages the cutting of raw lumber from a large forest owned by the company.
2. The Transportation Division is in charge of carrying the raw lumber from the forest area to a nearby harbor city.
3. The Finished Lumber Division, located in the harbor city, is in charge of turning the raw lumber into finished lumber to be sold to outside markets. One hundred board feet of raw lumber are needed to produce ninety board feet of finished lumber.

The total annual finished lumber production of 9,000 board feet resulting from the processing of 10,000 board feet of raw lumber is sold entirely to the outside market.

The cost and price information for each of the three divisions is shown in Figure 6.1.

Three pricing methods are considered:

Method A: Transfer price is set at 120 percent of variable costs.

Method B: Transfer price is set at 110 percent of absorption costs.

Method C: Transfer price is set at market prices.

The transfer prices per 100 board feet of finished lumber under each method are as follows:

Method A. 120 percent of variable costs:

• Raw Lumber Division to Transportation Division = 1.2($120) = $144.
• Transportation Division to Finished Lumber Division = 1.2($144 + $21) = $198.

```
┌─────────────────────────────────────────────────────┐
│ Raw Lumber Division of                              │          Market Price
│   Variable Costs per 100 Feet of Raw Lumber = $120  │    →  per 100 Feet
│   Fixed Costs per 100 Feet of Raw Lumber    = $150  │       of Raw Lumber
│   Absorption Costs per 100 Feet of Raw Lumber = $270│       = $300
└─────────────────────────────────────────────────────┘
```

```
┌─────────────────────────────────────────────────────┐
│ Transportation Division of                          │
│   Variable Costs per 100 Feet of Raw Lumber =  $21  │
│   Fixed Costs per 100 Feet of Raw Lumber    =  $40  │
│   Absorption Costs per 100 Feet of Raw Lumber = $61 │
└─────────────────────────────────────────────────────┘
```

Market Price per
100 Feet of Raw
Lumber Delivered

```
┌─────────────────────────────────────────────────────┐
│ Finished Lumber Division of                         │       to the Finished
│   Variable Costs per 100 Feet of Raw Lumber = $140  │  ←    Lumber Division
│   Fixed Costs per 100 Feet of Raw Lumber    = $ 60  │       by the
│   Absorption Costs per 100 Feet of Raw Lumber = $200│       Intermediate
└─────────────────────────────────────────────────────┘       Market = $400
```

External Sale

Market Price per 100 Feet of Finished

lumber sold to External Market

   = $600

Figure 6.1
Backwoods Lumber's Three Divisions

Method B. 110 percent of absorption costs:

- Raw Lumber Division to Transportation Division = 1.1($270) = $297.
- Transportation Division to Finished Lumber Division = 1.1($297 + $61) = $393.8.

Method C. Market price:

- Raw Lumber Division to Transportation Division = $300.
- Transportation Division to Finished Lumber Division = $400.

Table 6.1 illustrates the impact of the use of each of the transfer prices on the incomes of the three divisions and on the total income of the firm. Two points are worth considering:

1. The transfer price used has no impact on the total income of the firm. The total is equal to $1,290,000 under any of the three methods.
2. The transfer price method used has a definite impact on the operating income of each of the three divisions, fluctuating from huge losses to material profits for the Raw Lumber Division and the Transportation Division, and from huge profits to huge losses for the Finished Lumber Division. What this result implies is that the divisions whose managers are compensated on the basis of divisional incomes will strive to choose the transfer price that will generate positive divisional incomes.

These factors set the stage for divisional transfer pricing policies that may differ one division to another and that may result in a conflict situation.

6.3 TRANSFER PRICING METHODS

6.3.1 Market Price

A market price is the price at which the producing division would sell the product externally. In other words, the producing division charges the same price to their divisions as it would charge to outside customers in open market transactions. The market price has the advantage of providing an objective measure of value for goods or services exchanged, and it may result in the best information for use in performance evaluation of the profit centers. A transfer pricing system based on market price requires a competitive intermediate market, minimal interdependencies of the profit centers, and the availability of dependable market quotations.

There are also serious drawbacks to using a transfer price based on market price. First, in today's regulated economy, perfectly competitive markets are very rare. In an imperfect market, one seller or buyer, by itself, can affect the market price, rendering it inapplicable as an effective price.

Second, even if the intermediate is perfect, there is no guarantee that the market price is for a product strictly comparable in terms of grade and other relevant characteristics.

Third, a situation may arise in which the market price is a *distress price*. Should the transfer price be the distress price, or should it be a long-run average, or "normal," market price? Both prices are defensible. On one hand, the use of a

Table 6.1
Division Operating Income of Backwoods Raw Lumber per 10,000 Board Feet of Lumber

	Transfer Price Set at 120% of Variable Costs	Transfer Price Set at 110% of Absorption Costs	Transfer Price Set at Market Price
1. Raw Lumber Division			
Revenues			
$144, $297, $300 x 10,000 Feet of Raw Lumber	$1,440,000	$2,970,000	$3,000,000
Division Variable Costs			
$120 x 10,000 Feet of Raw Lumber	1,200,000	1,200,000	1,200,000
Division Fixed Cost			
$50 x 10,000 Feet of Raw Lumber	500,000	500,000	500,000
Division Operating Income	$ (260,000)	$1,270,000	$1,300,000
2. Transportation Division			
Revenues			
$198, $393.8, $400 x 10,000 Feet of Raw Lumber	$1,980,000	$3,938,000	$4,000,000
Division Variable Costs			
$21 x 10,000 Feet of Raw Lumber - - - - - - -	210,000	210,000	210,000
Division Fixed Costs			
$40 x 10,000 Feet of Raw Lumber - - - - - - -	400,000	400,000	400,000
Transferred-in Costs			
$144, $297, 300 x 10,000 Feet of Raw Lumber - -	1,440,000	2,970,000	3,000,000
Division Operating Income	$ (70,000)	$ 358,000	$ 390,000

	Transfer Price Set at 120% of Variable Costs	Transfer Price Set at 110% of Absorption Costs	Tranfer Price Set at Market Price
3. Finished Lumber Division			
Revenues			
$600 x 9,000 Feet of Raw Lumber	$5,400,000	$5,400,000	$5,400,000
Division Variable Costs			
$140 x 9,000 Feet of Finished Lumber	1,260,000	1,260,000	1,260,000
Division Fixed Cost			
$60 x 9,000 Feet of Finished Lumber	540,000	540,000	540,000
Transferred-in Costs			
$198, $393.8, $400 x 10,000 of Raw Lumber	1,980,000	3,938,000	4,000,000
Division Operating Income	$1,620,000	$ (338,000)	$ (400,000)
4. Total Company Income	$1,290,000	$1,290,000	$1,290,00

109

distress price may lead managers of the supplying division to dispose of productive facilities to affect positively the short-run ROI. However, this may reduce the activities of the buying division, which would be disadvantageous to the company as a whole. On the other hand, the use of the long-run average market price may penalize the buying division by forcing it to buy at a price higher than the market price. If the objective is to preserve the spirit of decentralization and if safeguards exist to prevent the supplying division from disposing of productive facilities, the distress price should be chosen.

Finally, there may be a problem if the goods or services transferred do not have a ready market price.

In spite of these limitations, the market price is considered the most effective transfer price because (1) it insures divisional autonomy, (2) it provides a good performance indication for use in performance evaluation, and (3) it creates a climate conducive to goal congruence.

6.3.2 Negotiated Price

A *negotiated transfer price* is the price set after bargaining between the buying and selling divisions. This system requires that these divisions deal with one another in the same way they deal with external suppliers and buyers. Thus, one basic requirement for the success of the bargaining process is the freedom of the divisions not only to bargain with one another, but also to deal with external markets if unsatisfied with the internal offers. This freedom will avoid the bilateral monopoly that exists when the divisions are only allowed to deal with themselves. In fact, the negotiated transfer price system works best when an intermediate market exists for the product or service transferred, providing the divisions with objective and reliable information for successful negotiations.

The literature contains several recommendations for the use of negotiated prices.[1] The writers maintain that prices negotiated in arm's-length bargaining by divisional managers help accomplish goal congruence. They view these prices as compatible with profit decentralization, insuring the division managers' freedom of action and increasing their accountability for profits. A survey conducted by R. K. Mautz indicates that about 24 percent of the participating diversified companies revealed *negotiation* as the basis for setting transfer prices between divisions.[2]

The negotiated transfer price system also may have a negative behavioral impact when personality conflicts arise between the bargainers; succeeding in the negotiation may become a more important goal than the company's profitability. Another drawback of the negotiated price system is that it can be time consuming. Division managers may lose an overall company perspective and direct their efforts to improve their divisional profit performance. In their attempts to obtain the best possible price, managers may find themselves in very lengthy argumentation.

When these conflicts arise, a transfer price should be set arbitrarily by a central decision of top management. This *arbitrary* or *imposed price* is the price felt to serve the overall company interests. Needless to say, the arbitrary price contradicts the spirit of decentralization, given the possible loss of divisional autonomy. Some authors in the accounting literature have fundamental objections to negotiation. R. Cyert and J. March viewed the organization as a coalition of interests and suggested that negotiation and renegotiation of transfer pricing can be expected to create conflict among the subunits constituting the coalition.[3] Nicholas Dopuch and D. F. Drake suggested that the negotiated price implies an evaluation of the power to negotiate rather than an evaluation of performance itself.[4]

6.3.3 Actual Cost

A transfer price based on actual absorption cost is a price based on the historical full cost of the product or service exchanged. It has the obvious advantage of being measurable, verifiable, and readily available.

When the actual costs are accepted for the determination of transfer prices, the problem remains of motivating the selling division to sell internally at a price other than the market price. One way of motivating the selling division is to set the transfer price at full actual cost plus some markup as a way of approximating the market price. The resulting *synthetic market price* may be better than the actual market price when the product existing in the intermediate market differs in terms of quality, grade, and other relevant characteristics from the product transferred.

The *full-cost-plus* or synthetic market price has been found to be the most popular approach under the following conditions: (1) an absence of competitive prices, (2) the presence of an interest in saving the cost of negotiating prices, and (3) the presence of a need to implement a policy of pricing the final product.[5]

There are several limitations inherent in the implementation of a transfer pricing model based on actual cost:

1. A transfer price based on actual cost is actually based on absorption cost in the sense that it includes all direct and indirect expenses (variable and allocated joint and fixed costs). As a result, this type of transfer price may transfer the inefficiencies of the selling division to the buying division, making it unwise to use divisional profit for divisional performance evaluation.
2. A transfer price based on actual cost may lessen the selling division's incentive to control costs.
3. Martin Shubik notes that cost-plus pricing of transfer goods can impede the search for technological progress by the manufacturing division.[6]

6.3.4 Standard Cost

We have seen that a transfer price based on actual cost can reinforce the inefficiencies of the selling division and lessen its motivation to control costs. A transfer price based on standard cost can correct for these problems. It reflects a normative position by expressing what costs should be under certain circumstances. As a result, a transfer price based on standard cost eliminates the inefficiencies of the selling division; when compared with actual cost, it may create an incentive to control costs.

6.3.5 Marginal or Variable Cost

A company using a transfer price based on either the full actual cost or the full standard cost may face at least two situations:

1. The full actual cost and the full standard cost may be higher than the market price.
2. The full actual cost and the full standard cost include both direct and indirect costs (variable and fixed). The indirect costs can result from arbitrary allocation procedures. The fixed costs can be committed costs that are incurred whether the selling division operates at full or at less-than-full capacity. Thus, the buying division may feel that either the indirect costs and/or the fixed costs should not be included in the determination of the transfer price. When this situation arises, it may be more motivating and important to maintain the spirit of decentralization and resort to a *transfer price based on partial cost,* which charges only a portion of the full actual or, preferably, full standard cost. Conceptually, this partial cost includes values between full cost and zero cost and refers to either the marginal cost or the variable cost.

The *marginal cost* is the incremental cost of producing additional units. In general, the buying division will be willing to buy as long as the marginal revenue is superior to the marginal cost. Although conceptually appealing, a transfer price based on marginal cost requires available information on all production levels. Because such figures are not always available, a surrogate for the marginal cost may have to be used—the *variable cost.*

The *variable cost* or the *variable cost plus a lump sum* can be used either as a surrogate for marginal cost or as a way of encouraging the use of some facilities' services. First, the variable cost can be used when marginal cost cannot easily be computed because of the absence of adequate information. Second, the use of the variable cost can encourage divisions to use the services of facilities with excess capacity until it becomes more profitable or advantageous to the selling division to switch to a full cost (actual or standard).

6.3.6 Dual Price

From the preceding discussion of transfer pricing alternatives, it can be seen that (1) the best motivating transfer price for the selling division is the market price, and (2) the most acceptable price for the buying division is the variable cost.

One way of meeting both of these optimal situations is to use a dual transfer price rather than a single transfer price. The dual price system allows the selling division to sell either at a market price or at a synthetic market price, hence creating a profit and motivating the selling division to sell. This system allows the buying division to buy inside the company at variable cost, which prevents the selling division from having excess capacity when the buying division buys outside at market prices equal to or lower than the variable cost. In short, the dual price system motivates both the buying and selling divisions to operate in the best interests of the company as a whole. One possible drawback of this system is the possibility that the divisions may no longer be motivated to control costs.

6.4 TRANSFER PRICING SYSTEMS ILLUSTRATED

To illustrate the transfer pricing systems, assume the Dowbing Company has two divisions (X and Y). For one of the company's products, division X produces a major subassembly, and division Y incorporates this subassembly into a final product. In the open market, similar subassemblies can be purchased at $150 each. Division Y currently buys the total output of division X and wants to increase purchases by 500 units. The following are some recent cost data for division X:

Subassembly	Standard Cost	Actual Cost
Direct material	$ 50	$ 60
Direct labor	20	25
Variable manufacturing overhead	15	15
Fixed manufacturing overhead	15	20
	$100	$120

1. Using the current market price, division X would transfer the parts at $150 each:

   500 units × $150 = $75,000.

2. Assume divisions X and Y agree after lengthy negotiations that the outside market price includes $10 of selling and advertising expenses. The negotiated price would be $140 ($150 − $10) each:

   500 units × $140 = $70,000.

3. Assume that divisions X and Y cannot agree on the amount of selling and administrative expenses and that top management has set an arbitrary dictated price of $130 per unit:

   500 units × $130 = $65,000.

4. Using the full actual cost, division X would transfer the parts at $120 each:

   500 units × $120 = $60,000.

5. Using the full standard cost, division X would transfer the parts at $100 each:

$$500 \text{ units} \times \$100 = \$50,000.$$

6. Assume division X is already operating at full capacity, and to produce the additional 500 units it must incur additional standard fixed costs of $5 per unit. The marginal cost of production per unit is computed as follows:

Direct material	$ 50
Direct labor	20
Variable manufacturing overhead	15
Fixed manufacturing overhead ($15 + $5)	20
	$105

$$500 \text{ units} \times \$105 = \$52,500.$$

7. Using the actual variable cost, division X would transfer the parts at $100 each:

$$500 \text{ units} \times \$100 = \$50,000.$$

8. Using a dual price system, division X can be given credit for the market price of $150, and division Y is charged at the variable cost of $100. Assuming that the variable cost of Y is $30 per unit, the profit of the division will be as follows:

Division X

Sales to division Y at $150	$ 75,000
Variable costs at $100	50,000
Contribution margin	$ 25,000

Division Y

Sales of finished product at $200 (assumed)	$100,000
Variable costs	
Division X at $100	50,000
Division Y at $30	15,000
Contribution margin	$ 35,000

Note that the profit of the company as a whole is less than the sum of the divisional profits. Some eliminations must be made before the total company profit can be determined. The total of the company is actually only $35,000 ($200 unit selling price of the final product − $130 total unit variable cost incurred in both divisions X and Y = $70 contribution margin per unit; $70 contribution margin per unit × 500 units = $35,000 total contribution margin). The $25,000 additional contribution reflected in the income statement of division X is due to division X to allow it to sell at market price; this, in fact, constitutes a corporate subsidy to motivate division X to sell to division Y.

6.5 GENERAL GUIDELINE FOR COMPUTING TRANSFER PRICES

The various methods discussed in the preceding sections illustrate the general infeasibility of using only one given method for all circumstances. There is, however, a general guideline that can be used as a benchmark in setting a transfer price: The minimum transfer price is as follows:

1. *The additional outlay cost per unit incurred to the point of transfer* (these costs may sometimes be approximated by the variable costs) *plus*

2. *The opportunity costs per unit to the firm as a whole* (contribution margin per unit on outside sales).

With this guideline, the transfer price would be equal to the variable costs in those cases where no alternative use of the resources existed and to the market price in the case of a strong external market for the product.

To illustrate the use of the guideline, assume that a multidivisional electronic company has a monitor division aimed at the external market. The monitor requires $400 in variable costs and sells for $700. The monitor division has a production capacity of 4,000 monitors. Another division, the computer division, needs a different monitor from the one currently produced by the monitor division. It can buy the monitor from an outside supplier at a price of $650 per monitor based on an order of 4,000 monitors. The monitor division has advised, however, that it would devote all its capacity to the production of the new monitor required by the computer division. The variable cost of the new monitor would be $300 per unit.

Applying the guideline to these data, the transfer price for the monitor division would be as follows:

Transfer price = $300 (variable cost of the new monitor)
+ $300 (the contribution margin lost to the monitor division as a result of giving up outside monitor sales: $700 selling price − $400 variable costs = $300)

Transfer price = $600.

The decision should be to authorize the computer division to buy the new monitor from the monitor division at $600 per unit rather than from an outside supplier at $650 per unit, given the prevailing market conditions.

6.6 MULTINATIONAL TRANSFER PRICING

As mentioned earlier in the chapter, the following three criteria are used for the setting of transfer prices:

1. Goal congruence
2. Divisional autonomy
3. Performance evaluation.

These criteria are, however, most dominant for domestic transfer pricing. Other factors stated by executives to be important in domestic transfer pricing include the following (in order of importance):

1. Performance evaluation—to measure the results of each operating unit.
2. Managerial motivation—to provide the company with a "profit-making" orientation throughout each organizational entity.
3. Pricing driven—to better reflect "costs" and "margins" that must be received from customers.
4. Market driven—to maintain an internal competitiveness so that the company stays in balance with outside market forces.[7]

In the case of multinational transfer pricing, however, other "external" conditions may exert influences in establishing procedures and policies for a firm's transfer pricing mechanism. Factors stated by executives to be important in international transfer pricing include the following (in order of importance):

1. Overall income to the company.
2. The competitive position of subsidiaries in foreign countries.
3. Performance evaluation of foreign subsidiaries.
4. Restrictions imposed by foreign countries on repatriation of profits or dividends.
5. The need to maintain adequate cash flows in foreign subsidiaries.
6. Maintaining good relationships with host governments.

While the above factors reflect the positions stated by executives, a book written on behalf of the European Center for Study and Information on Multinational Corporations states that transfer price has acquired a bad meaning because it "evokes the idea of systematic manipulation of prices in order to reduce profits artificially, cause losses, avoid taxes or duties."[8] The resulting situation may be summarized as the parent company's dictating what the transfer price should be. But the complexities of the situation may transform the transfer price problem into a major hurdle. As noted by Irving Fantl:

The first hurdle involves personal relations with foreign management: it is easier to explain the need for arbitrary pricing to a domestic executive and to discount its effects in evaluating its performance. The foreign manager starts from a basis of suspicion of the motives by the U.S. parent. Any system that would make him feel unappreciated or misunderstood can undermine the success of the foreign venture. For internal measurement purposes, transfer pricing becomes more crucial than in domestic relations.[9]

The whole situation is, in fact, created by one of the goals of multinational corporations which is the maximization of global after-tax profits. This is accomplished by minimizing the global income tax liability. Other things being the same, profits are increased by setting high transfer prices to take out profits from subsidiaries located in high tax countries and low transfer prices to move profits to subsidiaries domiciled in low tax countries. This arbitrary shifting of profits purely for tax avoidance is being challenged by most governments in the developing and developed countries through their enacting of appropriate legislation. In the United States, the main legislation restricting the internal-pricing policies of multinational corporations is contained within the 1954 Internal Revenue Code, Section 482, and the 1977 Regulation 861.

6.6.1 Intercorporate Transfer Pricing: Section 482

In any case of two or more organizations, trades, or businesses (whether or not incorporated, whether or not organized in the United States, and whether or not affiliated) owned or controlled directly or indirectly by the same interests, the secretary or his delegate may distribute, apportion, or allocate gross income, deductions, credits, or allowances between or among such organizations, trades, or businesses, if he determines that such distribution, appointment, or allocation is necessary to prevent evasion of taxes or to reflect clearly the income of such organizations, trades, or businesses.[10]

The purpose of Section 482 is to place a controlled taxpayer on a tax parity with an uncontrollable taxpayer by determining, according to the standards of an uncontrolled taxpayer, the true taxable income from the property and business of a controlled taxpayer. Basically, the Internal Revenue Service (IRS) is allowed to disallow an existing transfer pricing system and to reallocate income to reflect the "true taxable income." The *true taxable income* is described as the income resulting if each member were acting "at arm's length" from the others. Detailed regulations were issued, under the section, based on the principle that transactions between related parties should take place on an arm's-length basis. These regulations set forth three pricing methods to be used in determining the arm's-length price, namely, in order of preference, the comparable uncontrolled price method, the resale price method, and the cost-plus method.

The comparable uncontrolled price method determined the transfer price as the basis of "uncontrolled sales" made to buyers who are not part of the same controlled group. Guidelines for what constitutes a "comparable uncontrolled price" are provided in the regulations as follows:

Uncontrolled sales are considered comparable to controlled sales if the physical property and circumstances involved in the uncontrolled sales are identical to the physical property and circumstances involved in the controlled sales, or if such properties and circumstances are so nearly identical that any differences either have no effect on price, or such differences can be reflected by a reasonable number of adjustments to the price of uncontrolled sales. . . . Some of the differences which may affect the price of property are differences in the quality of the product, terms of sale, intangible property associated with the sale, time of sales, and the level of the market and the geographic market in which the sale takes place.[11]

Uncontrolled sales are defined to include sales made by the seller to an unrelated party, to the buyer by an unrelated party, or where neither party is a member of a controlled group. If there are no comparable uncontrolled sales, the regulations prescribe the use of the resale price method.

The resale price method is applicable when the buyer does not add a significant value to the product; that is, the buyer is simply a distributor. In such a case, the transfer price is equal to the resale price to unrelated parties less an appropriate markup, plus or minus certain adjustments. Basically, the resale price method establishes the arm's-length price by working back from a third-party selling price. The arm's-length price is equal to:

1. *The applicable resale price:* the price at which property purchased in the controlled sales is resold by the buyer, or ultimately resold by some late buyer, in an uncontrolled sale,

2. *Adjusted by the appropriate markup percentage:* equal to the percentage of gross profit earned by the reseller or another party on the resale of property that is both purchased and resold in an uncontrolled transaction similar to the controlled sale, and

3. *Property adjusted for any differences:* the functions or circumstances that have a definite and readily measurable effect on price, such as warranty or advertising contribution.[12]

The cost plus method is prescribed in those situations when both the comparable uncontrolled price and the resale price methods are not applicable. The cost plus price is equal to full cost (actual or standard) plus an appropriate profit percentage similar to that earned by the division or other companies in similar transactions with unrelated parties. In this case, the arm's-length price is equal to:

1. *The cost of production:* computed in a consistent manner in accordance with sound accounting practices for allocating or appropriating costs that neither favor nor burden controlled sales in comparison with uncontrolled sales,

2. *Add appropriate gross-profit percentage:* equal to the gross profit percentage earned by the seller or another party on uncontrolled sales that are most similar to the controlled sales in question, and

3. *Properly adjusted for any difference:* differences that have a definite and readily measurable effect on price that would warrant an adjustment of price in uncontrolled transactions.[13]

Besides these three methods, the regulations prescribe the use of some "appropriate method" of pricing if it is comparable to the pricing that would be charged to an unrelated party.

6.6.2 Allocation of Expenses: Section 861

Section 482 is intended to allocate the proper taxable income to the parent at arm's length, and Section 861 is intended to allocate corporate expenses to the foreign source income. Basically, it allocates and apportions all of a firm's expenses, losses, and other deductions to specific sources of income (sales, royalties, dividends) and then apportions the expenses between domestic and foreign source income.

6.7 CONCLUSION

In 1967 the National Industrial Conference Board managed 190 U.S. firms to find the type of transfer price most often used by companies. The study classified all prices into two main categories—cost or market-based prices—and confirmed the use of more than one transfer price within a single enterprise.[14] No method emerged as the "preferred price."[15] This lack of agreement emphasizes the need for a better solution to the transfer pricing problem.

Legal restrictions are major considerations for companies establishing a transfer price. For internal tax purposes, a transfer price must make commercial sense. Transfers to foreign subsidiaries ideally should be justifiable and should not be made to achieve a more favorable tax climate. Antitrust regulations also force large companies to use realistic transfer prices.

Reliable information for use in determining transfer prices should be available through the accounting discipline. However, in the context of transfer pricing there is no one accounting solution that is simultaneously appropriate for performance evaluation, decision making, and general financial statement purposes. The dual pricing approach is the best solution accounting can offer. The use of a synthetic market price for the selling division and some form of variable cost charged to the buying division reflects most fairly a division's performance and permits the purchasing division to make decisions that are advantageous to the firm. The synthetic market price and variable cost must be determined by a third party who is knowledgeable about the relevance and reliability of these prices. The major deficiency in the dual pricing approach to the transfer pricing problem is the undermining of divisional autonomy through the introduction of a third party.

The economic analysis of divisionalized firms cannot provide a simple solution for transfer pricing of intermediate goods. The initial theory developed by Jack Hirschleifer in 1956 was considered a pathfinding approach to the problem. It outlined the risk of dysfunctional decisions if divisions were allowed to operate as autonomous units. Marginal costs and marginal revenues can be used to predict the optimal situation for a firm as a whole, and they provide the meeting ground for cost-based and market-oriented transfer prices.[16]

The decomposition programming model (DPM) offers a systematic procedure for calculating the bonuses and penalties used in obtaining optimal use and pricing of resources. Using the central coordination of corporate headquarters, this method attempts to insure goal congruence by adjusting subprograms to the complexities of the overall firm. The DPM also eliminates interdivisional communication, thus minimizing the interpersonal conflicts that can otherwise arise. Performance evaluation focuses on the ability of division managers to adhere to the optimal plan. Although the degree of true divisional autonomy possible has been questioned, the decomposition procedure allows divisional responsibility and authority for the formulation and calculation of divisional programs.

It must be remembered that whatever solution is reached applies to a particular organizational environment. Each situation is unique and must be incorporated into the organizational philosophy. Without consideration for the behavioral aspect, no solution will succeed. "Users and uses must determine the transfer pricing technique to be selected."[17]

NOTES

1. Joel Dean, "Decentralization and Intracompany Pricing." *Harvard Business Review* (July–August 1955): 65–74; David H. Li, "Interdivisional Transfer Planning." *Management Accounting* (June 1965): 51–54; Timothy P. Haidinger, "Negotiate for Profits." *Management Accounting* (December 1970): 23–24; James M. Fremgen, "Transfer Pricing and Management Goals." *Management Accounting* (December 1970): 25–31; H. James Shaub, "Transfer Pricing in a Decentralized Organization." *Management Accounting* (April 1978): 33–36, 42.

2. R. K. Mautz, *Financial Reporting by Diversified Companies* (New York: Financial Executives Research Foundation, 1968), 36.

3. R. Cyert and J. March, *A Behavioral Theory of the Firm* (Englewood Cliffs, N.J.: Prentice-Hall, 1963), 276.

4. Nicholas Dopuch and D. F. Drake, "Accounting Implications of a Mathematical Programming Approach to the Transfer Price Problem." *Journal of Accounting Research* (Spring 1964): 13.

5. National Association of Accountants, *Research Report No. 30*, "Accounting for Intra-Company Transfers" (New York: NAA, 1954), 31–36.

6. Martin Shubik, "Incentives, Decentralized Control: The Assignment of Joint Costs and Internal Pricing," in *Management Controls: New Directions in Basic Research*, ed. C. P. Bonini, R. K. Jaedicke, and H. M. Wagner (New York: McGraw-Hill, 1964), 221–222.

7. Price Waterhouse, *Transfer Pricing Practices of American Industry* (New York: Price Waterhouse, 1984).

8. R. Tang, "Environmental Variables of Multinational Transfer Pricing: A U.K. Perspective." *Journal of Business Finance and Accounting* (Summer 1982): 182.

9. Irving Fantl, "Transfer Pricing—Tread Carefully." *The CPA Journal* 44 (December 1974): 44.

10. U.S. Internal Revenue Code (1954), Section 482.

11. Ibid., Section 482-1(e)(2)(ii).

12. Michael P. Casey, "International Transfer Pricing." *Management Accounting* (October 1985): 33.

13. Ibid., 34.

14. National Industrial Conference Board, *Interdivisional Transfer Pricing* (New York: National Industrial Conference Board, 1967).

15. I. Sharav, "Transfer Pricing, Diversity of Goals and Practices." *Journal of Accountancy* (April 1974): 56–62.

16. Jack Hirschleifer, "On the Economics of Transfer Pricing," *Journal of Business* (January 1956): 172–184.

17. Sharav, "Transfer Pricing," p. 61.

SELECTED READINGS

Abdel-Khalik, A. Rashad, and E. J. Lusk. "Transfer Pricing: A Synthesis." *Accounting Review* (January 1974): 9–23.

Anthony, Robert N., and J. Dearden. *Management Control Systems*. 3d ed. Homewood, Ill.: Irwin, 1976, chaps. 6–7.

Baumol, W., and T. Fabian. "Decompositions, Pricing of Decentralization and External Economies." *Management Science* (Spring 1964): 1–32.

Benke, Ralph L., Thomas E. Gibbs, and Richard G. Schroeder. "Should You Use Transfer Pricing to Create Pseudo-Profit Centers?" *Management Accounting* (February 1979): 29–34.

Berkwitt, G. J. "Do Profit Centres Really Work?" *Management Review* (August 1969): 15–20.

Bernhard, R. H. "Some Problems in Applying Mathematical Programming to Opportunity Costing." *Journal of Accounting Research* (Spring 1968): 143–148.

Bierman, H. "Pricing Intercompany Transfer." *Accounting Review* (July 1959): 429–432.

Bierman, H., and T. R. Dyckman. *Managerial Cost Accounting*. 2d ed. New York: Macmillan Co., 1976, chap. 19.

Cowen, Scott S., Lawrence C. Phillips, and Linda Stillabower. "Multinational Transfer Pricing." *Management Accounting* (January 1979): 17–22.

Dantzig, G. B., and P. Wolfe. "Decomposition Principle for Linear Programs." *Operations Research* (January–February 1960): 101–111.

Dearden, J. "Interdivisional Pricing." *Harvard Business Review* (January–February 1960): 117–125.

Dopuch, Nicholas, and Drake, D. F., "Accounting Implications of a Mathematical Programming Approach to the Transfer Price Problem," *Journal of Accounting Research* (Spring 1964): 10–21.

Fremgen, James M., "Transfer Pricing and Management Goals," *Management Accounting* (December 1970): 25–31.

Goetz, B. E., "Transfer Prices: An Exercise in Relevancy and Goal Congruence." *Accounting Review* (July 1967): 435–440.

Gordon, Myron J., "A Method of Pricing for a Socialist Economy," *Accounting Review* (July 1970): 427–443.

Hass, J. E., "Transfer Pricing in a Decentralized Firm," *Management Science* (February 1968): B-310, B-333.

Hirschleifer, Jack, "Economics of the Divisionalized Firm," *Journal of Business* (April 1957): 96–108.

Hirschleifer, Jack, "On the Economics of Transfer Pricing," *Journal of Business* (January 1956): 172–184.

Jennergren, P., "Decentralization on the Basis of Price Schedules in Linear Decomposable Resource-Allocation Problems," *Journal of Financial and Quantitative Analysis* (January 1972): 1407–1417.

Lucien, Kent, "Transfer Pricing for the Cost of Funds in a Commercial Bank," *Management Accounting* (January 1979): 23–24.

Lusch, Robert F., and Bentz, William F., "A Variance Approach to Analyzing Changes in Return on Investment," *Management Accounting* (February 1979): 29–33.

Madison, Roland L., "Responsibility Accounting and Transfer Pricing: Approach with Caution," *Management Accounting* (January 1979): 25–29.

Onsi, M., "A Transfer Pricing System Based on Opportunity Cost," *Accounting Review* (July 1970): 535–543.

Ronen, Joshua, and McKinney, George III, "Transfer Pricing for Divisional Autonomy," *Journal of Accounting Research* (Spring 1970): 99–112.

Samuels, J. M., "Opportunity Costing: An Application of Mathematical Programming," *Journal of Accounting Research* (Autumn 1965): 182–191.

Sharav, I., "Transfer Pricing, Diversity of Goals and Practices," *Journal of Accountancy* (April 1974): 56–62.

Shubik, Martin, "Incentives, Decentralized Control: The Assignment of Joint Costs and Internal Pricing," in *Management Controls: New Directions in Basic Research,* eds. C. P. Bonini, R. K. Jaedicke, and H. M. Wagner (New York: McGraw-Hill, 1964), 205–225.

Solomons, David, *Divisional Performance: Measurement and Control* (New York: Financial Executives Research Foundation, 1965).

Tang, Roger W., *Transfer Pricing Practices in the United States and Japan* (New York: Praeger, 1979).

Van Horne, J. C., *Financial Management and Policy,* 3d ed. (Englewood Cliffs, N.J.: Prentice-Hall, 1974), chap. 24.

Walker, W. E., "A Method for Obtaining the Optimal Dual Solution to a Linear Program Using the Dantzig-Wolfe Decomposition," *Operations Research* (March–April 1969): 368–370.

Watson, D. J. H., and Baumler, J. V., "Transfer Pricing: A Behavioral Context," *Accounting Review* (July 1975): 466–474.

Whinston, A., "Pricing Guides in Decentralized Organizations," in *New Perspectives in Organizational Research,* eds. W. W. Cooper et al. (New York: Wiley, 1964), chap. 22, 411–417.

Whisler, T. L.; Meyer, H.; Baum, B. H.; and Sorenson, P. F., "Centralization of Control: An Empirical Study of Its Meaning and Measurement," *Journal of Business* (January 1970): 10–26.

7

Planning Principles

Of all possible organizational styles of management, the ones most likely to create problems are the "fire fighting" and "tunnel vision" approaches. Fire fighting consists of reacting to events and crises when they appear; tunnel vision is a selective perception of what constitutes the organization's concern.

Planning is an effective mechanism to counter both the fire fighting and tunnel vision management styles. It allows the organization to define its relationship with the environment and is "a method of guiding managers so that their decisions and actions are set to the future of the organization in a consistent and rational manner, and in a way desired by top management."[1] Planning has also been defined as "a process which begins with objectives; defines strategies, policies and detailed plans to achieve them; which establishes an organization to implement decisions; and feedback to introduce a new planning cycle."[2]

These definitions describe planning as the process of collecting information on objectives and making decisions on the best way to achieve them. Planning is vital to an organization's future success. Stanley Thune and Robert House analyzed the planning function in thirty-six similar firms in six industries. They concluded that (1) those firms which rely on a formal planning department were more successful than those which rely on informal planning, and (2) those firms which rely on a formal planning department perform more successfully after the system is instituted than previously.[3] Planning prepares firms to operate in a dynamic world and to adapt to the ensuing changes in technology, financing, resource availability, economic conditions, and so forth. Because of the benefits of planning, it is not surprising that most firms of all sizes and industries rely on some type of formal planning system.[4]

This chapter elaborates on planning principles and examines budgeting as a formalization of planning in the organization. It illustrates the technical preparation of the master budget.

7.1 GOAL CONGRUENCE: THE MAIN OBJECTIVE OF PLANNING AND CONTROL

Cost accounting systems, also known as management control systems or control systems, consist of rules and procedures aimed at the accumulation and communication of relevant cost information for internal decision making. These control systems formalize the objectives of the organization and express them operationally as performance criteria to be met by the individuals in the organization. Central to the efficient working of the control systems is goal congruence, that is, the harmonization of the individual and group objectives within the organization and the objectives of the organization as a whole. Robert N. Anthony was perhaps the first to stress the importance of goal congruence. In 1964 he wrote

Essentially, therefore, the control system should be designed so that actions that it leads people to take, in accordance with their perceived self-interest, are actions that are also in the best interests of the company. In the language of social psychology, the system should encourage goal congruence. . . . Perfect congruence between individual goals and organizational goals does not exist, but as a minimum the system should not encourage the individual to act against the best interests of the company.[5]

Goal congruence is achieved when individuals in the organization strive or are induced to strive toward the company goals. This assumes, of course, that the individuals are aware of the company goals and the derivative performance criteria.

The essence of a company's goals is conveyed by the planning process, which expresses these goals in terms of *budgets,* standards, and other formal measures of performance. Management must tailor the planning activities to encourage goal congruence at various levels of management. To achieve goal congruence the following ideas are important.[6]

First, the firm should be viewed as a pluralist entity where coalitions of individuals seek to express their own aspirations within the structure of the firm. Personnel cannot be viewed only as people sharing the same goal, but also as people striving for such rewards as power, security, survival, and autonomy.[7] K. J. Arrow observes:

An organization is a group of individuals seeking to achieve some common goals, or, in different language, to maximize an objective function. Each member has objectives of his own, in general not coincident with those of the organization. Each member also has some range of decisions to make within limits set partly by the environment external to the organization and partly by the decisions of other members. Finally, some but not all observations about the workings of the organization and about the external world are communicated from one member to another.[8]

Second, while profit maximization has long been considered the single goal of the firm, in reality, corporations pursue a range of goals. For example, the General Electric Company emphasizes multiple goals by stressing that organizational performance be measured in the following eight areas: (1) profitability, (2) market position, (3) productivity, (4) product leadership, (5) personnel development, (6) employee attitudes, (7) public responsibility, and (8) a balance between short-range and long-range goals.

Third, the goals of the firm may also conflict with one another and with the individual and group objectives. A bargaining process may be necessary to reduce these conflicts in the goal-setting process.[9] In fact, the budget may be considered the key mechanism for the stabilization of that process, that is, "a bargaining medium through which individuals and groups try to further their own goals."[10]

7.2 FROM PLANNING TO BUDGETING

Anthony's decision systems framework, presented in chapter 1, distinguishes between planning and budgeting. Planning—or, precisely, strategic planning—takes place at the strategic planning level and principally involves elaboration of organizational goals and the strategies necessary to accomplish them. Planning reflects the organization's desire to face the future in a rational manner by providing a general guide to managerial decision making. In general, strategic planning is subdivided into two activities: business planning and diversification planning, which are defined as follows:

Business planning is the process of determining the scope of organizational activities that will be undertaken toward the satisfaction of a broad consumer need, of deciding on the objectives of the organization in its defined area of operation, and of evaluating the effectiveness with which varying magnitudes of resources may be committed toward achieving those objectives.

Diversification planning is the process of deciding on the objectives of a corporation, including the determination of which and how many lines of business to engage in, of acquiring the resources needed to attain those objectives, and of allocating resources among the different businesses in a manner intended to achieve those objectives.[11]

The strategic planning process is followed by a management control process the purpose of which is to insure that the long-term plans emerging from business and diversification planning are implemented over the years. The management control process, therefore, is a communication and interaction process for the implementation of strategic plans, and *its success rests on budgeting*. Budgeting, then, is the most conspicuous evidence of the planning process. The budget, the formal means by which the planning process takes shape, ties together the diverse activities of the firm that are related to specific goals and specifies the means for their realization. W. J. Vatter defines budgets as follows:

Budgets state formally—in terms of expected transactions—the decisions of all levels of management about the resources to be acquired, how they are to be used, and what ought to result. Budgets put the details of management plans for operations in money units, so that the results may be projected into expected financial statements.[12]

In short, planning precedes budgeting, and budgets are quantitative, and mostly monetary, short-term expressions of plans.

7.3 BUDGETING PRINCIPLES

7.3.1 Nature of Budgeting

Most companies, large or small, prepare budgets. The budget is a quantitative monetary expression of future activities covering a specific period of time, usually one year. The budget, also called a *master budget,* is used as a tool for planning in both centralized and decentralized firms. The following are among the purposes of budgets and budgeting:

1. The budget is used to plan and coordinate the overall activities of the firm, and it forces management to quantify their expectations.
2. The budget is used to communicate to all employees the goals and objectives of the firm and the means to be used to attain them.
3. The budget is used to assign to each employee the responsibility for the performance of a given activity, task, or program, and it serves as a final guide in evaluating the adequacy of the employee's performance.
4. The budget is used to give management a chance to examine environmental conditions and changes, thereby increasing their potential to reduce uncertainty and to shape the firm's future progress.
5. The budget is used to create a harmony between all functional areas of the firm (sales, marketing, production, purchasing, finance, personnel, and so forth) by specifying what each functional area manager must do to optimize the performance in other areas and in the firm as a whole.

7.3.2 Types of Budgets

Budgeting is sometimes referred to as *periodic budgeting* because budgets are usually prepared for specific time periods, such as one year or five years. The annual profit plan is the master budget, which may be broken down by months or quarters. The master budget is a *continuous budget* if a budget for one month (or one quarter) is added as one month (or one quarter) goes by. The firm then has an annual profit plan at all times. Budgets are not always connected to a time period. For example, a *project budget* or *product budget* serves as a general guideline to probable results of a project or product. It emphasizes the various stages of the project or product rather than the periods. There is a connection to periods, however, because the cash requirements for the project or product budgets are considered in the cash budget as a component of the master budget.

The *capital budget* specifies the future expenditures for fixed assets over a given number of years. It is a major component of the strategic plan outlining the long-term future of the firm. The capital budget also affects periodic budgeting because the cash requirements for the fixed asset purchases are periodically specified in the cash budget as a component of the master budget.

7.3.3 Advantages of Budgeting

The use of budgeting has many advantages. It may lead to better performance of individuals in the organization because of better performance by the managers. Budgets may motivate managers to accomplish the organizational objectives if they are used to communicate company objectives; establish subobjectives in accord with managerial objectives; and provide a thoroughly understood, common basis for performance measurement and feedback. Thus, budgets motivate people by providing information for the comparison of expected and actual performance. When such evaluation of performance is known to result in rewards and penalties, people are more often motivated to do their best.

Because budgets are quantitative plans for action, they may force management to examine carefully the available resources and determine how these can be used efficiently.

Budgets make expectations concrete by letting people know what is expected of them. They require specific quantification of ideas.

Budgets are essential tools of coordination. They provide an integration of all the production factors and all the departments and functions of an organization; thus, the organization's joint objectives are obtained, and a congruence is insured between the goals of the individual managers and the goals of the organization as a whole. By using budgets to coordinate activities, a firm is more likely to operate at an optimal level, given the constraints on its resources. Hence the budgeting of departmental activities insures their coordination, so bottlenecks do not occur and interdepartmental conflicts are reduced.

Budgets are essential tools to communicate expectations. When a budget is distributed to those responsible for various parts of it, the individual managers become more aware of where they fit in the organization.

7.3.4 Budgeting Procedures

The budgeting procedures and the construction of a master budget usually are supervised by a budget committee, which may include members representing the firm's divisions or functions (sales, marketing, production, purchasing, finance, personnel, and so forth). A budget director, generally the controller or the chief financial officer, serves as head of the budget committee.

Although they differ from one organization to another, the budgeting procedures are likely to resemble the following:

1. Top management develops the overall goals of the organization and includes them in the firm's strategic plan.

2. Keeping in mind the overall organizational goals, the budget committee determines the basic economic forecasts outlining the future progress of the company and communicates these long-term forecasts to the divisions or departments.

3. Each division or department determines its operating budgets in line with the overall goals and basic economic forecasts outlined for the company. These operating budgets then are communicated to the budget committee.

4. The budget committee reviews and coordinates the budgets and either asks for revision or approves the submitted budgets. When all the submitted budgets are approved, the budget committee puts the master budget in final form, which is then communicated to the various departments or divisions to serve as a guide for action and control.

7.4 THE MASTER BUDGET ILLUSTRATED

As an annual profit plan, the master budget expresses the company's *financial* position and *operational* performance for the next year. It is a coordinated set of detailed financial schedules and statements, including sales and expenses forecasts, cash receipts and disbursements, balance sheets, income statements, and a statement of changes in the financial position (see Figure 7.1).

The budgets constituting the master budget, accompanied by their detailed schedules, generally include the following components:

I. Operating budget
   A. Sales budget
   B. Production budget (for manufacturing companies)
      1. Production budget and changes in inventory levels budget
      2. Material usage and purchases budget
      3. Direct-labor budget
      4. Factory overhead budget
   C. Cost of goods sold budget
   D. Selling expense budget
   E. Administrative expense budget
   F. Budgeted income statement

II. Financial Budget
   A. Capital budget (long-range forecasts for specific projects)
   B. Cash budget (cash receipts and disbursements)
   C. Budgeted balance sheet
   D. Budgeted statement of changes in the financial position.

The relationships between these budgets is shown in Figure 7.1. First, note that strategic planning provides long-range sales forecasts that can be used in the sales budget. Second, notice that the operating budget focuses on the income statements and its supporting schedules and that the financial budget focuses on the impact that the operating budget and the capital budget have on the cash

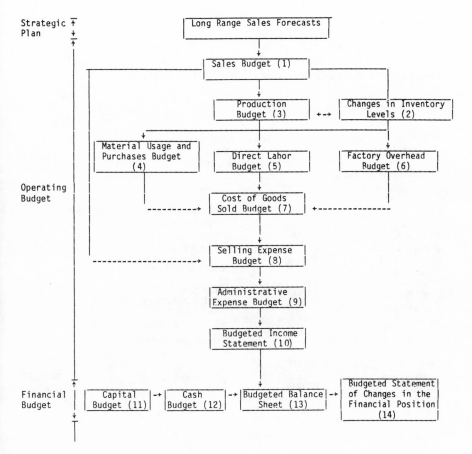

Figure 7.1
The Master Budget and Its Components

Note: Every step taken in the preparation of the master budget rests on the reliability and
accuracy of the sales forecasts in the sales budget (step 1). The next steps all
contribute to the budgeted financial statements (steps 8 to 14).

budget, the balance sheet position, and the statement of changes in the financial
position.

Section 7.4 provides a detailed description of the master budget of the Monti
Company. The basic data are used in a step-by-step procedure for the preparation
of the master budget. Although only one draft of the budget is presented, in
reality subsequent drafts may be required before a final master budget is chosen.

7.4.1 Basic Information

The Monti Company is preparing its master budget immediately after the close of the year 19XA. Mr. Ali Mabrouk, the budget director, together with a budget committee, has gathered the following data and requirements:

1. The balance sheet for the year just ended, 19XA, is given here:

Monti Company
Balance Sheet
December 13, 19XA

Assets			Equities		
Current Assets			**Current Liabilities**		
Cash	$ 10,000		Accounts Payable	$ 1,000	
Accounts Receivable	10,000		Wages Payable	1,000	
Material Inventory (10,000 Units)	10,000		Total Current Liabilities		$ 2,000
Finished Goods Inventory (2,500 Units)	10,000		**Stockholders' Equity**		
Total Current Assets		$ 40,000	Common Stock, No Par, 2,000 Shares Outstanding	$200,000	
			Retained Earnings	48,000	
Fixed Assets			Total Stockholders' Equity		248,000
Land	$150,000				
Buildings and Equipment	100,000		Total Equities		$250,000
Accumulated Depreciation	(40,000)	210,000			
Total Assets		$250,000			

2. The expected monthly gross sales for 19XB are as follows:

Month	Volume (in Units)	Unit Selling Price (in Dollars)
January	5,000	5
February	5,000	5
March	5,000	5
April	5,000	10
May	10,000	10
June	15,000	10
July	15,000	10
August	10,000	10
September	10,000	10
October	5,000	5
November	5,000	5
December	5,000	5
	95,000	
January 19XC	5,000	$5

3. The sales discounts, returns, and allowances are estimated to be 10 percent of gross sales. Net sales consists of 40 percent cash and 60 percent credit. All credit sales are collected in the month following the sales.

4. At the end of each month, the Monti Company desires an ending finished goods inventory equal to 50 percent of the sales of the following month.

5. There are no work-in-process inventories.

6. Each finished goods unit requires two units of a direct material (X), the price of which is estimated to be $1 per unit.

7. At the end of each month, the Monti Company desires an ending material inventory equal to 100 percent of the materials requirements for the following month. However, for April and May, the company wants to maintain an ending material inventory equal to 50 percent of the material requirements of the following month.

8. The purchase discounts, returns, and allowances are estimated to be equal to 10 percent of the gross purchases.

9. Each unit of finished goods requires 0.5 hour of direct labor at $2 per hour.

10. The Monti Company pays 40 percent of its direct-labor costs the same month they are incurred. It pays the 60 percent balance the following month.

11. Net purchases consist of 40 percent cash and 60 percent credit.

12. At the anticipated volume for 19XB, the company will incur the following costs:

Factory Overhead

Supplies	$10,000, to Be Paid 60% in June and 40% in December
Indirect Labor	20,000, to Be Paid 50% in June and 50% in December
Maintenance-Variable Portion	1,000, to Be Paid in June
Power-Variable Portion	1,500, to Be Paid in December
Property Taxes	500, to Be Paid in June
Depreciation	500
Payroll Fringe Costs	10,000, to Be Paid 50% in June and 50% in December
Maintenance-Fixed Portion	2,000, to Be Paid in June
Power-Fixed Portion	1,000, to Be Paid 50% in June and 50% in December
Miscellaneous-Fixed Portion	1,000, to Be Paid 50% in June and 50% in December
	$47,500

Selling and Administrative Overhead

Travel	$10,000, to Be Paid in December
Sales Commissions	4,000, to Be Paid in December
Salaries	12,000, to Be Paid $1,000 per Month
Depreciation	23,500
	$49,500

13. The Monti Company expects to issue common stock for $100,000 in August and bonds for $40,000 in December.

14. The Monti company expects to purchase a new machine for $150,000 in April to be paid three months later.

15. Two parcels of land will be purchased in February to be paid as follows: $50,000 in April, $35,000 in May, $50,000 in June, $50,000 in July, $70,000 in August, $50,000 in September, $25,000 in October, and $25,000 in November.

16. The company borrows or repays money in multiples of $100 at an interest rate of 10 percent per year. Borrowing is generally done at the beginning of the month and repayment at the end of the month. Any excess of total cash available over total cash needed is used to repay the maximum principal and the corresponding interest. Any deficiency is corrected by borrowing the necessary cash.

17. The Monti Company expects to maintain a minimum monthly cash balance of $30,000.

18. The sales for January 19XB will be 5,000 units at $5 per unit.

7.4.2 Sales Budget

The first step in budgeting is the determination of the sales budget. This sets the level of anticipated activity upon which inventory levels, production, and expenses are planned.

Table 7.1 shows the sales budget for the Monti Company for 19XB. The sales budget shown includes units expected to be sold; the selling price; the total expected gross sales; the sales discounts, returns, and allowances; the net sales; the cash and credit sales; the total cash collections; and the accounts receivable by month.

The preparation of the sales budget, therefore, depends on the estimation of the following information:

1. The sales forecast in units
2. The selling price or pricing policy of the firm
3. The proportion of cash sales or the sales credit policy of the firm
4. The cash collection policy, bad debt history, and average time lag between sales and collections
5. The proportion of sales discounts, returns, and allowances.

Note that the accuracy of the sales forecasts is crucial as it will determine the reliability of all the other schedules and budgets. Great care must be taken by the marketing department in the preparation of the sales budget, the basis of the master budget. The factors that may influence sales must be identified and accounted for in the determination of the sales forecasts. It is, however, a difficult task as future sales depend on such diverse factors as:

1. Past sales volume (last year's, last month's, the same month last year)
2. General economic, political, social, and industry conditions
3. Impact of economic indicators such as gross national product, money supply, disposable income, employment, price levels, and industrial production
4. Relative product profitability

5. Market research studies
6. Pricing policies
7. Population trends
8. Advertising and promotion policies
9. Quality of the sales force
10. Competition
11. Seasonal variations
12. Production capacity
13. Long-term sales trends for various products
14. Market share
15. Industry competition
16. Unfilled order backlogs.

Statistical tools such as *regression analysis, time series analysis, trend and cycle projection,* and *correlation analysis,* as well as *econometric models* of the industry or the nation may be used to improve the reliability of the sales forecasts.

Another method used to estimate sales is the *Delphi technique.* It consists of asking the members of the forecasting group to submit their individual estimates anonymously. After each member receives a copy of each of the individual forecasts, the group meets to discuss all the estimates. The differences are discussed. Then each individual member is asked to revise his or her estimate and to submit it again anonymously. All the estimates are again discussed by the whole group. The process is repeated until a clear consensus emerges.

7.4.3 Production Budget (Changes in Inventory Levels Budget)

Once the sales budget has been determined, the production budget can be prepared. Assuming the firm has a finished goods inventory policy, the desired monthly ending inventory can be compared with the monthly sales estimates to determine the monthly production. In equation form, the relationship is

Units to be produced = Desired ending inventory + Estimated sales − Desired beginning inventory.

Table 7.2 illustrates the Monti Company's production budget for 19XB. It includes the estimated sales, ending inventory, total units needed, beginning inventory, and units to be produced by month. The preparation of the production budget, therefore, rests on an estimation of:

1. The sales forecast in units (provided now by the sales budget)
2. The inventory objectives or inventory policy of the firm.

Note that the production budget is expressed in finished physical units.

Table 7.1
Monti Company Sales Budget for the Year Ending December 31, 19XB

	January	February	March	April	May
Volume	5,000	5,000	5,000	5,000	10,000
Selling Price	$ 5	$ 5	$ 5	$ 10	$ 10
Gross Sales	$25,000	$25,000	$25,000	$50,000	$100,000
Sales Discounts, Returns, and Allowances	$ 2,500	$ 2,500	$ 2,500	$ 5,000	$ 10,000
Net Sales	$22,500	$22,500	$22,500	$45,000	$ 90,000
Cash Sales, 40%	$ 9,000	$ 9,000	$ 9,000	$18,000	$ 36,000
Credit Sales, 60%	$13,500	$13,500	$13,500	$27,000	$ 54,000
Cash Collections					
1. Cash Sales This Month	$ 9,000	$ 9,000	$ 9,000	$18,000	$ 36,000
2. Credit Sales of Last Month Collected		$10,000	$13,500	$13,500	$13,500	$ 27,000
3. Total Collections	$19,000	$22,500	$22,500	$31,500	$ 63,000
Accounts Receivable	$13,500	$13,500	$13,500	$27,000	$ 54,000

7.4.4 Material Usage and Purchases Budget

Once the production budget is determined, the material usage and purchases budget can be prepared. On the basis of the estimated production and the number of units of material required to produce one unit of finished goods, the number of units of material needed for production is determined. Assuming the firm has a material inventory policy, the desired monthly ending material inventory can be compared with the monthly production estimates to determine the monthly material purchases. In equation form, the relationship is

$$\text{Units to be purchased} = \text{Desired ending material inventory} + \text{Units of material needed for production} - \text{Beginning material inventory.}$$

Table 7.3 illustrates the Monti Company's material usage and purchases budget for 19XB. It includes material usage; inventory levels; units to be purchased; gross purchases; purchase discounts, returns, and allowances; net purchases; cash and credit purchases; disbursements for purchases; and accounts payable. The preparation of the material usage and purchases budget rests on the estimation of the following information:

1. Production (now provided in the production budget)
2. The material requirement for each unit of finished goods, that is, the input mix
3. The proportion of cash purchases or the purchase credit policy
4. The purchase price of materials

Table 7.1
(Continued)

June	July	August	September	October	November	December	Total
15,000	15,000	10,000	10,000	5,000	5,000	5,000	95,000
$ 10	$ 10	$ 10	$ 10	$ 5	$ 5	$ 5	
$150,000	$150,000	$100,000	$100,000	$25,000	$25,000	$25,000	$800,000
$ 15,000	$ 15,000	$ 10,000	$ 10,000	$ 2,500	$ 2,500	$ 2,500	$ 80,000
$135,000	$135,000	$ 90,000	$ 90,000	$22,500	$22,500	$22,500	$720,000
$ 54,000	$ 54,000	$ 36,000	$ 36,000	$ 9,000	$ 9,000	$ 9,000	$288,000
$ 81,000	$ 81,000	$ 54,000	$ 54,000	$13,500	$13,500	$13,500	$432,000
$ 54,000	$ 54,000	$ 36,000	$ 36,000	$ 9,000	$ 9,000	$ 9,000	$288,000
$ 54,000	$ 81,000	$ 81,000	$ 54,000	$54,000	$13,500	$13,500	$428,500
$108,000	$135,000	$117,000	$ 90,000	$63,000	$22,500	$22,500	$716,500
$ 81,000	$ 81,000	$ 54,000	$ 54,000	$13,500	$13,500	$13,500	

5. The disbursement policy, the credit terms extended by suppliers, and the bill-paying habits of the firm

6. The proportion of purchase discounts, returns, and allowances

7. The inventory objectives or inventory policy.

7.4.5 Direct-Labor Budget

Once the production budget has been determined, the direct-labor budget can also be prepared. The total hours needed for production is determined on the basis of the estimated production and the number of direct-labor hours required to produce one unit of finished goods. The total direct-labor costs expected are based on a knowledge of the labor rates. Table 7.4 shows the direct-labor budget for the Monti Company for 19XB. It includes the labor usage, labor costs, and disbursements for wages. The direct-labor budget is based on an estimation of

1. Production (now provided in the production budget)

2. The labor rates

3. The payroll methods or wage disbursements policy

4. The payroll dates.

7.4.6 Overhead Budget

The overhead budget includes both a factory overhead schedule and a selling and administrative overhead schedule. Once the production level is known, the

Table 7.2

Monti Company Production Budget in Units for the Year Ending December 31, 19XB

	January	February	March	April	May
Estimated Sales	5,000	5,000	5,000	5,000	10,000
+ Ending Inventory	2,500*	2,500	2,500	5,000	7,500
= Total Needed	7,500	7,500	7,500	10,000	17,500
− Beginning Inventory	2,500	2,500	2,500	2,500	5,000
= Units to Be Produced	5,000	5,000	5,000	7,500	12,500

*0.5 × February sales of 5,000 units.

Table 7.3

Monti Company Material Usage and Purchases Budget for the Year Ending December 31, 19XB

	January	February	March	April	May
Finished Goods: Units to be Produced*	5,000	5,000	5,000	7,500	12,500
Units of Material Needed for Production	10,000	10,000	10,000	15,000	25,000
Ending Material Inventory	10,000	10,000	15,000	12,500	15,000
Total Needed	20,000	20,000	25,000	27,500	40,000
Beginning Material Inventory	10,000	10,000	10,000	15,000	12,500
Units to Be Purchased	10,000	10,000	15,000	12,500	27,500
Gross Purchases	$10,000	$10,000	$15,000	$12,500	$27,500
Purchase Discounts, Returns, and Allowances	$ 1,000	$ 1,000	$ 1,500	$ 1,250	$ 2,750
Net Purchases	$ 9,000	$ 9,000	$13,500	$11,250	$24,750
Cash Purchases, 40%	$ 3,600	$ 3,600	$ 5,400	$ 4,500	$ 9,900
Credit Purchases, 60%	$ 5,400	$ 5,400	$ 8,100	$ 6,750	$14,850
Disbursements for Purchases					
1. Cash Purchases	$ 3,600	$ 3,600	$ 5,400	$ 4,500	$ 9,900
2. Credit Purchases of Last Month	$ 1,000	$ 5,400	$ 5,400	$ 8,100	$ 6,750
3. Total Disbursements	$ 4,600	$ 9,000	$10,800	$12,600	$16,650
Accounts Payable	$ 5,400	$ 5,400	$ 8,100	$ 6,750	$14,850

*From the production budget (Table 5.2).

Table 7.4

Monti Company Direct-Labor Budget for the Year Ending December 31, 19XB

	January	February	March	April	May
Finished Goods: Units to Be Produced*	5,000	5,000	5,000	7,500	12,500
Total Hours Needed for Production	2,500	2,500	2,500	3,750	6,250
Total Labor Costs Expected	$5,000	$5,000	$5,000	$7,500	$12,500
Disbursements for Wages					
1. 40% of This Month's Expenses	$2,000	$2,000	$2,000	$3,000	$ 5,000
2. 60% of Last Month's Expenses	$1,000	$3,000	$3,000	$3,000	$ 4,500
3. Total Disbursements	$3,000	$5,000	$5,000	$6,000	$ 9,500

*From the production budget (Table 5.2).

Table 7.2
(Continued)

June	July	August	September	October	November	December	Total
15,000	15,000	10,000	10,000	5,000	5,000	5,000	95,000
7,500	5,000	5,000	2,500	2,500	2,500	2,500	47,500
22,500	20,000	15,000	12,500	7,500	7,500	7,500	142,500
7,500	7,500	5,000	5,000	2,500	2,500	2,500	47,500
15,000	12,500	10,000	7,500	5,000	5,000	5,000	95,000

Table 7.3
(Continued)

June	July	August	September	October	November	December	Total
15,000	12,500	10,000	7,500	5,000	5,000	5,000	95,000
30,000	25,000	20,000	15,000	10,000	10,000	10,000	190,000
25,000	20,000	15,000	10,000	10,000	10,000	10,000	162,500
55,000	45,000	35,000	25,000	20,000	20,000	20,000	352,500
15,000	25,000	20,000	15,000	10,000	10,000	10,000	162,500
40,000	20,000	15,000	10,000	10,000	10,000	10,000	190,000
$40,000	$20,000	$15,000	$10,000	$10,000	$10,000	$10,000	$190,000
$ 4,000	$ 2,000	$ 1,500	$ 1,000	$ 1,000	$ 1,000	$ 1,000	$ 19,000
$36,000	$18,000	$13,500	$ 9,000	$ 9,000	$ 9,000	$ 9,000	$171,000
$14,400	$ 7,200	$ 5,400	$ 3,600	$ 3,600	$ 3,600	$ 3,600	$ 68,400
$21,600	$10,800	$ 8,100	$ 5,400	$ 5,400	$ 5,400	$ 5,400	$102,600
$14,400	$ 7,200	$ 5,400	$ 3,600	$ 3,600	$ 3,600	$ 3,600	$ 68,400
$14,850	$21,600	$10,800	$ 8,100	$ 5,400	$ 5,400	$ 5,400	$ 98,200
$29,250	$28,800	$16,200	$11,700	$ 9,000	$ 9,000	$ 9,000	$166,600
$21,600	$10,800	$ 8,100	$ 5,400	$ 5,400	$ 5,400	$ 5,400	$102,600

Table 7.4
(Continued)

June	July	August	September	October	November	December	Total
15,000	12,500	10,000	7,500	5,000	5,000	5,000	95,000
7,500	6,250	5,000	3,750	2,500	2,500	2,500	47,500
$15,000	$12,500	$10,000	$7,500	$5,000	$5,000	$5,000	$95,000
$ 6,000	$ 5,000	$ 4,000	$3,000	$2,000	$2,000	$2,000	$38,000
$ 7,500	$ 9,000	$ 7,500	$6,000	$4,500	$3,000	$3,000	$55,000
$13,500	$14,000	$11,500	$9,000	$6,500	$5,000	$5,000	$93,000

Table 7.5
Monti Company Overhead Budget for the Year Ending December 31, 19XB

Factory Overhead at an Expected Activity Level of 47,000 Direct-Labor Hours

Supplies	$10,000	
Indirect Labor	20,000	
Maintenance-Variable Portion	1,000	
Power-Variable Portion	1,500	
Payroll Fringe Costs	10,000	
Total Variable Overhead		$42,500
Property Taxes	$ 500	
Depreciation	500	
Maintenance-Fixed Portion	2,000	
Power-Fixed Portion	1,000	
Miscellaneous-Fixed Portion	1,000	
Total Fixed Overhead		$ 5,000
Total Factory Overhead		$47,500
Expected Activity Level		47,500 Direct-Labor Hours
Predetermined Overhead Application Rate		$1.00 per Direct-Labor Hour

Selling and Administrative Overhead

Travel	$10,000
Sales Commissions	4,000
Salaries	12,000
Depreciation	23,500
	$49,500

overhead budget can be prepared, as it depends on the anticipated activity level and upon the behavior of the individual expense items in relation to the level of activity. The overhead budget can be set at an expected activity level and includes both variable and fixed expenses. Table 7.5 illustrates the Monti Company's overhead budget for 19XB. It includes a detailed list of the factory overhead items, the predetermined overhead application rate, and a detailed list of the selling and administrative overhead items. Its preparation depends on an estimation of:

1. The activity level (now provided in the production budget)

2. The behavior of the individual expense items in relation to the level of activity

3. The disbursement policy and credit terms extended by suppliers.

7.4.7 Cost of Goods Sold Budget

The cost of goods sold budget depends on all the information gathered in the production, material usage and purchases, direct-labor, and overhead budgets. The basic relationship is

Cost of goods sold = Total manufacturing costs + Beginning finished goods inventory − Ending finished goods inventory.

The Monti Company's cost of goods sold budget for 19XB is shown in Table 7.6.

Table 7.6
Monti Company Cost of Goods Sold Budget for the Year Ending December 31, 19XB

Direct Material Used (from the Material Usage and Purchases Budget)	$190,000
Direct Labor Used (from the Direct-Labor Budget)	95,000
Manufacturing Overhead (from the Factory Overhead Budget)	47,500
	$332,500
Less: Purchase Discounts, Returns, and Allowances (from the Material Usage and Purchases Budget)	(19,000)
Total Manufacturing Costs	$313,500
Add: Finished Goods Inventory, December 31, 19XA (from the Production Budget)	10,000*
Total Needed	$323,500
Less: Finished Goods Inventory, December 31, 19XB (from the Production Budget)	10,000*
Cost of Goods Sold	$313,500

*2,500 units × $4 = $10,000.

7.4.8 Cash Budget

The cash budget, or budgeted statement of cash receipts and disbursements, may be prepared once management has prepared the sales, production, material usage and purchases, direct-labor, and overhead budgets, as well as a list of anticipated acquisitions and dispositions of fixed assets, dividend and interest payments to investors, proceeds from new financing, and outflows from long-

Table 7.7
Monti Company Cash Budget for the Year Ending December 31, 19XB

	January	February	March	April	May
Beginning Cash Balance	$10,000	$30,000	$30,079	$33,422	$30,022
Receipts[a]					
1. Collections from Customers	19,000	22,500	22,500	31,500	63,000
2. Issuance of Common Stock	—	—	—	—	—
3. Issuance of Bonds	—	—	—	—	—
Total Available before Current Financing	29,000	52,500	52,579	64,922	93,022
Less Disbursements					
1. For Labor[b]	3,000	5,000	5,000	6,000	9,500
2. For Materials[c]	4,600	9,000	10,800	12,600	16,650
3. For Other Manufacturing Expenses	—	—	—	—	—
4. For Other Nonmanufacturing Expenses	1,000	1,000	1,000	1,000	1,000
5. For Machinery Purchase	—	—	—	—	—
6. For Land Purchase	—	—	—	50,000	35,000
7. Total Disbursements	8,600	15,000	16,800	69,600	62,150
Minimum Cash Balance	30,000	30,000	30,000	30,000	30,000
Total Cash Needed	38,600	45,000	46,800	99,600	92,150
Excess (Deficit)	(9,600)	7,500	5,779	(34,678)	872
Financing					
1. Borrowing	9,600	—	—	34,700	—
2. Repayment	—	(7,300)	(2,300)	—	(800)
3. Interest[d]	—	(121)	(57)	—	(13)
4. Total	9,600	(7,421)	(2,357)	34,700	(813)
Ending Cash Balance	30,000	30,079	33,422	30,022	30,059
Loan Payable	9,600	2,300	0	34,700	33,900

[a] From the Sales Budget (Table 5.1)
[b] From the Direct-Labor Budget (Table 5.4)
[c] From the Material Usage and Purchases Budget (Table 5.3)
[d] Interest calculations are as follows:

February:	$ 7,300 × 0.10 × 2/12 months = $ 121
March:	$ 2,300 × 0.10 × 3/12 months = $ 57
May:	$ 800 × 0.10 × 2/12 months = $ 13
August:	$ 33,900 × 0.10 × 5/12 months = $1,412
	11,200 × 0.10 × 3/12 months = $ 280
	70,300 × 0.10 × 2/12 months = $1,172

$115,400	$2.864
September: $ 17,800 × 0.10 × 3/12 months = $ 445	
October: $ 20,700 × 0.10 × 4/12 months = $ 690	
December: $ 11,800 × 0.10 × 2/12 months = $ 197	
Accrued interest payable, December 31. 19XB:	
$ 5,500 × 0.10 × 2/12 months = $ 92	

term debt retirement and stock repurchasing. The cash budget may be considered the most important part of the master budgeting process. It allows the firm to control for its continuous solvency; that is, to have the ability to pay bills when due and to avoid unnecessary idle cash or cash deficiencies by a timely borrowing, repayment, and short-term investment policy. The cash budget, or budgeted

Table 7.7
(Continued)

June	July	August	September	October	November	December
$ 30,059	$ 30,009	$ 30,009	$ 30,045	$30,100	$30,210	$30,010
108,000	135,000	117,000	90,000	63,000	22,500	22,500
—	—	100,000	—	—	—	—
—	—	—	—	—	—	40,000
138,059	165,009	247,009	120,045	93,100	52,710	92,510
13,500	14,000	11,500	9,000	6,500	5,000	5,000
29,250	28,800	16,200	11,700	9,000	9,000	9,000
25,500	—	—	—	—	—	21,500
1,000	1,000	1,000	1,000	1,000	1,000	15,000
—	150,000	—	—	—	—	—
50,000	50,000	70,000	50,000	25,000	25,000	—
119,250	243,800	98,700	71,700	41,500	40,000	50,000
30,000	30,000	30,000	30,000	30,000	30,000	30,000
149,250	273,800	128,700	101,700	71,500	70,000	80,500
(11,191)	(108,791)	118,309	18,345	21,600	(17,290)	12,010
11,200	108,800	—	—	—	17,300	—
		(115,400)	(17,800)	(20,700)	—	(11,800)
—	—	(2,864)	(445)	(690)	—	(197)
11,200	108,800	(118,264)	(18,245)	(21,390)	17,300	(11,997)
30,009	30,009	30,045	30,100	30,210	30,010	30,013
45,100	153,900	38,500	20,700	0	17,300	5,500

statement of cash receipts and disbursements, for the Monti Company is illustrated in Table 7.7. Note the following sections of the cash budget.

Total cash available before current financing. In general, this is equal to the beginning cash balance, collections from customers (from the sales budget), proceeds from new financing, proceeds—including interest—from marketable securities, and proceeds from dispositions of long-term assets.

Total disbursements. In general, this is equal to the cash outflow for operations (for purchases and other operations), routine outflows to investors (as dividend and/or interest payments), outflows for long-term debt retirement and treasury stocks, and outflows for acquisition of long-term assets.

Total cash needed. In general, this is equal to the toal disbursements and a minimum cash balance the firm wants to keep as a security.

Excess or deficit of cash. In general, this is equal to the total cash available before current financing *minus* the total cash needed.

Total effect of financing. In general, this is equal to the amount borrowed in case of a cash deficit, the interest and principal repaid in case of an excess of cash, and the investment in short-term marketable securities in case of an excess of cash.

Ending cash balance. This is equal to the excess or deficit of cash *minus* the total effect of financing *plus* the minimum cash balance.

Loan payable. This is equal to the outstanding loan *minus* the short-term loan repayments and interest.

The preparation of the cash budget rests on a knowledge of the following information:

1. Cash inflows and outflows from operations
2. Cash inflows and outflows from capital, financial, and tax activities
3. The minimum cash balance
4. The short-term borrowing, repayment, and investment policy. In the Monti Company example, a self-liquidating loan is assumed in the sense that cash borrowed is used for operations, and the cash inflows from operations are used to repay the loan. Known as the *working capital cycle,* this style of management consists of transforming cash into finished goods and into accounts receivable and/or cash.

7.4.9 Budgeted Income Statement

The budgeted income statement may be prepared once the sales, production, material usage and purchases, direct-labor, overhead, cost of goods sold, and cash budgets are available. Table 7.8 shows the budgeted income statement for the Monti Company for 19XB. It includes the following sections:

1. Gross sales (from the sales budget)
2. Sales discounts, returns, and allowances (from the sales budget)
3. Cost of goods sold (from the cost of goods sold budget)
4. Selling and administrative expenses (from the overhead budget)
5. Interest expense.

Table 7.8
Monti Company Budgeted Income Statement for the Year Ending December 31, 19XB

Gross Sales (from the Sales Budget)		$800,000
minus Sales Discounts, Returns, and Allowances (from the Sales Budget)		(80,000)
equals Net Sales		$720,000
minus Cost of Goods Sold (from the Cost of Goods Sold Budget)		313,500
equals Gross Margin		$406,500
Selling and Administrative Expenses (from the Overhead Budget)	$49,500	
Interest Expense	4,479[a]	
Operating Expenses		$ 53,979
Net Profit before Taxes		$352,521

[a] This was derived from the summation of interest accrued on the loan payable (121 + 57 + 13 + 2864 + 445 + 690 + 197 + 92).

7.4.10 Budgeted Balance Sheet

The last step in developing the master budget is the preparation of the budgeted balance sheet. Table 7.9 shows the Monti Company's budgeted balance sheet for 19XB. Each of the balance sheet items is derived from the previously computed budgets, namely, the sales, production, material and usage purchases, direct-labor, overhead, cost of goods sold, and cash budgets and the budgeted income statement. For example, the accrued interest payable would be computed by subtracting the interest expenditures (from the cash budget) from the interest expense (from the budgeted income statement).

7.5 CONCLUSION

Planning essentially involves the collection of environmental and internal information to derive an organization's objectives and make decisions on the best way to achieve them. Central to an efficient planning system is goal congruence, the harmonization of the individual and group objectives within the organization, and the objectives of the organization as a whole. The budget as a formalization of planning is a key mechanism for the creation of goal congruence; it serves as a bargaining medium through which individuals and groups try to further their own

Table 7.9
Monti Company Budgeted Balance Sheet, December 31, 19XB

Assets

Current Assets

Cash	$ 30,013	
Accounts Receivable	13,500	
Material Inventory	10,000	
Finished Goods Inventory	10,000	
Total Current Assets		$ 63,513

Fixed Assets

Land	$ 505,000	
Buildings and Equipment	250,000	
Depreciation	(64,000)	
Total Fixed Assets		691,000
Total Assets		$754,513

Equities

Current Liabilities

Interest Payable[a]	$ 92	
Accounts Payable[b]	5,400	
Loans Payable[c]	5,500	
Wages Payable[d]	3,000	
Total Current Liabilities		$ 13,992
Bonds Payable		40,000

Stockholders' Equity

Common Stock	$ 300,000	
Retained Income ($48,000 + $352,521)	400,521	
Total Stockholders' Equity		700,521
Total Equities		$754,513

[a] The interest payable on December 31 is the accrued amount payable on the outstanding loan of $5,000 (5,500 × 10% × 3 months = $92).
[b] From Material Usage and Purchases Budget (Table 5.3).
[c] From the Cash Budget (Table 5.7).
[d] From Direct-Labor Budget (Table 5.4), 60% December labor costs outstanding (60% × $5,000 = $3,000).

goals. The budget is also used as a tool of planning, control, coordination, and communication. Used wisely, it can motivate managers to accomplish the organizational objectives.

NOTES

1. David W. Ewing, *The Practice of Planning* (New York: Harper & Row, 1968), 16.
2. G. A. Steiner, *Top Management Planning* (New York: Macmillan Co. 1969), 32.
3. Stanley Thune and Robert House, "Where Long-Range Planning Pays Off." *Business Horizons* (October 1970): 81–87.
4. J. Bacon, *Planning and Forecasting in the Smaller Company* (New York: Conference Board, 1971). In a study of ninety-three companies, each with 2,000 or fewer employees, Bacon found that only four do not plan at all.
5. Robert N. Anthony, *Management Accounting.* 3d ed. (Homewood, Ill.: Irwin, 1964), 362.
6. Lee D. Parker, "Goal Congruence: A Misguided Concept." *Abacus* (June 1976): 3–13.
7. C. Perrow, *Complex Organizations: A Critical Essay* (Glenview, Ill.: Scott, Foresman, 1972), 160–163.
8. K. J. Arrow, "Control in Large Organizations." *Management Science* (April 1964): 397–408.
9. R. M. Cyert and J. G. March, *A Behavioral Theory of the Firm* (Englewood Cliffs, N.J.: Prentice-Hall, 1963), 4–43, 83–177.
10. C. Perrow, *Complex Organizations,* 162.
11. Robert N. Anthony, J. Dearden, and R. F. Vancil, *Management Control Systems: Text Cases and Readings* (Homewood, Ill.: Irwin, 1972), 466.
12. W. J. Vatter, *Operating Budgets,* (Belmont, Calif.: Wadsworth Publishing, 1969), 15–16.

SELECTED READINGS

Auger, B. Y. "Presenting the Budget." *Management Accounting* (May 1981): 22–27.
Becker, Selwyn, and David Green, Jr. "Budgeting and Employee Behavior." *Journal of Business* (October 1962): 392–402.
Beddingfield, Ronald. "Human Behavior: The Key to Success in Budgeting." *Management Accounting* (September 1969): 54–56.
Benke, Ralph L., Jr., and W. Timothy O'Keefe. "Organizational Behavior and Operating Budgets." *Cost and Management* (July–August 1980): 21–27.
Bennett, Robert B. "Motivational Aspects of Participation in the Planning and Control System." *Cost and Management* (September–October 1974): 37–40.
Bradley, Hugh E. "Setting and Controlling Budgets with Regression Analysis." *Management Accounting* (November 1969): 31–34, 40.
Bullock, James H., and Virginia H. Bakay. "How Las Vegas Casinos Budget." *Management Accounting* (July 1980): 35–39.
Cheng, Philip C. "Humanizing the Budget Process in a Total Management System." *Cost and Management* (July–August 1976): 24–28.

Cismoski, David R., and Frederick Toepfer. "How to Allocate the College Budget Objectively." *Management Accounting* (December 1979): 45–50.

Feldbush, Marvin A. "Participative Budgeting in a Hospital Setting." *Management Accounting* (September 1981): 43–48.

Gunders, Henry. "Better Profit Planning." *Management Accounting* (August 1965): 3–24.

Hanson, E. I. "The Budgetary Control Function." *Accounting Review* (April 1966): 239–243.

Irvine, V. Bruce, "Budgeting: Functional Analysis and Behavioral Implications," *Cost and Management* (March–April 1970): 6–16.

Leitch, Robert A.; Barrack, John B.; and McKinley, Sue H., "Controlling Your Cash Resources," *Management Accounting* (October 1980): 58–60.

Levine, Marc, "The Behavioral Implications of Participative Budgeting," *Cost and Management* (March–April 1981): 28–32.

Lowe, Larry S.; Roberts, C. Richard; and Cagley, James W., "Your Sales Forecast-Marketing Budget Relationship: Is It Consistent?" *Management Accounting* (January 1980): 29–33.

Newman, M. S., "The Essence of Budgetary Control," *Management Services* (January–February 1965): 19–26.

Parker, Lee D., "Participation in Budget Planning: The Prospects Surveyed," *Accounting and Business Research* (Spring 1979): 123–137.

Ridgeway, V. F., "Dysfunctional Consequences of Performance Measurement," *Administrative Science Quarterly* 1 (September 1956): 240–247.

Schiff, M., and Lewin, A. Y., "The Impact of People on Budgets," *Accounting Review* (April 1970): 259–268.

Suver, James D., and Helmer, F. Theodore, "Developing Budgetary Models for Greater Hospital Efficiency," *Management Accounting* (July 1979): 34–36, 39.

8

Control Principles: Part I

The process of *control* is the attempt by a manager or accountant to reach a state of control, where actual results conform to planned results. The process of control traditionally has been visualized as a series of examinations of the deviations between actual and planned performances. However, a manager may decide to bring about control by altering the planned results to conform to actual results—a *feedback control system*. Similarly, a manager may elect to adjust the anticipated results through a compensatory action—a *feedforward control system*. Each of these control systems has distinct conceptual and operational advantages over the traditional control system. This chapter will elaborate on the nature of the control process and on its use for the control of direct costs. Other aspects of the control process will be covered in chapters 9 and 10.

8.1 NATURE OF THE CONTROL PROCESS

8.1.1 Types of Control

Control is a central factor in the management of any organization. Leonard Sayles illustrates its importance:

After all controls are the techniques by which the manager decides how to expend his most valuable assets, his time. Be they formal or informal, it is through controls that he knows where things are going badly that require his intervention—and where and when he can relax because things are going well. All managers from presidents to foremen made use of controls, some more effectively than others.[1]

Sayles lists four distinct types of control that serve very different functions for the manager:

1. Reassurances to sponsors, whereby stakeholders are informed of the efficient conduct of operations

2. Closing the loop, whereby the managers are informed that both technical and legal requirements have been met

3. Guidance to subordinates from managers, whereby the subordinates are informed of "what is important and what they should concentrate on"

4. Guidance to lower-level management by higher-level management, whereby managers are informed of "where accomplishment is lagging and management action is needed."[2]

A more operational classification is provided by W. H. Newman, who recognizes three different types of control:

1. Steering controls, whereby management is provided signals indicating what will happen if it continues its present operations. Steering controls enable management to take either a corrective or an adaptive response before the total operation is completed. A corrective response implies the source of the error is inside the organization and can be corrected. An adaptive response implies that the source of the error is outside the organization and cannot be corrected. In the latter case, the solution is to redesign the operations to adapt to the new environmental situations.

2. Yes/no controls, whereby management is provided rules indicating the conditions that must be met before work may proceed to the next step. Yes/no controls provide management with checkpoints at different levels of the total operation. The technique is a defensive strategy aimed at controlling the size of the errors to be made by lower-level management and subordinates in general. In other words, yes/no controls are comparable to safety devices.

3. Postaction controls, whereby management is provided with performance reports or scorecards upon completion of the operations, indicating the differences or variances between the actual and planned performance. In general, postaction controls and steering controls make use of the feedback mechanism for the correction of any deviations, except that the response in the steering controls concerns the completion of the total operation. The steering controls may be labeled as a feedback control system, while the postaction controls are a traditional control system.[3]

8.1.2 Stages Of Control

The control process involves the following stages:

1. Setting of goals for the performance of the activity or function. These goals help direct and channel human efforts. Organizational goals are desired ends or states of affairs for whose achievement system policies are committed and resources allocated.[4]

2. Establishing standards of performance for each specified goal of the activity or function. Standards are basically statements of the results that will exist when the performance is satisfactory.

3. Monitoring or measurement of actual performance. Monitoring can be expressed in monetary and accounting terms such as profits, costs, and revenues; by other accounting indicators such as rate of return on investment or residual income; and in nonmonetary terms such as the quality of the product, the nature of the market response, or any

other social indicator. Measurement is accomplished by human or mechanical means such as *sensors*.

4. Reviewing and comparing the actual with the planned performance. This is also known as the *comparator process*, which determines whether differences exist between the activities and the results that are taking place and what should be occurring.

5. Investigating then correcting the deviations.

6. Administering rewards to motivate and reinforce good performance. This is known as the *evaluation/reward process*.

8.1.3 Nature of the Deviations

There are five possible causes that can lead to a difference between the actual and standard performance: implementation failure, prediction error, measurement error, model error, and random deviation.

1. An *implementation failure* is a human or mechanical failure to obtain or maintain a specific obtainable action or standard. For example, the ordering or the use of the wrong quantity of a given input, material, labor, or overhead will result in an implementation failure. Given that the standard is assumed to be obtainable, the deviation caused by the implementation failure may be immediately corrected once its existence is known. The decision to correct such a variance depends on a comparison between the cost of correction and the resulting savings.

2. A *prediction error* is a failure to correctly predict one of the decision model's parameter values. Again, the decision to correct the variance depends on a comparison between the cost of developing a better prediction model and the resulting cost savings.

3. A *measurement error* in determining the actual cost of operations occurs because of improper classification, recording, or counting. The correction of the variance involves improving the work habits of employees and motivating them to maintain proper records.

4. A *model error* arises from an incorrect function representation in the decision model, resulting in a failure to capture reality. The decision to correct the variance depends on a comparison between the cost of reformulating the model and the resulting cost savings.

5. A *random deviation* results from minor variations in the input or output process. Random variations are inevitable and need no corrective action.

8.2 TRADITIONAL CONTROL MODEL

A firm using a traditional control model first establishes performance standards for each operational activity in a budget-setting phase. At the end of the period, it compares these standards with the actual results, using the variance analysis techniques to assess (1) the nature of the obtained deviations and (2) the possibility of any corrective action. Therefore, a proper selection of the types of standards and the variance analysis technique is essential to the success of a traditional control system.

8.2.1 Standard Setting

A standard is a norm set for a given activity in the plan. It represents the best and most operational working method for the activity, given the state of the art. Consequently, the standard represents a normative expression of the performance related to a given activity, while the actual result represents a descriptive expression. The difference between standard performance and actual performance lies in the distinction defined by management between what should be and what is acceptable behavior.

To avoid semantic problems, the standard is generally considered a unit concept, while the budget is a total concept. For example, the standard cost of direct labor is $3 per direct-labor hour (DLH), whereas the budgeted cost of direct labor is $24,000 if 8,000 direct-labor hours are needed at a standard cost of $3 per direct-labor hour. In general, the standard cost is used for the control of direct material and direct labor, while the budgeted cost is used for the control of overhead. This is because prime costs are identifiable with individual units of output, whereas overhead is only identifiable with total production.

Different types of standards have been presented in the literature and in practice. Standards are either basic or current. Basic standards are historical performance standards that are not changed unless there are important modifications in the nature or sequence of the manufacturing operations. Current standards might be changed to reflect environmental changes. Basic standards are useful for long-term analysis of variances, while current standards are more useful to short-run analysis.

There are three different levels of current and basic standards: expected actual standards, normal standards, and theoretical standards. The expected actual standard is set for an expected capacity for the coming year and reflects predictions about the expected actual results. The normal standard, or currently attainable standard, is set for a normal capacity. This is the level of operations attainable by normal operating procedures, allowing for extraordinary events such as normal spoilage, ordinary machine breakdowns, and lost time. The theoretical, or ideal, standards is the standard set for a theoretical capacity, the level of operations possible under the best operating conditions without any unusual events. It is a perfect, maximum efficiency standard.

There are four broad classes of current and basic standards: imposed standards, standards set through participation, standards set with consultation, and standards reinforced by financial rewards. Imposed standards are derived without any input from subordinates. They reassert the superior's power in the budgeting process and emphasize the goals of the organization. Standards set through participation are derived with direct input from subordinates. They can increase motivation, and they emphasize both the organizational and individual goals.

Standards set with consultation are derived with indirect input from subordinates. They represent a trade-off between the imposed and the participative approaches to standard setting. Standards reinforced by financial rewards are derived with a commitment from subordinates secured by linking rewards to organizational performance. An often-cited example is the Scanlon plan.[5]

8.2.2 Types of Budgets and Types of Analysis of Variance

The standards as expressed in the master budget are static standards in the sense that they refer to a single planned level. That is why the master budget illustrated in chapter 6 may be referred to as a static budget. As shown in Table 8.1, a comparison of actual performance with the static (master) budget results in a static-budget variance. The assumption is that the standard performance is as formulated in the static (master) budget. The variances illustrated in Table 8.1 are just informative enough for a good control of the activities of the firm. What would be required at the end of the period is a flexible budget or variable budget that would indicate how the budget would be for a range of activity. The flexible budget is illustrated in Table 8.2 for the relevant range of from 1,200 to 1,700 units. Notice that these budgets are based on the mathematical function used to estimate the cost or formula: $10,000 fixed cost per month plus $30 variable cost per unit of product. With a knowledge of the flexible budget, the analysis of variance can proceed to different levels to identify two new variances as follows:

1. Sales volume variance: the difference between the flexible budget performance and the static (master) budget performance, with selling prices and unit variable costs held constant

2. Flexible budget variance: the difference between actual performance and the flexible budget performance based on the actual output achieved.

The computation of these two variances is shown in Table 8.3. The sales variances result from changes in sales unit, market share, and market size. They will be fully explained in chapter 10. The flexible budget variances for direct costs will be explained in this chapter; the flexible budget variance for overhead costs will be explained in chapter 9.

8.2.3 Expressions of Standards

Standard cost systems generally express output in terms of standard units of input allowed for a good output product where the input chosen is a common denominator for the type of activity in question. The standard unit of input allowed for good output is computed as follows:

> Units of good output × Input allowed per unit of output
> = Standard units of input allowed for good output.

Table 8.1
Variance Analysis Based on a Static Budget

	Budgeted Amount Per Unit	Static (Master) Budget (1)	Actual Performance (2)	Variance (2) - (1)
Units		1,000	1,500	500F
Revenue	$50	$50,000	$82,500	$32,500F
Variable Cost				
Direct Material	$10	$10,000	$12,000	$2,000U
Direct Labor	$5	$5,000	$9,000	$4,000U
Variable Factory Overload	$12	$12,000	$22,500	$10,500U
Variable Manufacturing Costs	$27	$27,000	$43,500	$16,500U
Variable Selling and Administrative Costs	$3	$3,000	$6,000	$3,000U
Total Variable Cost	$30	$30,000	$49,500	$19,500U
Contribution Margin	$20	$20,000	$33,000	$13,000F
Fixed Costs				
Manufacturing		$8,000	$10,000	$2,000U
Selling and Administrative		$2,000	$4,000	$2,000U
Total Fixed Costs		$10,000	$14,000	$4,000U
Total Costs		$40,000	$63,500	$23,500U
Operating Income		$10,000	$19,000	$9,000F

F=Favorable, U=Unfavorable effect on operating income

Table 8.2
Flexible Budget Performance

	Budgeted Amount Per Unit	Various Levels of Volume		
Units		1,200	1,500	1,700
Revenue	$50	$60,000	$75,000	$85,000
Variable Cost				
Direct Material	$10	$12,000	$15,000	$17,000
Direct Labor	$5	$6,000	$7,500	$8,500
Variable Factory Overload	$12	$14,400	$18,000	$20,400
Variable Manufacturing Costs	$27	$32,400	$40,500	$45,900
Variable Selling and Administrative Costs	$3	$3,600	$4,500	$5,100
Total Variable Cost	$30	$36,000	$45,000	$51,000
Contribution Margin	$20	$24,000	$30,000	$34,000
Fixed Costs				
Manufacturing		$8,000	$8,000	$8,000
Selling and Administrative		$2,000	$2,000	$2,000
Total Fixed Costs		$10,000	$10,000	$10,000
Total Costs		$46,000	$55,000	$61,000
Operating Income		$14,000	$20,000	$24,000

Table 8.3
Variance Analysis Based on Both Flexible Budget and Static Budget

	(1) Actual Results	(2)=(1)-(3) Budget Variance	(3) Flexible Budget	(4)=(3)-(5) Sales Volume Variance	(5) Static (Master) Budget
Units	1,500		1,500	500F	1,000
Revenue	$82,500	7,500F	$75,000	25,000F	$50,000
Variable Cost					
Direct Material	$12,000	3,000F	$15,000	5,000U	$10,000
Direct Labor	$9,000	1,500U	$7,500	2,500U	$5,000
Variable Factory Overload	$22,500	4,500U	$18,000	6,000U	$12,000
Variable Manufacturing Costs	$43,500	3,000U	$40,500	13,500U	$27,000
Variable Selling and Administrative Costs	$6,000	1,500U	$4,500	1,500U	$3,000
Total Variable Cost	$49,500	4,500U	$45,000	15,000U	$30,000
Contribution Margin	$33,000	3,000F	$30,000	10,000F	$20,000
Fixed Costs					
Manufacturing	$10,000	2,000U	$8,000		$8,000
Selling and Administrative	$4,000	2,000U	$2,000		$2,000
Total Fixed Costs	$14,000	4,000U	$10,000		$10,000
Total Costs	$63,500	8,500U	$55,000	15,000U	$40,000
Operating Income	$19,000	1,000U	$20,000	10,000F	$10,000

F=Favorable, U=Unfavorable effect on operating income

For example, if the manufacturing of a product required in the budget 5 units of material and 6 hours of labor and if the actual production was 1,000 good units produced, then:

The standard direct material allowed = 5 × 10,000 = 50,000 units.

The standard hours allowed = 6 × 10,000 = 60,000 hours.

Therefore, in this example, the standard direct material allowed represents the number of units of material that should have been used if actual production was known. Similarly, the standard hours allowed represent the number of hours that should have been used if actual production was known.

8.3 DIRECT-COST VARIANCES

8.3.1 Models of Variance Analysis

Actual performance and standard performance can be compared within three models in variance analysis: the one-way model, the two-way model, and the three-way model.

The *one-way model* appraises the total performance for a given activity by combining the effects of both price and quantity decisions. It is expressed by a unique variance figure as follows:

$$V_t = P_a Q_a - P_s Q_s,$$

where

V_t = total variance
P_a = actual price
Q_a = actual quantity
P_s = standard price
Q_s = standard quantity.

The *two-way model* appraises both the price and quantity performance for a given activity. It is expressed by both a price and a quantity variance as follows:

$$V_p = Q_a(P_a - P_s)$$

and

$$V_q = P_s(Q_a - Q_s),$$

where

V_p = price variance
V_q = quantity variance.

The *three-way model* formulates the price variance differently than the two-way model to pinpoint the joint responsibility through a joint price/quantity variance. The model is expressed by a price variance, a quantity variance, and a joint price/quantity variance as follows:

$$V_p = Q_s(P_a - P_s),$$
$$V_q = P_s(Q_a - Q_s),$$
$$V_{pq} = (P_a - P_s)(Q_a - Q_s),$$

where V_{pq} = joint price/quantity variance.

The usual breakdown of variances into only price and quantity variances, as advocated by the two-way model, is not conceptually correct because of the existence of a joint price/quantity variance. The graphic analysis of variance depicted in Figure 8.1 highlights these differences. The small area in the upper right corner may create problems, because a price-responsible agent may not accept responsibility for the price variance $Q_a(P_a - P_s)$, as computed in the two-way analysis of variances. However, any of the three analyses of variance models can be used to assess the performance of operational activities pertaining to the acquisition and use of direct manufacturing inputs.

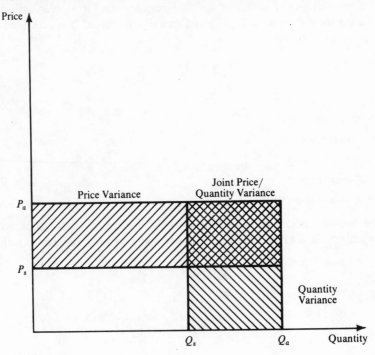

Figure 8.1
Graphic Analysis of Variances

8.3.2 Direct-Material Variances

The master budget must include two standards for material costs: a material price standard and a material quantity standard. A comparison between actual and planned material costs, using a two-way analysis of variance, leads to the computation and evaluation of both a material price variance and a usage variance (material quantity variance). The material price standards set by the purchasing department reflect current market prices. They are intended to be both an indicator of efficient conduct of the purchasing activities and an indicator of the effects of price changes on the company's profits. The material price standards can be used to evaluate the purchasing department's general performance. The material price variance is computed as follows:

$$\text{In a two-way model: } V_{mp} = Q_a(P_a - P_s),$$

$$\text{in a three-way model: } V_{mp} = Q_s(P_a - P_s),$$

where V_{mp} = material price variance.

The material quantity standard set by the production department reflects basic material specifications for routine production operations. Either the quantity standard at the time of purchase or at the time of usage can be used, and both are indicators of the efficient conduct of production activities. The usage variance is computed in both two- and three-factor models as follows:

$$U = P_s(Q_a - Q_s),$$

where U = usage variance.

8.3.3 Direct-Labor Variances

The master budget specifies two standards for labor: a labor price standard, or rate standard, and a labor quantity standard, or labor efficiency standard. A difference between the actual and planned labor performance will lead—in a two-way analysis of variance—to the computation of both a labor price variance, or labor rate variance, and a labor quantity variance, or labor efficiency variance. The rate standard set by the personnel department is the result of collective bargaining agreements, government regulations, and other factors. Consequently, rate variances are rare and occur only in unusual situations. The rate variance is computed as follows:

$$\text{In a two-way model: } R = Q_a(P_a - P_s),$$

$$\text{in a three-way model: } R = Q_s(P_a - P_s),$$

where R = rate variance.

The labor efficiency standard set by the production department reflects production specifications. The production department uses it to evaluate labor management efficiency. The labor efficiency variance can be computed as follows:

$$E = P_s(Q_a - Q_s),$$

where E = labor efficiency variance.

Table 8.4
Direct-Cost Variances

I. Analysis of Variance

    A. Total Material Variance
        ($5,000 × $15) − ($4,000 × $20)   = $5,000 (Favorable)

    B. Total Labor Variance
        ($2,000 × $20) − ($1,000 × $10)   = $30,000 (Unfavorable)

    C. Total Direct-Cost Variance
        $5,000 + ($30,000)   = $25,000 (Unfavorable)

II. Two-Way Analysis of Variance

    A. Material Variances
        1. Material Price Variance
           5,000 ($15 − $20)   = $25,000 (Favorable)
        2. Usage Variance
           $20 (5,000 − 4,000)   = $20,000 (Unfavorable)

    B. Direct-Labor Variances
        1. Rate Variance
           2,000 ($20 − $10)   = $20,000 (Unfavorable)
        2. Labor Efficiency Variance
           $10 (2,000 − 1,000)   = $10,000 (Unfavorable)

III. Three-Way Analysis of Variance

    A. Material Variances
        1. Material Price Variance
           4,000 ($15 − $20)   = $20,000 (Favorable)
        2. Usage Variance (as above)   = $20,000 (Unfavorable)
        3. Joint Price/Quantity Material Variance
           (5,000 − 4,000) × ($15 − $10)   = $5,000 (Favorable)
    B. Direct-Labor Variances
        1. Rate Variance
           1,000 ($20 − $10)   = $10,000 (Unfavorable)
        2. Labor Efficiency Variance
           $10 (2,000 − 1,000)   = $10,000 (Unfavorable)
        3. Joint Price/Quantity Labor Variance
           (2,000 − 1,000) ($20 − $10)   = $10,000 (Unfavorable)

8.3.4 Illustration of Direct-Cost Variances

Input	Actual Quantity	Standard Quantity	Actual Price	Standard Price
Direct Material	5,000 Units	4,000 Units	$15	$20
Direct Labor	2,000 DLH	1,000 DLH	$20	$10

The formal calculation of direct-cost variances is shown in Table 8.4.

8.4 STANDARD COST ACCOUNTING SYSTEM

A standard cost accounting system includes at least two phases: (1) the recording of standard costs in the regular accounting system and the isolation of variances and (2) the disposition of variances.

8.4.1 Isolating the Direct-Material Variances

The general ledger entries to record and isolate the material variances arising in a standard cost accounting system generally fit into three categories:

1. Material purchase price variance is recognized at the time of the input purchases, while material usage variance is recognized at the time of the issuance of the input.
2. Material usage price variance and material usage (quantity) variance are both recognized at the time of the input issuance.
3. Material purchase price variance is recognized at the time of the input purchases, while both material usage price variance and material usage (quantity) variance are recognized at the time of the input issuance.

To illustrate the three methods, assume the following data:

Standard Material Cost per Unit	$3.00
Purchases	1,000 Units at $2.50
Issuance for Production	500 Units
Standard Quantity Allowed	450 Units

Method 1. In the first method, the T accounts would appear as follows:

Material Inventory		Work-in-Process Inventory	
1. Beginning Inventory 2. Actual Quantity × Standard Price	3. Actual Quantity Requisitioned × Standard Price	3. Standard Quantity Requisitioned × Standard Price	

Accounts Payable		Direct-Material Purchase Price Variance		Direct-Material Usage Variance	
	2. Actual Quantity Purchased × Actual Price	2. Difference in Price × Actual Quantity		3. Difference in Quantity Issued × Standard Price	

The first method recognizes the material price variances at the time of incurrence or purchase and the usage variance at the time of issuance. Note that the variances are debited when unfavorable and credited when favorable.

The journal entry at the time of material incurrence would be

Material Inventory   3,000
    Accounts Payable   2,500
    Material Purchase Price Variance   500
To record the purchase of 1,000 units of direct material.

The journal entry at the time of material issuance would be

Work-in-Process   1,350
Material Usage Variance   150
    Material   1,500
To record the issuance of 500 units of direct material.

Method 2. In the second method, the T accounts would appear as follows:

Material Inventory		Work-in-Process Inventory	
1. Beginning Inventory 2. Actual Quantity × Standard Price	3. Actual Quantity × Standard Price	3. Standard Quantity Requisitioned × Standard Price	

Accounts Payable		Direct-Material Purchase Price Variance	
	2. Actual Quantity × Actual Price	2. Difference in Price × Actual Quantity Purchased	4. Difference in Price × Quantity Requisitioned

Direct-Material Usage Variance		Direct-Material Usage Price Variance	
3. Difference in Quantity Issued × Standard Price		4. Difference in Price × Quantity Requisitioned	

The third method recognizes the material purchase price variance at the time of purchase and both the material quantity and price variances at the time of issuance. The journal entry at the time of material incurrence would be

Material Inventory   3,000
    Accounts Payable   2,500
    Material Purchase Price Variance   500
To record the purchase of 1,000 units of direct material.

The entry at the time of material issuance would be

Work-in-Process   1,350
Material Quantity Variance   150
    Materials   1,500
To record the issuance of 500 units of direct material

The entry to record the material usage price variance would be

Materials Purchase Price Variance 250
    Materials Usage Price Variance 250

8.4.2 Isolating the Direct-Labor Variances

The general ledger entries to record and isolate the direct-labor variances arising in a standard cost accounting system generally fall under two categories: (1) direct labor incurred is recognized on the basis of actual values, and (2) standard direct labor distributed is recognized on the basis of standard values, and variances are isolated. To illustrate, assume the following data:

Actual Hours Worked	2,000 Hours
Actual Rate	$5 per Hour
Standard Hours Allowed	1,500 Hours
Standard Rate	$4 per Hour

To isolate the direct-labor variance, the T accounts would appear as follows:

Payroll		Work-in-Process Inventory		Accrued Payroll
1. Direct Labor Incurred	2. Actual Hours × Actual Rate	2. Standard Hours Allowed × Standard Rate		1. Direct Labor Incurred

Labor Rate Variance		Labor Efficiency Variance	
2. Difference in Rates × Actual Hours Worked		2. Difference in Quantities × Standard Rate	

The two journal entries are as follows. The entry at the time of labor incurrence would be

Payroll 10,000
    Accrued Payroll 10,000
To record the incurrence of direct labor.

The entry at the time of labor distribution would be

Work-in-Process 6,000
Labor Rate Variance 2,000
Labor Efficiency Variance 2,000
    Payroll 10,000
To record the distribution of direct labor.

8.5 FEEDBACK CONTROL SYSTEM

In the traditional control system, costs are classified by responsibility, budgeted, and then compared at the end of the period with the actual results, using the

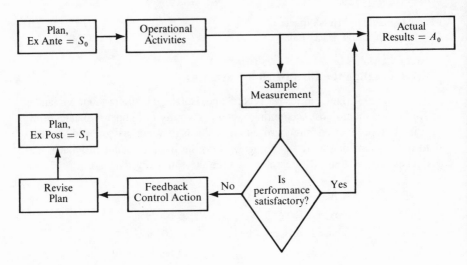

Figure 8.2
Feedback Control System

techniques of standard cost variance analysis. The traditional system does not include any monitoring system to detect and correct errors arising during the accounting period. It is an almost fatalistic approach in which the budget is perceived as a static rather than a continuous and dynamic process. A net separation between the budgeting and control phases dismisses the obvious complementarity of both operations.

One possible method of alleviating these shortcomings is the feedback control system, whereby an error in the system becomes the basis for the correction of the budget estimates. It is used after an error is detected and, therefore, represents a reaction to the error. As Figure 8.2 shows, the feedback control system consists of, first, an examination of a sample of operational activities; second, a feedback of observed error or confirmation; and, third, a revision of the budget in accordance with the deviations observed in the sample. Therefore, the feedback control system requires both the monitoring of errors and management action. R. N. Anthony and J. S. Reece observed:

Control reports are feedback devices, but they are only part of the feedback loop. Unlike the thermostat, which acts automatically in response to information about temperature, a control report does not by itself cause a change in performance. A change results only when managers take actions that lead to change. Thus, in a management control, the feedback loop requires both the control report plus management action.[6]

Feedback control systems may be applied to any business operation. For example, in the control of the purchasing manager, the accountant examines the actual prices paid to the supplier (sensor) and compares them to the budgeted prices (controller). If a variance emerges, the purchasing manager is advised to revise the budgeted price (actuator) to correct for the error.

J. S. Demski distinguishes between three types of results:

1. The ex ante budgeted performance (the original budgeted estimates)
2. The ex post budgeted performance (the revised budgeted performance after the feedback
3. The observed performance (the actual performance).[7]

The total traditional variance between the observed performance and the ex ante performance can be dichotomized as follows:

1. The difference between the ex ante and ex post results is a rough measure of the firm's forecasting ability. This is the difference between what the firm budgeted and what it should have budgeted.
2. The difference between the ex post and the observed results is a measure of the "opportunity cost to the firm" of not using its resources to maximum advantage.

Assuming

S_0 = ex ante performance.

S_1 = ex post performance.

A_0 = observed performance.

then

$$(A_0 - S_0) = (A_0 - S_1) + (S_1 - S_0),$$

where

$S_1 - S_0$ = indicator of the efficiency of the planning process.

$A_0 - S_1$ = "opportunity cost of nonoptimal capacity utilization."[8]

This feedback control system, also labeled the ex post control system, when based on a linear programming formulation of the planning process, was reported to have been successfully applied in conjunction with a petroleum refinery model in an effort to examine the system's feasibility.

The feedback control system does have some operational limitations. First, it depends heavily on the success of the error detection process. Second, there may be a time lag between the error detection, error confirmation, and error revision during which actual results may have changed again. The effectiveness of the feedback control system depends on the rapidity of the error response process.

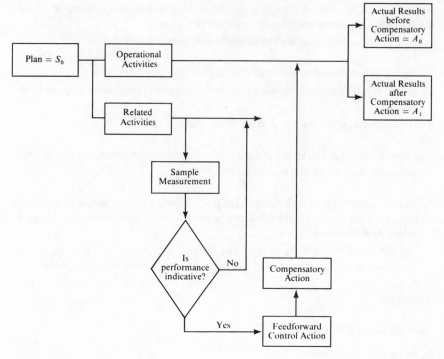

Figure 8.3
Feedforward Control System

8.6 FEEDFORWARD CONTROL SYSTEM

Feedback control systems must sense a specific error from a specific standard result before initiating a correction, and the process always occurs after the fact. Feedforward control systems do not rely on the examination of errors to recommend a correction. Instead, any correction is based on the anticipation of an error. As Figure 8.3 shows, a feedforward control system consists of, first, an examination of a "related" activity based on the anticipation of a possible deviation between the standard and actual performance; second, the feedforward or confirmation of the possibility of such an error; and, third, taking a compensatory action to maintain or adjust the operational activities. In other words, the information from the related activity acts as a surrogate for the operational activity and is fed forward to adjust the actual results through a compensatory action. Thus, the feedforward control system implies the possibility of predicting the effects of future actions and the very existence of a related activity:

Anticipation of deviations from standards depends upon the correlation of two systems such as the change in one enables prediction of change in the other. A controlling activity, which we shall call the "related activity," is ahead of the primary activity and "feeds forward" information to it.[9]

Norbert Wiener, the father of cybernetics, recognized the limitations of feedback control systems. He pointed out that where there are lags in the system, corrections ("the compensator") must predict or anticipate errors. He referred to this system as an "anticipatory feedback" system. In fact, feedforward control systems have been applied only to specialized engineering processes, mainly chemical processes.[10]

In a business setting, a feedforward control system might be used to adjust levels for inventories, production volume, purchase schedules, and employment as sales volume increases or decreases. A change in sales volume could automatically adjust the prescribed levels in the other factors in order to maintain a predetermined relationship of costs and activities to income.[11]

The typical feedforward control system goes through the following stages. At t − 1, an internal or external disturbance is detected by the controller (sensor). Given certain implied business relationships, the impact of such a disturbance on an organizational member's behavior at time t is postulated (controller). Appropriate information is fed forward to the given member for confirmation, and a compensatory action is taken that affects and governs the actual results (actuator).

To put such a system into operation, three figures are needed: the ex ante budgeted performance results (the originally budgeted results), the observed performance results (the actual results possible before the compensatory action), and the ex post actual performance results (the actual results after the compensatory action).

Feedforward control systems apply to management control as long as management can be provided information on forthcoming trouble in time for correction. For example, feedforward control can be used in cash planning, inventory control, and new product development. Mathematical models of these decisions programmed into a computer may be necessary to trace readily the influence of changes of input variables on cash flow, inventory level, and product development.[12] However, before feedforward can be applied as successfully in management control as it has been in engineering, several guidelines must be followed:

1. Thorough planning and analysis is required . . .
2. Careful discrimination must be applied in selecting input variables . . .
3. The feedforward system must be kept dynamic . . .
4. A model of the control system should be developed . . .
5. Data on input variables must be regularly collected . . .
6. Data on input variables must be regularly assessed . . .
7. Feedforward control requires action . . . [13]

The feedforward control system has two main limitations: It depends on the reliability of the relationship assumed between the related and operational activities, and it does not discriminate between usual or planned events and unusual events.

In fact, the feedforward and feedback control systems can be linked together, thus reducing the limitations attributed to each system. The general control process of usual events falls under the feedforward control system, while the control process for unusual events will be handled by the feedback control system:

Technical discussions also emphasize that while feedforward systems are useful in dealing with events which may be anticipated, such systems are best linked with feedback mechanisms to handle events which cannot be determined in advance.[14]

NOTES

1. Leonard Sayles, "The Many Dimensions of Control." *Organizational Dynamics* (Summer 1972): 21.

2. Ibid.

3. W. H. Newman, *Constructive Control and Use of Control Systems* (Englewood Cliffs, N.J.: Prentice-Hall, 1975), 6.

4. Joel S. Demski, *Information Analysis* (Reading, Mass.: Addison-Wesley, 1972), chap. 6.

5. F. C. Lesieur, ed. *The Scanlon Plan* (Cambridge, Mass.: MIT Press, 1958).

6. R. N. Anthony and J. S. Reece, *Management Accounting: Text and Cases* (Homewood, Ill.: Irwin, 1975), 780.

7. J. S. Demski, "An Accounting System Structured on a Linear Programming Model." *Accounting Review* (October 1967): 701–712.

8. Ibid., 704.

9. A. C. Filley, R. J. House, and S. Kerr, *Managerial Processes and Organizational Behavior* (Glenview, Ill.: Scott, Foresman, 1976), 441.

10. E. C. MacMullen and F. G. Shinskey, "Feedforward Analog Computer Control of a Superfractionator." *Control Engineering* 11 (1964): 69–74; F. G. Shinskey, "Feedforward Control of pH." *Instrumentation Technology* 15 (1968): 65–69; A. E. Nisenfield and R. G. Miyasaki, "Applications Feedforward Control to Distillation Columns." *Proceedings of the IFAC* (June 1972): 1–7.

11. Filley, House, and Kerr, *Managerial Processes*, 443.

12. Harold Koontz and Robert W. Bradspies, "Managing through Feedforward Control." *Business Horizons* (June 1972): 25–36.

13. Ibid., 36–37.

14. Filley, House, and Kerr, *Managerial Processes*, 463.

SELECTED READINGS

Barnes, John L. "How to Tell if Standard Costs Are Really Standard." *Management Accounting* (June 1983): 50–54.

Beerel, Annabel. "Strategic Financial Control Can Provide Light and Guidance." *Accountancy* (English) (June 1986): 70–74.

Christensen, John. "The Determination of Performance Standards and Participation." *Journal of Accounting Research* 20, no. 2, pt. 2 (Autumn 1982): 589–603.

Demski, Joel S. "Analyzing the Effectiveness of the Traditional Standard Cost Variance Model." *Management Accounting* (October 1967): 9–19.

Luh, F. S., "Controlled Cost: An Operation Concept and Statistical Approach for Standard Costing," *Accounting Review* (January 1968): 123–132.

Newman, W. H., *Constructive Control: Design and Use of Control Systems* (Englewood Cliffs, N.J.: Prentice-Hall, 1975).

Onsi, Mohamed, "Quantitative Models for Accounting Control," *Accounting Review* (April 1967) 321–330.

Sayles, Leonard, "The Many Dimensions of Control," *Organizational Dynamics* (Summer 1972) 21–31.

Control Principles: Part II

The analysis of variance procedure is expanded in this chapter to the control of factory overhead. The various overhead models are presented as well as the required journal entries. The disposition of material, labor, and overhead variances are also illustrated both in the case of no beginning inventory and in the case of beginning inventory.

9.1 FACTORY OVERHEAD VARIANCE

As automation increases and overhead leaves a higher part of the total manufacturing costs, the control of overhead becomes crucial in the management and controllable costs of the firm. The control of overhead resides in the determination and investigation of the factory overhead variances, which are equal to the differences between actual factory overhead and the standard factory overhead allowed for good output. The standard factory overhead allowed for good output is basically equal to the amount of overhead applied in the product costing process. The process for the determination of the applied overhead follows:

Step 1: Determine the volume base that is most highly associated with the variable factory overhead.

Step 2: In the budgetary process, determine the normal activity level and the corresponding factory overhead for the coming year. The estimated overhead is generally a semivariable cost composed of a fixed component and a variable component.

Step 3: Determine the budgeted variable factory overhead rate, the budgeted fixed factory overhead rate, and the budgeted total factory overhead rate.

Step 4: Apply the overhead to jobs and/or production on the basis of the actual activity level × budgeted total overhead rate.

Table 9.1 illustrates the computation of the predetermined or budgeted overhead rate and the resulting flexible budget. Assuming that 80 percent represents the

Table 9.1
Flexible Factory Overhead Budget

Capacity (Expressed as a Percentage of Normal)	40%	80%	100%
Direct-Labor Hours	5,000	10,000	15,000
Variable Factory Overhead			
Indirect Labor	$2,000	$ 3,000	$ 5,000
Indirect Material	1,000	4,000	5,000
Total Variable Factory Overhead	$3,000	$ 7,000	$10,000
Fixed Factory Overhead			
Machinery Depreciation	$1,000	$ 1,000	$ 1,000
Insurance	500	500	500
Property Taxes	500	500	500
Power and Light	800	800	800
Maintenance	200	200	200
Total Fixed Factory Overhead	$3,000	$ 3,000	$ 3,000
Total Factory Overhead	$6,000	$10.000	$13,000
Overhead Budget Formula	$3,000 + $.7 per Direct-Labor Hour		

normal capacity, the predetermined or budgeted overhead rate can be computed as follows:

$$\text{Budgeted overhead rate} = \frac{\$10,000}{100,000 \text{ hours}}$$

$$= \$.1 \text{ per standard direct-labor hour (SDLH).}$$

This determined rate may be divided into: (1) a fixed component: $3,000/10,000 hours = $.30 per SDLH and (2) a variable component: $7,000/10,000 hours = $.70 per SDLH. Although straightforward, the steps for computing the predetermined overhead rate present some conceptual problems in both the choice of the activity level and the specification of the denominator level.

The choice of the activity level rests on the choice of an expression of capacity. Depending on whether a long- or short-range viewpoint is adopted, the activity level can be expressed as either a normal capacity or as an expected annual capacity.

The normal capacity is the level of capacity utilization that will meet average and trend variations. It covers a period long enough to average consumer demand over a number of years and includes seasonal, cyclical, and trend variations. Its timespan is sufficiently long to average out sizable changes in activity and allow a trend for sales.

The expected annual capacity is the anticipated level of capacity utilization for the coming year. Needless to say, the resulting overhead rate will vary from one period to another with changes in the short-term production levels. It may be easily argued that the use of normal capacity avoids capricious changes in unit costs.

The denominator level expressing the activity level must be a useful common denominator for measuring production in all departments. Given the differences in the outputs of different departments, the activity level should be expressed uniformly. There must be a causal relationship between the denominator base and the overhead costs, and the denominator level should be measured in terms of outputs rather than inputs. In general, the denominator level is expressed in terms of standard hours of input allowed for good output produced. That is, if 1 unit of output requires 2 standard direct-labor hours, 800 units of output achieved may be expressed as 1,600 (800 × 2) standard hours of input allowed for good output produced.

9.2 OVERHEAD VARIANCE MODELS

9.2.1 One-Way Variance Model

Jobs and products in a standard cost system are charged with overhead on the basis of standard inputs allowed for actual outputs. An example of standard input is the standard hour allowed for one good output. At the end of a period, the applied overhead is compared with the actual overhead incurred. In the one-way variance model, the difference between the actual factory overhead and the applied factory overhead constitutes the total factory overhead variance.

Consider the following example. The Rocchi Company has prepared the following estimates for 19XA:

Budgeted overhead: $3,000 + $.7 per DLH.

Normal capacity in DLH: 10,000 units × 1 DLH per unit = 10,000 DLH.

Standard total overhead rate: $\dfrac{\$3,000 + \$.7(10,000 \text{ DLH})}{10,000 \text{ DLH}}$ = $1 per DLH.

$$= \$.3 \text{ fixed per DLH} + \$.7 \text{ variable per DLH}.$$

In 19XA the actual data are

Variable Overhead	$4,500
Fixed Overhead	$4,000
Units Produced	8,000 Units
Direct-Labor Hours	8,700 DLH

Thus, during 19XA the factory overhead applied to production, based on standard hours allowed for actual production, is equal to 8,000 units × 1 DLH per unit = 8,000 DLH. The total factory overhead variance will be computed as follows:

Total factory overhead variance = Actual factory overhead
                                 − Applied factory overhead

The computation of the one-way variance model for the Rocchi Company can be illustrated as follows:

Actual Factory Overhead **Based on Actual Activity** (8,700 DLH)		**Applied Factory Overhead** **Based on Standard Hours for Actual Output** (8,000 DLH × $1 per DLH)
Fixed $4,000		$2,400
Variable $4,500		$5,600
Total $8,500		$8,000
	Factory Overhead Variance	

$500 Unfavorable

This total factory overhead variance needs further analysis to identify the exact causes of its incurrence and help management choose a corrective action. Further analysis may be made by (1) the two-way variance model A or B, (2) the three-way variance model A or B, or (3) the four-way variance model.

9.2.2 Two-Way Variance Model A

The two-way variance model A is analogous to that used for direct costs (material and labor). The total overhead variance is divided into an overhead price variance and an overhead efficiency variance. The computation of the two-variance model A for the Rocchi Company is as follows:

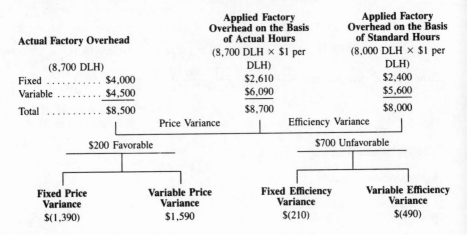

Actual Factory Overhead (8,700 DLH)		**Applied Factory Overhead on the Basis of Actual Hours** (8,700 DLH × $1 per DLH)	**Applied Factory Overhead on the Basis of Standard Hours** (8,000 DLH × $1 per DLH)
Fixed $4,000		$2,610	$2,400
Variable $4,500		$6,090	$5,600
Total $8,500		$8,700	$8,000
	Price Variance		Efficiency Variance

$200 Favorable $700 Unfavorable

Fixed Price Variance $(1,390)	**Variable Price Variance** $1,590	**Fixed Efficiency Variance** $(210)	**Variable Efficiency Variance** $(490)

9.2.3 Two-Way Variance Model B

The two-way variance model B distinguishes between a controllable variance and a volume variance (uncontrollable). The computation of the two-way variance model B for the Rocchi Company is as follows:

Actual Factory Overhead	Budgeted Overhead for Standard Hours	Applied Factory Overhead on the Basis of Standard Hours
	$3,000 + $.7(8,000 DLH)	(8,000 DLH × $1 per DLH)
(8,700 DLH)		
Fixed $4,000	$3,000	$2,400
Variable $4,500	$5,600	$5,600
Total $8,500	$8,600	$8,000

| Controllable Variance | Uncontrollable Variance |

          $100 Favorable $600 Unfavorable

The controllable variance and the volume variance can be computed differently. The controllable variance is due to the variable overhead and can be computed as follows:

Variable Overhead at Normal Capacity	$7,000
Standard Hours Allowed (8,000 DLH)	× 80%
Allowable Variable Overhead	$5,600
Actual Variable Overhead ($8,500–$3,000)	5,500
Controllable Variance	$ 100 (Favorable)

The uncontrollable (or volume) variance is due to the fixed overhead and can be computed as follows:

Normal Capacity	10,000 DLH
Standard Hours	− 8,000 DLH
Capacity Unused	2,000 DLH
Fixed Overhead Rate	×$ .3
	$ 600 (Unfavorable)

The controllable variance is the responsibility of the department manager, given that it is possible to control the causes of the variance. The uncontrollable or volume variance arises from the failure to use the total capacity or from the inefficient use of the available capacity.

9.2.4 Three-Way Variance Model A

In the three-way variance model A, the total factory overhead variance is divided into (1) an overhead spending variance, (2) an overhead capacity variance (or idle capacity variance), and (3) an overhead efficiency variance. The three-way variance model A for the Rocchi Company can be computed as follows:

Actual Factory Overhead	Budgeted Overhead for Actual Hours $3,000 + \$.7(8,700\ DLH)$	Applied Overhead on the Basis of Actual Hours (8,700 DLH × \$1 per DLH)	Applied Overhead on the Basis of Standard Hours (8,000 DLH × \$1 per DLH)
(8,700 DLH)			
Fixed \$4,000	\$3,000	\$2,610	\$2,400
Variable \$4,500	\$6,090	\$6,090	\$5,600
Total \$8,500	\$9,090	\$8,700	\$8,000

Spending Variance	Idle Capacity Variance	Efficiency Variance
\$590 Favorable	\$390 Unfavorable	\$700 Unfavorable

The idle capacity variance can be computed as follows:

Normal Capacity	10,000 DLH
Actual Capacity	− 8,700 DLH
Capacity Unused in Planning	1,300 DLH
Fixed Overhead Rate	×\$ .3
	\$ 390 (Unfavorable)

The spending variance is again the responsibility of the departmental manager. Performance based on the spending variance appears to be more favorable than performance based on the controllable variance (\$100 versus \$590) because the budgeted overhead is based on the actual rather than the standard hours.

The idle capacity variance is due to the underabsorption or overabsorption of overhead arising from differences between the actual capacity and the normal capacity, on which the overhead rate was based. The efficiency variance results from the differences between the actual hours and the standard hours allowed for actual production. These differences reflect inefficiencies in labor usage if the capacity level is expressed in terms of labor hours, and they reflect inefficiencies in material usage if the capacity level is expressed in terms of machine hours.

9.2.5 Three-Way Variance Model B

The three-way variance model B makes a distinction between overhead spending variance, overhead efficiency variance, and overhead capacity variance. The computation of the three-way variance model B for the Rocchi Company is illustrated as follows:

Actual Factory Overhead	Budgeted Overhead for Actual Hours $3,000 + \$.7(8,700\ DLH)$	Budgeted Overhead for Standard Hours $3,000 + \$.7(8,000\ DLH)$	Applied Overhead on the Basis of Standard Hours (8,000 DLH × \$1 per DLH)
(8,700 DLH)			
Fixed \$4,000	\$3,000	\$3,000	\$2,400
Variable \$4,500	\$6,090	\$5,600	\$5,600
Total \$8,500	\$9,090	\$8,600	\$8,000

Spending Variance	Efficiency Variance	Idle Capacity Variance
\$590 Favorable	\$490 Unfavorable	\$600 Unfavorable

9.2.6 Four-Way Variance Model

The four-way variance model is identical to the three-way variance model A, except that the efficiency variance is separated into fixed efficiency variance and variable efficiency variance. The four-way variance model for the Rocchi Company is computed as follows:

Actual Factory Overhead	Budgeted Overhead for Actual Hours	Applied Overhead on the Basis of Actual Hours	Applied Overhead on the Basis of Standard Hours
	$3,000 +	(8,700 DLH	(8,000 DLH
(8,700 DLH)	$.7(8,700 DLH)	× $1 per DLH)	× $1 per DLH)
Fixed $4,000	$3,000	$2,610	$2,400
Variable $4,500	$6,090	$6,090	$5,600
Total $8,500	$9,090	$8,700	$8,000

Spending Variance	Idle Capacity Variance	Efficiency Variance
$590 Favorable	$390 Unfavorable	$700 Unfavorable

Fixed Efficiency Variance	Variable Efficiency Variance
$.3 × (8,700 − 8,000 DLH)	$.7 × (8,700 − 8,000 DLH)
$210 Unfavorable	$490 Unfavorable

Note that the sum of the spending variance ($590 favorable) and the variable efficiency variance ($490 unfavorable) equals the controllable variance ($100) of the two-way variance method B. Similarly, the sum of the idle capacity variance ($390 unfavorable) and the fixed efficiency variance ($290 unfavorable) equals the uncontrollable or volume variance ($600) of the two-way variance method B. Table 9.2 summarizes the factory overhead variance analysis methods.

9.3 JOURNAL ENTRIES FOR OVERHEAD VARIANCES

The general ledger entries to record and isolate the overhead variances arising in a standard cost accounting system include the following steps:

1. Factory overhead incurred is recognized on the basis of actual values.
2. Factory overhead is applied to the Work-in-Process Inventory (sometimes referred to as Work-in-Process) on the basis of standard or budgeted values.
3. Overhead variances are isolated.

To illustrate, assume the following data (used previously in section 9.2.3 to illustrate the computation of overhead variances).

Standard overhead = $3,000 + $.7 per SDLH.

Table 9.2
Summary of Factory Overhead Variance Analysis Methods

Method	Actual Factory Overhead	Budgeted Overhead for Actual Hours	Budgeted Overhead for Standard Hours	Actual Hours × Standard Rate	Standard Hours × Standard Rate
Two-Way Variance Method A	$8,500			$8,700	$8,000
Two-Way Variance Method B	8,500		$8,600		8,000
Three-Way Variance Method A	8,500	$9,090		8,700	8,000
Three-Way Variance Method B	8,500	9,090	8,600		8,000
Four-Way Variance Method	8,500	9,090	8,600	8,700	8,000

Normal capacity = 10,000 SDLH.

Total predetermined overhead rate (TPOR) = $\dfrac{\$10,000}{10,000}$ = $1 per SDLH.

Variable predetermined overhead rate (VPOR) = $\dfrac{\$7,000}{10,000}$ = $.7 per SDLH.

Fixed predetermined overhead rate (FPOR) = $\dfrac{\$3,000}{10,000}$ = $.7 per SDLH.

Actual overhead = $4,000 fixed + $4,500 variable = $8,500.

Actual capacity = 8,700 DLH.

Standard hours for actual production = 8,000 SDLH.

The journal entries obtained by using the four-way variance method are as follows. At the time of factory overhead incurrence, the entry is

Factory Overhead Control   8,500
    Cash, Accounts Payable, Accrued Expenses   8,500
To record the incurence of actual factory overhead.

Table 9.2
(Continued)

Variances for Each Method	Total Overhead Variance
Price Variance = Col. 1 − Col. 4 = $200 Favorable. Efficiency Variance = Col. 4 − Col. 5 = $700 Unfavorable.	$500 (Unfavorable)
Controllable Variance = Col. 1 − Col. 3 = $100 Favorable. Volume Variance = Col. 3 − Col. 5 = $600 Unfavorable.	$500 (Unfavorable)
Spending Variance = Col. 1 − Col. 2 = $590 Favorable. Idle Capacity Variance = Col. 2 − Col. 4 = $390 Unfavorable. Efficiency Variance = Col. 4 − Col. 5 = $700 Unfavorable.	$500 (Unfavorable)
Spending Variance = Col. 1 − Col. 2 = $590 Favorable. Efficiency Variance = Col. 2 − Col. 3 = $490 Unfavorable. Idle Capacity Variance = Col. 3 − Col. 5 = $600 Unfavorable.	$500 (Unfavorable)
Spending Variance = Col. 1 − Col. 2 = $590 Favorable. Idle Capacity Variance = Col. 2 − Col. 4 = $390 Unfavorable. Variable Efficiency Variance = Col. 2 − Col. 3 = $490 Unfavorable. Fixed Efficiency Variance = $210 Unfavorable.	$500 (Unfavorable)

At the time of factory overhead application the entry is

Work-in-Process	8,000	
Variable Efficiency Variance	490	
Fixed Efficiency Variance	210	
Factory Overhead Control		8,700

To record the application of factory overhead.

To record the other variances and close the $200 credit balance of Factory Overhead, the entry is

Factory Overhead	200	
Idle Capacity Variance	390	
Spending Variance		590

Another possible accounting treatment for the second and third entries is as follows:

Work-in-Process	8,000	
Factory Overhead Control		8,000
Variable Efficiency Variance	490	
Fixed Efficiency Variance	210	
Idle Capacity Variance	390	
Spending Variance		590
Factory Overhead		500

9.4 STANDARD-COST ACCOUNTING: PRORATING THE VARIANCES

9.4.1 Methods of Treating Variances

Both the normal and standard costing systems produce accounts valued at standard costs, and a set of variances may be treated as follows: (1) They can be carried as deferred charges or credits on the balance sheet, (2) they can appear as charges or credits on the income statements, and (3) they can be allocated to inventories and cost of goods sold. Each of these methods will be dealt with in turn.

The deferral of variances is supported on the grounds that if the standards in use are based on normal levels of price, efficiency, and output, then positive and negative variances can be expected to offset one another in the long run. Because variance account balances at a given time are due to recurring seasonal and business cycle fluctuations, and because periodic reporting requirements result in arbitrary cutoff dates, variance account balances at a particular cutoff date are not assignable to the operating results of the period then ended. They will cancel out over recurring seasonal and business cycle fluctuations and, therefore, should be carried to the balance sheet. This method is appropriate for interim statements, no matter what method is used for annual statements.

If variances appear as charges or credits on the income statement, they are regarded as appropriate charges or credits in the period in which they arise because they are considered to be the result of favorable or unfavorable departures from normal (standard) conditions. These variances are disclosed separately from cost of goods sold at standard cost and thus provide management with unobscured information permitting immediate corrective action. Inventory valuations and cost of goods sold should not be distorted by variances that represent abnormal efficiencies or inefficiencies. A standard cost represents the amount that is reasonably necessary to produce finished products and, therefore, should be considered the best measure of cost of goods manufactured and inventory valuation as long as the underlying operating conditions remain unchanged.

Those who advocate allocation of variances to inventories and cost of goods sold regard standard costs as a useful tool for purposes of managerial control rather than as substitutes for actual historical costs in the financial statements. These people believe that only actual historical costs should be used for financial reporting, even though these costs are greater or less than standard costs and without regard to the reasons for the historical costs' differences from standard costs. Standard cost variances are not gains or losses; they are costs (or reductions thereof) of goods manufactured and, as such, should be allocated to inventories and cost of goods sold. To treat standard cost variances as gains or losses in the period in which they arise distorts both the inventory and gross profit figures. This distortion would be even greater if the standards lacked accuracy or reliability. Further, to substitute standard costs for actual historical costs in the financial statements represents an unwarranted sacrifice of objectivity. In fact, *Accounting Research Bulletin* 43 requires that standard costs, to be acceptable for financial reporting purposes, be "adjusted at reasonable intervals to reflect current conditions so that at the balance-sheet date standard costs reasonably approximate costs computed under one of the recognized bases."[1] The recognized bases are first in, first out (FIFO); last in, first out (LIFO); and weighted average cost-flow patterns.

Table 9.3
Data for a Fictional Example

Standard Cost of Product

Materials: 2 pounds at $5 = $10
Conversion Costs   20
Total $30

Production and Sales Data

	Units	Standard Cost of Material at $10	Standard Conversion Cost at $20	Total Standard Costs
Units Sold	30,000	$300,000	$600,000	$900,00
Finished Goods, Ending Inventory	20,000	200,000	400,000	600,000
Work-in-Process, Ending Inventory				
Materials, 6,000 Units 100% complete		60,000		
Conversion Costs, 6,000 Units 80% complete			96,000	
Total Work-in-Process				156,000

Material Data

The inventory of materials at the end of the period was 20,000 pounds with a standard cost of $100,000. There were no beginning inventories.

Variance Data

Material Price Variance:	$ 40,000 unfavorable
Material Usage Variance:	60,000 favorable
Conversion Cost Variance:	100,000 unfavorable

Table 9.4
Schedule of Proration of Variances, No Beginning Inventory

	Total	Material Usage Variance	Material Inventory	Work-in Process Inventory	Finished Cost Inventory	Cost of Goods Sold
1. Standard Cost of Materials	$ 600,000	($60,000)	$100,000	$60,000	$200,000	$300,000
2. Percentage of Total		10.00%	16.66%	10.00%	33.34%	50.00%
3. Proration of Material Price Variance	40,000	(4,000)	$ 6,664	4,000	13,336	20,000
4. Adjusted Usage Variance		$(64,000)				
5. Percentage of Total	$ 560,000	--	--	10.714%	35.714%	53.572%
6. Proration of Material Usage Variance		$(64,000)	--	$(6856.96)	$(22,856.96)	$(34,286.08)
7. Standard Conversion Cost	$1,096,000	--	--	$96,000	$400,000	$600,000
8. Percentage of Total				8.760%	36.496%	54.744%
9. Proration of Conversion Cost Variance	100,000			8.760%	36,486	54,744
10. Actual Cost	--	--	$106,664	$161,903.04	$626,975.04	$943,457.92

9.4.2 Prorating Variances: No Beginning Inventory

As a general rule, each variance on a given factor (labor, material, or overhead) is prorated to each relevant ending inventory and cost of sales proportionally to the standard cost for that factor in each account. The first example to be used assumes that there are no beginning inventories to simplify the presentation. The data for a fictional example appears in Table 9.3. The allocation of the variances, shown in Table 9.4, was accomplished on the basis of the following steps:

1. The materials price variances were prorated proportionally to the standard costs of materials in each affected account: usage variance, materials inventory, work-in-process inventory, finished goods inventory, and cost of sales. Note that the allocation to the usage variance was negative because the usage variance was favorable.

2. The usage variance is then adjusted before being prorated to the work-in-process inventory and the finished goods inventory and to the cost of goods sold.

3. The conversion cost variances are then prorated in proportion to the standard costs in each of the affected accounts, namely, finished goods inventory, work-in-process inventory, and cost of goods sold.

9.4.3 Prorating Variances: With Beginning Inventory

With beginning inventory present, a cost-flow assumption becomes very important. The example to be used assumes that FIFO is used, meaning that (1) all beginning material inventory is used in production first, (2) all beginning work-in-process inventory is completed first, and (3) all beginning finished goods inventory is sold first. The data for the fictional example appears in Table 9.5. The allocation of the variances proceeds as follows:

1. The materials price variance is allocated first to the ending inventory of materials as follows:

   • Ending inventory of materials: 40,000 gallons

   • Materials price variance per gallon: ($50,000/50,000): $1

   • Materials price variance allocated to ending inventory: $40,000 (40,000 gallons × $1)

   • Materials price variance remaining ($50,000 − $40,000): $10,000.

2. The next step is to determine where the current period equivalent production for materials and conversion cost finished. The computation may proceed as follows:

	Disposition of Current Period Production	
	Materials	*Conversion Costs*
Total Equivalent Production for Period	30,000	27,000
Equivalent Units in		
Ending Inventory of Work-in-Process	15,000	10,000
Ending Inventory of Finished Goods	8,000	8,000
Total Current Period Equivalent Production in Ending Inventory	23,000	18,000
Equivalent Production in Cost of Sales	7,000	9,000

3. The third step is to prorate the materials price variance proportionally to the standard costs of materials in (1) the usage variance, (2) the work-in-process inventory, (3) the finished goods inventory, and (4) the cost of goods sold. The results are shown in Table 9.6.

4. The fourth step is to prorate the adjusted usage variance proportionally to the standard

costs of materials in (1) the work-in-process inventory, (2) the finished goods inventory, and (3) the cost of goods sold. The results are shown in Table 9.6.

5. The conversion costs are then prorated in proportion to the standard conversion costs in (1) the work-in-process inventory, (2) the finished goods inventory, and (3) the cost of goods sold. The results are shown in Table 9.7.

Table 9.5
Data for Illustration

Standard Cost per Unit

Materials:	$1.50	
Conversion Costs:	3.00	
	$4.50	

Equivalent Production

	Materials	Conversion Costs
Completed	18,000	18,000
Ending Inventory	15,000	10,000
Beginning Inventory	(3,000)	(1,000)
Equivalent Production	30,000	27,000

Inventories

	Materials	Finished Costs
Beginning Inventory	20,000	10,000
Added during period	50,000	18,000
Used or sold	(30,000)	(20,000)
Ending Inventory	40,000	8,000

Variances

Material price :	$50,000 unfavorable
Usage :	10,000 favorable
Conversion cost:	20,000 unfavorable

Table 9.6
Schedule of Proration of Variances, with Beginning Inventory

	Total	Usage Variance	Work-in Process Inventory	Finished Cost Inventory	Cost of Goods Sold
1. Standard Cost of Materials	$35,000	$(10,000)	$22,500	$12,000	$10,500
2. Percentage of Total	100%	(28.57%)	64.28%	34.28%	30%
3. Proration of Material Price Variance	$10,000	(2,857)	6,428	3,428	3,000
4. Unadjusted Usage Variance	$10,000				
5. Adjusted Usage Variance	$ 2,857				
6. Percentage of Total	100%	--	50%	26.66%	23,33%
7. Proration of Usage Variance	$12,857	--	(6,428.5)	(3,497.67)	(2,999.54)
8. Standard Conversion Cost	$81,000	--	$30,000	$24,000	27,000
9. Percentage of Total	100%	--	37.03%	29.62%	3.33%
10. Proration of Conversion Cost Variance	$20,000		7,406	5,924	6,666

6. The variances are prorated to determine the actual costs of materials inventory, work-in-process inventory, finished goods inventory, and cost of goods sold. The results are shown in Table 9.7. Note that the standard figure used for cost of sales is total cost of sales at standard costs rather than just the standard cost of sales related to current period production.

9.5 CONCLUSION

This chapter illustrates the principles of standard cost accounting, namely, (1) the computation of variances and (2) the isolation and proration of variances. Standard cost accounting is an essential managerial tool for any firm concerned with the control of all of its activities. It requires an information system geared to the timely production and dissemination of the variances illustrated in this chapter.

Table 9.7
Proration Variances

	Materials Inventory	Work-in Process Inventory	Finished Cost Inventory	Cost of Goods Sold
Standard Cost	$45,000	$52,500	$36,000	$90,000
Material Price Variance	40,000	6,428	3,428	3,000
Material Usage Variance		(6,428.5)	(3,427.67)	(2,999.54)
Conversion Cost Variance		7,406	5,924	6,666
Actual Costs	$85,000	$59,906	$41,924	$96,666

NOTE

1. Committee on Accounting Procedure, *Accounting Research Bulletin No. 43, Restatement and Revision of Accounting Research Bulletins* (New York: American Institute of Certified Public Accountants, 1953), 17.

10

Control Principles: Mix, Yield, and Investigation

The subject of control and the use of variance analysis are continued in this chapter to cover the following five advance control subjects: (1) control of nonmanufacturing variance through the analysis of contribution mix variance and sales variances (sales volume variance, sales quantity variance, and sales mix variance), (2) the analysis of market size and market share variances, (3) the analysis of production mix variances using the partial linear substitution model, (4) the analysis of production mix variances using the fixed proportion substitution model, and (5) the problem of when to investigate a variance.

10.1 CONTROL OF NONMANUFACTURING ACTIVITIES

The analysis of variance can be extended to nonmanufacturing activities in general and to sales and profit analysis in particular. Because organizations generally produce more than one product or service, the analysis will rely on the sales mix which is the relative proportion or combination of the quantities of products that compose total sales.

10.1.1 Total Marketing Variance

The first variance used to control nonmanufacturing activities is the total marketing variance. It is computed as follows:

Total marketing variance: $\sum\limits_{i=1}^{n}$ [(Actual sales volume $\times$ Actual contribution

margin per unit) $-$ (Standard sales volume

$\times$ Standard contribution margin per unit)]

where n = number of products i in the sales mix.

10.1.2 Contribution Margin Variance and Sales Volume Variance

The total marketing variance is equal to the sum of the contribution margin variance and the sales volume variance. These are computed as follows:

$$\text{Contribution margin variance} = \sum_{i=1}^{n} [(\text{Actual number of units sold})$$

$$\times (\text{Actual contribution margin per unit}$$

$$- \text{Standard contribution margin per unit})]$$

where n = number of products in the sales mix.

The total contribution margin variance is a measure of the variation caused by the differences between the actual and standard contribution margin per unit of each product.

$$\text{Sales volume variance} = \sum_{i=1}^{n} [(\text{Actual sales volume} - \text{Standard sales volume})$$

$$\times (\text{Standard contribution margin per unit})]$$

where n = number of products i in the sales mix.

The sales volume variance shows the impact of a change in unit sales measured at the standard contribution margin per unit of each product.

10.1.3 Sales Quantity Variance and Sales Mix Variance

The sales volume variance can be decomposed into a sales quantity variance and a sales mix variance. In other words, a favorable (unfavorable) sales volume variance may be due to either an increase (decrease) in the total number of units sold to be measured by the sales activity variance or to a favorable (unfavorable) mix of products to be measured by the sales mix variance. These variances are computed as follows:

$$\text{Sales quantity variance: } \sum_{i=1}^{n} [(\text{Actual sales volume}$$

$$- \text{Static budgeted sales volume})$$

$$\times (\text{Standard average contribution margin per unit})]$$

where n = number of products i in the sales mix.

The sales quantity variance will be favorable or positive only if actual sales exceed standard sales. It is a measure of the variation caused uniquely by the sale of more or fewer units of products.

Sales mix variance: $\sum_{i=1}^{n}$ [(Actual sales mix percentage − Standard sales mix

percentage) × Actual total sales volume of all products)

× (Standard individual contribution margin per unit

− Standard average contribution margin per unit)]

where n = number of products i in the sales mix.

The sales mix variance is a measure of the variation in the total contribution margin caused by the differences between the actual and standard sales mix, taking into account how the product's contribution margin differs from the standard average contribution margin per unit. The products that have a contribution margin greater than the average standard contribution margin are known as "high-profit products," and those that have a lower than average margin are known as "low-profit products." Consequently, a move from low-profit products to high-profit products will increase profits and vice versa.

10.1.4 Illustration of the Control of Nonmanufacturing Activities

To illustrate the control of nonmanufacturing activities, let us use the example of a chain of cookie stores with four kinds of cookies: chocolate chip, oatmeal raisin, coconut, and peanut butter. The data for 19X5 are as follows:

Input Data: Control of Nonmanufacturing Activities

Kinds of Cookies	Standard Sales	Actual Sales	Standard Contribution Margin	Actual Contribution Margin	Total Standard Contribution Margin	Total Actual Contribution Margin
Chocolate Chip	200	180	$ 60	$ 56	$12,000	$10,080
Oatmeal Raisin	120	128	68	72	8,160	9,216
Coconut	60	56	80	68	4,800	3,808
Peanut Butter	20	28	140	136	2,800	3,808
Total	400	392			$27,760	$26,912

The analysis of variance may proceed as follows:

Total Marketing Variance:

$$\$26,912 - \$27,760 = \$(848) \text{ unfavorable.}$$

Contribution Margin Variance:

Chocolate chip: ($56 − $60)   × 180 = (720) unfavorable

Oatmeal raisin: ($72 − $68)   × 128 = .512 favorable

Coconut: ($68 − $80)   ×   56 = (672) unfavorable

Peanut butter: ($136 − $140) × 28 = (112) unfavorable

Total contribution margin variance: (992) unfavorable.

Sales Volume Variance:

Chocolate chip: (180 − 200) × $60 = $(1,200) unfavorable

Oatmeal raisin: (128 − 120) × $68 = $544 favorable

Coconut: (56 − 60)   × $80 = $(320) unfavorable

Peanut butter: (28 − 20)   × $140 = $1,120 favorable

Total sales volume variance: $144 favorable

Notice that the total marketing variance of $(848) (unfavorable) is equal to the sum of the total contribution margin of $(992) and the sales volume variance of $144.

Sales Quantity Variance:

The standard average contribution margin per unit is equal to $\dfrac{\$27,760}{400} =$ $69.4. Therefore, the sales quantity variances are computed as follows:

Chocolate chip: (180 − 200) × $69.4 = $(1,388) unfavorable

Oatmeal raisin: (128 − 120) × $69.4 = $555.2 favorable

Coconut: (56 − 60) × $65.4 = $(277.6) unfavorable

Peanut butter: (28 − 20) × $69.4 = $555.2 favorable

Total sales quantity variance: $(555.2) unfavorable

Sales Mix Variance (Formula 1):

Chocolate chip: $\left[\left(\dfrac{180}{392} - \dfrac{200}{400} \right) \times 392 \right] (\$60 - \$69.4)$

$$= \$150.4 \text{ favorable}$$

Oatmeal raisin: $\left[\left(\dfrac{128}{392} - \dfrac{120}{400} \right) \times 392 \right] (\$68 - \$69.4)$

$$= \$(14.56) \text{ unfavorable}$$

Coconut: $\left[\left(\dfrac{56}{392} - \dfrac{60}{400} \right) \times 392 \right] (\$80 - \$69.4)$

$$= \$(29.68) \text{ unfavorable}$$

Peanut butter: $\left[\left(\dfrac{28}{392} - \dfrac{20}{400} \right) \times 392 \right] (\$140 - \$69.4)$

$$= \dfrac{\$593.04 \text{ favorable}}{\$699.20 \text{ favorable}}$$

10.2 MARKET SIZE AND MARKET SHARE VARIANCES

The overall market demand for the products of an industry as well as the company's ability to maintain its market share are important to a company. Hence the sales quantity variance of a company can be subdivided into (1) a market size variance and (2) a market share variance.[1] They may be computed as follows:

Market size variance: (Standard market share percentage) × (Actual industry sales volume in units − Standard industry sales in units) × (Standard average contribution margin per unit).

Market share variance: (Actual market share percentage − Standard market share percentage) × (Actual industry sales volume in units) × (Standard average contribution margin per unit).

To illustrate these variances, let us return to the example used before for the computation of nonmanufacturing variances. Let us also assume that the standard sales of 400 units represents 1 percent of the expected industry sales of 40,000 units and that the actual sales of 392 units represents 1.25 percent of the actual industry sales of 31,360 units. What follows are the computations of the market size and market share variances:

Market size variance = $(0.01) (31,360 - 40,000) \times \$69.4$
$$= \$5996.16 \text{ unfavorable}$$

Market share variance = $(0.0125 - 0.01) (31,360) \times \$69.4$
$$= \dfrac{5440.96 \quad \text{favorable}}{\$552.2 \text{ unfavorable}}$$

Note that the total of market share variance and market size variance is equal to the sales quantity variance of $552.2 unfavorable obtained earlier.

10.3 PRODUCTION MIX AND YIELD VARIANCES: THE PARTIAL LINEAR SUBSTITUTION MODEL

Various manufacturing operations require a combination of a number of different direct materials or a material mix and a number of different direct labor types or a labor mix. What is expected from the use of these mixes is a yield which refers to the quantity of output most probable by the use of material and labor mixes. The variances may result in this situation. The first variance is the mix variance, which refers to the difference between the input quantities expected to be used and the input quantities actually used. The second variance is the yield variance, which refers to the difference between the output expected to be obtained and the output actually obtained. More specifically, the mix variance results from using an actual mix in quantities of input (materials or labor) different from the standard mix. The yield variance results from obtaining a yield (a measure of output) different from the one expected based on the standard input.

The computation of the mix variance and yield variance depends on the assumptions made about the production function, which is the technical relationship among inputs and between input quantities and output quantities. In general, the production function may be such (1) it allows partial linear substitution among input materials or labor (linear production function), (2) it requires usage of input materials or labor in a fixed proportion only (fixed proportion function), or (3) it allows substitution among inputs at varying rates (nonlinear production function).

10.3.1 Quantity Variance and Mix Variances

If partial linear substitution is assumed, the following variances may be used:

Quantity variance = (Standard quantity of input − Actual quantity) × standard price.
The quantity variance is equal to the sum of the mix variance and yield variance.

The mix variances are computed as follows:

Material mix variance = [(Actual material mix percentage − Standard material mix percentage) × (Actual total units of material inputs used) × (Standard individual price per unit of material input − Standard average price per unit of material input)]

Labor mix variance = [(Actual labor mix percentage − Standard labor mix percentage) × (Actual total units of labor inputs used) × (Standard individual price per unit of labor input − Standard average price per unit of labor input)]

The material variance for materials (or labor) is a measure of the cost variation caused by using a different mix of materials (or labor). The materials (or labor) that have a standard price higher than the average standard price of materials (or labor) are known as "high-cost inputs," and those that have a standard price lower than the average standard price are known as "low-cost inputs." A move from high-cost inputs to low-cost inputs will render the mix variance more favorable.

10.3.2 Yield Variances

The yield variances in the case of materials can be computed by using the following formulas:

Material yield variance (first formula):

$$\sum_{i=1}^{n} [(\text{Standard units of material input allowed for actual outputs} - \text{Actual units of material input used}) \times (\text{Standard average price per unit of material input})]$$

Material yield variance (second formula):
(Actual quantity of all material input × Average standard cost of all material input) − (Actual quantity of output produced × standard material cost of output units)

Material yield variance (third formula):
(Expected output − Actual output) × Unit output material cost.

Yield variances in the case of labor can be computed by using the following formulas:

Labor yield variance (first formula):

$$\sum_{i=1}^{n} [(\text{Standard units of labor input allowed for actual outputs} - \text{Actual units of labor inputs used}) \times (\text{Standard average price per unit of labor input})]$$

Labor yield variance: (second formula):
(Actual quantity of all labor inputs × Average standard cost of all labor inputs) − (Actual quantity of output produced × Standard labor cost of output units)

Labor yield variance: (third formula):
(Expected output − Actual output) × Unit output labor cost.

10.3.3 Illustration for Production Mix and Yield Variances for Material

Let us use the example of a chemical company which requires the use of two types of materials. The standard quantities and prices per unit of output are:

Materials	Standard Quantity	Standard Price	Total Standard Cost
A	.20	$ 6	$1.20
B	.12	10	1.20
Total	.32		$2.40

The information was based on a standard production of 2,000 good units of output.

The actual quantities and prices for the production of 2,200 units of output are as follows:

Material	Actual Quantity	Actual Price	Actual Material Cost for a Total Production of 2,200
A	240	$ 7.00	$1,680
B	124	11.00	1,364
Total	364		$3,044

The analysis of variance may proceed as follows:

1. Material usage variance: (Actual quantity − standard quantity) × Standard price.

$$A: (240 - 440) \times \$\ 6 = \$1,200 \text{ favorable}$$
$$B: (124 - 264) \times \$10 = \$1,400 \text{ favorable}$$
$$\text{Total} \qquad\qquad\qquad \$2,600 \text{ favorable}$$

Note that the standard quantity used is the standard quantity allowed, that is, the standard quantity to be used for actual production. For example, for material A, it is equal to 2,200 units of output × 0.20 = 440 standard quantity allowed.

2. Materials mix variance: First, the average standard price of all material input is computed as follows:

$$P^* = \frac{\$2.40}{.32} = \$7.5.$$

Second, the material mix variances are computed as follows:

Material A: $\left[\left(\frac{240}{364} - \frac{.20}{.32} \right) \times 364 \right]$ [$ 6 − $7.5] = $18.75 favorable.

Material B: $\left[\left(\frac{124}{364} - \frac{.12}{.32} \right) \times 364 \right]$ [$10 − $7.5] = $31.25 favorable.

3. Material yield variance; Three formulas may be used to determine the material yield variance: The first formula is as follows:

Materials yield variance:

$$\text{Material A: } (240 - 440) \times \$7.5 = \$1,500 \text{ favorable}$$
$$\text{Material B: } (124 - 264) \times \$7.5 = \$1,050 \text{ favorable}$$
$$\text{Total} \qquad\qquad\qquad\qquad \$2,550 \text{ favorable}$$

The second formula is as follows:

Materials yield variance = (Actual quantity of all inputs × Average standard cost of all inputs) − (Actual activity of output produced × standard material cost of output units)

$$= (364 \times \$7.5) - (2,200 \times \$2.40)$$
$$= (\$2,730 - \$5,280) = \$2,550.$$

The third formula is as follows:

Materials yield variance = (Expected output − Actual output) × (Unit output material cost).

To find the expected output, consider the following relationship:

$$\frac{\text{Standard quantity of material input}}{\text{Standard output}} = \frac{\text{Actual quantity of material input}}{\text{Expected output}}$$

therefore Expected output = $\dfrac{\text{Standard output} \times \text{Actual quantity of material input}}{\text{Standard quantity of material input}}$

in other words, Expected output = $\dfrac{2,000 \times 364}{(.32 \times 2,000)}$

or Expected output = 1,137.5 units.

Given that the unit output material cost is $2.40 per unit of output, the material yield variance will be

Material yield variance = (1,137.5 − 2,200) × $2.40 = $2,550 favorable.

10.3.4 Illustration for Production Mix and Yield Variances for Labor

Let us use the example of a manufacturing company who requires the use of two types of labor: semiskilled and skilled labor.

The standard quantities and prices are as follows:

Labor	Standard hours per Unit of Output	Standard Labor Rate	Standard
Semiskilled	2.50	$ 5 per hour	$12.5
Skilled	2.50	30 per hour	75
Total	5.00		$87.5

The average standard price of labor is then $17.50 (87.50/5.00). The above information was based on a standard production of 1,000 units of output.

The quantities and prices for the actual production of 1,100 units of output follows:

Labor	Actual Labor in Hours	Actual Labor Rate	Actual Labor for the Total Production of 1,100 Units
Semiskilled	2,480	$10.50	$ 26,040
Skilled	2,640	33.00	87,120
Total	5,120		$113,160

The analysis of variance may proceed as follows:

1. Labor quantity variance (labor efficiency variance).

Labor efficiency variance = (Actual hours − Standard hours) × Standard rate.

Semiskilled:	(2,480 − 2,750) × $ 5 =	$1,350 favorable
Skilled:	(2,640 − 2,750) × $30 =	$3,300 favorable
Total		$4,650 favorable

Note that the standard quantity used is the standard quantity allowed, that is, the standard quantity to be used for actual production. For example, for semiskilled labor, it is equal to 1,100 units of output × 2.50 = 2,750 standard hours allowed. For skilled labor, it is also equal to 2,750 (1,100 × 2.50).

2. Labor mix variance.

$$\text{Semiskilled} = \left[\left(\frac{2,480}{5,120} - \frac{2.50}{5.00} \right) \times 5,120 \right] \left[\$ 5 - \$17.50 \right] = \$1,000 \text{ unfavorable.}$$

$$\text{Skilled} = \left[\left(\frac{2,640}{5,120} - \frac{2.50}{5.00} \right) \times 5,120 \right] \left[\$30 - \$17.50 \right] = \$1,000 \text{ unfavorable.}$$

3. Labor yield variance: Three formulas may be used to determine the labor yield variance. The first formula is as follows:

Labor yield variance:

Semiskilled:	(2,480 − 2,750) × $17.50 =	$4,725 favorable
Skilled:	(2,640 − 2,750) × $17.50 =	$1,925 favorable
Total		= $6,650 favorable

The second formula is as follows:

Labor yield variance = (Actual quantity of all inputs × Average standard cost of all inputs) − (Actual quantity of output produced × Standard labor cost of output units) = (5,120 × $17.50) − (1,100 × $87.50) = $6,650.

The third formula is as follows:

Labor yield variance = (Expected output − Actual output) × (Unit output labor cost).

To find the expected output, consider the following relationship:

$$\frac{\text{Standard quantity of labor input}}{\text{Standard output}} = \frac{\text{Actual quantity of labor input}}{\text{Expected output}}$$

$$\text{therefore, Expected output} = \frac{\text{Standard output} \times \text{Actual quantity of labor input}}{\text{Standard quantity of labor input}}$$

$$\text{in other words, Expected output} = \frac{1,000 \times 5,120}{(5 \times 1,000)}$$

$$\text{or Expected output} = 1,102.4 \text{ units.}$$

therefore the labor yield variance is equal to

$$(1,024 - 1,100) \times \$87.5 = \$6,650 \text{ favorable.}$$

10.4 PRODUCTION MIX AND YIELD VARIANCES: THE FIXED PROPORTION SUBSTITUTION MODEL

Under a fixed proportion substitution model, the following formula may be used:

1. The mix variance is computed as follows:

Mix variance = (Expected quantity of one input − Actual quantity of one input) × Standard price of one input.

2. The yield variance is computed as follows:

Yield variance = (Expected output − Actual output) × Unit output cost.

To illustrate the application of the formula to material, let us return to the example used in section 10.3.3. The variances, assuming a fixed proportion substitution model, are as follows:

1. Mix variance. To compute the mix variance, the expected quantity of one input has to be computed. The following relationship may be used.

$$\frac{\text{Standard quantity of one input}}{\text{Standard quantity of another input}} = \frac{\text{Expected quantity of one input}}{\text{Actual quantity of another input}}$$

therefore, the Expected quantity of one input = (Standard quantity of one input × Actual quantity of another input)/(Standard quantity of another input).
It follows that

$$\text{Expected quantity of material A} = \frac{(.20 \times 2{,}200) \times 124}{(.12 \times 2{,}200)} = 206.66.$$

Therefore, the mix variance of material A = (206.66 − 240) × \$6 = \$200.00 unfavorable.

2. Yield variance. To compute the yield variance, the expected output is needed. The following relationship may be used.

$$\frac{\text{Total standard quantity of input}}{\text{Actual output}} = \frac{\text{(Expected quantity of one input + Actual quantity of another input)}}{\text{Expected output}}$$

$$\frac{(.32 \times 2{,}200)}{2{,}200} = \frac{206.66 + 124}{\text{Expected output}}$$

Expected output = 1,033.3125 units

therefore, the yield variance is computed as follows:

(1033.3125 − 2,200) × \$2.40 = 2,800.04 favorable.

Note that the sum of the mix variance of \$200.04 (unfavorable) and the yield variance of \$2,800.04 (favorable) is equal, as expected, to the material usage variance of \$2,600 favorable.

To illustrate the application of the formula to labor, let us return to the example used in section 10.3.4. The variances, assuming a fixed proportion substitution model, are as follows:

1. Mix variance. To compute the mix variance, the expected quantity of one input has to be computed. The following relationship may be used.

$$\frac{\text{Standard quantity of one input}}{\text{Standard quantity of another input}} = \frac{\text{Expected quantity of one input}}{\text{Actual quantity of another input}}$$

Therefore, the Expected quantity of one input = (Standard quantity of one input × actual quantity of another input)/(Standard quantity of another input).
It follows that

$$\text{Expected quantity of skilled labor} = \frac{(2.50 \times 1,100) \times 2,480}{(2.50 \times 1,100)} = 2,480.$$

Therefore, the labor mix variance of skilled labor = (2,480 − 2,640) × $30 = $4,800 unfavorable.

2. Yield variance. To compute the yield variance, the expected output is needed. The following relationship may be used.

$$\frac{\text{Total standard quantity of input}}{\text{Actual output}} = \frac{(\text{Expected quantity of one input} + \text{Actual quantity of another input})}{\text{Expected output}}$$

$$\frac{(5.00 \times 1,100)}{(1,100)} = \frac{2,480 + 2,480}{\text{Expected output}}$$

Expected output = 992 units.

therefore, the labor yield variance is computed as follows: (992 − 1,100) × $87.5 = $9,450 favorable.

Note that the sum of the mix variance of $4,800 unfavorable and the yield variance of $9,450 favorable is equal, as expected, to the material usage variance of $4,650 favorable.

10.5 WHEN TO INVESTIGATE A VARIANCE: THE ROLE OF BREAKEVEN PROBABILITIES

The basis of any control decision, although not explicitly stated, is that the benefits to be realized from investigation will exceed the costs of the investigation. The decision rule will be to choose the act (investigate versus do not investigate) that minimizes the expected costs. Therefore the decision to investigate a variance can be represented by a two-state-action problem as follows:

States of Nature:	I. In control process random variation	II. Out of control process nonrandom variation
Actions		
1. Investigate and correct (a_1)	Cost = c Type I error	Cost = C + M Correct decision
2. Do not investigate (a_2)	Cost = 0 Correct decision	Cost = L Type II error

where

C = Cost of investigating a variance

M = Cost of correcting a variance

L = Opportunity cost, which can be thought of as the future cost savings that might have been realized had the variance being investigated been found to be nonrandom and eliminated; this can be labeled "out-of-control loss."

Let us now assume that f_1 is the prior probability that the process is in control or that the variance is due to random and noncontrollable causes and that f_2 is the prior probability that the process is out of control or that the variance is due to nonrandom and controllable causes.

The expected cost of each act is calculated by multiplying each conditional cost by its respective probability and by summing the results. The expected costs from the investigate (a_1) and do not investigate (a_2) actions are as follows:

$$\text{Investigate: } E(a_1) = (C)P_1 + (C + M)P_2$$

$$\text{Do not investigate: } E(a_2) = (0)\,P_1 + (L)P_2.$$

Therefore, a firm would be indifferent toward investigation if the expected cost of each action were equal, that is, when

$$CP_1 + (C + M)P_2 = LP_2$$

or

$$C(1 - P_2) + (C + M)P_2 = LP_2.$$

Solving for P_2 yields the breakeven or critical probability, that is, the probability at which the expected value of a decision to investigate a variance is equal to the expected value of the loss through a failure to investigate. The breakeven probability P^*_2 is

$$P_2^* = \frac{C}{L - M}$$

or, alternatively,

$$P^*_1 = 1 - \frac{C}{L - M}.$$

Therefore, if

$$P_2 > P^*_2 \text{ or } P_1 < P^*_1,$$

the decision is to investigate the variance.

If

$$P_2 < P^*_2 \text{ or } P_1 > P^*_1,$$

the decision is not to investigate the variance.

For example, assume the following information on a manufacturing process:

C = \$ 3,600 = Cost of investigation
L = \$16,000 = Present value of incremental costs that would have been incurred if corrective action were not taken
M = \$10,000 = Cost of corrective action
P_1 = 0.8 = Prior probability of the process being in control
P_2 = 0.2 = Prior probability of the process being out of control.

The breakeven probability is

$$P_1^* = 1 - \frac{\$3,600}{\$16,000 - \$10,000} = 0.4.$$

Therefore the variance is investigated only when the probability of the system's being in control drops below 0.4. Given that P_1 = 0.8, the decision is not to investigate the process. It is important, however, to note that the model used to determine the critical probability assumes (1) that the out-of-control process stays out of control and (2) that after being corrected the out-of-process control stays in control until the end of the cost period. The model is also limited to a two-state-two actions situation and assumes risk-neutral decision makers. The academic literature offers more complex models[2] and critical comments on their relevance.[3]

10.6 CONCLUSION

This chapter adds to the use of variances for control by covering the following new variances: contribution margin variance, sales volume variance, sales quantity variance, sales mix variance, market size variance, market share variance, production mix variance, and production yield variance. Those variances allow a more complete evaluation of the performance of an entity when more than one product is produced and more than one input is used.

The decision to investigate a variance is also examined with an emphasis on the use of the breakeven probability and the use of a simple decision rule.

NOTES

1. J. Shank and N. Churchill, "Variance Analysis: A Management-Oriented Approach." *Accounting Review* (October 1977): 955.

2. F. Jacobs and R. Marshall, "A Note on the Choice Structure of Cost Variance Investigation Models." *Journal of Accounting Literature* (Spring 1984): 73–83.

3. G. Boa, "Solutions in Search of a Problem: The Case of Budget Variance Investigation Models." *Journal of Accounting Literature* (Spring 1984): 47–69.

SELECTED READINGS

Adelberg, A. "An Improved Analysis of Production-Mix Variances." *Production and Inventory Management* (Fourth quarter, 1984): 35–41.

Becker, E. A., and K. J. Kim, "Direct Material Variances: Review of the Mix and Yield Variances." *Issues in Accounting Education* (Spring 1988): 1–16.

Boa, G. "Solutions in Search of a Problem: The Case of a Budget Variance Investigation Model." *Journal of Accounting Literature* (Spring 1984): 47–49.

Brown, G. M. "Energy Costs and Variance Analysis." *CIMA Management Accounting* 66, no. 1 (January 1988): 42–43.

Capettini, Robert, and Dennis Collins. "The Investigation of Deviations from Standard Costs in the Presence of Unequal State Variances." *Journal of Business, Finance and Accounting* 5, no. 4 (Winter 1978): 335–352.

Dittman, David, and Prem Prakash. "Cost Variance Investigation: Markovian Control versus Optimal Control." *Accounting Review* 54, no. 2 (April 1979): 358–373.

Jacobs, Fredric H. "An Evaluation of the Effectiveness of Some Cost Variance Investigation Models." *Journal of Accounting Research* 16, no. 1 (Spring 1978): 190–203.

Jacobs, F. "When and How to Use Statistical Cost Variance Investigation Techniques." *Cost and Management* (January–February, 1983): 26–32.

Jacobs, F., and R. Marshall. "A Note on the Choice Structure of Cost Variance Investigation Models." *Journal of Accounting Literature* (Spring 1984): 73–83.

Kaplan, Robert S. "The Significance and Investigation of Cost Variances: Survey and Extensions." *Journal of Accounting Research* 13, no. 2 (Autumn 1975): 311–337.

Manes, Rene P. "Demand Elasticities: Supplements to Sales Budget Variance Reports." *Accounting Review* 58, no. 1 (January 1983): 143–156.

Shank, J., and N. Churchill. "Variance Analysis: A Management-Oriented Approach." *Accounting Review* (October 1977): 66–74.

Zebda, Awni. "The Investigation of Cost Variances: A Fuzzy Set Theory Approach." *Decision Sciences* 15, no. 3 (Summer 1984): 359–388.

11

Cost Estimation and Regression Analysis

Chapter 3 provides the fundamentals of cost estimation by comparing some of the practical techniques available to the cost accountant. This chapter extends the cost estimation analysis by introducing the use of regression analysis in cost estimation.

Regression analysis is a formal statistical technique aimed at determining the cost estimation equation. In single regression analysis, there is only one *independent variable* to explain the change in the *dependent variable* of cost. In multiple regression analysis, there is more than one independent variable to explain the changes in the dependent variable of cost. Both single and multiple regression analyses for cost estimation are presented in this chapter.

11.1 SIMPLE REGRESSION METHOD

The regression method is a statistical estimating technique which determines relationships between variables. In its simplest form, the *simple regression method*, it relates one dependent variable to one independent variable:

$$y = \alpha + bx + \mu.$$

The total variation in y (described as the dependent, endogenous, regressed, or explained variable) is equal to systematic variation associated with variation in the independent variable (x) and a random variation (μ) attributed to unknown factors. μ is also termed *the residual,* the *disturbance term,* or the *error term.* It is the deviation of the actual value of y from the regression line.

In the technique's more complex form, the *multiple regression method*, it relates one dependent variable to more than one independent variable. Both simple and multiple regression analyses determine the equation relating the independent variable to the dependent variable(s) by estimating the unknown parameters a and b. The mathematical technique used is the *least squares method* or, more precisely, the ordinary least squares (OLS) regression method.

11.1.1 Least Squares Method

The least squares regression method is a mathematical technique that estimates the regression parameters a and b and provides an exact fit between the independent and dependent variables. This method determines a straight line that minimizes the sum of the squared deviations $(\Sigma\mu_i^2)$.

The mathematics of the least squares method are as follows:

1. The least square linear model is written as

$$y_i = a + bx_i + \mu_i,$$

where y_i denotes the dependent variable and x_i, the independent variable.

2. The deviations μ_i, which are the vertical distances between the observations y_i and the regression line, are written as

$$\mu_i = y_i - (a + bx_i)$$
$$= y_i - a - bx_i.$$

3. The regression parameters a and b are obtained by minimizing the sum of squared deviations as follows:

$$\Sigma\mu_i^2 = \Sigma(y_i - a - bx_i)^2\epsilon \text{ (\$WL) a minimum.}$$

4. By taking the partial derivatives with respect to a and b and setting them equal to zero for minimizing the sum of squares, "normal equations" will be obtained:

$$\frac{\partial \sum_{i=1}^{n} \mu_i^2}{\partial a} = -2 \sum_{i=1}^{n} (y_i - a - bx_i) = 0$$

and

$$\frac{\partial \sum_{i=1}^{n} \mu_i^2}{\partial b} = -2 \sum_{i=1}^{n} X_i (y_i - a - bx_i) = 0.$$

The two normal equations also can be stated as follows:

$$\Sigma y = na = b\Sigma x.$$
$$\Sigma xy = a\Sigma x + b\Sigma x^2.$$

These normal equations can be solved either by successive substitution or by using matrix algebra.

5. Successive substitution (or *Cramer's rule*) produces the following:

$$a = \frac{(\Sigma y)(\Sigma x^2) - (\Sigma x)(\Sigma xy)}{n(\Sigma x^2) - (\Sigma x)^2}$$

and

$$b = \frac{n(\Sigma xy) - (\Sigma x)(\Sigma y)}{n(\Sigma x^2) - (\Sigma x)^2}.$$

By inserting the values from the JABEX problem from chapter 3, the values of a and b will equal

$$a = \frac{(120)(158) - (40)(441)}{12(158) - (40)^2} = \$4.45.$$

$$b = \frac{(12)(441) - (40)(120)}{12(158) - (40)^2} = \$1.66.$$

Table 11.1 shows the detailed computations. Placing the values of a and b in the equation of the least squares line produces y' = \$4.45 + \$1.66x, where y' is the predicted production cost for a given month and x the direct-labor hours (y' is shown in Figure 11.1). The least squares equation may be used for prediction. Thus, for estimated direct-labor hours of 10, the predicted production costs will equal \$4.45 + \$1.66 × 10 = \$21.05.

Table 11.1
JABEX, Inc.: Computation for Least Squares

(1)	(2)	(3)	(4)	(5)
Month (*t*)	Labor Hours (*x*)	Production Costs (*y*)	*xy*	*x²*
1	2	7	14	4
2	1	5	5	1
3	3	10	30	9
4	4	12	48	16
5	2	8	16	4
6	3	11	33	9
7	5	13	65	25
8	6	15	90	36
9	2	9	18	4
10	4	10	40	16
11	5	11	55	25
12	3	9	27	9
n = 12	x = 40	y = 120	xy = 441	x² = 158

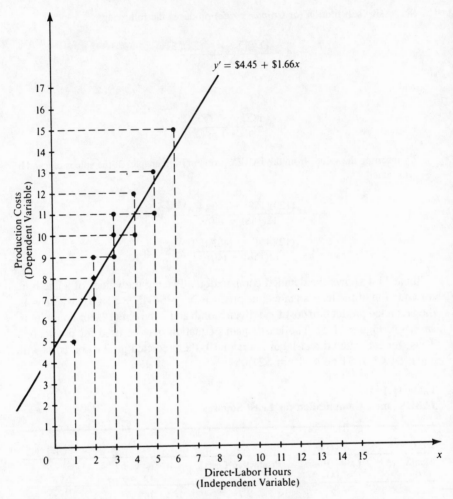

Figure 11.1
JABEX, Inc.: The Least Squares Regression Line

6. In matrix form, the system of equations becomes

$$\begin{bmatrix} n & \Sigma x \\ \Sigma x & \Sigma x^2 \end{bmatrix} \begin{bmatrix} a \\ b \end{bmatrix} = \begin{bmatrix} \Sigma Y \\ \Sigma xY \end{bmatrix}$$

or

$$(X'X)B = [X'Y]$$
$$(X'X)^{-1}(X'X)B = (X'X)^{-1}(X'Y)$$
$$B = (X'X)^{-1}(X'Y).$$

By inserting the values from the JABEX example, we obtain:

$$
\overset{X^1}{\begin{bmatrix} 1 & 1 & \ldots & 1 & 1 \\ 2 & 1 & \ldots & 5 & 3 \end{bmatrix}}
\quad
\overset{X}{\begin{bmatrix} 1 & 2 \\ 1 & 1 \\ \cdot & \cdot \\ \cdot & \cdot \\ \cdot & \cdot \\ 1 & 5 \\ 1 & 3 \end{bmatrix}}
=
\overset{X^1X}{\begin{bmatrix} 12 & 40 \\ 40 & 158 \end{bmatrix}}.
$$

$$
\overset{X'}{\begin{bmatrix} 1 & 1 & \ldots & 1 & 1 \\ 2 & 1 & \ldots & 5 & 3 \end{bmatrix}}
\quad
\overset{Y}{\begin{bmatrix} 7 \\ 5 \\ \cdot \\ \cdot \\ \cdot \\ 11 \\ 9 \end{bmatrix}}
=
\overset{X\,Y}{\begin{bmatrix} 120 \\ 441 \end{bmatrix}}.
$$

$$
B = (X^1X)^{-1}(X'Y)
$$

$$
= \begin{bmatrix} 12 & 40 \\ 40 & 158 \end{bmatrix}^{-1} \begin{bmatrix} 120 \\ 441 \end{bmatrix} = \begin{bmatrix} 0.53378 & -0.13513 \\ -0.13513 & 0.04054 \end{bmatrix} \begin{bmatrix} 120 \\ 441 \end{bmatrix}
$$

$$
= \begin{bmatrix} 4.45 \\ 1.66 \end{bmatrix}.
$$

11.1.2 Assumptions in Regression Analysis

Although apparently mechanical and objective, the regression method is reliable only when the assumptions of regression are met. The assumptions on the disturbance term or deviation in a regression model are as follows:

1.
$$E(\mu_i) = 0, \; i = 1, 2, \ldots, N$$

specifies that the expected value of μ_i is zero for any value of the dependent variable x_i.

2.
$$E(\mu_i\mu_j) = 0, \; i \neq j$$

means that no two μs are correlated. The distribution is referred to as *free from serial correlation*.

3.
$$E(\mu_i\mu_i) = 6_\mu^2, \; i = j$$

means that the standard deviation and variance of the μs are constant. This constancy of variance is known as the *homoscedasticity* assumption.

4.
$$E(x_i\mu_j) = 0$$

specifies that x_i is independent of μ_i. It specifically implies that the direction of dependence is from x to y, and no feedback effect from y to x exists.

5. $\mu_i \approx N(0,6^2)$

specifies that μ_i is normally distributed and hence permits statistical testing and inferences.

Specification analysis, the process of insuring that these assumptions are met, is essential before valid inferences can be made from sample data about population relationships. If any of these conditions are not met, the results of regression analysis are inappropriate for cost estimation and prediction. When these assumptions are satisfied, the regression coefficients obtained through the examined sample of observations are the best available estimate of the population parameters.

11.1.3 Descriptive Statistics in Regression Analysis

The preceding sections demonstrated how the least squares regression method can be used to compute the relationship between a dependent and an independent variable. For the JABEX, Inc., example presented in Figure 11.1, the regression summarized the relationship as $y = \$4.45 + 1.66 + \mu$. When the assumptions of regression analysis are met, the next steps determine (1) the degree of association between the variables and (2) the reliability of the estimates provided by the least squares equation.

Coefficient of Determination (R²)

The values on the equation line (y') differ from the actual values (y). These variations depend partially on chance and partially on the relationship between x and y. The coefficient of determination (R^2) measures the degree of association between the variables, or *goodness of fit*. Operationally, it measures closeness as the percentage of total variation in the dependent variable explained by the regression line. Figure 11.2 illustrates the explained and unexplained variations for a given observation. The explained variation is the difference between the mean ($\bar{y}$) and the value on the line (y'). The unexplained variation is the difference between the actual value (y) and the value on the line (y'). In other words, ($y' - \bar{y}$) is explained by x, while ($y - y'$) is unexplained by x.

The formal definition of R^2 is the following:[1]

$$R^2 = 1 - \frac{\text{Unexplained variation}}{\text{Total variation}}$$

$$= 1 - \frac{\Sigma(y - y')^2}{\Sigma(y - \bar{y})^2}$$

The range of R^2 is $0 \leq R^2 \leq 1$.

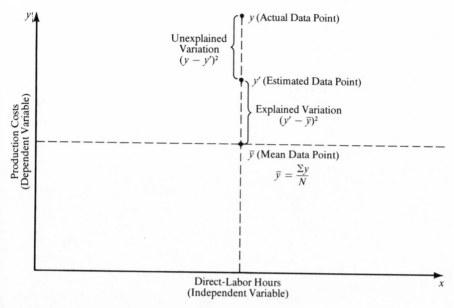

Figure 11.2
Variations around the Mean ȳ

Table 11.2 presents a worksheet for the computation of the coefficient of determination for the JABEX, Inc., problem. Direct-labor hours explained about 85.18 percent of the change in total production costs, leaving 14.82 percent unexplained.

Relying exclusively on R^2 and goodness of fit can lead to inclusion of a variable that has no *economic plausibility*. In other words, the regression equation should make sense as a *plausible* model of the relationship between cost and the independent variable. *Data mining*, that is to say, the sole reliance on R^2 as a criterion for the choice of the independent variable, is dangerous if that choice does not make economic sense.

Standard Error of Estimate

How accurate is the least squares line for prediction? This question arises because the least squares line is based on a sample of observations rather than the total population of observations. In other words, using the JABEX, Inc., problem, $4.45, $1.66, and y = $4.45 + $1.66x are only estimates of the true values of the total fixed cost, unit variable cost, and total cost, respectively. The accuracy of each of these estimates must be determined.

The standard error of estimate (S_e) measures the accuracy of the regression line. It indicates the size of the forecasting errors which may result from the use

Table 11.2
JABEX, Inc.: Correlation Analysis

(1)	(2)	(3)	(4)	(5)	(6)
Month (t)	Labor Hours (x)	Production Costs (y)	y'	$(y - y')^2$	$(y - \bar{y})^2$
1	2	7	7.77	0.5929	9
2	1	5	6.11	1.2321	25
3	3	10	9.43	0.3249	0
4	4	12	11.09	0.8281	4
5	2	8	7.77	0.0529	4
6	3	11	9.43	2.4649	1
7	5	13	12.75	0.0625	9
8	6	15	14.41	0.3481	25
9	2	9	7.77	1.5129	1
10	4	10	11.09	1.1881	0
11	5	11	12.75	3.0625	1
12	3	9	9.43	0.1849	1

$n = 12 \qquad \Sigma x = 40 \qquad \Sigma y = 120 \qquad\qquad \Sigma(y - y')^2 = 11.854 \qquad \Sigma(y - \bar{y})^2 = 80$

$$R^2 = 1 - \frac{11.854}{80} = 0.8518$$

of a given regression equation and measures the scatter of the actual observations (y values) about the values on the y′ line. The S_e is computed as follows:

$$S_e = \sqrt{\frac{\text{Unexplained variation}}{n - 2}}$$

$$= \sqrt{\frac{\Sigma(y - y')^2}{n - 2}},$$

where n is the size of the sample. The n − 2 represents the degrees of freedom around the regression line because, based on the sample of observations, the values of two regression coefficients, a and b, were estimated.

If all the assumptions of regression analysis are met, the following confidence in the predictions can be stated:

$y'_i \pm 1S_e$ has a 68 percent chance of including the actual value.

$y'_i \pm 2S_e$ has a 95 percent chance of including the actual value.

$y'_i \pm 3S_e$ has a 99.7 percent chance of including the actual value.

Thus, for the JABEX, Inc., problem, the standard error of estimate is computed as

$$S_e = \sqrt{\frac{\Sigma(y - y')^2}{n - 2}} = \sqrt{\frac{11.852}{12 - 2}} = 1.08.$$

Similarly, for seven direct-labor hours, the total cost and confidence intervals will be as follows:

$$y' = \$4.45 + \$1.66(7) = 16.07,$$

and

1. $16.07 \pm 1 \times 1.08$ ($\$17.15 \geq y' \geq \$14.99$) has a 68 percent chance of including the actual value.
2. $16.07 \pm 2 \times 1.08$ ($\$18.23 \geq y' \geq \$13.91$) has a 95 percent chance of including the actual value.
3. $16.07 \pm 3 \times 1.08$ ($\$19.31 \geq y' \geq \$12.83$) has a 99.7 percent chance of including the actual value.

Sampling Errors and Regression Coefficients

As stated earlier, the regression line y is based on a sample of observations rather than the total population. How well does each of the coefficients a and b explain the relationships between x and y? If there were no relationship, b would equal zero. The problem, then, becomes to test the null hypothesis that $b = 0$ and the alternate hypothesis that $b \neq 0$.[2]

To test these hypotheses, compute the standard error of the b regression coefficient as follows:

$$S_b = \frac{S_e}{\sqrt{\Sigma x^2 - \bar{x}\,\Sigma x}}$$

or

$$S_b = \frac{S_e}{\sqrt{\Sigma(x - \bar{x})^2}}.$$

S_b is a measure of the sampling error of the regression coefficient. In our example, the standard error of b is

$$S_b = \frac{1.08}{\sqrt{24.67}} = 0.217.$$

Accordingly, to test the hypothesis that b = 0, a t value is computed as follows:

$$t_b = \frac{b - 0}{S_b} = \frac{\$1.66 - 0}{0.217} = 7.649.$$

The table value of t for df (12 − 2) at the 95 percent confidence level is 2.228. The statistical evidence indicates that it is safe to reject the null hypothesis at the 95 percent confidence level for b. For the 10 degrees of freedom, the confidence interval equals b ± $t_{0.025}$ S_b = 1.66 ± 2.228(0.217) = 1.66 ± 0.483.

Similarly, the t value for a may be computed as follows:

$$S_a = S_e \sqrt{\frac{1}{n} + \frac{\bar{x}^2}{\Sigma(x - \bar{x})^2}}.$$

$$S_a = 1.08 \sqrt{\frac{1}{12} + \frac{10.98}{24.48}} = 0.77.$$

$$t_a = \frac{4.45 - 0}{0.77} = 5.7.$$

The statistical evidence again indicates that it is safe to reject the null hypothesis a = 0 at the 95 percent confidence level. For 10 degrees of freedom, the confidence interval is computed as follows: a ± $t_{0.025}$ S_a = 4.45 ± 2.228 (0.77) = 4.45 ± 1.715.

11.2 MULTIPLE REGRESSION COST ESTIMATION MODEL

Cost estimation is a determinant step in the budgeting process. The cost object as a dependent variable is subject to the influence of independent variables, and multiple regression techniques enable the cost accountant to estimate these relationships. Although very helpful to estimation and prediction of cost, the techniques can lead to useless results if the assumptions are not satisfied and the limitations not recognized.

11.2.1 Description of a General Regression Cost Estimation Model

Multiple regression analysis as a technique enables the cost accountant to estimate the amount by which various cost-causing factors affect costs. For example, the cost C_j for Branch j during a given accounting period may be described as

$$C_j = b_1 + b_2x_{2j} + b_3x_{3j} + \ldots + b_mx_{mj} + \mu_j \text{ for } j = 1, 2, \ldots, n.$$

The operating cost C_j is assumed to be a linear function of $m - 1$ variables (causal variables) x_{ij} plus a disturbance term μ_j arising from unexplainable variations in the model. Such a disturbance term may be explained by the regression model's failing to include all the explanatory variables affecting the costs. It also could be the result of measurement errors in the causal variables of the model.

The terms b_1, b_2, ..., b_m represent the *net regression coefficients*. Each measures the changes in C_j per unit change in each explanatory variable while holding all the others constant. As an example, suppose that a given firm manufactures a widget and several other products, using the services of different departments.[3] In one department, two products are produced: Gammas and Alphas. Gammas are produced in batches, while Alphas are assembled singly. Weekly observations of cost and output are punched on cards. A graph is prepared that indicates the presence of a linear relationship. Furthermore, the cost of producing Gammas is not believed to be a function of Alpha production or other causal variables. Therefore, the following regression is computed:

$$\hat{C} = 110.3 = 8.21N - 7.83B + 12.32D + 235S + 523W - 136A$$
$$(40.8) \quad (0.53) \quad (1.69) \quad (2.10) \quad (100) \quad (204) \quad (154)$$

Where

$\hat{C}$ = expected cost

N = number of Gammas

B = average number of Gammas in a batch

D = number of Alphas

S = summer dummy variable, where S = 1 for summer, 0 for other seasons

W = winter dummy variable, where W = 1 for winter, 0 for other seasons

A = autumn dummy variable, where A = 1 for autumn, 0 for other seasons

R^2 = 0.892 (the coefficient of multiple determination)

Number of observations = 156

Standard error of estimate = 420.83, which is 5 percent of the dependent variable cost.

The numbers in parentheses beneath the coefficients are the standard errors of the coefficients. For example, 0.53 is the sampling error associated with the estimate 8.21, or the standard error of the coefficient 8.21. This standard error of the coefficient, 0.53, allows assessment of a probability of 0.67 that the "true" marginal cost is between 7.68 and 8.74 (8.21 ± 0.53) and a probability of 0.95 that it is between 7.15 and 9.27 (8.21 ± 1.06).[4]

The predictive ability of the explanatory variable can be ascertained by computing t. In this case, the t value of N is $8.21 \div 0.53 = 15.49$. Such a high value of t demonstrates the importance of the variable N.

The regression can be used in forecasting. For example, suppose the following were production levels for a given week: N = 532, B = 20, D = 321, and S = summer = 1. If this week were representative of past experience, total costs would be $110.3 + 8.21(532) - 7.83(20) + 12.32(321) + 235(1) = 8,511.14$.

The forecast amount does not necessarily equal the actual amount. However, we can compute the probability that actual cost is within some range around the expected cost. Given an adjusted standard error of estimate equal to 592.61, we can assess a probability of 0.67 that the actual costs incurred will be between 7,918.53 and 9,103.75 ($8,511.14 \pm 592.61$); a probability of 0.95 that they will be between 9,696.36 and 7,325.92 ($8,511.14 \pm 2 \times 592.61$); and a probability of 0.99 that they will be between 10,288.97 and 6,733.31 ($8,511.14 \pm 3 \times 592.61$).

11.2.2 Determination of the Model Parameters

The regression equation for the cost of Branch j with m independent variables can be expressed as follows: $y_j = a + b_1x_{1j} + b_2x_{2j} + ... + b_{mj}x_{mj} + e_j$, where y is the variable to be predicted; $x_{1j}, x_{2j}, ..., x_{mj}$ are the independent variables on which the prediction is to be based; $a, b_1, b_2, ..., b_m$ are unknown regression coefficients of the explanatory variables; and e_j is the disturbance term including the effects of all other variables.

Using matrix notation, the cost estimation model may be stated as follows: $y = X B + C$, where for n branches and m variables we have:

$$
\begin{bmatrix} Y_1 \\ Y_2 \\ Y_3 \\ \cdot \\ \cdot \\ \cdot \\ Y_n \end{bmatrix}
=
\begin{bmatrix}
1 & X_{11} & X_{12} & \cdots & X_{1m} \\
1 & X_{21} & X_{22} & \cdots & X_{2m} \\
1 & X_{31} & X_{32} & \cdots & X_{3m} \\
\cdot & \cdot & \cdot & & \cdot \\
\cdot & \cdot & \cdot & & \cdot \\
\cdot & \cdot & \cdot & & \cdot \\
1 & X_{n1} & X_{n2} & & X_{nm}
\end{bmatrix}
\begin{bmatrix} a \\ b_1 \\ b_2 \\ b_3 \\ \cdot \\ \cdot \\ b_m \end{bmatrix}
+
\begin{bmatrix} e_1 \\ e_2 \\ e_3 \\ \cdot \\ \cdot \\ e_m \end{bmatrix}
$$

$y = a (n \times 1)$, vector of observations on the dependent variables.

$X = a (n \times m + 1)$, matrix of observations on the independent variables.

$B = a (k + 1 \times 1)$, vector of the regression coefficients.

$e = a (n \times 1)$, vector of the error terms.

The regression coefficients in B are not known and must be estimated using reported branch data for the accounting period to arrive at least squares estimates b_i for $i = 1, 2, ..., n$. The least squares estimates are given by the following:

$$B = \begin{bmatrix} a \\ b_1 \\ b_2 \\ \cdot \\ \cdot \\ \cdot \\ b_n \end{bmatrix} = (X'X)^{-1} X'Y.$$

Computer programs could provide these estimates with high speed and accuracy.

Once the regression line is found, determine how well it estimates y given some value of x. The relevant statistics presented for the simple regression analysis are computed in the multiple regression analysis as follows:

1. The standard error of the estimate can still be found as

$$S_e = \sqrt{\frac{\Sigma(y - y')^2}{n - m - 1}}.$$

2. The standard error of the b_j regression coefficients may be expressed as

$$S_{bj} = S_e \sqrt{S_{jj}},$$

where S_{jj} is the jth diagonal element of the $(X'X)^{-1}$ matrix. Accordingly, the t test used to determine if the b_j value is significantly different from zero is $t = b_j/S_{bj}$, which has a t distribution with $n - m - 1$ degrees of freedom. The confidence interval equals

$$b_j \pm t_{(1-\alpha)/2} \, S_{bj}.$$

3. Just as the t ratio is used to test the null hypothesis $b_j = 0$, the F ratio allows the cost analyst to test for the simultaneous effects of all the independent variables by computing the ratio of the mean squares of the sum of squares regression (SSR) and the sum of squares error (SSE):

$$F = \frac{\dfrac{SSR}{m}}{\dfrac{SSE}{n - m - 1}} = \frac{\dfrac{\Sigma(Y' - \bar{Y})^2}{m}}{\dfrac{\Sigma(Y - Y')^2}{n - m - 1}},$$

which has an F distribution with m and $n - m - 1$ degrees of freedom. If the F ratio is greater than the F statistic (obtainable from an F table), the null hypothesis that the regression coefficients of the cost model taken into combination are equal to zero can be rejected.[5]

11.3 DATA PROBLEMS IN REGRESSION ANALYSIS

Certain data requirements must be met to insure the usefulness of the regression analysis. If the data originate in the cost accounting recording system, the user should be aware of all possible data problems.

11.3.1 Data Characteristics

To be useful, the data on both the dependent and the independent variables should represent the same periods, which in turn should meet the following general criteria:

1. The periods should be long enough to allow a proper matching of the output produced in a period with its related production costs. Any lag in reporting either costs or production must be corrected. The periods also should be small enough to catch wide variation in the production during the period, which may obscure the true relationship between the cost and the independent variables.

2. There should be a sufficient number of time periods. In general, the number of observations should exceed the number of coefficients in the regression by one. In other words, the number of degrees of freedom equals the number of observations minus the number of coefficients in the regression being estimated. Naturally, many more observations are needed to assess the significance of the "true" relationship between the cost and cost-related factors.

3. The periods should represent the widest possible range of variability. A greater variation from period to period in the dependent and independent variables will insure a better estimation of the "true" relationship.

4. All cost-related factors should be specified and included in the analysis. For example, changes in the price of the input factors require adjustment of the data to account for the specific price changes. Similarly, changes in technology and capacity, seasonal differences, and other change factors must be accounted for by the inclusion or exclusion of variables in the regression model.

All these requirements emphasize the necessity of properly defining the time periods in terms of their length and number and the range of observations. As a rule of thumb, time periods of no longer than one month and no shorter than one week allow effective analysis of the relationship between cost and the independent variables.

11.3.2 Data Forms

The data used in every previous example are known as *time series data* since they have been generated for a single costing unit at different points in time. When analysts seek knowledge of the cost behavior patterns of other costing units, they use cross-sectional data generated from several similar but different costing units at different points in time. Regression analysis techniques and interpretations are similar for both time series data and cross-sectional data. However, certain requirements must be kept in mind:

1. The costing units should be homogeneous enough to allow pooling of the data, which implies that technological and even behavioral factors be sufficiently similar.
2. When the costing units are observed at a single point in time (which may often be the case), behavior is more random than when the costing units are observed over time. As a result, independent and dependent variables have more systematic movements in time series data, leading to a higher coefficient of determination (R^2).
3. The assumption of the homogeneity of variances is violated more often in cross-sectional data than in time series data.

11.3.3 Measurement Errors

The dependent and independent variables are subject to measurement errors, and they must be measured accurately. The impact of these errors on the usefulness of regression analysis varies. If an inaccurate measurement of the dependent variable, cost, includes an error (∂), then the cost equation will be as follows:

$$C + \partial = b_0 + b_1 x_1 + \mu$$

or

$$C = b_0 + b_1 x_1 + \mu - \partial.$$

As we see from the equation, only the disturbance term and the predictive ability of the cost equation are affected—the estimate of the regression coefficient is not.

If, instead, any independent variable (x) is inaccurately measured and includes an error (ϕ), then the cost equation will be as follows:

$$C = b_0 + b_1(x_1 + \phi) + \mu$$

or

$$C = b_0 + b_1 x_1 + b_1 \phi + \mu.$$

Inaccurate measurement of x affects the regression coefficient, leading to correlation between the independent variable and the residual μ, as well as an underestimation of the regression coefficient. The measurement errors may be caused by either one of the following:

1. The failure to record the production costs in the same period the output was produced. Benston gives as an example overtime pay for production workers in the week following their work.

2. Recording errors, such as recording costs in the wrong account or wrong period, failing to expense previously capitalized costs, or allocating specific cost accounts to time periods bearing no relation to production.

11.3.4 Dummy Variables

Although most independent variables included in cost models are quantitative, some qualitative variables are often used. Seasonal adjustment is a good example in the cost estimation model: Production costs hypothetically differ between the seasons. To measure the impact of qualitative variables, *dummy variables* included in the regression equations take the value of 1 for the presence of the qualitative attribute and 0 for the absence of the given attribute. For example, if a company wanted to measure the impact of the regional location of its divisions on the behavioral pattern of their production costs, the following model may be assumed:

$$C_i = b_0 + b_1 R_i(1) + b_2 R_i(2) + b_3 R_i(3) + \mu_i,$$

where

C_i = Production costs of division i.

R_i = Region of the division i
$$\begin{cases} \rule{1cm}{0.4pt}\ 1 = \text{Northeast.} \\ \rule{1cm}{0.4pt}\ 2 = \text{Midwest.} \\ \rule{1cm}{0.4pt}\ 3 = \text{West.} \\ \rule{1cm}{0.4pt}\ 4 = \text{South.} \end{cases}$$

$R_i(1)$ = 1 if the division is in region 1.
       = 0 otherwise.
$R_i(2)$ = 1 if the division is in region 2.
       = 0 otherwise.
$R_i(3)$ = 1 if the division is in region 3.
       = 0 otherwise.

From equation C_i we may derive the following statements:

$E(C_i) = b_0$ when $R_1^i(1) = R_1^i(2) = R_1^i(3) = 0$, that is, the ith division belongs to region 4.

$E(C_i) = b_0 + b_1$ when the ith division belongs to region 1.

$E(C_i) = b_0 + b_2$ when the ith division belongs to region 2.

$E(C_i) = b_0 + b_3$ when the ith division belongs to region 3.

This example serves as a warning about what is known as the *dummy variable trap*. In general, whenever dummy variables are included using the zero-one technique (binary dummy variables) and there is an intercept term in the equation, such as b_0 in this example, the number of such dummy variables should be one less than the number of different ways in which the dummy variable under consideration is expected to affect the dependent variable.

11.3.5 Lagged Factor Relation

In cost estimation we can sometimes assume that cost today depends on what happened yesterday. As an example, the production costs in a given period may be partly determined by the patterns of production in previous periods.[6] Such a model, in which the dependent variables are lagged values, is known as an *autoregressive model*. The simplest case of such a model can be expressed as follows:

$$C_t = b_0 + b_1 x_{t-1} + \mu_y, \, t = 1, 2, ..., T.$$

Such a model often violates the assumptions of regression analysis. It is likely that the residuals and the dependent variables are not independent, so special estimating techniques are required. Given the complexity of the problem, the reader should consult references on autoregressive and lag models.

11.4 REQUIREMENTS FOR THE IMPLEMENTATION OF THE REGRESSION MODEL

Because of the data problems discussed in previous sections, adjustments and preparatory steps are necessary before the accounting data can be used in a regression analysis cost estimation model. The data should be examined to detect any bias introduced by the accounting policies. To do so, some guidelines must be followed:

1. The cost data and the activity data should be of the same period.
2. The data should be properly classified by costing unit.
3. The extent to which the costs of the costing unit are the result of accounting allocations should be determined.
4. The time period under consideration should be long enough to permit collection of meaningful data but short enough to reflect different rates of activity.
5. The data should be examined to determine if they come from a stationary or homogeneous process. They should be homogeneous.
6. The independent variables should be selected on the logical basis of physical or reasonable evidence.
7. The data are plotted to determine the nature of the relationship between the cost factor and the output or decision variables presumed to be causal variables.

11.5 STATISTICAL PROBLEMS IN REGRESSION ANALYSIS

11.5.1 Heteroscedasticity

If the homoscedasticity assumption of constant variance of the disturbance term is violated, the test of significance for the efficiency of the estimating coefficients is not appropriate. In this condition, referred to as heteroscedasticity, the disturbance variance increases with the square of one of the explanatory variables; that is, $E(\mu_j) = 6^2 f_{ij}$.

The practical significance of heteroscedasticity derives from its tendency to inflate the sampling errors of the least squares estimators of b_{1j}, b_{2j}, ..., b_{mj}, μ_j. Traditional tests of hypotheses concerning these estimators can no longer be made, since their sampling variances are biased.

Testing for heteroscedasticity is essential to the successful application of the regression analysis cost estimation mode. Different tests have been advocated in the literature.[7]

11.5.2 Multicollinearity

Multicollinearity exists when the independent variables in a regression coefficient are highly correlated with one another. The computed coefficients of the independent variables are entangled and have very large standard errors. In cost estimation models, multicollinearity exists in varying degrees. As a rule of thumb, Lawrence R. Klein suggests that multicollinearity is severe if $r_{ij} > R_y$, where r_{ij} = zero-order correlation between the two independent variables x_j and x_j ($i \neq j$), and R_y = multiple correlation coefficient between the dependent variable (y) and all the independent variables (x).[8]

To understand the multicollinearity problem, consider the hypothetical observations in Table 11.3 on the number of direct-labor hours worked on refrigerators, freezers, and washing machines. The production times, in terms of direct-labor hours for each week, reflect a construct ratio of 3:1:2. In this extreme case, an increase in the size of the standard errors of the estimated coefficients

Table 11.3
Direct-Labor Hours Worked on Refrigerators, Freezers, and Washing Machines during a Five-Week Period

Week	Refrigerator	Freezer	Washing Machine
1	6	2	4
2	12	4	8
3	15	5	10
4	9	3	6
5	6	2	4

makes it more likely that the correlated independent variables will be found to be not significantly different from zero.

One test for multicollinearity is based on the correlation coefficients between the dependent variables. For example, consider the following fictional results:

	Production Costs	Direct-Labor Hours	Number of Units Produced
Production Costs	1,000	0.8636	0.8540
Direct-Labor Hours	0.8636	1,000	0.9050
Number of Units Produced	0.8540	0.9050	1.000

Assuming the correlation coefficients have a bivariate normal distribution with $n - m - 1$ degrees of freedom, the t statistic is as follows:

$$t = \frac{R}{\sqrt{\dfrac{1 - R^2}{n - 2 - 1}}}.$$

The multicollinearity between the direct-labor hours and machine hours may be tested on the basis of the following computed t value (assuming $n = 10$):

$$t = \frac{0.9050}{\sqrt{\dfrac{1 - 0.9050^2}{10 - 2 - 1}}} = 5.63.$$

The confidence interval at the 95 percent level of significance for a two-tail test and 10 degrees of freedom is

$$P(5.63 - 2.228 < t < 5.63 + 2.228) = 0.95.$$

$$P(3.40 < t < 7.86) = 0.95.$$

Therefore, the t coefficient of 5.63 is significant; it indicates the existence of multicollinearity between direct-labor hours and the number of units produced. Different methods been proposed to eliminate multicollinearity:

1. When multicollinearity is suspected, omit one of the highly correlated variables from the regression.

2. George J. Benston suggests that one construct an index of output in which the different types of output are weighted by a factor (such as labor hours) that serves to describe their relationship to cost.[9] For example, our firm produced 300 refrigerators, 100 freezers, and 200 washers. The 600 units produced are equivalent to 100 units of the product mix 3:1:2, that is, a "bundle" of output in a mix of 3:1:2.

3. Benston also suggests that one first allocate cost to cost centers where a single output is produced, and second compute a regression for each cost center.[10]

4. Collect new information: The variables may be multicollinear in one sample but not in another.

5. Transform the observed time series data to first differences.

11.5.3 Serial Correlation

Serial correlation, or autocorrelation, refers to the correlation of successive residual terms. The correlation is positive or negative, depending on whether the residual terms are positively or negatively correlated. Autocorrelation causes an underestimation of the standard error of the regression coefficient, which influences the accuracy of the outcome of the hypothesis-testing procedure.

In general, autocorrelation is tested by the *Durbin-Watson statistic* (d), which has the following formulation:

$$d = \sum_{i=1}^{n} (\mu_t - \mu_{t-1})^2 \Big/ \sum_{i=1}^{n} \mu_t^2,$$

where μ_t = residual term = $y_t' - y_t$, for t = 1, 2, 3, ..., n.

A Durbin-Watson table is used. If correlation is a problem, then $M_t = \rho M_{t-1}$ = error when $|\rho| < 1$. The null hypothesis is $H_0:\rho = 0$ against the alternate hypothesis $H_1:\rho > 0$. The Durbin-Watson table is used as follows: If $d < d_L$, reject H_0; if $4 - d < d_L$, reject H_0; and if $d_u < d < 4 - d_u$, accept H_0.

As an example, assume that n = 15, k = 2 (number of independent variables), and that the Durbin-Watson statistic is 1.85. The d_L and d_u values are, respectively, $1.85 < 0.83$, $4 - 1.85 < 0.83$, and $1.40 < 1.85 < 4 - 1.40$. Consequently, the d statistic is not significant, and there is no serial correlation.

Different solutions have been proposed for the problem of serial correlation. It may be resolved by the addition of a dummy variable. Another possible solution is the "first difference method," in which the changes in the dependent variables are regressed against the changes in the independent variables. Other methods—the Cochrane-Orcutt method, the generalized least squares method, and the Durbin method—may be found in any standard econometric textbook.[11]

11.6 CONCLUSION

This chapter elaborated on the use of simple and multiple regression analyses in cost estimations. Assuming that economic plausibility is verified, the relationship between the dependent variable of cost and one or more independent variables can be determined and its statistical significance ascertained.

Be attentive to the potential technical and data requirements and limitations of each method of analysis: Check the data and statistical properties before you draw inferences from the cost estimation model. You should fully understand two requirements:

1. Properly defined structural relationships between costs and the chosen independent variable guarantee economic plausibility.

2. Properly defined data should precede the use of the many available computer programs on estimation.

NOTES

1. R^2 can be derived as follows:

   a. The total variation relationship can be expressed as $y - \bar{y} = (y - y') + (y' - \bar{y})$. Total variation = unexplained variation + explained variation.

   b. The goodness of fit relationship for all observations can be expressed as follows:

   $$\Sigma(y - \bar{y})^2 = \Sigma(y - y')^2 + \Sigma(y' - \bar{y})^2.$$

   Total sum of squares (TSS) = sum of squares regression (SSR) + sum of squares error (SSE), or

   $$1 = \frac{\Sigma(y - y')^2}{\Sigma(y - \bar{y})} + \frac{\Sigma(y' - \bar{y})^2}{\Sigma(y - \bar{y})^2}.$$

   1 = unexplained sum of squares + explained sum of squares.

   c. R^2 can be derived as equal to the explained sum of squares, as follows:

   $$R^2 = 1 = \frac{\Sigma(y - y')^2}{\Sigma(y - \bar{y})^2} + \frac{\Sigma(y' - \bar{y})^2}{\Sigma(y - \bar{y})^2}.$$

   d. $r = \sqrt{R^2}$ is often given as the sample correlation coefficient.

2. An explanation of hypothesis testing is available in all statistics books.

3. Adapted with permission from George J. Benston, "Multiple Regression Analysis of Cost Behavior." *Accounting Review* (October 1966): 670–671.

4. The statements about probability are based on a Bayesian approach, with normality and diffuse distribution assumed.

5. The degrees of freedom are expressed by two numbers, the first equal to the number of regression coefficients in the cost model and the second equal to number of observations on the cost data (n) minus the number of regression coefficients found in the cost model.

6. In the economics "habit formation" hypothesis, the consumption of nondurable goods and services is affected by patterns of consumption in previous periods.

7. For an expanded discussion of this problem, see M. Dutta, *Econometric Methods* (Cincinnati, Ohio: South-Western Publishing, 1975), chap. 5; and S. M. Goldfield and R. E. Quandt, "Some Tests for Homoscedasticity." *Journal of the American Statistical Association* (July 1966): 539–547.

8. Lawrence R. Klein, *An Introduction to Econometrics* (Englewood Cliffs, N.J.: Prentice-Hall, 1962): 64, 101.

9. Benston, "Multiple Regression Analysis of Cost Behavior," 666–667.

10. Ibid.

11. Dutta, *Econometric Methods,* 117–126.

SELECTED READINGS

Association of American Railroads. *A Guide to Railroad Cost Analysis*. Washington, D.C.: Bureau of Railway Economics, AAR, 1964.

Benston, George J. "Economics of Scale and Marginal Costs in Banking Operations." *National Banking Review* (July 1965): 507–549.

Benston, George J. "Multiple Regression Analysis of Cost Behavior." *Accounting Review* (October 1966): 657–672.

Cerullo, Michael J. "Use a Flow Chart to Interpret Regression Analysis Computer Output." *Cost and Management* (May–June 1979): 37–41.

Chan, K. H., F. L. Sbrocchi, and N. R. VanZante. "Forecasting Methods and the Management Accountant." *Cost and Management* (January–February 1980): 40–45.

Dutta, M. *Econometric Methods*. Cincinnati, Ohio: South-Western Publishing, 1975.

Gynther, R. S. "Improving Separation of Fixed and Variable Expenses." *NAA Bulletin* (June 1963): 25–38.

Hicks, J. "The Application of Exponential Smoothing to Standard Cost Systems." *Management Accounting* (September 1980): 28–32, 53.

Jensen, Robert. "A Multiple Regression Model for Cost Control: Assumptions and Limitations." *Accounting Review* (April 1967): 265–273.

Johnson, J. *Statistical Cost Analysis*. New York: McGraw-Hill, 1960.

Knapp, Robert A. "Forecasting and Measuring with Correlation Analysis." *Financial Executive* (May 1963): 13–19.

Leininger, W. E., *Quantitative Methods in Accounting* (New York: Van Nostrand, 1980), chap. 6.

McClenon, Paul R., "Cost Finding through Multiple Correlation Analysis," *Accounting Review* (July 1963): 540–547.

Naphtali, Michael W., "Improving Cost Forecasting," *Cost and Management* (June 1974): 13–20.

National Association of Accountants, *Accounting Practice Report No. 10*, "Separating and Using Costs as Fixed and Variable" (New York: NAA, 1960), in *NAA Bulletin* (June 1960), sec. 3.

Oliver, F. R., "A Cross-section Study of Marginal Cost," *Applied Statistics* (June 1962): 65–78.

Pierce, Richard F., "The Importance of the Distinction between Fixed and Variable Costs," *NAA Bulletin* (May 1964): 19–26.

Tingey, Sherman, "Difficulties in Identifying Fixed and Variable Costs," *Budgeting* (March–April 1968): 25–28.

12

Cost Accumulation for Product Costing: Job-Order Costing

A cost accounting system includes a set of activities for product costing and a set of activities for planning and control purposes. Product costing is the accumulation of costs and the assignment of these costs to cost objects. The two major cost objects are the department and the units of products because a cost accounting system emphasizes the determination of unit costs and the control of costs. Determination of unit costs for inventory valuation is essential to profit determination, and determination of departmental costs and assignment of responsibility is essential to the control process.

In sum, the product costing part of a cost accounting system assigns costs to two major cost objects as follows: first, by accumulation of costs by responsibility centers for control purposes and, second by application of these costs to physical units that are produced in the department for product costing purposes. There are two basic approaches—the *job-order cost system* and the *process cost system*—and each has many variations. This chapter describes the difference between job-order costing and process costing and the elements and techniques of cost accumulation and recording in a job-order costing system.

12.1 TECHNIQUES OF COST RECORDING

Cost recording techniques involve accounting entries and the allocation of costs to costing objects by means of an averaging process. These two phases provide the data bank with recorded costs that can be used for both product costing and decision making.

12.1.1 General and Subsidiary Ledger Relationships

Cost accounting has two objectives: inventory valuation and control. Therefore, the accounting system and its supporting documents consist of these components: the *general ledger* and a set of *subsidiary ledgers* and the supporting documentation (see Figure 12.1). The general ledger is a summary device that

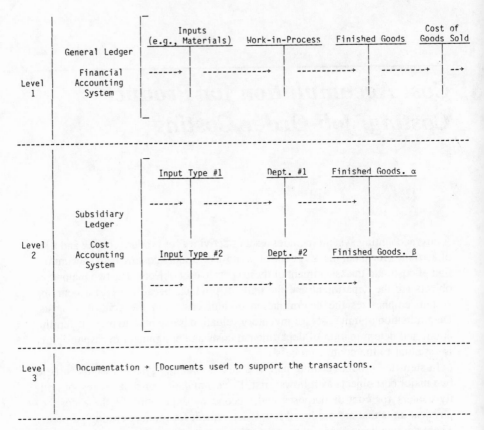

Figure 12.1
Total Accounting System

portrays the general accounting relationship of the cost accounting cycle in a system of financial accounts. Its ultimate output is inventory valuation and profit determination. Using double-entry bookkeeping, total costs are recorded first to show the transfer of inputs to a Work-in-Process Inventory account (sometimes referred to as Work-in-Process or W-I-P), and second to portray the transfer of finished goods to a Finished Goods account. These total entries are supported by detailed entries in the subsidiary ledger. Thus, the general ledger, a part of the financial accounting system, is composed of a set of accounts to summarize the detailed operations of the costing system. Postings to it are made from subsidiary ledger totals.

In general, the control accounts in the general ledger and their corresponding subsidiary ledgers of records are as follows:

1. The *Materials account* controls the *materials cards* in a perpetual inventory system.

2. The *Factory Overhead account* controls the *expense ledger* or *departmental expense analysis sheet*, also called the departmental overhead cost sheet.

3. The *Work-in-Process account* controls the *job-order cost sheet* in a job-order costing system and the *production reports* in a process costing system.

4. The *Finished Goods account* controls the *finished goods ledger cards*.

Although conceptually subordinate to the financial accounting system, the cost accounting system is more flexible in the sense that it can be adapted to produce information useful for decision making. Using the cost accounting system, it is always possible to record additional cost accounting information outside the constraints of double-entry bookkeeping, for example, to record memorandum data on opportunity costs. The control account–subsidiary ledger combination can be used to gather information on every possible segment of the firm.

The documentation comprises the third part of the cost recording system. It consists of a series of source documents used to justify the incurrence and the accuracy of the general ledger and the corresponding subsidiary ledger entries. The documents include the following:

1. The *approved invoice* as a source document for the purchase of raw materials or supplies

2. The *material requisition cards* as a source document for the issuance of direct and indirect materials for use in the production process

3. The *time tickets* and the *labor cost summary* (also called *labor cost distribution summary* or *payroll recapitulation*) as source documents for the distribution of labor costs

4. The *clock cards* and *individual withholding* from *payroll sheets* (or payroll register) as source documents for the payment of salaries

5. The *memorandum for the office*, the *approve invoices*, the *accrual memorandum*, *depreciation schedule*, *insurance register*, or *memorandum from insurance officers* as source documents for the incurrence of actual factory overhead

6. The *schedule portraying the determination of the predetermined overhead rate* as a source document for the application of factory overhead

7. The *production report* as a source document for the completion of jobs

8. The *sales invoice* as a source document for the revenue realized from the sales of jobs

9. The *sales invoice* and the *finished goods card* as source documents for the costs of goods sold.

All these source documents may exist only in the form of computer records and are entered via terminals. The principles remain the same. The flow of the *main* documents in a job-order costing system is shown in Figure 12.2.

12.1.2 Averaging Process

The association of costs with products depends on the degree of traceability to the product and the nature of the production center. The product costs are either direct or indirect in terms of their ease of traceability with regard to the product.

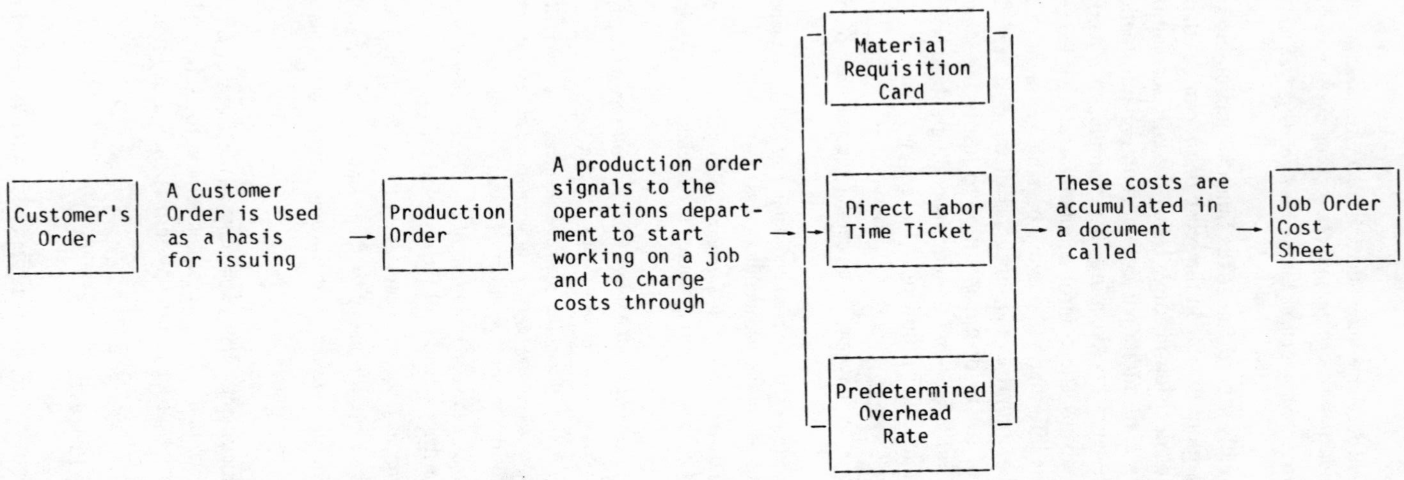
Customer's Order
A Customer Order is Used as a basis for issuing
Production Order
A production order signals to the operations department to start working on a job and to charge costs through
Material Requisition Card
Direct Labor Time Ticket
Predetermined Overhead Rate
These costs are accumulated in a document called
Job Order Cost Sheet

Figure 12.2
Flow of Main Documents in a Job-Order Costing System

The production center produces as output either *homogeneous* units (not distinguishable from one another during a production process) or *heterogeneous* units (identifiable as individual units or lots).

The direct costs in either homogeneous or heterogeneous cost accounting situations can be traced easily to the appropriate product accounts. However, a few calculations may be necessary in the allocation of the indirect costs.

First, with a homogeneous output, the indirect costs can be assigned directly to the appropriate product by an averaging process used on the physical output of the producing department. Hence if a producing department incurred a total indirect cost of $50,000 for a production volume of 5,000 widgets, the average indirect cost per widget is simply $50,000/5,000 = $10. Second, with a heterogeneous output, the indirect costs can be assigned to each appropriate product only by an averaging process applied to some identifiable and common basis of allocation, usually the direct-labor hours used by each product.

12.2 DIFFERENCES BETWEEN JOB-ORDER AND PROCESS COSTING

The two main product costing methods are *job-order costing* and *process costing*. Both can be used with an actual- or standard-cost system.

Job-order costing has been appropriately defined as a method of cost accounting whereby costs are accumulated for a specific quantity of products, equipment, repairs, or other services that move through the production processes as a continuously identifiable unit. It is used by companies with heterogeneous products or where an order is produced to a customer's specifications (batch production). Whether the batch production is in the form of individual units or lots, it is characterized by the need to accumulate costs by job. Accordingly, job-order cost accounting can be defined as the system of cost accumulation by individual jobs. The method applies to such diverse industries as the construction, printing, aircraft, furniture, shipbuilding, foundry, and machine tool industries.

Process costing is used by companies with products manufactured in a relatively continuous operation or with homogeneous products. This method can be applied in such diverse industries as the textile, oil, brewery, food processing, paint, carpeting, paper, and many other industries. It is appropriate where there is mass production of standardized units requiring a continuous, uniform set of production processes or operations. Costs are accumulated by cost centers or processes periodically, rather than by jobs. Accordingly, process cost accounting can be defined as a system of cost accumulation for products undergoing a continuous production process.

The difference between the job-order and process costing methods centers on the nature of the demand, the product, and the production process. Process costing involves situations where (1) production is initiated by future market demand rather than a specific customer order; (2) the individual units are homogeneous, like units requiring the same input, technology, and effort; and (3) the production process can be characterized by mass production with task specialization under standard operating procedures.

12.3 JOB-ORDER COSTING

12.3.1 Job-Order Procedures

In job-order costing, each job is an object of costing in the sense that it is assigned materials, labor, and overhead. The cost information on each job is recorded in the appropriate column of a *job-order cost sheet* (also called job-order or job-cost record), the basic document for the accumulation of product costs which the cost accounting department sets up for each job. The totals in the file of cost sheets are periodically posted to the Work-in-Process account; the cost sheets are subsidiary records to the Work-in-Process account.

In the discussion that follows, assume that the ABEL Manufacturing Company uses a job-order costing system. Its main products are custom-made chairs and desks. To clarify the explanation, cost accounting procedures have been divided into accounting for materials, accounting for labor, accounting for overhead, and accounting for jobs completed and cost of goods sold. Each phase will be discussed in terms of the general ledger entries, the subsidiary ledger entries, and the nature of the supporting source documents. Assume that the ABEL Manufacturing Company accepts two orders to manufacture a custom-made chair and desk during January. It assigns job numbers 1 and 2 to these orders. The following transactions took place during January:

1. Materials are purchased as follows:

	Type A	Type B	Supplies	Total
Materials	$1,000	$1,000	$1,000	$3,000

2. Materials are issued to the factory as follows:

	Factory Overhead	Job 1	Job 2	Total
Materials, Type A		$500	$400	$ 900
Materials, Type B		200	400	600
Supplies	$300			300
	$300	$700	$800	$1,800

3. Labor costs are incurred as follows:

	Factory Overhead	Job 1	Job 2	Total
Direct Labor		$300	$300	$600
Indirect Labor	$200			200
Total	$200	$300	$300	$800
Labor Hours		25	25	

4. Other costs are incurred as follows:

Depreciation of Equipment	$ 50
Light, Heat, and Power	100
Miscellaneous	110
Total	$260

An *absorption costing system* will be used which means that the product cost will include direct materials, direct labor, variable factory overhead, and fixed factory overhead. It is so named because it provides for the absorption of all costs. It is also called the full cost approach.

12.3.2 Accounting for Materials

Accounting for materials in a job-order costing system involves three main transactions: the purchase of materials and supplies, the issuance of direct materials for production use, and the issuance of supplies (indirect materials) for production use.

All entries start when, upon receipt of a *customer's order,* the sales department notifies the production department of all necessary production details. These data are then used by the production department to prepare a *production order* authorizing the manufacturing process. At the same time, the cost accounting department sets up the appropriate number of *job cost sheets* (in this case, job cost sheets 1 and 2). The production order, including detailed requirements for production, is used to prepare a schedule of the required materials in a document called a *bill of materials.* A copy of the bill of materials is forwarded to the storekeeper to verify the availability of an adequate amount of materials on hand for completing the order. At this stage, procedures are implemented for the purchase of raw materials and supplies. These procedures originated when, through a *purchase requisition,* a warehouse clerk or a material ledger clerk notified the purchasing agent of the need for a particular material. On the basis of the purchase requisition, the purchasing agent issued a *purchase order* to a supplier. Upon receipt of the materials, the receiving department issued a *receiving report.* Finally, upon receipt of copies of the receiving report, the purchase order, and the *approved vendor's invoice,* the accounting department originated the following entries:

1. General Ledger
   Materials Inventory Control $3,000
       Accounts Payable $3,000
   To record the purchase of raw materials (types A and B and supplies).
2. Subsidiary Ledger
   Materials Card A (Received Column) $1,000
   Materials Card B (Received Column) 1,000
   Supplies Card (Received Column) 1,000

Each individual materials card shows at least the quantity on hand and the cost of the materials.

The purpose of this double-counting procedure at the accounting department is to insure maximum control and to meet the two cost objectives, namely, the control objective and the product costing objective. The balance of the Materials Inventory account and the total of the materials card (in a materials ledger or stores ledger) are compared periodically to identify any discrepancies.

The issuance of materials originates when, through a *materials requisition card*, a production clerk notifies the storekeeper to deliver materials to a given department. Upon receipt of a sufficient number of materials requisitions, the accounting department originates the following entries:

1. General Ledger
   Work-in-Process Inventory Control $1,500
   Materials Inventory Control   1,500
   To record the issuance of direct material.

In the cost department, the materials requisition cards bearing the job numbers are used to assign the materials to the appropriate job by entering the amount in the Materials column of the appropriate cost sheet and the Issued column of the materials card as follows:

2. Subsidiary Ledger
   Job-Order Cost Sheet 1 (Custom Chair) $700
   Job-Order Cost Sheet 2 (Custom Desk)   800
   Materials Card A (Issued Column)   900
   Materials Card B (Issued Column)   600

The issuance of supplies for departmental use involves the same entries as the issuance of materials (direct materials), except the Factory Overhead Control account is debited instead of the Work-in-Process Control account. This treatment is justified by the "indirect" nature of supplies, which cannot be traced directly to a particular job. Similarly, in the subsidiary ledger, the amount is debited to an Indirect Material column of a department overhead cost sheet. Thus, the accounting department originates the following entries:

1. General Ledger
   Factory Overhead Control $300
   Materials Inventory Control   300
   To record the issuance of indirect materials.
2. Subsidiary Ledger
   Department Overhead Cost Sheet (Indirect Material Column) $300
   Supplies Card (Issued Column)   300

12.3.3 Accounting for Labor

Accounting for labor includes at least two phases: (1) the recording and payment of labor and (2) the distribution of labor. *Time tickets, clock cards,* and a

```
                    Clarkson Manufacturing Co.
                       Grinding Department

    Employee No.          1064

    Employee  Name   Robert Davidson
```

Job	Time			
Job No. 101	0.15	0.5	1	1.15
	1.50	1.75	2	2.15
	2.50	2.75	3	3.15 .
Job No. 101	0.15	0.5	1	1.15
	1.50	1.75	2	2.15
	2.50	2.75	3	3.15
Job No. 101	0.15	0.5	1	1.15
	1.50	1.75	2	2.15
	2.50	2.75·	3	3.15
Job No. 101	0.15	0.5	1	1.15
	1.50	1.75	2	2.15
	2.50	2.75	3	3.15

```
Superintendent
Signature
```

Figure 12.3
Time Ticket

payroll register usually are used to record the number of hours and the cost of direct and indirect labor. (Figure 12.3 shows a time ticket.) Time tickets are collected daily, checked with the clock cards, and used by the payroll clerk to post to the payroll record the number of hours worked by each employee the previous day. At the end of each payroll period, the payroll department determines the net amount payable to each employee.

The information for the distribution of labor in the time tickets is first recorded in a *labor cost summary* (or labor distribution manual), which distinguishes between direct and indirect labor as well as regular time, overtime, and idle time. The labor cost summary is basically a summary of the time tickets that will be used by the cost clerk in the accounting department to originate the following entries:

1. General Ledger
   Work-in-Process Inventory Control $600
   Factory Overhead Control (Indirect Labor) 200
       Factory Payroll   800
   To record the distribution of direct and indirect labor.
2. Subsidiary Ledger
   Job-Order Cost Sheet 1 (Direct-Labor Column) $300
   Job-Order Cost Sheet 2 (Direct-Labor Column) 300
   Department Overhead Cost Sheet (Indirect-Labor Column) 200

The payment of payroll is accomplished periodically at such time as the accounting department originates the following entries

1. General Ledger
   Accrued Payroll $800
       Cash   800

12.3.4 Accounting for Manufacturing Overhead

Accounting for manufacturing overhead involves three phases: the purchase of overhead, the estimation of overhead, and the application of overhead.

Purchase of Actual Factory Overhead

Besides indirect material and indirect labor, other factory overhead expenses are incurred during the production cycle. Examples of indirect manufacturing expenses are rent, insurance, property taxes, utilities, depreciation, lubricants, and so forth. These factory expenses are recorded both on the departmental overhead cost sheet and in the Factory Department Overhead Control account in the general ledger. The accounting department originates the following entries:

1. General Ledger
   Factory Department Overhead Control $260
       Accumulated Depreciation   50
       Cash, Payables, or Prepaids   210
   To record the incurrence of factory overhead.
2. Subsidiary Ledger (Departmental Overhead Cost Sheet)
   Depreciation Column $50
   Heat, Light, and Power Column 100
   Miscellaneous Column 110

Note that a single departmental cost sheet with individual columns to record each kind of expense is used in this example. A possible alternative would be to use separate expense ledger sheets for each kind of expense, with individual columns to show a departmental classification.

Estimation of Overhead

Given the heterogeneous nature of the output in a job-order costing situation, overhead cannot be traced directly to the particular jobs, so an averaging process is necessary. Thus, factory overhead will be entered in the job cost sheets on the basis of a predetermined overhead rate based on a justified relationship between the overhead costs and an activity index. The predetermined overhead rate is established based on past experience and the budget for the period. A popular activity index used in accounting for overhead is direct-labor hours. Direct-labor costs and machine hours are also frequently used. For example, suppose that the ABEL Manufacturing Company has estimated its manufacturing overhead to be $100,000 and direct labor to be 10,000 hours. The predetermined overhead rate is then equal to $100,000/10,000 = $10. This rate is used in charging a share of overhead to each job. Notice that the budgeted overhead rate is equal to: total budgeted overhead/table budgeted volume.

To avoid fluctuations in the budgeted level of activity from one year to another, most companies base the budgeted level of activity on the *normal* or average activity level that spans many periods—past, present, and future. The predetermined overhead rate obtained by dividing the budgeted overhead costs of a period by the normal level of activity for the same period is called a *normalized overhead* rate. Therefore a *normalized overhead rate* is the predetermined rate based on the long-run average (normal) level of activity rather than on the expected level of activity.

Another point to remember is that this example is for a small company that uses a single overhead rate (called a *plant-wide overhead rate*). Large companies in general use *multiple overhead rates,* given that a single rate may not be accurate in handling the overhead costs of different departments.

Application of Overhead

Overhead is then applied to each job by multiplying the job's direct-labor hours by the predetermined overhead rate and entering the resulting amount, which is the *applied factory overhead,* in the Overhead column of the job cost sheets. Similarly, the overhead rate is used to apply overhead to any job in process by the end of the accounting period. The total overhead assigned to all jobs is recorded in the general ledger by the following entry:

Work-in-Process Inventory Control $500
    Factory Department Overhead Control .... 500 (50 Hours × $10)
To apply factory overhead to jobs at the rate of $10 per direct-labor hour.

Similarly, in the subsidiary ledger overhead is applied to the appropriate job by entering the amount of applied overhead in the Manufacturing Overhead column of the appropriate cost sheet:

Job-Order Cost Sheet 1 .... $250 (25 Hours × $10)
Job-Order Cost Sheet 2 .... 250 (25 Hours × $10)

Table 12.1
Summary of Factory Overhead Costs

---

1. *Budgeted Overhead Costs*:	This is the amount of overhead factory estimated by management at the beginning of the period using any of the cost estimation techniques covered in Chapters 3 and 12. This amount of budgeted overhead costs is divided by the budgeted value to yield the predetermined overhead rate. The period could be a year or month.
2. *Actual Overhead Costs*:	This is the amount of annual factory overhead actually incurred for the period.
3. *Applied Overhead Costs*:	This is the amount applied to the current production by multiplying actual activity of the period by the predetermined overhead rate. The difference between the actual overhead costs and the applied costs is either an under- or an overapplied overhead. If actual overhead costs are higher than applied overhead costs, the difference amounts to an underapplied overhead. If actual overhead costs are lower than applied overhead costs, the difference amounts to an overapplied overhead.

Please note here the basic differences between the budgeted factory overhead, the actual factory overhead, and the applied factory overhead (see Table 12.1).

12.3.5 Accounting for Jobs Completed and Cost of Goods Sold

Suppose jobs 1 and 2 for the custom-made chair and desk are completed; cost sheets 1 and 2 will be transferred in the subsidiary ledger to a finished goods file. In the general ledger an entry is originated as follows:

Finished Goods Inventory Control		$2,600
Work-in-Process Inventory Control	2,600	
To record the completion of jobs 1 and 2.		

If job 1 is sold, the sale is recorded as follows:

Accounts Receivable		$2,000
Cost of Goods Sold		1,250
Finished Goods Inventory Control	1,250	
Sales	2,000	
To recognize the sales revenue and the cost of goods sold of job 1.		

Table 12.2
Year-End Balance of Factory Department Overhead T Account

Factory Department Overhead

Indirect Materials	$300	Applied	$500
Indirect Labor	200		
Accumulated Depreciation	50		
Miscellaneous	210		
Total	$760		
Balance: Underapplied	$260		

12.3.6 Disposition of Overapplied or Underapplied Overhead

The actual overhead costs have either a debit or credit balance because of estimation errors in the computation of the predetermined overhead rate. If the difference is a debit balance, it is known as an *underapplied overhead;* if it is a credit balance, it is an *overapplied overhead.* In the case of the ABEL Manufacturing Company, the balance of the factory department overhead is equal to $260 (see Table 12.2). Different accounting treatments can be used for the disposition of the underapplied or overapplied overhead.

A first, expedient solution is to charge the total underapplied or overapplied overhead as an adjustment of the Cost of Goods Sold as follows:

Cost of Goods Sold $260
    Factory Overhead Control 260
To close and charge underapplied overhead to the Cost of Goods Sold.

Note that, if it were an overapplied overhead, it would instead be credited to Cost of Goods Sold.

A second solution would be to prorate the underapplied or overapplied overhead between the balance amounts of the Work-in-Process Control account, the Finished Goods Control account, and the Cost of Goods Sold account in the general ledger and the individual job orders in the subsidiary ledger. For ABEL Manufacturing Company, the Work-in-Process, Finished Goods Inventory, and Cost of Goods Sold accounts have balances equal to 0, $135, and $125, respectively. Consequently, the following entry is recorded in the general ledger to reflect the proportional allocation of the underapplied overhead:

Work-in-Process 0

Finished Goods .... $135 \left(260 \times \dfrac{1,350}{2,600} \right)$

Cost of Goods Sold .... $125 \left(260 \times \dfrac{1,250}{2,600} \right)$

Factory Overhead Control 260

To close and prorate the underapplied overhead to the Work-in-Process Inventory, Finished Goods, and Cost of Goods Sold.

Table 12.3
Year-End Disposition of Underapplied Factory Department Overhead

		Solution One: Immediate Write-Off			
Factory Overhead		Product Costs Before Write-Off			Product Costs After Write-Off
Incurred:	$760	Work-in-Process	$ 0	-----→	0
Applied:	500	Finished Goods	1350	-----→	1,350
Underapplied:	$260 --→	Cost of Goods Sold	1250	-----→	1,510

		Solution Two: Proration Among Inventory			
Factory Overhead		Product Costs Before Proration		Amount Prorated	Product Costs After Prorated
Incurred:	$760	Work-in-Process	$ 0	$ 0	0
Applied:	500	Finished Goods	1350	135	1,485 (1,350 + 135)
Underapplied:	$260 --→	Cost of Goods Sold	1250	125	1,375 (1,250 + 125)

These two solutions are compared in Table 12.3. The choice of either solution or accounting treatment for the disposition of over- or underapplied overhead again depends on the magnitude and materiality of the overapplied or underapplied overhead and also on the particular managerial objective use of the resulting data.

Table 12.4 and Figure 12.4 summarize all the entries that have taken place in the ABEL Manufacturing Company example in both the general and subsidiary ledgers.

12.4 OVERVIEW OF JOB-ORDER COSTING SYSTEM

The transactions involved in a job-order costing system are numerous and call for the creation of source documents and the making of general ledger and

Table 12.4
Summary of Cost Flows for ABEL Manufacturing Co.: General Ledger

Materials Inventory

Debit	Credit
(a.) 1.500	(b.) 1.500
(c.) 300	

Accounts Payable

Debit	Credit
	(a.) 3.000

Factory Overhead Control

Debit	Credit
(c.) 300	(h.) 500
(e.) 200	(k.) 260
(f.) 260	

Cash, Payables, Prepaids

Debit	Credit
	(f.) 210

Accumulated Depreciation

Debit	Credit
	(f.) 50

Work-in-Process

Debit	Credit
(b.) 1.500	(i.) 2.600
(e.) 600	
(g.) 500	

Factory Payroll

Debit	Credit
(d.) 800	(e.) 800

Accrued Payroll

Debit	Credit
	(d.) 800

Finished Goods

Debit	Credit
(i.) 2.600	(j.) 1.250
(k.) 135	

Cost of Goods Sold

Debit	Credit
(j.) 1.250	
(k.) 125	

Sales Revenue

Debit	Credit
	(j.) 2.000

Factory Overhead Applied

Debit	Credit
(h.) 500	(g.) 500

Accounts Receivable

Debit	Credit
(j.) 2.000	

Explanation of Entries
(a.) Purchase of materials and supplies.
(b.) Issuance of materials for production.
(c.) Issuance of supplies for production.
(d.) Recording of payroll.
(e.) Recording of distribution of direct and indirect labor.
(f.) Purchase of factory overhead.
(g.) Application of overhead.
(h.) Closing of Applied Factory Overhead.
(i.) Transfer of cost of goods manufactured into Finished Goods.
(j.) Sale of finished goods.
(k.) Proration of underapplied overhead.

a. Job Cost Sheet #1

Job Number ___1___
Department ___Finishing___
Item ___Chair___

Materials		Direct Labor			Manufacturing Overhead		
Req. No.	Amount	Card	Hours	Amount	Hour	Rate	Amount
x1	700	13	100	300	250	$1	250

Cost Summary	
Materials	$ 700
Direct Labor	$ 300
Overhead	$ 250
Total Cost	$1,250

b. Job Cost Sheet #2

Job Number ___2___
Department ___Finishing___
Item ___Desk___

Materials		Direct Labor			Manufacturing Overhead		
Req. No.	Amount	Card	Hours	Amount	Hour	Rate	Amount
x1	800	15	100	300	250	$1	250

Cost Summary	
Materials	$ 800
Direct Labor	$ 300
Overhead	$ 250
Total Cost	$1,350

Figure 12.4
Summary of Cost Flows for ABEL Manufacturing Co.: Subsidiary Ledger

c. Department F, Overhead Cost Sheet

Indirect Material	Indirect Labor	Depreciation	Heat, Light, and Power	Miscellaneous
$300	$200	$50	$100	$110

d. Raw Materials Subsidiary Ledger

Material A

Received	Issued	Balance
$1,000	$900	$100

Material B

Received	Issued	Balance
$1,000	$600	$400

Supplies C

Received	Issued	Balance
$1,000	$300	$700

Figure 12.4
(Continued)

subsidiary ledger entries. A summary of all the possible transactions and their corresponding general ledger and subsidiary ledger entries and source documents is shown in Table 12.5 as an overview of a job-order costing system. Use this exhibit for any review of the accounting entries for job-order costing.

Notice that the assignment of overhead is done on the basis of a budgeted overhead rate, whereas the assignment of material and labor is done on the basis of actual values. This system is known as a *normal absorption costing system*. In contrast, a system that used actual values uniquely is called an *actual absorption costing system*. A job-order costing system relies generally on the normal absorption costing system. The differences between the two approaches will affect the Work-in-Process Inventory as follows:

Actual Absorption Costing	Work-in-Process Inventory	Normal Absorption Costing	Work-in-Process Inventory
Actual Direct Materials		Actual Direct Materials	
Actual Direct Labor		Actual Direct Labor	
Actual Variable Factory Overhead		Applied Variable Factory Overhead	
Actual Fixed Factory		Applied Fixed Factory	

Table 12.5
Elements of Job-Order Costing

Transaction	General Ledger Entries	Subsidiary Ledgers	Source Documents	Additional Cost Accumulation Tasks
1. Purchase of Raw Materials or Supplies	Raw Materials Inventory Control (Dr.) Accounts Payable (Cr.)	Dr. Materials Card "Received Column"	Approved Invoice	
2. Issuance of Direct Materials	Work-in-Process Inventory Control (Dr.) Raw Materials Inventory Control (Cr.)	Dr. Job Cost Sheet, "Direct Material Column" Cr. Materials Cards' "Issued Column"	Materials Requisition Cards	The requisitions are periodically summarized and classified by Department for periodic direct materials usage reports
3. Issuance of Indirect Materials (or Supplies)	Factory Department Overhead Control (Dr.) Raw Materials Inventory Control (Cr)	Dr. Department Overhead Cost Sheets, Indirect Material Column Cr. Supplies Cards "Issued Column"	Materials Requisition Cards	The requisitions are periodically summarized and classified by Department for periodic indirect materials usage reports
4. Distribution of Labor Costs	Work-in-Process Inventory Control (Dr.) Factory Department Overhead Control (Dr.) Accrued Payroll (Cr.)	Dr. Job Cost Sheet. "Direct Labor Column" Cr. Department Overhead Cost Sheets, "Indirect Labor Column"	Summary of time tickets. The document is called Labor Cost Summary, Labor Cost Distribution Summary or a Payroll Recapitulation	
5. Payment of Salaries	Accrued Payroll (Dr.) Witholdings Payable (Cr.) Cash (Cr.)		Summay of Clock Cards and individual witholdings from payroll sheets (or payroll register)	This entry is made periodically following the payment of salaries

240

Transaction	General Ledger Entries	Subsidiary Ledgers	Source Documents	Additional Cost Accumulation Tasks
6. Payment of Withholdings	Withholdings Payable (Dr.) Cash (Cr.)			
7. Employer Payroll Taxes	Factory Department Overhead Control (Dr.) Employee Payroll Taxes Payable (Cr.)			
8. Actual Factory Overhead Incurred	Factory Department Overhead Control (Dr.) Miscellaneous Credits (Cr.)	Dr. Department Overhead Cost Sheet, "Appropriate Column" Examples of Columns a. Utilities b. Depreciation on Factory Equipment c. Factory Insurance Written Off	Approved invoices; accrual over or under, "depreciation schedule and insurance register or memorandum from insurance officer	
9. Applications of Factory Overhead	Work-in-Process Inventory Control (Dr.) Factory Department Overhead Control (Cr)	Dr. Job Cost Sheets, "Factory Overhead Column"	Schedule portraying the determination of the predetermined factory overhead rate	
10. Completion of Jobs	Finished Goods Inventory Control (Dr.) Work-in-Process Inventory Control (Cr.)	Dr. Finished Goods Cards "Received Column" Cr. Job Cost Sheets	Production Report	The Job Cost sheets may be used as Finished Goods Cards.

(Continued)

Table 12.5
(Continued)

Transaction	General Ledger Entries	Subsidiary Ledgers	Source Documents	Additional Cost Accumulation Tasks
11. Sale of Jobs: Revenue	Accounts Receivable Control (Dr.) Sales (Cr.)	Dr. Account Receivable Subsidiary Ledger	Sales Invoice (Copy)	
12. Sale of Jobs: costs	Cost of Goods Sold (Dr.) Finished Goods Inventory Control (Cr.)	Dr. Cost of Goods Sold Sheet. Cr. Finished Goods Card "Issued Column"	Sales Invoice Finished Goods Cards.	
13. Year-End Handling of Over- or Under-applied Overhead	a) For Underapplied Overhead Factory: Overhead (Dr.) Cost of Goods Sold (Cr.) Work-in-Process Inventory Control(Cr.) b) For Overapplied Overhead Cost of Goods Sold (Dr.) Work-in-Process Inventory Control (Dr.) Finished Goods Inventory Control (Dr.) Factory Department Overhead Control (Cr.)		General Ledger Balances	

Dr. = debit
Cr. = credit

Therefore, the normal product cost (or normalized product cost) is composed of actual direct materials, actual direct labor, and applied factory overhead. Needless to say, the year-end proration of over- or underapplied factory overhead leads to the results under actual costing.

12.5 CONCLUSION

This chapter covered one cost accumulation technique: job-order costing. It is used in those manufacturing concerns where units of products differ from each other. The costs of each job are accumulated in a job-order cost sheet, a subsidiary ledger document. The total of the job cost sheet should be equal to the debit balance in the Work-in-Process Inventory account.

A normal absorption costing system is used in the sense that direct materials and direct labor are valued at actual values while overhead is applied on the basis of a normalized predetermined overhead rate. The year-end proration of the over- or underapplied overhead reconcile the figures to the results under an actual absorption costing system.

13

Process Costing

This chapter continues the discussion of product costing by covering *process costing*. As mentioned in chapter 12, process costing is used in those situations that apply costs to homogeneous products that are produced in a continuous process through a series of production steps. It is used in industries that produce such homogeneous products as petroleum, steel, chemicals, flour, glass, and paint; in companies that make products in large batches in assembly-type operations, such as cars, bicycles, and typewriters; and in utilities that produce gas, water, and electricity. As a result, while the job-costing system accumulates costs for two cost objects—departments and specific jobs—the process costing system accumulates costs by department before allocating them evenly to the units produced.

The purpose of this chapter is to continue the discussion of product costing that was started in chapter 12 and to include, in this chapter, the specific procedures called for by a process costing system.

13.1 NATURE OF PROCESS COSTING

Process costing presents similarities and differences from job-order costing. Some of these similarities and differences may be viewed in Figure 13.1. First, while different jobs (nos. 1, 2, and 3) are worked on during the period in job-order costing, with each one of them requiring different production needs (in terms of material, labor, and overhead), process costing presents the production of a single product on a continuous basis in a series of departments (departments X, Y, and Z). Second, while the cost of each individual job is accumulated in a *job-order cost sheet* in the subsidiary ledger for the job-order system; under a process costing system, the costs of each department and for each period are accumulated in a *department cost of production report* (department production reports X, Y, and Z). Third, while the job-order cost sheet under job-order costing shows the cost of each individual job, the department cost of production report shows the costs of each department for each period.

Note that the general ledger entries for material, labor, and overhead, under both systems, follow the same sequence: first in the Work-in-Process account,

A. Job Order Costing

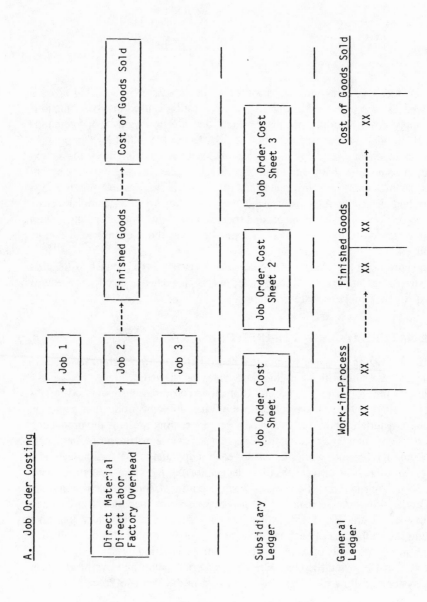

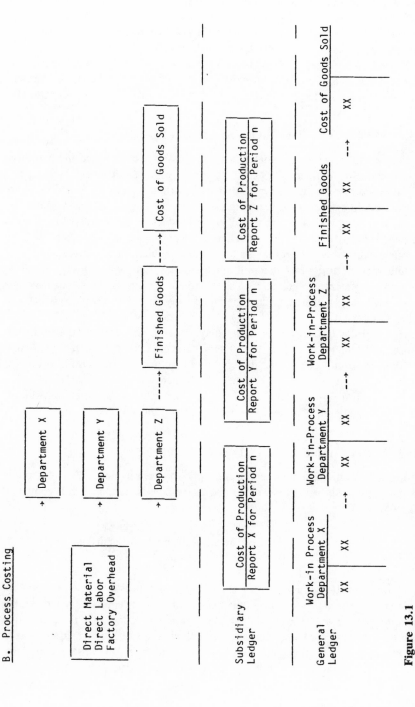

Figure 13.1
Comparison of Job-Order and Process Costing

247

second in the Finished Goods account, and third in the Cost of Goods Sold account.

Under process costing, the costs for each department are accumulated periodically and are then divided by the quantity to yield the average unit cost for the particular department and the particular period. The department production report stands as a pivotal subsidiary ledger in process costing system in the same way that the job-order cost sheet occupies a pivotal role in job-order costing.

13.2 NATURE OF THE PROCESS COST FLOWS

Each of the steps in a manufacturing process is accomplished in an autonomous processing department. Therefore, a *processing department* is any step and place in the manufacturing process where a certain type of work and tasks are performed on a product (or one of the stages of a product) and where materials, labor, and overhead costs are added to the product. Consequently, in a process costing system, costs are accumulated by departments in conformity with an existing work flow, which may be sequential, parallel, or selective.

In a *sequential product flow,* all units undergo transformation in each of the processing centers. As Figure 13.2 shows, the recording of costs goes from one Work-in-Process account to another and finally to a Finished Goods account when completed.

In a *parallel product flow,* units may undergo transformation in different processing centers. As Figure 13.2 shows, costs are initially recorded in different Work-in-Process accounts and then brought together in a final Work-in-Process before being transferred to a Finished Goods account.

Finally, in a *selective product flow,* costs are charged to different Work-in-Process accounts in conformity with the existing output mix (see Figure 13.2).

13.3 EQUIVALENT UNITS OF PRODUCTION

In each cost of production report, the unit cost of production in that department before being assigned to the work in the department is computed. It is computed as follows:

$$\text{Unit cost} = \frac{\text{Cost incurred in the department}}{\text{Equivalent units}}.$$

Notice that the denominator or department's output is expressed in terms of *equivalent units of production.* Equivalent units as a concept refers to the number of units produced in a given department in a given period as if the production process in that department resulted in completed units of product. It amounts to determining the completed units and then adjusting them for partially completed work in the Work-in-Process Inventory. Basically, if thirty units were started at

Sequential Product Flow

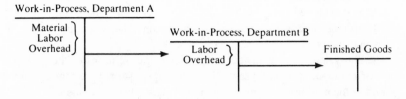

A Parallel Product Flow

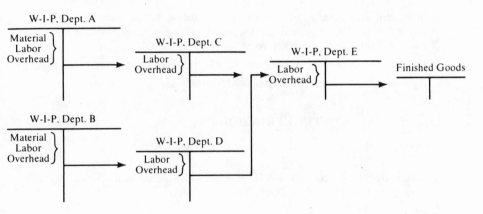

Selective Product Flow

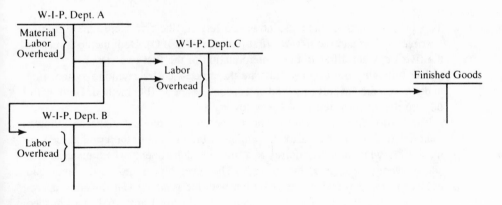

Figure 13.2
Process Cost Flows

the beginning of a period and each was 60 percent completed at the end of the period, then the cumulative work done in the partially completed thirty units would be considered as equivalent to the work done on eighteen units (60 × 30% = 18). In other words, thirty units 60 percent completed corresponds to eighteen equivalent units.

The equivalent unit means the amount of output in terms of the quantities of each of the input applied thereto. To be more precise, suppose thirty units were started at the beginning of the period in a department where one unit of material is added at the beginning of the period, and labor and overhead are added evenly during the period. If, at the end of the period, the thirty units were 70 percent completed, the equivalent units would be computed as follows:

1. Equivalent units in terms of material: 30 × 100% = 30 equivalent units. Because material is asked at the beginning of the period, the degree of completion at the end of the period is by definition 100 percent.

2. Equivalent units in terms of labor: 30 × 70% = 21 equivalent units.

3. Equivalent units in terms of overhead: 30 × 70% = 21 equivalent units.

13.4 PROCESS COSTING PROCEDURES

Process costing involves the following five major steps:

1. Summarize the total costs to be accounted for, which are the total debits in Work-in-Process (that is, the costs applied to Work-in-Process).

2. Summarize the flow of physical units.

3. Compute the output in terms of equivalent units.

4. Compute the cost per equivalent unit.

5. Apply the total costs to units completed and units in Work-in-Process Inventory.

Two process costing methods, however, rely on the five steps: the *weighted average method* and the *first-in, first-out method* (FIFO). Both methods rely on the five steps but differ in their interpretation of the first two steps.

The following discussions illustrate the process cost accounting system first under a weighted average method and second under a FIFO method. Both methods are described in terms of the following example.

The ABEL Manufacturing Company produces a product alpha as follows: Material A is introduced at the beginning of the process in the grinding department, after which it is transferred to a finishing department, where material B is added evenly throughout the process. The other processing costs, labor and overhead, are also added evenly during both the grinding and finishing operations. The output of the finishing department, alpha is transferred to a Finished Goods account. Data for the January 19X5 cost period are as follows:

	Grinding Department	Finishing Department
Beginning Work-in-Process Inventory		
Units	3,000 (⅓)	2,000 (¼)
Material	$3,000	$9,250
Labor	$15,500	$9,750
Overhead	$15,000	$10,250
Transferred In		$19,000
Units Started in January	30,000	18,000
Units Completed and Transferred	18,000	14,000
Ending Work-in-Process Inventory		
Units	15,000 (⅔)	6,000 (⅓)
Current Costs		
Material	$30,000	$38,750
Labor	$40,500	$54,250
Overhead	$27,000	$69,750
Transferred In	—	?

Compute the cost of goods transferred out of department A, the ending inventory costs for goods remaining in department A, the cost of goods transferred out of department B to finished goods, and the ending inventory costs for goods remaining in department B for the month of January. Use weighted average product costing and FIFO product costing.

What the requirements really amount to is the preparation of the cost of production reports for department A and department B for the month of January under both the weighted average product costing method and the FIFO costing method.

13.5 WEIGHTED AVERAGE METHOD: THE FIRST DEPARTMENT

A company using the weighted average method can be characterized by two distinct assumptions from a product costing point of view:

1. The production equations depicting the flow of physical units is expressed as follows:

$$\begin{matrix} \text{Number of units} \\ \text{in the beginning} \\ \text{Work-in-Process} \\ \text{Inventory} \end{matrix} + \begin{matrix} \text{Units started in} \\ \text{the period} \end{matrix} = \begin{matrix} \text{Units completed} \\ \text{in the period} \end{matrix} + \begin{matrix} \text{Number of units} \\ \text{in the ending} \\ \text{Work-in-Process} \\ \text{Inventory.} \end{matrix}$$

2. The unit cost for a period is expressed as follows:

$$\text{Unit input cost} = \frac{\text{Beginning Work-in-Process Inventory costs} + \text{Current costs of the period}}{\text{Number of equivalent units}}.$$

Both characteristics amount to the implicit assumption made under the weighted average product costing method to consider the beginning Work-in-Process Inventory as if it were started in the current period.

Given those two characteristics, we can return to the ABEL Company problem and use the five-step procedure to account for process cost in the grinding department A.

Follow the application of the five-step procedure in Table 13.1 which depicts the cost of production report for the month of January in the grinding department.

1. The first step is to accumulate the costs of material, labor, and overhead for the grinding department. These costs include both the costs of the beginning Work-in-Process and the current costs of the period. (Keep in mind that this is one of the requirements of the weighted average method.) The beginning Work-in-Process of the grinding department includes $3,000 of direct material, $15,500 of direct labor, and $15,000 of overhead. The current costs for the month of January include $30,000 of direct material, $40,500 of direct labor, and $27,000 of factory overhead.

2. The second step is to summarize the flow of physical units in the grinding department for the month of January. Notice, following a requirement of the weighted average method, that the production equation depicting the flow of physical units specifies that the number of units in the beginning inventory (3,000 units) plus the units started in the period (30,000) equals the units completed in the period (18,000 units) plus the number of units in the ending Work-in-Process Inventory (15,000 units).

3. The third step is to compute the output in terms of equivalent units. The equivalent units are computed for both the units completed in the period (18,000 units) and the ending Work-in-Process Inventory (15,000 units). The rationale goes as follows:
   • For the 18,000 units completed in the period, the total completion of these units required 18,000 equivalent units of material, labor, and overhead.
   • Because the 15,000 units in the ending Work-in-Process Inventory are only two-thirds complete, 15,000 equivalent units of material were used (keep in mind that the material is added at the beginning of the process), and only 10,000 equivalent units of labor and overhead were required (in other words, two-thirds of 15,000 units, because the ending Work-in-Process is two-thirds complete and because labor and overhead are added evenly throughout the process; only 10,000 equivalent units— two-thirds of 15,000—are required). Therefore, the total equivalent units are 33,000 equivalent units of material, 28,000 equivalent units of labor, and 28,000 equivalent units of overhead.

4. The fourth step is to compute the cost per equivalent unit. Using the total cost information obtained in step 1 as the numerator and the equivalent units obtained in step 3 as the denominator, the equivalent unit processing costs can now be computed. They are $1 per unit for material, $2 per unit for labor, and $1.50 per unit for overhead.

5. The fifth step is to apply the total costs of $131,000 to units completed and units in the ending Work-in-Process Inventory, which, in this case, amount to $81,000 to goods completed and $50,000 to ending Work-in-Process Inventory.

All these steps are summarized in one document, the cost of production report of the grinding department for the month of January.

Table 13.1
ABEL Manufacturing Company, Ltd., Grinding Department Cost of Production Report for the Month Ended January 31, 19X5 (Weighted Average Method)

1. Costs Charged to the Department

	Material	Labor	Overhead	Total
Current Costs	$30,000	$40,500	$27,000	$ 97,500
Beginning Work-in-Process	3,000	15,500	15,000	33,500
Total Costs to Be Accounted for	$33,000	$56,000	$42,000	$131,000

2. Equivalent Unit Processing Costs

	Total Units	Equivalent Units		
		Material	Labor	Overhead
Beginning Work-in-Process (1/3)	3,000			
Units Started	30,000			
To Account for	33,000			
Units Completed	18,000	18,000	18,000	18,000
Ending Work-in-Process (2/3)	15,000	15,000	10,000	10,000
Equivalent Units	33,000	33,000	28,000	28,000
Total Costs to Be Accounted for		$33,000	$56,000	$42,000
Equivalent Unit Processing Costs		$1.00	$2.00	$1.50

3. Costs Applicable to the Work of the Department

Goods Completed: 18,000 ($1.00 + $2.00 + $1.50)	$ 81,000
Ending Work-in-Process	50,000[a]
	$131,000

[a] The ending Work-in-Process is computed by deducting the Costs of Goods Completed from the Total Costs. It is, however, appropriate to check the accuracy of the figure as follows:
Material: 15,000 × $1.00 = $15,000
Labor: 10,000 × $2.00 =   20,000
Overhead: 10,000 × $1.50 =   15,000

$50,000

13.6 WEIGHTED AVERAGE METHOD: TRANSFER TO ANOTHER DEPARTMENT

In the case of a transfer of a product to another department, an additional cost is considered besides the material, labor, and overhead added in the new department. These costs are called *transferred-in costs*. They are exactly the costs incurred by the product in the previous department before being transferred to the

Table 13.2
ABEL Manufacturing Company, Ltd., Finishing Department Cost of Production Report for the Month Ended January 31, 19X5 (Weighted Average Method)

1. Costs Charged to the Department

	Material	Labor	Overhead	Transferred In	Total
Current Costs	$38,750	$54,250	$69,750	$ 81,000	$243,750
Beginning Work-in-Process	9,250	9,750	10,250	19,000	48,250
Total Costs to Be Accounted for	$48,000	$64,000	$80,000	$100,000	$292,000

2. Equivalent Unit Processing Costs

	Total Units	Equivalent Units			
		Material	Labor	Overhead	Transferred In
Beginning Work-in-Process (1/4)	2,000				
Units Started	18,000				
To Account for	20,000				
Units Completed	14,000	14,000	14,000	14,000	14,000
Ending Work-in-Process (1/3)	6,000	2,000	2,000	2,000	6,000
Equivalent Units		16,000	16,000	16,000	20,000
Total Costs to Be Accounted for		$48,000	$64,000	$80,000	$100,000
Equivalent Unit Processing Costs		$3.00	$4.00	$5.00	$5.00

3. Costs Applicable to the Work of the Department

Goods Completed: 14,000 ($3.00 + $4.00 + $5.00 + $5.00)	$238,000
Ending Work-in-Process	54,000*
	$292,000

*Ending Work-in-Process:

Material:	2,000 × $3.00 =	$ 6,000
Labor:	2,000 × $4.00 =	8,000
Overhead:	2,000 × $5.00 =	10,000
Transferred In:	6,000 × $5.00 =	30,000
		$54,000

new department. Therefore, the computations and the procedures will be the same except for the addition of a new input, which is the transferred-in costs.

Given this new addition, we can now return to the ABEL Company problem and use the five-step procedure to account for process cost in the finishing department. Follow the application of the five-step procedure in Table 13.2, which depicts the cost of production report for the month of January in the finishing department.

1. The first step is to accumulate not only the costs of material, labor, and overhead but *also* the transferred-in costs from the previous department. These costs naturally include the costs of the beginning Work-in-Process and the current costs of the period. (Keep in mind that this is one of the requirements of the weighted average method.) The current costs of the finishing department includes $38,750 of direct material,

$54,250 of labor, $69,750 of overhead, and $81,000 of transferred-in costs. While the costs of direct material, direct labor, and overhead are given, the $81,000 of transferred-in costs are the costs incurred in the grinding department before being transferred to the finishing department. (To check, notice in Table 13.1 that the costs of goods completed and transferred are exactly $81,000.)

The beginning Work-in-Process of the finishing department includes $9,250 of direct material, $9,750 of direct labor, $10,250 of overhead, and $19,000 of transferred-in costs. All these costs are given because they have been incurred in the finishing department in an earlier period. For the results of step 1 in the finishing department, see Table 13.2.

2. The second step is to summarize the flow of physical units in the finishing department for the month of January. Notice again, following a requirement of the weighted average method, that the production equation depicting the flow of physical units specifies that the number of units in the beginning inventory (2,000 units) plus the units started in the period (18,000 units) equal the units completed in the period (14,000 units) plus the ending Work-in-Process (6,000 units).

3. The third step computes the output in terms of equivalent units. The equivalent units are computed for both the units completed in the period (14,000 units) and the ending Work-in-Process inventory (6,000 units). The rationale goes as follows:
   - For the 14,000 units completed in the period, the total completion of these units required 14,000 units of material, labor, and overhead in the finishing department and *earlier* required 14,000 units of transferred-in the grinding department before being transferred to the finishing department.
   - Because the ending Work-in-Process was one-third completed in the finishing department, the 6,000 units only required 9,000 units of material, labor, and overhead (6,000 units × ⅓ completion). The equivalent units for transferred-in are, however, 6,000 units as these units received their full share of costs in the grinding department before being transferred to the finishing department. Therefore, the total equivalent units are 16,000 equivalent units for material, labor, and overhead and 20,000 equivalent units for transferred-in costs.

4. The fourth step is to compute the cost per equivalent unit. Using the total cost information for each input obtained in step 1 as the numerator and the equivalent units information each input as the denominator, the equivalent unit processing costs are computed. They are $3.00 ($48,000/16,000) for overhead and $5.00 ($100,000/20,000) for transferred-in costs.

5. The fifth step is to apply the total costs of $292,000 to units completed and units remaining in the ending Work-in-Process Inventory, which in this case results in $238,000 applied to goods completed and $54,000 applied to ending Work-in-Process Inventory. All those steps are naturally summarized in the document, the cost of production report of the finishing department for the month of January, which is shown in Table 13.2.

13.7 FIFO METHOD: THE FIRST DEPARTMENT

A company using the FIFO method can be characterized by two distinct assumptions from a product costing point of view:

1. The production equation depicting the flow of physical units is expressed as follows:

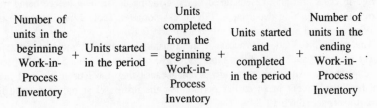

Number of units in the beginning Work-in-Process Inventory + Units started in the period = Units completed from the beginning Work-in-Process Inventory + Units started and completed in the period + Number of units in the ending Work-in-Process Inventory

2. The average unit cost of the period is as follows:

$$\text{Average unit input cost} = \frac{\text{Current costs of the period}}{\text{Number of equivalent units}}.$$

In other words, a company using the FIFO method would consider the units in the beginning Work-in-Process as completely separate and distinct from the units started and completed in the period. The units in the beginning inventory are completed first before production starts on new units. Consequently, only the current costs are used as a numerator in the computation of the equivalent unit processing costs.

Given these two assumptions, we can now return to the ABEL Company problem and use the five-step procedure to account for process cost in the grinding department. Follow the application of the five step procedure in Table 13.3, which depicts the cost of production report for the month of January in the grinding department.

1. The first step is to accumulate the costs of material, labor, and overhead for the grinding department. These costs include *only* the current costs of the period. (Keep in mind that this is one of the requirements of the FIFO method). The current costs include $30,000 of direct material, $40,500 of labor, and $27,000 of overhead for a total of $97,500. Notice that the total costs of beginning inventory is considered here as a *start-up cost* of $33,500. (These start-up costs do not enter in the computation of the equivalent unit processing costs but are shown here because ultimately they would need to be applied to the costs of goods completed in step 5. Watch carefully for them.)

2. The second step is to summarize the flow of physical units in the grinding department for the month of January. Notice, following a requirement of the FIFO method, that the production equation depicting the flow of physical units specifies that the number of units in the beginning inventory (3,000 units) plus the units started (30,000 units) equal the units completed from the beginning inventory (3,000 units) plus the units started and completed in the period (15,000) plus the ending Work-in-Process (15,000 units).

3. The third step is to compute the output in terms of equivalent units. The equivalent units are computed for the units completed from the beginning Work-in-Process Inventory (3,000 units), the units started and completed in the period (15,000 units), and

Table 13.3
ABEL Manufacturing Company, Ltd., Grinding Department Cost of Production Report for the Month Ended January 31, 19X5 (FIFO Method)

1. Costs Charged to the Department

	Material	Labor	Overhead	Start-up	Total
Current Costs	$30,000	$40,500	$27,000	—	$ 97,500
Beginning Work-in-Process	—	—	—	$33,500	33,500
Total Costs to Be Accounted for	$30,000	$40,500	$27,000	$33,500	$131,000

2. Equivalent Unit Processing Costs

	Total Units	Equivalent Units		
		Material	Labor	Overhead
Beginning Work-in-Process (1/3)	3,000			
Units Started	30,000			
To Account for	33,000			
Units Completed				
Beginning Inventory (1/3)	3,000	—	2,000	2,000
Started and Completed	15,000	15,000	15,000	15,000
Ending Work-in-Process (2/3)	15,000	15,000	10,000	10,000
Equivalent Units		30,000	27,000	27,000
Total Costs to Be Accounted for		$30,000	$40,500	$27,000
Equivalent Unit Processing Costs		$1.00	$1.50	$1.00

3. Costs Applicable to the Work of the Department

Goods Completed	
Beginning Work-in-Process: 33,500 + 2,000 ($1.50 + $1.00)	$ 38,500
Started and Completed: 15,000 ($1.00 + $1.50 + $1.00)	52,500
	$ 91,000
Ending Work-in-Process ($131,000 − $91,000)	40,000*
	$131,000

*Ending Work-in-Process:
Material: 15,000 × $1.00 = $15,000
Labor: 10,000 × $1.50 = 15,000
Overhead: 10,000 × $1.00 = 10,000

                     $40,000

the units in the ending Work-in-Process (15,000 units). The rationale for the computation of the equivalent units is as follows:

- The 3,000 units in the beginning Work-in-Process inventory are one-third completed at the beginning of the period. To be fully completed in the period, no material is needed as material has been added in the previous period, and 2,000 equivalent units of labor and overhead are needed. The 2,000 equivalent units of labor and overhead are obtained by multiplying 3,000 by two-thirds as one additional two-thirds completion is needed.
- For the 15,000 units started and completed in the period, the total completion of these units requires 15,000 units of material, labor, and overhead.
- Because the 15,000 units in the ending Work-in-Process are two-thirds completed, 15,000 equivalent units of material were used (keep in mind that the material in this example is added at the beginning of the period), and only 10,000 equivalent units of labor and overhead were required (in other words, two-thirds of 15,000 units because the ending work-in-process is two-thirds completed and both labor and overhead are added evenly throughout the process; only 10,000 equivalent units—two-thirds of 15,000—are required).

Therefore, the total equivalent units are 30,000 equivalent units of material, 27,000 equivalent units of labor, and 27,000 equivalent units of overhead.

4. The fourth step is to compute the cost per equivalent unit. Using the total cost information obtained in step 1 as the numerator and the equivalent units obtained in step 3 as the denominator, the equivalent unit processing costs can now be computed. They are $1.00 per unit of material ($30,000/30,000), $1.50 per unit of labor ($40,500/27,000), and $1.00 per unit of overhead ($27,000/27,000).

5. The fifth step is to apply the total costs of $131,000 to the units completed and the units remaining in the Work-in-Process, which, in this case, amounts to $91,000 for the costs of goods completed and $40,000 for the ending Work-in-Process. Note in Table 13.3 that the costs of goods completed include both the costs of goods completed from the beginning inventory ($38,500) and the costs of the units started and completed in the period ($52,500). Notice again that the costs of goods completed from the beginning inventory include the start-up costs of $33,500 plus the costs incurred during the period.

All these steps are summarized in one document, the cost of production report of the grinding department for the month of January.

13.8 FIFO METHOD: TRANSFER TO ANOTHER DEPARTMENT OR TO FINISHED GOODS

In the case of a transfer of a product to another department, an additional cost is considered besides the material, labor, and overhead in the new department. These costs are, as you should know by now, called *transferred-in costs*. They are exactly the costs incurred by the product in the previous department before being transferred to the new department. As we saw before, under the weighted average method, the transferred-in costs are submitted under the FIFO method to

Table 13.4
ABEL Manufacturing Company, Ltd., Finishing Department Cost of Production Report for the Month Ended January 31, 19X5 (FIFO Method)

1. Costs Charged to the Department

	Material	Labor	Overhead	Transferred In	Start-up	Total
Current Costs	$38,750	$54,250	$69,750	$91,000	—	$253,750
Beginning Work-in-Process	—	—	—	—	$48,250	48,250
Total Costs to Be Accounted for	$38,750	$54,250	$69,750	$91,000	$48,250	$302,000

2. Equivalent Unit Processing Costs

	Total Units	Material	Labor	Overhead	Transferred In
		Equivalent Units			
Beginning Work-in-Process (1/4)	2,000				
Units Started	18,000				
To Account for	20,000				
Units Completed					
Beginning Inventory (1/4)	2,000	1,500	1,500	1,500	—
Started and Completed	12,000	12,000	12,000	12,000	12,000
Ending Work-in-Process	6,000	2,000	2,000	2,000	6,000
Equivalent Units		15,500	15,500	15,500	18,000
Total Costs to Be Accounted for		$38,750	$54,250	$69,750	$91,000
Equivalent Unit Processing Costs		$2.50	$3.50	$4.50	$5.0555

3. Costs Applicable to the Work of the Department

Goods Completed	
Beginning Inventory: 48,250 + 1,500 ($2.50 + $3.50 + $4.50)	$ 64,000
Units Started and Completed: 12,000 ($2.50 + $3.50 + $4.50 + $5.0555)	186,666
	$250,666
Ending Work-in-Process: $302,000 − $250,666 =	51,334*
	$302,000

*Ending Work-in-Process:
Material:	2,000 × $2.50 =	$ 5,000
Labor:	2,000 × $3.50 =	7,000
Overhead:	2,000 × $4.50 =	9,000
Transferred In: 6,000 × $5.0555 =		30,334
		$51,334

the same treatment as the material, labor, and overhead added in the new department.

Given this new knowledge, we can now return to the ABEL Company problem and use the five-step procedure to account for process cost in the finishing department under the FIFO method. Follow the application of the five-step procedure in Table 13.4, which depicts the cost of production report for the month of January in the finishing department.

1. The first step is to accumulate not only the costs of material, labor, and overhead added this period but also the transferred-in costs from the previous department. These costs include *only* the current costs of the period. (Keep in mind again that this is one of the requirements of the FIFO method.) Therefore, the current costs of the finishing department include $38,750 of direct material, $54,250 of direct labor, $69,750 of overhead, and $91,000 of transferred-in costs. While costs of direct material, direct labor, and overhead are given, the $91,000 of transferred-in costs are the costs incurred in the grinding department before being transferred to the finishing department. (To check, notice in Table 13.4 that the costs of goods completed and transferred are exactly $91,000.)

   The beginning Work-in-Process costs are kept separate as a $48,250 start-up cost. (The start-up costs do not enter into the computation of the equivalent unit processing costs but are shown in Table 13.4 because ultimately they would need to be applied to the cost of goods completed in step 5. Watch carefully for them.)

2. The second step is to summarize the flow of physical units in the finishing department for the month of January. Notice again, following a requirement of the FIFO method, that the production equation depicting the flow of physical units specifies that the number of units in the beginning inventory (2,000 units) plus the units started in the period (18,000 units) equal the units completed in the period from the beginning inventory (2,000 units) plus the units remaining in the ending inventory (6,000 units).

3. The third step is to compute the output in terms of equivalent units. The equivalent units are computed for the units completed from the beginning inventory (2,000 units), the units started and completed (12,000 units), and the units in the ending Work-in-Process (6,000 units). The rationale for the computation of the equivalent units is as follows:

   - The 2,000 units in the beginning inventory are one-fourth completed at the beginning of the period. To be fully completed in the period, 1,500 equivalent units of material, labor, and overhead are needed. (The 1,500 equivalent units are obtained by multiplying the 2,000 by three-fourths as an additional three-fourths completion is needed.) Notice that 0 equivalent units of transferred-in is used as the units in the beginning inventory had received their share of transferred-in costs in the previous period.
   - For the 12,000 units started and completed in the period, the total completion of these units requires 12,000 equivalent units of material, labor, and overhead.
   - Because the 6,000 units in the ending Work-in-Process Inventory are one-third completed, 2,000 equivalent units of material, labor, and overhead are needed. (In other words, one-third of the 6,000 units have been completed in terms of material, labor, and overhead; only 2,000 equivalent units—one-third of 6,000—are required.) However, 6,000 equivalent units of transferred-in costs are needed as these represent units just transferred from the previous department and should represent the full cost borne in the previous department. Therefore, the total equivalent units are 15,500 equivalent units for material, labor, and overhead and 18,800 equivalent units for transferred-in costs.

4. The fourth step is to compute the cost per equivalent unit. Using the total cost information obtained in step 1 as the numerator and the equivalent units obtained in step 3 as the denominator, the equivalent unit processing costs can now be computed. They are $2.50 per unit of material ($38,750/15,500), $3.50 per unit of labor

($54,250/15,500), $4.50 per unit of overhead ($69,750/15,500), and $5.0555 per unit of transferred-in costs ($91,000/18,000).

5. The fifth step is to apply the total costs of $302,000 to the units completed from the beginning inventory, the units started and completed in the period, and the units remaining in the ending inventory, which, in this case, amounts to $64,000 to the units in the beginning inventory, $186,666 for the units started and completed in the period, and $51,334 to the ending Work-in-Process inventory. Note in Table 13.4 that the costs of goods completed include both the $64,000 of units completed from the beginning inventory and the $186,666 from the units started and completed during the period. Note again that the costs of goods completed from the beginning inventory include the start-up costs of $48,250 for the costs incurred during the period.

All these steps are summarized in one document, the cost of production report of the finishing department for the month of January.

13.9 JOURNAL ENTRIES IN A PROCESS COST SYSTEM

The journal entries for the ABEL Manufacturing Company example are as follows:

	Weighted Average		FIFO	
Work-in-Process—Grinding Department	97,500		97,500	
Raw Material Inventory		30,000		30,000
Factory Payroll		40,500		40,500
Factory Overhead		27,000		27,000
To record the input of material and conversion costs.				
Work-in-Process—Finishing	81,000		91,000	
Work-in-Process—Grinding		81,000		91,000
To record the costs of goods finished and transferred to the finishing department.				
Work-in-Process—Finishing	162,750		162,750	
Raw Material Inventory		38,750		38,750
Factory Payroll		54,250		54,250
Factory Overhead		69,750		69,750
To record the input of material and conversion costs.				
Finished Goods Inventory	238,000		250,666	
Work-in-Process—Finishing		238,000		250,666
To record the cost of goods finished and transferred to Finished Goods.				

13.10 RECONCILING THE COMPUTATION OF EQUIVALENT UNITS

The difference in equivalent units obtained by the weighted average and the FIFO methods arises from the two different assumptions about the production equation and the average unit costs. In brief, the beginning Work-in-Process Inventory in the FIFO method is viewed as a batch of goods separate and distinct

Table 13.5
Reconciliation of the Computations of Equivalent Units

Equivalent Units

Grinding Department	Total Units	Material	Labor	Overhead	Trans-ferred In
Beginning Work-in-Process (1/3)	3,000				
Units Started	30,000				
To Account for	33,000				
Units Completed	18,000	18,000	18,000	18,000	
Ending Work-in-Process (2/3)	15,000	15,000	10,000	10,000	
Equivalent Units (Weighted Average)		33,000	28,000	28,000	
Less Old Equivalent Units for Work Done on Beginning Inventory		3,000	1,000	1,000	
Equivalent Units (FIFO)		30,000	27,000	27,000	
Finishing Department					
Beginning Work-in-Process (1/4)	2,000				
Units Started	18,000				
To Account for	20,000				
Units Completed	14,000	14,000	14,000	14,000	14,000
Ending Work-in-Process (1/3)	6,000	2,000	2,000	2,000	6,000
Equivalent Units (Weighted Average)		16,000	16,000	16,000	20,000
Less Old Equivalent Units for Work Done on Beginning Inventory		500	500	500	2,000
Equivalent Units (FIFO)		15,500	15,500	15,500	18,000

from the units started and completed. Thus, the main difference between the equivalent units in the FIFO and the weighted average methods relates to the fact that the FIFO method excludes the old equivalent units for work done on beginning inventories. In other words,

$$\begin{array}{c}\text{Equivalent units} \\ \text{(weighted average)}\end{array} - \begin{array}{c}\text{Old equivalent units} \\ \text{for work done on} \\ \text{beginning inventory}\end{array} = \text{Equivalent units (FIFO)}.$$

The application of this reconciliation formula is illustrated in Table 13.5 based on the data from the ABEL Manufacturing Company example.

13.11 STANDARD COSTS AND PROCESS COSTING

Standard costing can be used in both job-order and process cost situations. It is more appropriate, however, in situations where operations are amenable to the

Table 13.6
**ABEL Manufacturing Company, Ltd., Grinding Department Process Cost
Summary for the Month Ended January 31, 19X5 (Standard Costs)**

1. Standard Costs Charged to the Department

	Material	Labor	Overhead	Start-up	Total
Current Costs	$45,000	$27,000	$54,000	—	$126,000
Beginning Work-in-Process	—	—	—	$13,500	13,500
Total Costs to Be Accounted for	$45,000	$27,000	$54,000	$13,500	$139,500

2. Equivalent Unit Processing Costs

	Total Units	Equivalent Units		
		Material	Labor	Overhead
Beginning Work-in-Process (1/3)	3,000			
Units Started	30,000			
To Account for	33,000			
Units Completed				
Beginning Inventory (1/3)	3,000	—	2,000	2,000
Started and Completed	15,000	15,000	15,000	15,000
Ending Work-in-Process (2/3)	15,000	15,000	10,000	10,000
Equivalent Units		30,000	27,000	27,000

3. Costs Applicable to the Work of the Department

Goods Completed
Beginning Inventory: $13,500 + 2,000 ($1.00 + $2.00) $ 19,500
Units Started and Completed: 15,000 ($1.50 + $1.00 + $2.00)   67,500

                                                            87,000
Ending Work-in-Process: ($139,500 − $87,000)   52,500*

                                                            $139,500

*Ending Work-in-Process:
Material: 15,000 × $1.50 = $22,500
Labor: 10,000 × $1.00 = 10,000
Overhead: 10,000 × $2.00 = 20,000

                    $52,500

4. Summary of Variances (Actual Performance − Standard Performance)

Material: $30,000 − $45,000 $15,000 Favorable
Labor: $40,500 − $27,000 13,500 Unfavorable
Overhead: $27,000 − $54,000 27,000 Favorable

                              $28,500 Favorable

establishment of physical standards, usually continuous mass production processes. One of the main advantages of standard costs used in process costing is the elimination of the conflicts between the weighted average and FIFO costing methods.

To illustrate the application of standard costs in process costing, assume that the following standard costs have been determined for the grinding department of the ABEL Manufacturing Company:

	Per Unit
Direct Material	$1.50
Direct Labor	1.00
Overhead	2.00
	$4.50

The beginning Work-in-Process Inventory = 3,000 units, one-third complete (material $4,500, labor $3,000, overhead $6,000) = $13,500. Units started and completed = 15,000 units. The ending Work-in-Process Inventory = 15,000 units, two-thirds complete.

The process cost summary for the grinding department using standard costs is shown in Table 13.6. Not only does the use of standard costs eliminate the need to compute the equivalent unit cost, it also facilitates control through the computation of the summary of variances. Notice that the computation of equivalent units for standard costing corresponds to the FIFO-based equivalent units.

13.12 CONCLUSION

Process costing is used in those situations that apply costs to homogeneous products that are mass produced in a continuous process through a series of production steps. The basic subsidiary ledger document used to accumulate costs in a process cost system is the cost of production report. It is used to accumulate costs incurred in a given department for a given period, with the objective of determining the costs of the ending Work-in-Process Inventory. Five steps are used to determine the content of the cost of production report. These methods of process costing used in practice are presented in this chapter, namely, the weighted average method, the FIFO method, and the standard cost method. More complex situations involving process costing will be covered in chapter 14.

14

Accounting for Quality Costs

Chapters 12 and 13 assume the absence of any quality problem affecting the production process. In reality, production processes may encounter several quality problems generally identified as scrap and waste, defective work, spoilage, and lost units. This chapter elaborates on the methods used to account for these quality costs. In addition, the chapter introduces the new manufacturing accounting intended to reduce or eliminate these quality costs and to insure a zero defect policy.

14.1 ACCOUNTING FOR LACK OF QUALITY

Most manufacturing operations are expected to be subject to possible production losses due to scrap, spoilage, defective work, and lost units. To be fully informative, a good cost accounting system must recognize such losses.

14.1.1 Scrap and Waste

Scrap and *waste* are material residues of manufacturing operations that are believed to have minor resale value to scrap dealers. If the amount of scrap is relatively significant, scrap tickets are prepared to support entries to scrap reports usually expressed in terms of quantities of scrap delivered to the storeroom. At the time of sale, the possible entries are as follows.

Cash (or Accounts Receivable)   xxx
    Income from sale of scrap (or Department Factory Overhead
    Control account)   xxx

This entry shows that, in case the scrap is not identifiable to a particular job or department, the credit entry can be made either to a special income account or to reduce the Department Factory Overhead account. The posting made to the subsidiary ledger is recorded in the Sale of Scrap column on the departmental cost sheet.

Cash (or Accounts Receivable)   xxx
    Work-in-Process   xxx

If the scrap is identifiable to a specific job or department, an alternative treatment is to credit the appropriate Work-in-Process account. This treatment is justifiable when an agreement exists between the manufacturer and the customer that specifies the crediting of jobs with all scrap or spoilage losses. Accordingly, the posting made to the subsidiary ledger is recorded in the specific job-order cost sheet.

From a critical point of view, timely and continuous reporting of scrap losses is advisable for the proper functioning of a responsibility accounting system. At the time of occurrence, the recording of not only the scrap quantity but also the scrap value at an "estimated" resale value may even be advisable. The entry would be

Scrap Inventory   xxx
    Factory Overhead (or Work-in-Process)   xxx

This last entry is more justifiable when there is a significant time lag between the incurrence and sale of scrap.

Scrap as an aspect of the total manufacturing cost should not be ignored. It needs to be identified, monitored, and the full expense segregated in department, plant, division, and corporate management reports. Operating measures that can be used to monitor scrap include quality incoming material inspection, material cost as a percentage of total cost, actual scrap, scrap by part/production/ operation, and scrap percentage of total cost.[1] Beyond monitoring, the objective should be to eliminate scrap:

Ironically, if the new manufacturing environment really means high incoming quality and tight in-process control, then you should expect that scrap would be at a minimum. That is the ultimate goal and, in fact, more world class manufacturers have set zero scrap as their objective. That means no scrap allowances. Until a manufacturer gets there, however, the measurement of scrap is critical.[2]

14.1.2 Defective Work

Defective goods result from failure to meet the production standard established for a good unit. When they occur, the supervisor can authorize either rework or resale. If the decision is to rework the defective units at added cost of materials, labor, and overhead, the accounting treatment will depend on whether the cost of defective units is to be charged to the total production and, consequently, debited to the Department Factory Overhead Control account, or if it is to be charged to a specific job and, consequently, to Work-in-Process. In either case, the entries will be as follows:

    Department Factory Overhead (or Work-in-Process)   xxx
    Materials   xxx
    Labor   xxx
    Overhead Applied   xxx

14.1.3 Spoilage

Spoilage and *lost units* result from either (1) production that does not meet the standard established for good units, that cannot be reworked, and, consequently, that is sold for disposal value, or (2) shrinkage or evaporation of the materials used so completed production has a smaller volume than the total of basic inputs. *Normal spoilage* is an expected, inherent result of the production process that cannot be controlled. It should be internalized logically in the computation of the predetermined overhead rate to be prorated to the total period production. *Abnormal spoilage* is an unexpected production loss resulting from controllable factors; as such, it should be recognized by a loss account called Loss from Abnormal Spoilage.

To illustrate, assume the following example:

Units Completed:		2,200 Units
Good Units	2,000	
Normal Spoilage	50	
Abnormal Spoilage	150	
Total	2,200 Units	

Unit Cost: $3

The accounting entries for this example could be as follows:

Work-in-Process		6,600
Material, Factory Payroll, Manufacturing Overhead	6,600	
To record the input of material and conversion costs.		
Cost of Spoiled Goods		600
Work-in-Process	600	
To record the spoilage of 200 units.		
Finished Goods		6,000
Work-in-Process	6,000	
To record the completion of 2,000 units.		
Finished Goods		150
Cost of Spoiled Goods	150	
To record the normal spoilage of 50 units.		
Loss from Abnormal Spoilage		450
Cost of Spoiled Goods	450	
To record the abnormal spoilage of 150 units.		

Note that the second entry recognizes a cost of spoiled goods and is, in a way, a clearing account which allows the recognition of both normal and abnormal spoilage as product costs first, and then as either a loss or an expense. In practice, such an entry can be skipped for expediency.

14.1.4 Lost Units

Accounting for *lost units* depends on whether the units were lost in the first department or after the first department. If the units are lost in the first department, the number of units decreases; this leads to a higher unit cost, and no adjustments are necessary. If the units are lost in subsequent departments, an adjustment for lost units must be made. Such an adjustment can be computed according to two possible methods.

Method 1

The adjustment for lost units is equal to the difference between the new unit cost and the old unit cost, where the unit cost is computed as follows:

$$\text{New unit cost} = \frac{\text{Transferred-in cost}}{\begin{array}{c}\text{Units transferred from}\\ \text{preceding department}\end{array} - \text{Lost units}}.$$

Method 2

The adjustment for lost units is computed by allocating the total cost lost over the number of units actually produced:

$$\text{Adjustment for lost units} = \frac{\text{Lost units} \times \text{Old unit cost}}{\begin{array}{c}\text{Units transferred from}\\ \text{preceding department}\end{array} - \text{Lost units}}.$$

As an example, assume the following information for departments 1 and 2:

Transferred-in Costs from Department 1	$120,000
Units Transferred from Department 1	30,000
Units Lost in Department 2	6,000

The adjustment for lost units is computed using method 1 as follows:

$$\text{New unit cost: } \$120,000/(30,000 - 6,000) = \$5.$$

$$\text{Old unit cost: } \$120,000/30,000 = \$4.$$

$$\text{Adjustment: } \$5 - \$4 = \$1.$$

Using method 2,

$$\text{Adjustment: } \frac{6,000 \times \$4}{30,000 - 6,000} = \$1.$$

Besides requiring an adjustment to the unit cost, the possibility of units lost in production or units added in the process requires an adjustment in the flow of units in the production equation. Hence the production equation will be as follows for the weighted average method:

$$\begin{array}{c}\text{Units in process} \\ \text{at the beginning}\end{array} + \begin{array}{c}\text{Units} \\ \text{started}\end{array} + \begin{array}{c}\text{Units} \\ \text{added}\end{array} = \begin{array}{c}\text{Units} \\ \text{completed}\end{array} + \begin{array}{c}\text{Units still} \\ \text{in process} \\ \text{at the end}\end{array} + \begin{array}{c}\text{Units} \\ \text{lost}\end{array}.$$

For the FIFO method, the production equation will be

$$\begin{array}{c}\text{Units in} \\ \text{process} \\ \text{at the} \\ \text{beginning}\end{array} + \begin{array}{c}\text{Units} \\ \text{started}\end{array} + \begin{array}{c}\text{Units} \\ \text{added}\end{array} = \begin{array}{c}\text{Units} \\ \text{completed} \\ \text{from the} \\ \text{beginning} \\ \text{inventory}\end{array} + \begin{array}{c}\text{Units} \\ \text{started and} \\ \text{completed}\end{array} + \begin{array}{c}\text{Units} \\ \text{still in} \\ \text{process} \\ \text{at the} \\ \text{end}\end{array} + \begin{array}{c}\text{Units} \\ \text{lost}\end{array}.$$

Notice that units added increases the left side of the production equation, while units lost increases the right side. Using method 1, the following adjustment for lost units is made for another example:

New unit cost: $300,000/(60,000 - 12,000) = \$6.25.$

Old unit cost: $300,000/60,000 \qquad = \$5.00.$

Adjustment for lost units: $\$6.25 - \$5 \qquad = \$1.25.$

Using method 2,

$$\text{Adjustment for lost units} = \frac{18{,}000 \text{ units} \times \$5}{60{,}000 - 12{,}000} = \$1.25.$$

14.2 PROCESS COSTING AND SPOILAGE (SHRINKAGE, EVAPORATION, WASTE, AND LOST UNITS)

14.2.1 Initial and Terminal Spoilage

Process costing for spoilage (shrinkage, evaporation, waste, and lost units) differs depending on where in production the spoilage takes place. If spoilage occurs at the beginning of operations, the condition is called *initial spoilage*. The costs of spoiled goods from normal spoilage are allocated to good production and units in the Ending Work-in-Process Inventory. If spoilage occurs at the end of operations, the condition is called *terminal spoilage,* and the costs of spoiled goods from normal spoilage are only allocated to the Units Completed and Transferred Out of the Department. The following example illustrates the accounting treatment of spoilage in a process cost system under either the FIFO or the weighted average method and assuming either initial or terminal spoilage.

Assume that the ABEL Manufacturing Company produces a product alpha with costs accumulated on a process cost basis. Material for alpha are added in at the beginning of the process, and the conversion costs are added evenly throughout the process. Normal spoilage represents about one-tenth of the good output. Additional relevant production statistics for December are as follows:

Beginning Inventory	
Number of Units	2,000 (¼ Complete)
Total Costs	$29,250
Material	$17,000
Labor	$ 8,500
Overhead	$ 3,750
Processing Costs	
Total Costs	$90,000
Material	$60,000
Labor	$24,000
Overhead	$ 6,000
Production	
Units Started	5,000
Units Completed	5,000
Ending Inventory (Units)	1,000 (½ Complete)
Normal Spoilage (Units)	500
Abnormal Spoilage (Units)	500

Tables 14.1 and 14.2 show the process cost summary under the weighted average method and the FIFO method, respectively. On the basis of these two process cost summaries, accounting for spoilage (either initial or terminal) can be initiated.

If the spoilage in the ABEL Manufacturing Company was an initial spoilage, the costs of spoiled goods from normal spoilage would be allocated to good production and units in the Ending Work-in-Process. The allocation using the weighted average results would be as follows:

1. Ending Work-in-Process before normal spoilage: $14,250.
2. Goods Completed before normal spoilage loss: $87,500.
3. Normal spoilage per unit ($8,750/6,000 units): $1.458.
4. Normal spoilage allocated to Goods Completed ($1.458 × 5,000): $7,292.
5. Normal Spoilage allocated to Ending Work-in-Process ($1.458 × 1,000): $1,458.
6. Goods Completed after normal spoilage (2 + 4): $94,790.
7. Ending Work-in-Process after normal spoilage (1 + 5): $15,708.

The allocation using the FIFO results would be as follows:

1. Ending Work-in-Process before normal spoilage: $14,500.
2. Goods Completed before normal spoilage loss: $87,750.
3. Normal spoilage per unit ($8,500/6,000 units): $1.416.

4. Normal spoilage allocated to Goods Completed ($1.416 × 5,000): $7,084.
5. Normal spoilage allocated to Ending Work-in-Process ($1,416 × 1,000): $1,416.
6. Goods Completed after normal spoilage (2 + 4): $94,835.
7. Ending Work-in-Process after normal spoilage (1 + 5): $15,917.

The journal entries will be as follows:

	Weighted	Average	FIFO	
Work-in-Process	90,000		90,000	
Raw Material Inventory		60,000		60,000
Factory Payroll		24,000		24,000
Factory Overhead		6,000		6,000
To record the input of material and conversion costs.				
Cost of Spoiled Goods	17,500		17,000	
Work-in-Process		17,500		17,000
To record the spoilage of 1,000 units.				
Finished Goods	87,500		87,750	
Cost of Spoiled Goods		87,500		87,750
To record the completion of 5,000 units.				
Finished Goods	7,292		7,084	
Work-in-Process	1,458		1,416	
Cost of Spoiled Goods		8,750		8,500
To allocate normal spoilage to good production and units in the Ending Work-in-Process.				
Loss from Abnormal Spoilage	8,750		8,500	
Cost of Spoiled Goods		8,750		8,500
To record the abnormal spoilage of 500 units.				

If the spoilage in the ABEL Manufacturing Company was a terminal spoilage, the costs of spoiled goods from normal spoilage would be allocated only to the units completed and transferred out of the department. In such a case, the journal entries would be as follows:

	Weighted	Average	FIFO	
Work-in-Process	90,000		90,000	
Raw Material Inventory		60,000		60,000
Factory Payroll		24,000		24,000
Factory Overhead		6,000		6,000
To record the input of material and conversion costs.				
Cost of Spoiled Goods	17,500		17,000	
Work-in-Process		17,500		17,000
To record the spoilage of 1,000 units.				
Finished Goods	87,500		87,750	
Work-in-Process		87,500		87,750
To record the completion of 5,000 units.				
Finished Goods	8,750		8,500	
Cost of Spoiled Goods		8,750		8,500
To record the normal spoilage of 500 units.				
Loss from Abnormal Spoilage	8,750		8,500	
Cost of Spoiled Goods		8,750		8,500
To record the abnormal spoilage of 500 units.				

Table 14.1
ABEL Manufacturing Company, Ltd., Process Cost Summary (Weighted Average Method)

1. Costs Charged to the Department

	Material	Labor	Overhead	Total
Current Costs	$60,000	$24,000	$6,000	$ 90,000
Beginning Work-in-Process	17,000	8,500	3,750	29,250
Total Costs to Be Accounted for	$77,000	$32,500	$9,750	$119,250

2. Equivalent Unit Processing Costs

	Total Units	Equivalent Units		
		Material	Labor	Overhead
Beginning Work-in-Process (1/4)	2,000			
Units Started	5,000			
To Account for	7,000			
Units Completed	5,000	5,000	5,000	5,000
Ending Work-in-Process (1/2)	1,000	1,000	500	500
Spoilage	1,000	1,000	1,000	1,000
Equivalent Units		7,000	6,500	6,500
Total Costs to Be Accounted for		$77,000	$32,500	$9,750
Equivalent Unit Processing Costs		$11.00	$5.00	$1.50

3. Costs Applicable to the Work of the Department

Goods Completed:	5,000 ($11 + $5.00 + $1.50)		$ 87,500
Ending Work-in-Process			
Material:	1,000 ($11.00)	$11,000	
Conversion Costs:	500 ($6.50)	3,250	14,250
Normal Spoilage:	500 ($17.50)		8,750
Abnormal Spoilage:	500 ($17.50)		8,750
Total Costs Accounted for			$119,250

14.3 ACCOUNTING FOR LABOR

Accounting for labor involves (1) the distribution of labor costs to the appropriate cost objects such as jobs, processes, and so forth; (2) the withholding of different types of taxes and the payment of employees; and (3) the remittance of all the withholdings and the payments of different labor-related costs such as

Table 14.2
ABEL Manufacturing Company, Ltd., Process Cost Summary (FIFO Method)

1. Costs Charged to the Department

	Material	Labor	Overhead	Start-up	Total
Current Costs	$60,000	$24,000	$6,000	—	$ 90,000
Beginning Work-in-Process	—	—	—	$29,250	29,250
Total Costs to Be Accounted for	$60,000	$24,000	$6,000	$29,250	$119,250

2. Equivalent Unit Processing Costs

		Equivalent Units		
	Total Units	Material	Labor	Overhead
Beginning Work-in-Process (1/4)	2,000			
Units Started	5,000			
To Account for	7,000			
Units Completed				
Beginning Inventory	2,000	—	1,500	1,500
Started and Completed	3,000	3,000	3,000	3,000
Ending Work-in-Process (1/2)	1,000	1,000	500	500
Spoilage	1,000	1,000	1,000	1,000
Equivalent Units		5,000	6,000	6,000
Total Costs to Be Accounted for		$60,000	$24,000	$6,000
Equivalent Unit Processing Costs		$12.00	$4.00	$1.00

3. Costs Applicable to the Work of the Department

Goods Completed			
Beginning Inventory:	29,250 + 1,500 ($4.00 + $1.00)		$ 36,750
Started and Completed:	3,000 ($17.00)		51,000
Normal Spoilage:	500 ($17.00)		8,500
Abnormal Spoilage:	500 ($17.00)		8,500
Ending Work-in-Process			
Materials:	1,000 ($12.00)	$12,000	
Conversion Costs:	500 ($ 5.00)	2,500	14,500
Total Costs Accounted for:			$119,250

vacation pay, sick pay, retirement benefits, insurance benefits, employee training, and so forth. These entries can be illustrated as follows:

Factory Payroll	100,000	
Accrued Payroll		100,000
To record the incurrence of labor costs.		
Work-in-Process Control	50,000	

Factory Overhead Control	30,000	
Selling Expense Control	10,000	
Administrative Expense Control	10,000	
Factory Payroll		100,000

To record the distribution of labor costs.

Accrued Payroll	100,000	
Withheld Income Taxes Payable (Assume 20%)		20,000
Withheld FICA Taxes Payable (Assume 5%)		5,000
Vouchers Payable or Cash		75,000

To record the withholding of taxes and the payment of earnings to employees.

Withheld Income Taxes Payable	20,000	
Withheld FICA Taxes Payable	5,000	
Vouchers Payable or Cash		25,000

To record the remitting of withholdings.

Work-in-Process Control	1,000	
Factory Overhead Control	500	
Liability for Vacation Pay, Bonuses, Etc.		1,500

To accrue vacation pay, bonuses, and other fringe benefits.

Liability for Vacation Pay, Bonuses, Etc.	1,500	
Vouchers Payable or Cash		1,500

To record the payment of fringe benefits.

It may also be expedient to regard the fringe benefits as essentially indirect costs, in which case the fifth entry will be as follows:

Factory Overhead Control	1,500	
Liability for Vacation Pay		1,500

To record the payment of fringe benefits.

14.4 INSPECTION AT A DEGREE OF COMPLETION

The example so far assumes that the spoilage is either initial or terminal. However, the spoilage may be detected at a certain degree of completion. In such a case, the cost of spoilage will receive a percentage of the conversion costs equal to the degree of completion. For example, assume that the spoilage has been detected with an inspection at 40 percent of the ABEL Manufacturing Company operations. In such a case, the equivalent units for spoilage under the weighted average method should be 1,000 units for material and 400 units (1,000 units × 40 percent) of conversion costs. Similarly, the equivalent units for spoilage under the FIFO method would be 0 units of material and 150 units [(.40 − .25)1,000] of conversion costs if we assume that the spoiled units originated from the beginning inventory or 1,000 units of material and 400 units of conversion costs if we assume that the spoiled units originated from the units started in the period. The assignment of the cost of normal spoilage when the inspection is done at a certain degree of completion (40 percent in this case) would depend on one of two situations:

1. If the ending inventory was less than the degree of completion as far as the production cycle was concerned, then the cost of normal spoilage will be assigned only to the units that have passed inspection.

2. If the ending inventory was more than the degree of completion as far as the production cycle was concerned, then the cost of normal spoilage will be assigned to both the completed units and the ending inventory.

Thus, a comparison of the stage in operations at which inspection occurs and the stage of completion of the ending inventory is crucial in deciding whether to allocate some of the costs of normal spoilage to the partially completed units in the ending inventory. Tables 14.3, 14.4, and 14.5 show the process cost remaining under the weighted average method and the FIFO method.

Under different conditions, the results would be as follows.

14.4.1 Condition 1

Table 14.3 shows the process cost summary using the weighted average method. The spoilage is assumed to have been discovered at 40 percent of the operations of the firm. The allocation using the weighted average method results and assuming that the ending inventory was more than 40 percent completed are as follows:

1. Ending Work-in-Process before normal spoilage: $14,579.325.
2. Goods Completed before normal spoilage: $90,793.25.
3. Normal spoilage per unit ($6,931.73/6,000 units): $1.1552.
4. Normal spoilage allocated to Goods Completed ($1.1552 × 5,000): $5,776.
5. Normal Spoilage allocated to Ending Work-in-Process ($1.1552 × 1,000): $1,155.20.
6. Goods Completed after normal spoilage (2 + 4): $96,569.25.
7. Ending Work-in-Process after normal spoilage (1 + 5): $15,734.525.

14.4.2 Condition 2

Table 14.4 shows the process cost summary using the FIFO method, assuming that the spoiled units come from the beginning inventory. The spoilage is assumed to have been discovered at 40 percent of the firm's operations. The allocation using the FIFO method results and assuming that the ending inventory was more than 40 percent completed are as follows:

1. Ending Work-in-Process before normal spoilage: $17,912.57.
2. Goods Completed before normal spoilage: $100,463.13.
3. Normal spoilage per unit ($436.8855/6,000): $0.0728.

4. Normal spoilage allocated to Goods Completed ($0.0728 × 5,000): $364.

5. Normal spoilage allocated to Ending Work-in-Process ($0.0728 × 1,000): $72.80.

6. Goods Completed after normal spoilage (2 + 4): $100,827.13.

7. Ending Work-in-Process after normal spoilage (1 + 5): $17,985.37.

Table 14.3
ABEL Manufacturing Company, Ltd., Process Cost Summary (Weighted Average Method)

1. Costs Charged to the Department

	Material	Labor	Overhead	Total
Current Costs	$60,000	$24,000	$6,000	$ 90,000
Beginning Work-in-Process	17,000	8,500	3,750	29,250
Total Costs to Be Accounted For	$77,000	$32,500	$9,750	$119,250

2. Equivalent Unit Processing Costs

	Total Units	Equivalent Units		
		Material	Labor	Overhead
Beginning Work-in-Process (1/4)	2,000			
Units Started	5,000			
To Account For	7,000			
Units Completed	5,000	5,000	5,000	5,000
Ending Work-in-Process (1/2)	1,000	1,000	500	500
Spoilage	1,000	1,000	400	400
Equivalent Units		7,000	5,900	5,900
Total Costs to Be Accounted For		$77,000	$32,500	$9,750
Equivalent Unit Processing Costs		$11.000	$5.5084	$1.65025

3. Costs Applicable to the Work of the Department

Goods Completed:	5,000($11+$5.5084+$1.65025) =	$90,793.25
Ending Work-in-Process		
Material:	1,000($11) = $11,000	
Conversion Costs:	500($5.5084+$1.65025)=$3,579.325	$14,579.325
Normal Spoilage:	(500x11) + 200x($5.5084+$1.65025)	6,931.73
Abnormal Spoilage:	(500x11)+200($5.5084+$1.65025)	6,931.73

Table 14.4
ABEL Manufacturing Company Ltd., Process Cost Summary (FIFO Method)

1. Costs Charged to the Department

	Material	Labor	Overhead	Start up	Total
Current Costs	$60,000	$24,000	$6,000	---	$ 90,000
Beginning Work-in-process	---	---	---	$29,250	$ 29,250
Total Costs To Be Accouted For	$60,000	$24,000	$6,000	$29,250	$119,250

2. Equivalent Unit Processing Cost

	Total Units	Equivalent Units		
		Material	Labor	Overhead
Beginning Work-in-Process (1/4)	2,000			
Units Started	5,000			
To Account For	7,000			
Units Completed				
Beginning Inventory (1/4)	2,000	--	1,500	1,500
· Started and Completed	3,000	3,000	3,000	3,000
Ending Work-in-Process (1/2)	1,000	1,000	500	500
Spoilage	1,000	--	150	150
Equivalent Units		4,000	5,150	5,150
Total Costs to Be Accounted For		$60,000	$24,000	$6,000
Equivalent Unit Processing Costs		$15	$4.6601	$1.16504

3. Costs Applicable to the Department

Goods Completed:
Beginning Inventory:	$29,250+1,500(44.6601+$1.16504) =	$37,987.71
Started and Completed:	3,000($15+$4.6601+$1.16504) =	$62,475.42
Normal Spoilage:	75($4.6601+$1.16504) =	$436.8855
Abnormal Spoilage:	75($4.660+$1.16504) =	$436.8855
Ending Work-in-Process		$17,912.57
Materials:	1,000x$15 = $15,000	
Conversion Costs:	500($4.6601+$1.16504) = $2,912.57	

Table 14.5
ABEL Manufacturing Company, Ltd., Process Cost Summary (FIFO Method)

1.   Costs Charged to the Department

	Material	Labor	Overhead	Startup	Total
Current Costs	$60,000	$24,000	$6,000	---	$90,000
Beginning Work-in-Process	----	---	---	$29,250	$29,250
Total Costs to be Accounted For	$60,000	$24,000	$6,000	$29,250	$119,250

2.   Equivalent Unit Processing Cost

Equivalent Unit

	Total Units	Material	Labor	Overhead
Beginning Work-in-Process (1/4)	2,000			
Units Started	5,000			
To Account For	7,000			
Units Completed				
Beginning Inventory (1/4)	2,000	---	1,500	1,500
Started and Completed	3,000	3,000	3,000	3,000
Ending Work-in-Process (1/2)	1,000	1,000	500	500
Spoilage	1,000	1,000	400	400
Equivalent Units		5,000	5,400	5,400
Total Costs to be Accounted for		$60,000	$24,000	$6,000
Equivalent Unit Processing Cost		$12	$4.4444	$1.1111

3.   Costs Applicable to the Department
Goods Completed $90249.75
    Beginning Inventory: $29,250+1,500($4.4444+$1.1111)=$37583.25
    Started and Completed: 3,000($12+$4.444+$1.11111)=$52666.5
Normal Spoilage:500($12)+200($4.4444+$1.1111)= $7111.1
Abnormal Spoilage:500($12)+200($4.4444+$1.1111)= $7111.1
Ending Work-in-Process $14777.75
    Materials: 1000($12)=$12,000
    Conversion Costs: 500($4.4444+$1.1111)=$2777.75

14.4.3 Condition 3

Table 14.5 shows the process cost summary using the FIFO method, assuming that the spoiled units come from the units started in the period. The spoilage is assumed to have been discovered at 40 percent of the firm's operations. The allocation using the FIFO method results and assuming that the ending inventory was more than 40 percent completed are as follows:

1. Ending Work-in-Process before normal spoilage: $14,777.75.

2. Goods Completed before normal spoilage: $90,249.75.

3. Normal spoilage per unit ($7,111.10/6,000): $1.1851.

4. Normal spoilage allocated to Goods Completed ($1.1851 × 5,000): $5,925.50.

5. Normal spoilage allocated to Ending Work-in-Process ($1.1851 × 1,000): $1,185.10.
6. Goods Completed after normal spoilage (2 + 4): $96,175.25.
7. Ending Work-in-Process after normal spoilage (2 + 5): $15,962.85.

14.5 NEW MANUFACTURING ACCOUNTING

New manufacturing accounting has emerged as a result of new technologies and intense global competition. Examples of these technologies include computer-integrated manufacturing (CIM) systems, the flexible manufacturing system (FMS), and just-in-time (JIT) systems. Their introduction is motivated by the need to increase product quality and reduce product costs. The new manufacturing accounting is considered to be the cause of the superior performance of some Japanese manufacturing firms. Some of the improvements brought by the new manufacturing accounting are explored in this section.

14.5.1 Inventory and Production Control Systems

Two new systems, the push system and the pull system, reflect the extreme points of inventory and production control systems.

The push system has been defined as follows:

A push system in reality is simply a schedule-based system. That is, a multi-period schedule of future demands for the company's products (called a master production schedule) is prepared and the computer breaks that schedule down into detailed schedules for making or buying the component parts. It is a push system in that the schedule pushes the production people into making the required parts and then pushing the parts out and onward. The name given to this push system is material requirements planning (MRP).[3]

Under the push system, following a forecast of demand, production begins in the first department (or subassembly) and is pushed to the Work-in-Process buffer inventory separating the department from the next one. The present department production is pushed to another buffer inventory. The sequence started in the first department continues until the end of the assembly line. The Work-in-Process Inventories accumulated between departments or work stations serve as a cushion for inaccurate forecasting, line imbalances, and inefficiencies. The workers are left decoupled from each other and the production goals.

Under the pull system, or JIT control system, the production is controlled by a forecast of current demand and the level of finished goods inventory. When the finished goods inventory falls below a specified level, production is started. The Work-in-Process buffer between work stations is kept low or at zero. The last worker dictates the pace of the job. As he or she completes his or her part of the subassembly, removing it from the Work-in-Process buffer inventory, the next-to-last worker indicates the production of his or her part of the subassembly. Production is therefore pulled from the end of the subassembly line. Unlike the push system, the workers under the pull system are tightly coupled and sensitive to the production goal.

In short, under the pull system, the production system initiates the work in a component immediately as needed by the next step in the production line. The main objective is to have a zero inventory system, which explains the other terms given to the JIT system: materials as needed (MAN), minimum inventory production system (MIPS), pull through production (PTP), and zero inventory production system (ZIPS). (The pull system–based production control technique is also known as the kanban system.) This system has the advantage of eliminating and reducing inventory cost. Traditionally, the cost of inventory is perceived to be a financial cost—the inventory in hand multiplied by the cost of capital. In fact, other indirect and qualitative costs are associated with holding inventory:

Examples include: increased space requirements, increased materials handling costs, increased recordkeeping costs, increased insurance and tax obligations, slower throughput, higher scrap and obsolesence, and more costly inventory write-downs.[4]

Reducing these costs frees up cash for investment in productive assets and improves profitability.

Just-in-time is more than a technique; it is a philosophy. George Foster and Charles Horngren delineate the four aspects pivotal of a JIT system:

- The elimination of all activities that do not add value to a product or service. In the context of JIT, "not adding value" is a buzz phrase loosely used to describe any activities or resources that are targets for reduction or elimination.
- A commitment to a high level of quality. Doing things right the first time is crucial if no time is allowed for rework.
- A commitment to continuous improvement in the efficiency of an activity.
- Simplification and increased visibility to identify activities that do not add value.[5]

A good example of the type of new manufacturing environment is provided by Nummi (New United Motors of Manufacturing Inc.), a General Motors–Toyota venture. At their plant, a team concept allows the workers to be involved in manufacturing planning. The system known as "management by stress," "team concept," or "synchronous manufacturing" centers on target specifications and monitoring the low jobs to be done, tight control of work, and JIT manufacturing. A description of the system follows:

Under management by stress, the aim is to methodically locate and remove protections against glitches. Glitches are in fact welcomed because they identify the system's weak points. Breakdowns indicate where methods must be changed, perhaps a way found to perform a particular bottleneck operation more quickly. Just as important, points that never break down are assumed to waste resources. They are targeted as well—human or material resources are removed until the station can keep up, but just barely.[6]

A lighted board above the assembly line, called the andon board, is used to show the status of each work station. If a worker cannot keep up, he pulls a cord to ring a bell and light up the board, allowing management to redesign the job to make it more efficient. An unlighted board indicates inefficiencies, and management has to speed up the line to stress the system and thereby find the inefficiencies. The system is assumed to allow for "kaizen," or continuous improvement.

Management by stress is, in fact, a reinforcement of Taylorism with a bigger role for the workers themselves.

In fact, management by stress is an intensification of Taylorism. Engineers and group and team leaders break the required assembly tasks down into the tiniest of separate "acts" and come up with a detailed written specification of how each worker is to do each job. This chart is posted near the line so the group leader can check to see that the worker does not vary his or her methods. Workers are not allowed to work faster for a short time to create some breathing space—although the jobs are so "loaded" that this is not possible anyway. If they discover a method, on their own, that makes the job easier, they must ask the supervisor's permission to use it. The catch, of course, is that another task will be found to fill the time.[7]

14.5.2 Costing under a JIT Production System

Under a JIT production system, there are no Work-in-Process and Finished Goods inventories. Basically, the amount produced conforms exactly to the customers' orders and is shipped immediately to the customers. The costing system, known as JIT costing, is definitively simpler than the costing procedures examined in the last three chapters. Basically, under JIT costing, department costs are accumulated for control purposes before being charged directly to the cost of goods sold. The procedures may be as follows:

First, for the raw material, a JIT costing system will combine the new material accounts and Work-in-Process account into a *resources in process* account. The new in-process account will be debited by the material purchases and credited for the raw materials assigned directly to the finished goods. A comparison of the journal entries between JIT costing and operation costing follows. Operations costing, or specification costing, collects both direct labor and factory overhead to operations by using a simple average unit conversion cost for the operation. Accounting for material uses the same procedures used in the JIT costing system.

Operation Costing

Stores	$10,000	
Accounts Payable		10,000

To record the purchases.

Work-in-Process	$10,000	
Stores		10,000

To record the issuance of material.

| Finished Goods | $9,500 | |
| Work-in-Process | | 9,500 |

JIT Costing

Raw and In-Process		
Inventory	$9,500	
Accounts Payable		9,500

To record the purchases.

Finished Goods	$9,500	
Raw and In-Process		
Inventory		9,500

Second, conversion costs are charged to departments upon occurrence and are then applied directly to the cost of goods sold as follows:

| Cost of Goods Sold | $5,000 | |
| Applied Factory Overhead | | 5,000 |

Third, at the end of each period, an adjustment is made for the overhead applicable to raw and in-process inventory and finished goods as follows:

Raw and in-process inventory	$200	
Finished Goods	800	
Cost of Goods Sold		1,000

To reallocate irrelevant costs from Cost of
Goods Sold to ending inventory.

In the above illustration, the figures are assumed. The journal entries shown are not necessarily the only approach available under JIT costing.[8] Other approaches will surely be devised in the future.

14.5.3 Quality Control Systems

The systems of quality control, the process-based system and the output-based system, reflect extreme points of quality control systems.

Under the *output-based quality control system,* the product is inspected for quality when it leaves the assembly line. At the time of this inspection, detective products, scrap, and spoilage are identified. This system engenders a suspicion that, because of uncooperative relationships between production and quality control people, problems undetected by quality control people may be deliberately ignored by production people, resulting in inefficiency and heavy losses to companies.[9]

Under the *process-based quality control system,* or "jikoda," the responsibility for quality control is given to the production worker who can stop the total production process when he or she detects a production problem. Quality control, therefore, takes place at each stage of the process because each worker checks every part sent to him or her to detect any errors before proceeding to work on it. This system is assumed to have eliminated all errors in output in many Japanese manufacturing firms. The situation in many U.S. manufacturing firms is different.

In contrast, in many U.S. firms, management tries very hard to avoid downtime and workers who persist in pointing out problems leading to downtime may be chastised. Worker-based process quality control results in relatively high performance efficiency (i.e., the ratio of good output to total output) because errors are detected and converted before completion of the output. In contrast, output-based quality control has relatively lower performance efficiency because errors are not necessarily detected and converted before the output is completed. Thus, in this latter case, a lower percentage of the total output may not be good output.[10]

14.5.4 Total Quality Control

The Japanese have revamped their concepts of quality control into a set of techniques labeled total quality control (TQC). When implemented in concert with a JIT system and various other productivity improvements, the TQC has the potential to improve industrial management. The emphasis in a TQC system is as follows:

1. A goal of continual quality improvement, project after project (rejection of the Western notion of an "acceptable quality level").
2. Worker (not QC Department) responsibility.
3. Measurers of quality that are visible, visual, simple, and understandable, even to the casual observer.
4. Automatic quality measurement derives (self-development).[11]

Seven basic principles included in quality control include (1) process control, (2) easy-to-see quality, (3) insistence on compliance, (4) line stop, (5) correcting one's own errors (6) 100 percent check, and (7) project-by-project improvement.[12]

1. Process control focuses on checking the quality of the product while the work is being done.
2. Easy-to-see quality refers to the display of easy to understand, visual, obvious indicators of quality, resulting in a principle of "measurable standards of quality" at every process.
3. Insistence on compliance refers to an uncompromising position on quality first and output second.
4. Line stop refers to giving each worker the authority to stop the production line to correct quality problems.
5. Correcting one's own errors makes the worker who made the bad product responsible for performing any rework required.

6. A 100 percent check refers to the inspection of every item, rather than just a random sample, and to the rejection of lot acceptance inspection.

7. Improvement is accomplished on a project basis.

14.5.5 Measuring and Reporting Quality Costs

If a final product fails to meet the appropriate chemical specifications, it does not meet quality standards, specifically, it fails quality conformance. Quality costs are associated with quality of conformance, namely, prevention costs, appraisal costs, internal failure costs, and external failure costs.[13] These costs have been defined as follows:

Prevention costs are the costs associated with designing, implementing, and maintaining the quality system. These costs include engineering quality control systems, quality planning of various departments, and quality training programs. Appraisal costs use the costs incurred to insure that materials and products meet quality standards.

These costs include inspection of raw materials, laboratory tests, quality audits, and field testing. Internal failure costs are the costs associated with materials and products that fail to meet quality standards and result in manufacturing losses. They include the costs of scrap, repair, and rework of defective products identified before they are shipped to consumers.

Table 14.6
Quality Cost Report

	Current Month's Lost	% of Loss
Prevention Costs		
Quality Training	$ 3000	1.5%
Reliability Engineering	15000	7.5%
Pilot Studies	6000	3%
System Development	9000	4.5%
Total Prevention	$33,000	16.5%
Appraisal Costs		
Materials Inspection	$ 8,000	4%
Supplies Inspection	4,000	2%
Reliability Testing	6,000	3%
Laboratory	28,000	14%
Internal Failure Costs:		
Scrap	13,000	6.5%
Repair	23,000	11.5%
Rework	13,000	6.5%
Downtime	7,000	3.5%
Total Internal Failure	$56,000	28%
External Failure Costs:		
Warranty Costs	$13,000	6.5%
Out of Warranty Repairs & Replacement	7,000	3.5%
Customer Complaints	10,000	5%
Product Liability	10,000	5%
Transportation Losses	25,000	12.5%
Total External Failure	$65,000	39.5%
Total Costs of Nonconformance	$200,000	100.0

External failure costs are the costs incurred because inferior quality products are shipped to consumers. They include the costs of handling complaints, warranty replacement, repairs of returned products, and so forth.[14]

These costs must be measured and reported to highlight the costs of quality of conformance. An example of a quality cost report is shown in Table 14.6. It shows the cost of nonconformance as an aggregation of all the implicit costs that are attributable to manufacturing a nonquality product.[15]

14.6 QUALITY COST RELATIONSHIP

A model proposed by J. T. Godfrey and W. R. Pasework views quality costs as being composed of defect control costs, failure costs, and cost of lost sales.[16]

14.6.1 Defect Control Costs

Defect control costs (Q) are defined as equal to prevention costs (K) plus appraisal costs (A), or $Q = K + A$.

14.6.2 Failure Costs

Failure costs (F) are defined as equal to rework costs, profit lost by selling units as defective, and the cost of processing customer returns. The profit lost by selling units as defective (Z) is equal to

$Z =$ [Total defective units (D) − Number of units reworked (Y)] * [Profit for good units (p1) − Profit for defective units (p2)]

or

$$Z = (D - Y) * (p1 - p2).$$

The rework costs (R) are equal to the costs of reworking a unit (r) multiplied by the number of units reworked, or $R = r*Y$.

The cost of processing customer returns (W) is equal to the cost of a single customer return (w) multiplied by the number of defective units returned by customers (D2), or $W = w*D2$.

Therefore, the total failure costs (F) are equal to

$$F = R + Z + W$$

or

$$F = (r*y) + [(D - Y) * (p1 - p2)] + (w*D2).$$

14.6.3 Cost of Lost Sales

Cost of lost sales (L) is defined as the cost of current and future sales that will be lost if defective units are received by customers.

14.6.4 Total Quality Costs

Total quality costs (T) can now be expressed as

$$T = K + A + R + Z + W + L$$

or

$$T = K + A + (Y*r) + [(D - Y)(p1 - p2) + (D2*w)] + L.$$

Appraisal costs, rework costs, profit foregone by selling units as defective, cost of processing customers' returns, and cost of lost sales increase as the percentage of defective units increases. However, prevention costs decrease as the percentage of defective units increase.

Assuming that the number of defective units discovered by customers is a constant percentage of total defective units, the quality cost relationships may be illustrated as shown in Table 14.7. Management, in this case, would opt for case D, where the total quality costs are minimized at $220.00.

Table 14.7
Quality Cost Relationships

Case	Defect Control Costs		Percent Defective	Failure Costs			Cost of Lost Sales ((L)	Total Quality Costs
	Prevention Costs (K)	Appraisal Costs (A)		Rework Costs (R)	Cost of not Re-work ing (Z)	Cost of pro-cess ing (W)		
A	$250	$ 50	2.5%	$25.0	$2.5	$1.25	$3.25	$332.00
B	260	45	2.00%	20.0	2.0	1.00	3.00	331.00
C	270	40	1.50%	15.0	1.5	0.75	2.25	329.50
D	275	32	1.00%	10.0	1.0	0.50	1.50	220.00
E	290	30	0.50%	5.0	0.5	0.25	0.30	325.60
F	320	20	0.00%	0.0	0.0	0.00	0.00	340.00

14.6.5 Zero Defect Policy

In the section 14.1, we assumed that scrap and waste, defective work that had to be reworked, spoilage, and lost units are unavoidable phenomena in the production process. That assumption explains the attitude known as "produce-and-rework-if-defective," a policy that expects that a certain level of error is compatible with a tolerance level set by managers. This assumption is, however, severely criticized in favor of a zero defect policy, which expects every produced unit to be a good unit. Any spoilage resulting in rework is therefore treated as an abnormal spoilage and is written off as a loss.

14.7 CONCLUSION

This chapter identified the main problem associated with accounting for quality costs. It also served as an introduction to the new manufacturing accounting aimed at completely eliminating these quality costs.

NOTES

1. Robert A. Howell and Stephen R. Soucy, "Operating Controls in the New Manufacturing Environment." *Management Accounting* (October 1987): 13.

2. Ibid. 15.

3. Richard J. Schonberger, *Japanese Manufacturing Techniques* (New York: The Free Press, 1982): 220.

4. Robert A. Howell and Stephen R. Soucy, "The New Manufacturing Accounting: Major Trends for Management Accounting." *Management Accounting* (July 1982): 16.

5. George Foster and Charles T. Horngren, "Cost Accounting and Cost Management Issues." *Management Accounting* (June 1987): 19.

6. Mike Parker and Jane Slaughter, "Behind the Scenes at Nummi Motors." *New York Times Sunday* (December 4, 1988): 2F.

7. Ibid. 2F.

8. R. Hunt, L. Garrett, and C. M. Mertz, "Direct Labor Cost Not Always Relevant at H.P." *Management Accounting* (February 1985): 61.

9. R. H. Hayes, "Why Japanese Factories Work." *Harvard Business Review* (July–August, 1981): 57–66.

10. Mark S. Young, Michael D. Shields, and G. Wolf. "Manufacturing Controls and Performance: An Experiment." *Accounting, Organizations and Society* (October 1988): 610.

11. R. J. Schonberger, *Japanese Manufacturing Techniques: Nine Hidden Lessons in Simplicity* (London: The Free Press, 1982): 7.

12. Ibid. 55.

13. Harold P. Roth and Wayne J. Moore, "Let's Help Measure and Report Quality Costs." *Management Accounting* (August 1983): 50–53.

14. Ibid. 50.

15. See also John Clark, "Costing for Quality at Celanese." *Management Accounting* (March 1985): 42–46.

16. James T. Godfrey and William R. Pasework, "Controlling Quality Costs." *Management Accounting* (March 1988): 48–51.

SELECTED READINGS

Chalos, P. "High-Tech Production: The Impact on Cost Reporting Systems." *Journal of Accountancy* (March 1986): 106–112.

Clark, John "Costing for Quality at Celanese." *Management Accounting* (March 1985): 42–46.

Clark, Ronald L., and James B. McLaughlin. "Controlling the Cost of Product Defects." *Management Accounting* (August 1986): 32–35.

Crosby, P. *Quality without Tears.* New York: McGraw-Hill, 1984.

Foster, George, and Charles T. Horngren, "Cost Accounting and Cost Management Issues." *Management Accounting* (June 1987): 19–25.

Howell, Robert A., and Stephen R. Soucy, "The New Manufacturing Accounting: Major Trends for Management Accounting." *Management Accounting* (June 1982): 16.

Young, Mark S., Michael D. Shields, and G. Wolf. "Manufacturing Controls and Performance: An Experiment." *Accounting, Organizations and Society* (October 1988): 610.

15

Direct versus Absorption Costing: Inventory and Decision Making

The issue of whether inventories should be costed at variable or full cost remains a subject of debate in both the academic and business worlds. The controversy centers mainly on two inventory valuation methods: the *direct* or *variable costing* method and the *absorption* or *full costing* method. The costing problem encompasses many conceptual and operational dimensions, mainly in the areas of asset valuation, income determination, and decision making. This chapter elaborates on (1) a definition of the problem, (2) the arguments in the controversy, (3) the reconciliation of the two inventory valuation methods, and (4) the relevance for decision making.

15.1 NATURE OF THE PROBLEM

15.1.1 Asset-Expense Dichotomy

The central problem in asset valuation, and particularly in inventory valuation, is making a clear distinction between assets and expenses. A cost is recognized as an asset if it results from the acquisition of future potential services. A determinant of an asset lies in its revenue-producing powers. The term *asset* has been approximately defined as follows:

Assets are economic resources devoted to business purposes within a specific accounting entity; they are aggregates of service potential available for or beneficial to expected operation. The significance of some assets may be uniquely related to the objectives of the business entity and will depend upon enterprise continuity.[1]

For example, inventories and prepaid expenses are viewed as assets, since they both constitute realizable aggregates of service potential.

An expense, however, results from the use or expiration of a resource that is an asset. In other words, when assets no longer have service potential, they are expired and called *expenses*. For example, the prepaid rent of $3,000 for three years, recognized initially as an asset, is reduced by $1,000 rent expense at the end of the first year to reflect the expiration of some of the rights to use the property.

The central problem in the asset-expense dichotomy is that, while the definition of asset as an acquisition of an aggregate of service potential is accepted, the definition of expense as the expiration of some of this service potential is subject to different interpretations. The accounting profession has adopted two principles to resolve the expiration problem: the *costs attach* principle and the *matching* principle.[2] A proper conceptual definition of these principles is necessary for an understanding of the asset-expense dichotomy or, more precisely, the acquisition-expiration process.

Costs Attach Principle

The costs attach principle implies that, if accounting is to be a good description of events occurring in the real world, all the related costs should "attach" to the units produced. In other words, all costs actually expended in the production process are to be attached directly to the product. A. W. Paton and A. C. Littleton stated:

It is a basic concept of accounting that costs can be marshalled into new groups that possess real significance. It is as if costs had a power of cohesion when properly brought into contact. Accounting assumes that acquisition costs are mobile and may be reapportioned or regrouped, and that costs reassembled have a natural affinity for each other which identify them with the group. Some costs, like manufacturing overhead, in which an affinity with a product can be detected, are allocated directly to a product. . . .

The purpose of reassembling is to trace the efforts made to give materials and other components additional utility.[3]

The costs attach principle specifies that those costs that are essential to the very existence of the product are to be inventoried with the product. They constitute the economic attributes of the product and would expire only with the loss of these attributes.

Matching Principle: Product versus Period Matching

While the costs attach principle specifies the requirements for a cost to be inventoried and attached to a product or asset, the matching principle specifies the requirements for the recognition of the expense. Consider the following definition:

Costs (defined as product and service factors given up) should be related to revenues realized within a specific period on the basis of some discernible positive correlation of such costs with the recognized revenues.[4]

Thus, the matching principle requires the determination of a proper association between expenses and the revenues of the period.

Two methods conventionally used are the direct, or *product matching,* method and the indirect, or *period matching,* method. The direct, or product matching, method consists of at least two steps. First, some costs (known as product costs) are attached to the product or asset and inventoried according to a costs attach criterion. Second, some of these product costs are released as expenses at the time of reporting the associated revenues. The indirect, or period matching, method consists of reporting some costs (known as period costs) as expenses during the period they are used. The rationale lies in the association of these expenses with the period rather than with the revenues. Whether an item constitutes a product cost (and hence an asset) or a period cost (and hence an expense) depends on the choice between the two inventory valuation methods: absorption costing and direct costing.

15.1.2 Accounting for Fixed Manufacturing Overhead

The main issue in the inventory valuation controversy is the classification of costs as either product or period costs. Thus,

1. The absorption costing method is a total input concept in the sense that all the manufacturing costs, whether variable or fixed, are treated as product costs and hence inventoried with the products. The cost of an item, then, includes the cost of direct material, the cost of direct labor, and an apportioned share of manufacturing overhead. Consequently, under absorption costing, the period costs are limited to both selling and administrative overhead.

2. The direct costing method is a variable input concept in the sense that only the variable manufacturing costs are treated as product costs and inventoried. The period costs include not only the selling and administrative overhead, but also the fixed manufacturing overhead.[5]

The main difference between product costing methods lies in the accounting treatment of the fixed manufacturing overhead. Under the direct costing method, the fixed manufacturing overhead is regarded as a period cost (that is, an expired cost to be immediately charged against the period sales). Figure 15.1 highlights the differences between these two inventory valuation techniques.

To illustrate the operational differences, consider the following example. The XYZ Company produces 4,000 units of a single product per year. The costs related to the product are

	Cost per Unit of Product
Direct-Material Cost	$ 5
Direct-Labor Cost	$ 3
Variable Manufacturing Overhead	$ 2
Fixed Manufacturing Overhead	$20,000

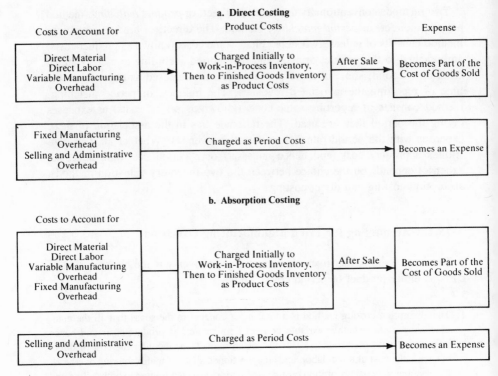

Figure 15.1
Comparison of the Flow of Costs

Assume that you are required to compute the unit cost of a product under both the absorption costing method and the direct costing method. Correct computations follow:

Absorption Costing

Direct Material	$ 5
Direct Labor	3
Variable Manufacturing Overhead	2
Fixed Manufacturing Overhead ($20,000 ÷ 4,000)	5
Total Cost per Unit	$15

Direct Costing

Direct Material	$ 5
Direct Labor	3
Variable Manufacturing Overhead	2
Total Cost per Unit	$10

The items in the ending inventory of finished goods will be valued at $15 under the absorption costing method and at $10 under the direct costing method.

The $20,000 fixed manufacturing overhead will be released as period expenses against income under the direct costing method.

15.1.3 Comparison of Absorption and Direct Costing Results

This section will illustrate the impact of absorption and direct costing on inventory valuation and income determination. For consistency, the income determination format resulting from the use of absorption costing for inventory valuation will be labeled as the *traditional method,* and the format resulting from the use of direct costing will be called the *contribution method.* Income statements prepared under both methods are presented in Tables 15.1 and 15.2. The cost characteristics used to prepare these statements follow:

Normal Capacity	10,000 Units
Standard Direct-Material Cost per Unit	$ 1
Standard Direct-Labor Cost per Unit	$ 2
Standard Variable Manufacturing Overhead per Unit	$ 4
Standard Fixed Manufacturing Overhead per Year	$50,000
Standard Fixed Manufacturing Overhead per Unit ($50,000 ÷ 10,000)	$ 5
Fixed Selling and Administrative Overhead per Year	$20,000
Work-in-Process Inventories	0 Units
Sales Price per Unit	$ 20
Variable Selling and Administrative Overhead per Unit	$ 1

Similarly, the actual production, sales, and finished goods inventory in units are

	Year 1	Year 2	Year 3	Three Years Together
Beginning Inventory	0	0	2,000	0
Production	10,000	12,000	6,000	28,000
Sales	10,000	10,000	8,000	28,000
Ending Inventory	0	2,000	0	0

There were no variances from the standard variable costs, and volume variance is written off directly at year-end as an adjustment to Cost of Goods Sold.

The following generalizations can be made from the results shown in Tables 15.1 and 15.2:

1. When the sales and production volumes are equal, the profits under absorption and direct costing are equal. In year 1, the profit under both methods is equal to $50,000 due to the fact that, under both methods, the $50,000 fixed manufacturing overhead is charged off in total against income as a period expense.

2. When the production volume exceeds the sales volume, absorption costing yields a higher profit, as shown in the results for year 2. The reason is that while the total fixed manufacturing overhead of $50,000 is released as a period expense under direct costing, only a portion of it is charged off as a period expense, and the rest is charged to inventory to be deferred to future periods under absorption costing.

Table 15.1
Profit Figures under the Traditional Method (Absorption Costing)

Income Statement	First Year	Second Year	Third Year	Three Years Together
Sales	$200,000	$200,000	$160,000	$560,000
Direct Material	$ 10,000	$ 12,000	$ 6,000	$ 28,000
+ Direct Labor	20,000	24,000	12,000	56,000
+ Variable Factory Overhead	40,000	48,000	24,000	112,000
+ Fixed Factory Overhead	50,000	60,000	30,000	140,000
Cost of Goods Manufactured	$120,000	$144,000	$ 72,000	$336,000
+ Beginning Inventory @ $12	0	0	24,000	0
Available for Sale	$120,000	$144,000	$ 96,000	$336,000
− Ending Inventory @ $12	0	24,000	0	0
Cost of Goods Sold	$120,000	$120,000	$ 96,000	$336,000
+ Volume variance[a]	0	(10,000)[c]	20,000	10,000
Adjusted Cost of Goods Sold	$120,000	$110,000	$116,000	$346,000
Gross Margin	$ 80,000	$ 90,000	$ 44,000	$214,000
− Selling and Administrative Expenses	30,000[b]	30,000[b]	28,000[d]	88,000[e]
Net Operating Income	$ 50,000	$ 60,000	$ 16,000	$126,000

[a] Volume variance resulting from a normal capacity of 10,000 units: Second year: $(12,000 - 10,000) \times \$5 = \$10,000$ overapplied. Third year: $(10,000 - 6,000) \times \$5 = \$20,000$ underapplied. Three years together: $(30,000 - 28,000) \times \$5 = \$10,000$ underapplied.
[b] $20,000 + ($1.00 × 10,000 units sold).
[c] Another possible alternative is to prorate the volume variance between the Inventory and Cost of Goods Sold.
[d] $20,000 + ($1.00 × 8,000 units sold).
[e] ($20,000 × 3) + ($1.00 × 28,000 units sold).

3. When the sales volume exceeds the production volume, direct costing yields a higher profit, as seen in the results for year 3. Fixed costs previously deferred to inventory under direct costing are now charged off against income as a period expense.

4. The profit under costing fluctuates in proportion to sales, as shown by a comparison of the results of year 1 and year 2. Hence, given a constant sales volume in year 1 and year 2, the profit under direct costing is constant in both years, while the profit under absorption costing from year 1 to year 2 is affected by the direction and amount of the changes in inventory.

5. The difference in profits between the two methods in each of the three years is attributable to the differences in accounting for fixed manufacturing overhead and the imbalances between sales and production. Under absorption costing, the fixed manufacturing overhead is transferred from one year to another as a product or inventoried cost. Under direct costing, the fixed manufacturing overhead is indirectly charged as a

Table 15.2
Profit Figures under the Contribution Method (Direct Costing)

Income Statement	First Year	Second Year	Third Year	Three Years Together
Sales	$200,000	$200,000	$160,000	$560,000
Direct Material	$ 10,000	$ 12,000	$ 6,000	$ 28,000
+ Direct Labor	20,000	24,000	12,000	56,000
+ Variable Manufacturing Overhead	40,000	48,000	24,000	112,000
Variable Cost of Goods Manufactured	$ 70,000	$ 84,000	$ 42,000	$196,000
+ Beginning Inventory @ $7	0	0	14,000	0
Available for Sale	$ 70,000	$ 84,000	$ 56,000	$196,000
− Ending Inventory @ $7	0	14,000	0	0
Variable Cost of Goods Sold	$ 70,000	$ 70,000	$ 56,000	$196,000
+ Variable Selling and Administrative Overhead	10,000	10,000	8,000	28,000
− Total Variable Expenses	$ 80,000	$ 80,000	$ 64,000	$224,000
Total Contribution Margin	$120,000	$120,000	$ 96,000	$336,000
Fixed Manufacturing Overhead	$ 50,000	$ 50,000	$ 50,000	$150,000
+ Fixed Selling and Administrative Overhead	20,000	20,000	20,000	60,000
Total Fixed Expenses	$ 70,000	$ 70,000	$ 70,000	$210,000
Net Operating Income	$ 50,000	$ 50,000	$ 26,000	$126,000

period expense. The following formula computes the differences between the net profits of absorption and direct costing:

$$\begin{array}{ccc} \text{Absorption} & \text{Direct} & \text{Fixed} & \text{Changes in} \\ \text{costing} & - \text{ costing} = & \text{manufacturing} \times & \text{inventory} \\ \text{profit} & \text{profit} & \text{overhead per unit} & \text{in units.} \end{array}$$

When applied to the XYZ Company example, the formula yields the following results:

	Year 1	Year 2	Year 3	Three Years Together
Absorption Costing Profit	$50,000	$60,000	$ 16,000	$126,000
− Direct Costing Profit	50,000	50,000	26,000	126,000
= Difference in Profit	$ 0	$10,000	$(10,000)	$ 0
Fixed Manufacturing Overhead per Unit	$ 5	$ 5	$ 5	$ 5
× Changes in Inventory Units	0	2,000	(2,000)	0
= Difference in Profit	$ 0	$10,000	$(10,000)	$ 0

These generalizations do not hold in all cases and, as will be indicated, depend on the cost flow assumptions.[6]

The real controversy between the direct and absorption costing methods concerning income fluctuations is whether income should be affected by the production or inventory policies. While direct costing advocates say that income should not be affected, the absorption costing advocates maintain that the profit is the result of the total activity of the firm, including both production and sales.

15.2 RECONCILIATION OF DIRECT AND ABSORPTION COSTING PROFITS

15.2.1 Differences between Direct and Absorption Costing Profits

The difference between the full- and direct-cost profits was defined as being equal to the changes in inventory multiplied by the unit fixed manufacturing cost. This generalization holds only under the last-in, first-out (LIFO) and the standard-cost methods of inventory costing.[7] Table 15.3 shows the correct generalizations for the various inventory costing methods.

15.2.2 Formats for Reconciliation

Given the relative merit of and the controversy surrounding the use of the direct and absorption costing methods, a format providing a reconciliation of both methods may be appropriate. In fact, firms can elect to keep their accounting records on a direct costing basis and make a reconciliation of both methods at the end of the year.

One-Factor Model

Table 15.4 presents a format for reconciling both direct and absorption costing. Up to the entry "Total Contribution" it is based on a direct costing approach. The section following "Total Contribution" reconciles both methods.

The example assumes an opening inventory of 5,000 units, a production volume of 10,000 units, a sales volume of 6,000 units, and an ending inventory of 9,000 units. Assume also that (1) an FIFO actual inventory valuation method is used; (2) the variable cost per unit is $50 for the previous and current periods; and (3) the fixed manufacturing cost per unit decreased from $15 in the previous period to $10 in the current period. The sales price per unit is $100.

The adjustment to absorption costing equals the difference between the fixed overhead charged to Ending Inventory and the fixed overhead charged to Beginning Inventory. Consequently, the following results can be noted:

1. When the fixed overhead charged to Ending Inventory is equal to the amount in Beginning Inventory, both inventory valuation methods will charge the same amount of fixed costs against revenues.

Table 15.3
Differences between Full- and Direct-Cost Profit Inventory Costing Methods (PF-PD)

Inventory Costing Methods	$(PF-PD)$
Average	$\dfrac{ws}{w+s}\left[\dfrac{MN}{s}-\dfrac{BN}{w}\right]$
FIFO with $s \geq w^-$	$w\left[\dfrac{MN}{q}-\dfrac{BN}{w}\right]$
FIFO with $s \leq w^-$	$s\left[\dfrac{MN}{s}-\dfrac{BN}{w^-}\right]$
LIFO with $s \leq q$	$(w-w^-)\dfrac{MN}{q}$
LIFO with $s \geq q$	$(w-w^-)\dfrac{BN}{w^-}$
Standard	$\alpha^*(w-w^-)$

Notation is as follows:
PF = Profit under full costing (absorption costing).
PD = Profit under direct costing.
MN = The fixed cost portion of the current period's manufacturing cost.
BN = The fixed portion of beginning inventory.
w = Ending inventory quantity.
w^- = Beginning inventory quantity.
s = Current period's quantit; sold.
q = The quantity produced in the current period.
α^* = Standard fixed cost per unit.

Source: Yuji Ijiri, Robert K. Jaedicke, and John L. Livingstone, "The Effect of Inventory Costing Methods on Full and Direct Costing," *Journal of Accounting Research* (Spring 1965), pp. 63–74. Reprinted by permission.

2. When the fixed overhead charged to Ending Inventory is greater than the amount in Beginning Inventory, absorption costing will yield a higher profit than direct costing.

3. When the fixed overhead charged to Ending Inventory is less than the amount in Beginning Inventory, direct costing will yield a higher profit than absorption costing.

Two-Factor Model

The reconciliation format presented in Table 15.5 takes into account only the difference in profits during the time periods in which the fixed manufacturing overhead costs incurred in a given period are charged as a period cost. This format considers only a single determinant of the difference in the profits under both inventory valuation techniques. This profit difference can be separated into

Table 15.4
Modified Direct Costing Format (Fictional Example), One-Factor Model

	Net Sales (6,000 × $100)	$600,000
minus	Variable Cost of Goods Sold (6,000 × $50)	300,000
equals	Contribution Margin	$300,000
minus	Fixed Costs	100,000
equals	Total Contribution	$200,000
plus	Adjustment to Absorption Costing Fixed Costs for Ending Inventory (9,000 × $10) .... $90,000 *Less:* Fixed Costs for Beginning Inventory (5,000 × $15) 75,000	15,000
equals	Net Profit under Absorption Costing	$215,000

Table 15.5
Modified Direct Costing Format, Two-Factor Model

	Net Sales (6,000 × $100)	$600,000
minus	Variable Costs of Goods Sold	300,000
equals	Contribution Margin	$300,000
minus	Fixed Costs	100,000
equals	Total Contribution	$200,000
plus	Adjustment to Absorption Costing .... Changes in Fixed Cost Due to a Decrease in Fixed Manufacturing Overhead Rate (5,000 × $5) .... $25,000 Changes in Fixed Cost Due to an Increase in Inventory (4,000 × $10) 40,000	15,000
equals	Net Profit under Absorption Costing	$215,000

two components: (1) the change due to the difference in the physical quantity of inventory and (2) the change due to the difference in the fixed manufacturing overhead rate between the two periods.

Using the same example as the one-factor model, the two-factor model shows the change in fixed costs due to (1) an increase (or decrease) in the fixed manufacturing overhead rate and (2) an increase (or decrease) in inventory volumes.

15.3 ARGUMENTS IN THE CONTROVERSY

Inventory valuation focuses on a product and its costs and, consequently, affects both the external and internal uses of the resulting data. The external uses include asset measurement, income determination, and external reporting, whereas the internal uses refer to internal decision making. Thus, the arguments in the controversy between absorption and direct costing center mainly on the methods' relative merits to income determination, asset measurement, external reporting, and decision making.

15.3.1 Period/Product Question for Income Determination

The central issue affecting income determination is whether fixed manufacturing costs are product or period costs. Two views exist in the literature.[8]

According to one view, known as the *period cost concept,* the fixed manufacturing costs are viewed as period costs. This view associates the expiration of fixed manufacturing costs with the passage of time rather than with the flow of units produced. Its main assumption is that the fixed manufacturing costs are continuously incurred for each time period to create a productive capacity, regardless of the state of the production process:

Proponents of variable costing maintain that fixed factory overhead provides capacity to produce. Whether that capacity is used to the fullest extent or not used at all is usually irrelevant insofar as the expiration of fixed cost is concerned.

. . . As the clock ticks, fixed costs expire, to be replenished by new bundles of fixed costs that will enable production to continue in succeeding periods.[9]

According to the other view of fixed manufacturing costs, known as the *product cost concept,* all manufacturing costs are viewed as product costs. They are assumed to be associated with and assigned to the product rather than the period. An extreme position in support of the product cost concept follows:

In theory, there is no such thing as a true period cost. All costs incurred by a firm, including non-manufacturing costs, are costs of the product. For the product of a firm is not merely a physical commodity from a production line, it is a bundle of economic utilities, which include time and place as well as form. Thus, in theory, distribution and administrative costs are just as much costs of the product as are factory costs. The product is not complete until it is in a form and place and at a time desired by the customer; and this product completion involves distribution just as essentially as it does manufacturing.[10]

15.3.2 Nature of Service Potential for Asset Measurement

The product cost method of costing pertains mainly to the choice of an inventory valuation method and, consequently, to the choice of an asset valuation method. Assets have been defined as "aggregates of service potential available for or beneficial to expected operation." The link between assets and service potential can be used to resolve the controversy between absorption and direct costing. In other words, the test for determining whether fixed manufacturing overhead is a product or period cost is to determine whether the costs are beneficial to the operations of future periods. There are two possible interpretations of the concept of service potential: the *cost obviation concept* and the *revenue production concept*.

According to the cost obviation concept, the measurement of assets should include those costs that will be obviated in the future as a result of their incurrence in the past. In other words, assets have service potential if the costs included will not need to be incurred in the future. Advocates of direct costing point out that the incurrence of variable manufacturing costs avert their future incurrence, while the incurrence of fixed manufacturing costs does not. They maintain that the production of goods for inventory may create a revenue potential for the future without a reincurrence of the variable costs of producing the same inventory of goods. Only the variable costs of production should be inventoried, given that the fixed costs of production do not result in future cost avoidance. Robert B. Wetnight argued as follows:

If this test of future benefit is applied to the two methods of costing under discussion, it can be seen that direct costing most closely fits the requirements. In the first place, there is a future benefit from the incurrence of variable costs. These costs will not need to be incurred in a future period. However, in the case of fixed costs, no future benefits exist, since these costs will be incurred during the future period, no matter what the level of operations.[11]

According to the revenue production concept of service potential, the measurement of assets should include those costs that will contribute to the production of revenues in the future. This concept defines a product cost as a cost conducive to the realization of revenue in the future. James M. Fremgen contended:

Any cost essential to the production of a product that may reasonably be expected to be sold and, thus generate revenue, is a cost of obtaining such revenue and should be deferred in inventory so that it may be matched with the revenue in the determination of income for the period of sale.[12]

This revenue production concept can be used to argue for either direct or absorption costing, depending on whether or not an association—logical or empirical—can be established between fixed manufacturing costs and revenue. Thus, any costs essential to the production of goods that reasonably can be expected to be sold in the future should be considered product costs.

15.3.3 Impact of the Choice of Various Denominator Levels

The activity level or denominator level chosen for the computation of the predetermined total overhead rate in general and predetermined fixed rate in particular has an impact on the operating income result under absorption costing.

Although the choice of the denominator level is an outcome of capital budgeting decisions, it is influenced by the need to determine the correct capacity of the firm, one that takes into account the impact of two factors on future demands: (1) seasonal and cyclical fluctuations in demand and (2) upward trends in demand. Basically, four expressions of capacity are available for the choice:

1. Theoretical capacity: a maximum or ideal capacity that encompasses the production of output for 100 percent of the time.
2. Practical capacity: a measure of capacity that reduces theoretical capacity for Sundays, holidays, overtime, and changeover time and acts as a maximum level at which the firm's manufacturing units can operate efficiently.
3. Normal capacity: a measure of capacity that reduces practical capacity of provisions for seasonal, cyclical, and trend factors affecting demand and, consequently, satisfies average consumer demand for at least five years or more.
4. Master-budget volume or projected annual capacity: a measure of expected capacity for the coming year.

The income statement effects of the choice of any of these expressions of capacity as denominators for overhead application may be indicated by the following example.

A company XYZ has a budgeted priced factory overhead for 19X1 of $720,000. The different capacities were 80,000 direct-labor hours for the master-budget volume, 90,000 direct-labor hours for the normal volume, and 100,000 direct-labor hours for the practical capacity. As a result, the budgeted fixed factory overhead rate per hour are

1. $9.00 using a master-budget volume denominator based rate ($720,000/80,000 direct-labor hours)
2. $8.00 using a normal capacity denominator based rate ($720,000/90,000 direct-labor hours)
3. $7.20 using a practical capacity denominator based rate ($720,000/100,000 direct-labor hours).

The actual production in 19X1 was 85,000 units (in 85,000 actual and standard hours allowed) and 70,000 units were sold. There were no beginning inventories, and the actual fixed factory overhead cost is equal to the budgeted fixed overhead. The impact of the choice of the denominator volume is shown in Table 15.6. Operating income and ending inventory values are different under the three methods. Operating income is the highest when the master-budget volume is used as the denominator level. It is the highest when the practical capacity is used as the denominator level.

The journal entry at the end of 19X1 would appear as follows:

When the denominator volume is based on a master-budget volume:

Fixed Factory Overhead Applied	$765,000	
Production Volume Variance		$ 45,000
Actual Fixed Factory Overhead		$720,000

When the denominator volume is based on normal capacity:

Fixed Factory Overhead Applied	$680,000	
Production Volume Variance		40,000
Actual Fixed Factory Overhead		$720,000

When the denominator volume is based on practical capacity:

Fixed Factory Overhead Applied	$612,000	
Production Volume Variance		108,000
Actual Fixed Factory Overhead		$720,000

Given the impact on inventory and profit, the choice of the denominator volume under absorption costing is important if management wants to avoid fluctuations in their overhead applications and the resulting mispricing of their product. Reasoning for the choice of any of the capacity expressions follows:

1. If management wants to run at full or practical capacity, to conform to the portion of the Internal Revenue Service (IRS) that forbids variable costing, and to obtain a higher unit of fixed factory overhead as a tax deduction, then it will choose practical capacity as the denominator volume. The risks are lower unit cost for inventory purposes and continuous underapplied production volume variance, sometimes treated on the invoice statement as "Idle Capacity Loss."

2. If management wants to choose a period by enough to average out the seasonal and cyclical fluctuations in demand as well as account for trends in sales, it would choose normal capacity as the denominator volume. Overapplications of fixed factory overhead are expected to be over the period offset by underapplications of fixed factory overhead. They are theoretically carried forward on the balance sheet but are practically closed to income summary to conform to IRS regulations.

3. If management is leery about the difficulty of forecasting normal capacity, focuses on planning and control for the current year, and highlights the current year's goals, then the master-budget volume will be chosen. The rationale here is that normal capacity and practical capacity are out of phase with current year's concerns.

Table 15.6

Income Statement Effects of Choosing Different Expressions for Capacity for the Denominator Level

	Master-Budget Volume (80,000 Hours)	Normal Volume (90,000 Hours)	Practical Capacity (10,000 Hours)
	Fixed Overhead per hour = $9.00	Fixed Overhead Rate = $8.00 per hour	Fixed Overhead Rate = $7.2 per hour
Sales	$xxx	$xxx	$xxx
Production Costs			
Direct Material, Direct Labor, Variable Overhead	$ xxx	$ xxx	$ xxx
Applied Fixed Overhead[1]	765,000	680,000	612,000
Total Production Costs (85,000 Units)	$ xxx	$ xxx	$ xxx
Ending Inventory, Fixed Overhead Component (10,000 units)[2]	90,000	80,000	72,000
Total Fixed Overhead Component of Cost of Goods Sold	$675,000	$600,000	$540,000
Production Volume Variance[3]	(45,000)	40,000	108,000
Total Fixed Overhead Charged to the Period's Sales	$630,000	$640,000	$648,000
Operating Income	Highest	Middle	Worst

[1] 85,000 x $9.00 and 85,000 x $8.00 and 85,000 x $7.2 respectively.
[2] 10,000 x $9.00 and 10,000 x $8.00 and 10,000 x $7.2 respectively.
[3] (80,000-85,000) x $9.00 and (90,000-85,000) x $8.00 and (100,000-85,000) x $7.2.

15.4 INVENTORY VALUATION AND REGULATION

Various regulatory agencies encourage the adoption of the full absorption method of accounting for reasons similar to those that will be described in this section.

The general acceptability of direct costing as an accounting principle for external reporting purposes is ambiguously expressed in the AICPA's *Accounting Research Bulletin No. 43*, which states:

The exclusion of all overhead from inventory costs does not constitute an accepted procedure. The exercise of judgment in an individual situation involves a consideration of the adequacy of the procedures of the cost accounting system in use, the soundness of the principles thereof, and their consistent application.[13]

The ambiguity of that paragraph led first to the acceptance of various alternative methods of allocating overhead costs to inventory under absorption costing, and second to the possibility that direct costing could be recognized as a generally accepted accounting principle. In spite of this possible recognition of direct costing, absorption costing remains the predominant method for external reporting purposes, and it is preferred in generally accepted accounting principles.

The Securities and Exchange Commission (SEC) relies on the accounting profession to set generally accepted accounting principles and hence favors absorption costing as the basis of valuation in SEC filings. Any departure following the adoption of some form of direct costing must be fully disclosed:

Sometimes the omission of overhead from inventory does not have a material effect either on the financial position or on the results of the operations during the period under report. In that case the SEC has accepted registration statements containing financial statements which disclosed the facts and stated that the statements had not been adjusted.[14]

In September 1973, the IRS promulgated rules and regulations governing the allocation of indirect costs to inventories:

In order to conform as nearly as may be possible to the best accounting practices and to reflect income (as required by section 471 of the code) both direct and indirect production costs must be taken into account in the computation of inventoriable costs in accordance with the "full absorption" method of inventory pricing.[15]

These regulations specify which indirect costs should be included. Regulation 1.471.11 divides typical overhead costs into three classifications:

1. Category 1 costs include overhead items that must be capitalized (that is, included in the computation of cost inventory regardless of their financial statements treatment). The items are repair costs; maintenance; utilities; rent; indirect materials and supplies;

tools and equipment not capitalized; quality control; inspection; and indirect labor and production supervision wages, including basic compensation, overtime pay, vacation and holiday pay, sick leave pay (with exceptions), shift differential, payroll taxes, and contributions to a supplemental unemployment benefits plan.

2. Category 2 costs include overhead items that can be included at the taxpayer's option, regardless of their financial statement treatment: marketing costs, advertising costs, selling costs, other distribution costs, interest, research and development, specified casualty and other losses, excess of percentage depletion over costs, excess of tax over book depreciation, income taxes on inventory sales, past service cost as pension contributions, general and administrative overall activities, and officer's salaries and overall management activities.

3. Category 3 costs include overhead items governed by the financial statements, provided that the statements are prepared in accordance with generally accepted accounting principles: property and other local and state taxes; book depreciation and cost depletion; costs attributable to strikes, rework labor, scrap, and spoilage; factory administrative costs; production officers' salaries; insurance costs; and employee benefits (current pension service costs; worker's compensation; wage continuation; nonqualified pension, profit sharing, and stock bonus—to an extent taxable to employees—life and health insurance premiums; safety and medical treatment; cafeteria; recreational facilities; and membership dues).

Despite the popular use of direct costing for internal segment reporting, the FASB seems to support absorption costing as a basis for segment profit reporting, as shown in *Statement No. 14*.[16]

15.5 CONCLUSION

This chapter presented two fundamentally conflicting methods of reporting the same information, which are considered equally correct. The advocates of both direct costing and absorption costing support the usefulness of the results of their method with both practical and theoretical justifications.

From the theoretical point of view, both methods appear to be internally consistent. Under absorption costing, the fixed manufacturing overhead costs are perceived as product costs, inventoried as part of the cost of finished goods, and only released for matching with the revenues realized as part of the cost of goods sold. Similarly, under the direct costing approach, the fixed manufacturing overhead costs are perceived as period costs and are released immediately against the revenues of the period. On one hand, the fluctuation of the profit with both sales and production volume and the inclusion of a fair share of fixed manufacturing overhead in asset valuation under absorption costing and, on the other hand, the fluctuation of the profit with sales volume only and the valuation of assets on the basis of variable costs only are consistent with one another.

From the practical point of view as well, both methods have merit. Thus, there is no absolute answer to whether a cost is a product or a period cost. Theoretically, all costs incurred are ultimately costs of the products produced and sold. The accountant is forced into the time period assumption to provide a rationale for differentiating between product and period costs.

Given that it is difficult to make a value judgment on which method gives proper recognition to the true nature of costs, either method can be used, and either maintains a full disclosure in the sense that a reconciliation is made to adjust the results from one method to the other. More research on the behavioral impact of both methods is necessary to ultimately assess the relevance of either method.

NOTES

1. Committee on Concepts and Standards Underlying Corporate Financial Statements, "Accounting and Reporting Standards for Corporate Financial Statements, 1957 Revision." *Accounting Review* (October 1957): 538.

2. George H. Sorter and Charles T. Horngren, "Asset Recognition and Economic Attributes: The Relevant Costing Approach." *Accounting Review* (July 1962): 391–399.

3. A. W. Paton and A. C. Littleton, *An Introduction to Corporate Accounting Standards* (Evanston, Ill.: American Accounting Association, 1940), 13–14.

4. American Accounting Association 1964 Concepts and Standards Research Study Committee, "The Matching Concept." *Accounting Review* (April 1965): 369.

5. Under the third approach, known as *prime costing*, manufacturing overhead is not considered to be a product cost, and both variable and fixed manufacturing overhead are considered period costs. Although not recognized in North America, this approach is considered appropriate for various circumstances in the United Kingdom.

6. Furthermore, the accuracy of the generalizations is subject to the additional assumptions that there are no variations in the unit fixed manufacturing cost.

7. Yuji Ijiri, Robert K. Jaedicke, and John L. Livingstone, "The Effect of Inventory Costing Methods on Full and Direct Costing." *Journal of Accounting Research* (Spring 1965): 63–74.

8. James M. Fremgen, "The Direct Costing Controversy: An Identification of Issues," *Accounting Review* (January 1964): 43–51.

9. Charles T. Horngren and George H. Sorter, "'Direct' Costing for External Reporting." *Accounting Review* (January 1961): 88.

10. James M. Fremgen, "Variable Costing for External Reporting: A Reconsideration." *Accounting Review* (January 1962): 78.

11. Robert B. Wetnight, "Direct Costing Passes the 'Future Benefit Test.'" *NAA Bulletin* (August 1958): 84.

12. Fremgen, "Direct Costing Controversy," 50.

13. American Institute of Certified Public Accountants, *Accounting Research Bulletin No. 43* (New York: AICPA, 1953), chap. 4, par. 5.

14. Louis H. Rappaport, *SEC Accounting Practice and Procedure*, 2d ed. (New York: Ronald Press, 1963), chap. 21, p. 2.

15. *Internal Revenue Code* (September 1973), sec. 471, 1.471.11, par. 1.

16. Financial Accounting Standards Board, *Statement of Financial Accounting Standards No. 14*, "Financial Reporting for Segments of Business Enterprises" (Stamford, Conn.: FASB, 1976).

SELECTED READINGS

Ajinkya, Bipim, Rowland Atiase, and Linda Smith Bamber. "Absorption versus Direct Costing: Income Reconciliation and Cost-Volume-Profit Analysis," *Issues in Accounting Education* (Fall 1986): 268–281.

Brumett, R. Lee. "Direct Costing: Should It Be a Controversial Issue?" *Accounting Review* (July 1955): 439–443.

Fremgen, James M. "The Direct Costing Controversy: An Identification of Issues." *Accounting Review* (January 1964): 43–51.

Horngren, Charles T., and Sorter, George H. "'Direct' Costing for External Reporting." *Accounting Review* (January 1961): 84–93.

Ijiri, Yuji, Robert K. Jaedicke, and John L. Livingstone. "The Effect of Inventory Costing Methods on Full and Direct Costing." *Journal of Accounting Research* (Spring 1965): 63–74.

Staubus, George J. "Direct, Relevant or Absorption Costing?" *Accounting Review* (January 1963): 64–73.

Swalley, R. W. "The Benefits of Direct Costing." *Management Accounting* (September 1974): 13–16.

Williams, Bruce R. "Measuring Costs: Full Absorption Cost or Direct Cost?" *Management Accounting* (January 1976): 23–24, 36.

16

Relevant Costing and Pricing Decisions

Management must make short-run, tactical, and operational decisions. These decisions generally involve a choice among various alternative courses of action necessary for accomplishing a given goal or objective. That choice involves the use of a decision model. The decision model to be used in this chapter follows the concept of differential incremental or relevant costs and is termed *differential analysis*. It is illustrated in this chapter for the evolution of such common tactical decisions as analysis of serial contracts, segment analysis, make-or-buy analysis, and product pricing.

16.1 CRITERIA OF RELEVANCE

16.1.1 Cost Concepts for Decision Making

Costs may be either relevant or irrelevant for decision making purposes. Their relevance depends on the identification of costs as:

1. Sunk versus out-of-pocket costs
2. Marginal, incremental, or differential costs
3. Historical versus opportunity costs
4. Escapable versus inescapable costs.

Sunk costs are past expenditures already incurred and not relevant to a particular decision; *out-of-pocket costs* are the possible outlays resulting from a decision. A sunk cost is irrelevant to any decision because it cannot be changed by a present or future decision. For example, outlays already spent on research and development are sunk costs for the purpose of deciding whether to produce a product.

Incremental or *differential costs* are the expected future costs that differ as a consequence of choosing one alternative over another. The change in costs resulting from a change in the operating level is an incremental cost. The *marginal cost* is a unit concept; it refers to the cost created by the production of one additional unit. In other words, if Y1 and Y2 are the costs and the output levels are X1 and X2, then

$$Y2 - Y1 = \text{incremental cost}$$

and

$$\frac{y2 - y1}{x2 - x1} = \text{marginal cost.}$$

To explore the use of incremental or differential costs, assume that five years ago the Briston Manufacturing Company purchased a cutting machine for $20,000; it has an accumulated depreciation of $10,000 and has five remaining years of useful life. The machine may be sold for $5,000 now and will have no disposal value at the end of the five years. The management, realizing that the old machine no longer has its original operating advantages, has decided to buy a new machine. After detailed analysis, management is considering a new machine, costing $12,000, which has a useful life of five years, would reduce the operating costs from $6,000 to $4,000 annually, and would have a $5,000 disposal value at the end of the five years. Table 16.1 presents a summary of the cost comparison for the equipment replacement. The book value of the old equipment is irrelevant to the decision and does not appear in the analysis. The disposal values of both the old and the new equipment are relevant as future revenues that differ with the two alternatives. The difference columns show that

Table 16.1
Cost Comparison for Replacement of Equipment

	Five Years Together			One-Year Analysis		
Accounts	**Old Machine**	**New Machine**	**Difference**	**Old Machine**	**New Machine**	**Difference**
Cash Operating Costs	$30,000	$20,000	$10,000	$6,000	$4,000	$2,000
Old Equipment (Book Value)						
Periodic Depreciation	10,000			2,000		
or						
Write-off		10,000ᵃ			2,000	
Disposal Value (Old Equipment)		−5,000ᵃ	+5,000		−1,000	+1,000
New Machine						
Periodic Depreciation		12,000	−12,000		2,400	−2,400
Disposal Value (New Equipment)		−5,000	+5,000		−1,000	+1,000
Total Costs	$40,000	$32,000	$8,000	$8,000	$6,400	$1,600

ᵃThe two items may be combined as Loss on Disposal of $5,000.

the purchase of the new machine yields an $8,000 five-year cost savings, or a cost savings of $1,600 a year.[1] Although the book value of the old equipment did not appear in the above analysis, it will appear in the computation of the formal income statement. Hence, the income statement will show a $5,000 loss on disposal ($5,000 disposal value, $10,000 book value). Notice that a manager may be reluctant to replace the equipment to avoid recognizing this loss on disposal. Needless to say, such an attitude emphasizing short-run profit is a form of suboptimization harmful to the company.

Opportunity costs refer to the benefits foregone by the choice of one alternative over the next best alternative. Because resources are limited, any decision to produce a given commodity implies doing without some other commodity. As an example on the social level, when a tank is produced, an implicit decision has been made not to produce ten tractors with the material, labor, and overhead used by the production of the tank. Thus, the opportunity cost of the tank is ten tractors. The opportunity cost doctrine prevalent in economic analysis views problems of social choice in terms of all alternatives of economic progress. At the microeconomic level, the doctrine may be used in the context of profit maximization. Hence, the opportunity cost may be the difference between the profits earned in two managerial alternatives in a profit situation, or the difference in the costs incurred in a cost situation. Suppose a firm either uses a machine to make product X or product Y. The production of Y can be sold for $20,000 with corresponding direct costs of $15,000. The opportunity cost of producing X is, therefore, $5,000 ($20,000 − $15,000). Thus, the opportunity cost of using the machine to produce X is the sacrifice of earnings from Y that might be produced by using the machine.

An *escapable cost* can be incurred by a structural or operational change. For example, if the cost of labor is reduced by a curtailment of activities, such a cost may be considered an escapable or avoidable cost. The opposite inescapable cost must be incurred in spite of structural or operational changes.

In the context of an abandonment situation, the concept of attributable cost is the cost per unit that could be avoided, on the average, if a product or function were discontinued entirely without changing the supporting organization structure. The costing unit may be either a physical product or a unit of service performed. Attributable cost, the long-run equivalent to avoidable cost, includes both variable out-of-pocket costs and fixed departmental costs that may result from the abandonment of a product.

In general, the out-of-pocket, the incremental, the marginal, the opportunity, and the escapable costs are relevant costs for decision making.

16.1.2 Marginal Analysis: Economic Approach

Economists use the marginal classification of costs in decision making.[2] *Marginal cost analysis* attempts to determine pricing and output decisions. *Economic analysis* assumes that a firm is trying to maximize its total profits. Marginal

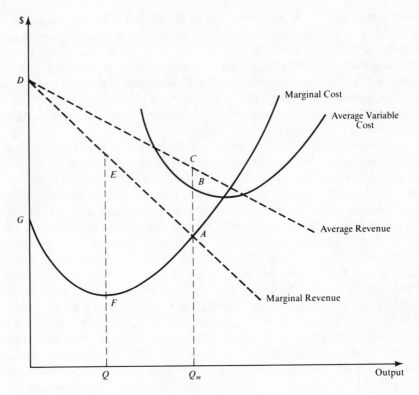

Figure 16.1
Graphic Presentation of Marginal Analysis

analysis proposes that no firm can achieve its maximum profit until its marginal cost and marginal revenue are equal, in other words, unless the cost of the additional unit of output produced brings enough additional revenue to make the marginal profitability equal zero.

Marginal analysis may be explained with aid of Figure 16.1. At any rate of output, OQ total revenue is expressed by the area OQED under the marginal revenue curve. Total cost is expressed by the area OQFG under the marginal cost curve. The profit, which is equal to the difference between the areas of total revenue and total cost, is expressed by area FEGD. It is obvious that moving Q to the right will increase the profit FEGD to the point Q_m where it will reach a maximum. At point Q_m, the marginal cost is equal to the marginal revenue.

The marginal analysis may also be performed algebraically. Assume a demand function $P = 200 - 0.02Q$, where Q is the weekly production, and a total cost function $C = 60Q + 20,000$. It is easy to deduce the following:

$$\text{Total revenue} = PQ = 200Q - 0.02Q.$$

$$\text{Marginal revenue} = dPQ/Q = 200 - 0.04Q.$$

$$\text{Marginal cost} = \frac{dC}{dQ} = 60.$$

The marginal analysis requires, as a profit maximization objective, that marginal costs equal marginal revenue. Thus, $60 = 200 - 0.04 Q$, or $Q = 140/0.04 = 3,500$ units per week. Consequently, the price will be $P = 200 - 0.02Q = \$130$, and total profit per week will be $u = PQ - C = (\$130 \times 3,500) - (20,000 + 60 \times 3,500) = \$225,000$.

16.1.3 Differential Analysis: Accounting Approach

The accountant uses the incremental classification of costs in decision making. *Differential* or *incremental cost analysis* is similar to the economist's marginal analysis except that the accountant is interested in the additional cost of a change in the level of production rather than the cost of an additional unit. This approach has also been labeled the *relevant cost approach*. It is particularly applicable to short-term decisions such as dropping or adding products, setting prices, selecting equipment, selling manufactured products or processing them further, special order decisions, rationing scarce capacity, and make-or-buy decisions. The differential analysis approach consists of determining the relevant costs, those expected future costs that will differ among alternatives. For example, suppose that firm X decides to increase its level of production because the sales price offered, $4, was more than the new per-unit cost of production. The following information was provided:

	Cost of Production	
	Old Activity Level	*New Activity Level*
	(20,000 Units)	*(30,000 Units)*
Variable Costs	$20,000	$45,000
Fixed Costs	20,000	30,000
	$40,000	$75,000
Cost per Unit	$2.00	$2.50

The differential analysis will proceed as follows:

Added Revenues (10,000 × $4)	$40,000
Incremental Costs ($75,000 − $40,000)	35,000
Added Contribution	$ 5,000

If we make the assumption that all incremental costs are out-of-pocket costs, then, the decision to increase the level of production is beneficial because it increases the firm's total wealth.

16.1.4 More on Differential Analysis

Management must make decisions that involve a choice among competing alternatives. The approach generally used is differential analysis. Basically, differential analysis is the process of estimating the consequences of alternative actions facing managers. It follows that differential costs are those costs that are expected to differ between competing alternatives. Differential costs are the relevant costs for decision making. That is why differential analysis is sometimes referred to as a relevant cost analysis. Differential costs may include variable costs and fixed costs.

Variable costs are differential costs when the decision involves a change in volume. Fixed costs may be differential in the long run when changes in capacity are involved. They may be differential also in the short run as we will see in section 16.2.3, concerning make-or-buy analysis.

Beware of the hasty conclusion that all variable costs are relevant and all fixed costs are irrelevant. Relevant or differential costs are those costs (variable or fixed) that are expected to differ in the choice between alternative actions.

For example, when one buys a new car, the purchase price and the operating costs of the model are differential and relevant costs. After one buys the car, the operating costs are still relevant costs, but the original purchase price is not.

The original purchase price or historical cost of the car is termed a sunk cost: a cost that has been incurred and cannot be altered. Sunk costs are therefore irrelevant for decision making. The historical cost of an asset may be considered relevant given that it will have an impact on taxes through book gains or losses on disposition or through taxes saved through depreciation.

16.1.5 Illustration of Differential Analysis

Assume the following data for Benjamin Company, which makes a particular type of typewriter known as the CD-1350:

Units sold	100 units per month
Maximum production and sales capacity	150 units per month
Selling price	$60
Variable manufacturing cost per unit	$10
Variable manufacturing cost per unit	$5
Fixed manufacturing costs per month	$3,000
Fixed selling and administrative costs per month	$2,000

The CEO of the Benjamin Company wants to increase volume by 50 percent per month by decreasing the selling price from $60 to $50 per unit. The proposal would involve an increase of $6,000 in the fixed manufacturing overhead costs. Would the proposal be implemented? Differential cost analysis, as shown in Table 16.2, indicates that the proposal will increase the profit. Notice that in large scale both variable costs and fixed costs are found to be differential, incremental, or relevant costs.

Table 16.2
Benjamin Company: Differential Cost Analysis

	Option 1: Sell 1,000 units at $60	Option 2: Sell 1,500 units $50	Difference
Sales	$60,000	$75,000	$15,000
less Variable Costs	(15,000)	(22,500)	(7,500)
Total Contribution			
Margin	$45,000	$52,500	$7,500
less Fixed Costs	(5,000)	(11,000)	(6,000)
Operating Profit	$40,000	$41,500	$1,500

16.2 COMMON TACTICAL DECISIONS

Proponents of direct costing base their beliefs mainly on its relevance to internal decision making. They assume that separate reporting of fixed and variable costs facilitates incremental profit analysis and removes from income the effect of inventory changes. These advantages have been summarized in the NAA *Research Series No. 23* as follows:

1. Cost-volume-profit relationship data wanted for profit planning purposes is easily obtained from the regular accounting statement. Hence management does not have to work with two separate sets of data to relate one to the other.
2. The profit for a period is not affected by changes in absorption of fixed expenses resulting from building or reducing inventory. Other things remaining equal (e.g., selling prices, costs, sales mix), profits move in the same direction as sales when direct costing is in use.
3. Manufacturing cost and income statements in the direct cost form follow management's thinking more closely than does the absorption cost form for these statements. For this reason, management finds it easier to understand and to use direct cost reports.

4. The impact of fixed costs on profits is emphasized because the total amount of such costs for the period appears in the income statement.

5. Marginal income figures facilitate relative appraisal of products, territories, classes of customers, and other segments of the business without having the results obscured by allocation of joint fixed costs.

6. Direct costing ties in with such effective plans for cost control as standard costs and flexible budgets. In fact, the flexible budget is an aspect for direct costing and many companies thus use direct costing method for this purpose without recognizing them as such.

7. Direct cost constitutes a concept of inventory cost which corresponds closely with the current out-of-pocket expenditure necessary to manufacture the goods.[3]

As a result of these advantages, various firms elect to adopt a cost accounting system based on direct costing. This system, known as *contribution margin reporting,* consists of reporting variable and fixed costs separately to facilitate decision making, for example, analysis of special price contracts, segment analysis, and make-or-buy analysis.

16.2.1 Analysis of Special Contracts

The differentiation between the fixed and variable components of costs is useful in the appraisal of the impact of changes in activity volume. It can be applied in decisions sensitive to volume changes, such as the acceptance of special orders.

For example, every year, the ABEL Manufacturing Company produces and sells 100,000 units of a product for $10 per unit. The variable manufacturing cost per unit and the total fixed manufacturing costs are $6 and $200,000, respectively. The fixed selling and administrative expenses are $100,000. The absorption costing profit follows:

Sales (100,000 Units @ $10/Unit)	$1,000,000
Cost of Goods Sold (100,000 Units @ $8/Unit)	800,000
Gross Profit	$ 200,000
Selling and Administrative Expenses (Fixed)	100,000
Net Income	$ 100,000

The ABEL Manufacturing Company has received an order for an additional 50,000 units at $7 per unit, and acceptance would not require additional capacity. On the basis of the absorption costing results, the order would not be accepted, given that the unit production cost of $8 is higher than the offered contract price of $7. However, under direct costing, it can be assumed that the fixed manufacturing expenses are period expenses that would not be affected by the additional sale. The following table shows the net income with and without the special order:

Contribution Income Statement

	Without Special Order	With Special Order	Combined
Sales	$1,000,000	$350,000	$1,350,000
Variable Cost of Goods Sold ($6 Each)	600,000	300,000	900,000
Contribution Margin	$ 400,000	$ 50,000	$ 450,000
Fixed Manufacturing Costs			200,000
Fixed Selling and Administrative Costs			100,000
Net Income			$ 150,000

The direct costing approach to the problem shows that the net income will increase by $50,000 as a result of the acceptance of the special order.

16.2.2 Segment Analysis

A *segment* of a firm is any portion of the organization about which costs and/or revenues can be accumulated, such as a division, product line, sales territory, region of the country, or a portion differentiated by the degree of domestic and foreign operations. In examining the profitability of a company's segments, management may have to decide whether or not to add or to discontinue a particular segment.

To illustrate the usefulness of contribution margin reporting to segment analysis, consider this example. The Poduch Company produces and sells three different products: Ex, Why, and Zee. Cost analysis reveals that (1) production costs are 50 percent variable and 50 percent fixed and (2) selling and administrative costs are 60 percent variable and 40 percent fixed. Projected income statements by product line are prepared on an absorption costing basis as follows:

	Ex	Why	Zee	Total
Revenues	$400,000	$300,000	$200,000	$900,000
Cost of Goods Sold	200,000	150,000	150,000	500,000
Gross Profit	$200,000	$150,000	$ 50,000	$400,000
Selling and Administrative Expenses	100,000	100,000	60,000	260,000
Net Income	$100,000	$ 50,000	$(10,000)	$140,000

When faced with a decision on whether to discontinue product Zee, management of the Poduch Company elected first to prepare the income statements on a direct costing basis, taking into account the fact that the fixed costs cannot be traced adequately to the individual products on a cause-and-effect basis. The contribution income statements follow:

	Ex	Why	Zee	Total
Revenues	$400,000	$300,000	$200,000	$900,000
Variable Costs and Expenses				
Production	$100,000	$ 75,000	$ 75,000	$250,000
Selling and Administrative Expenses	60,000	60,000	36,000	156,000
Total	$160,000	$135,000	$111,000	$406,000
Contribution Margin	$240,000	$165,000	$ 89,000	$494,000
Fixed Expenses (Not Traceable)				
Production				$250,000
Selling and Administrative Expenses				104,000
Total				$354,000
Net Income				$140,000

The direct costing approach to the problem reveals that product Zee contributes $89,000 to the total income rather than creating a $10,000 loss. Thus, if Zee is discontinued, not only will the net income drop drastically, but the productive capacity used by Zee will be idle.

16.2.3 Make-or-Buy Analysis

Management often faces the problem of whether to make or buy component parts or tools. When faced with a make-or-buy decision, management should evaluate the qualitative factors important to the decision. One factor supporting a decision to buy a part would be problems of availability of know-how, technology, skilled labor, materials, and so forth. A second factor favoring buying the part would be the desire to secure long-term relationships with suppliers rather than destroying them by an erratic decision to make the part in good (profitable) times and to buy the part in bad (unprofitable) times. A factor supporting a decision to make a part would be the desire to secure and maintain high-quality parts.

Management should also evaluate the quantitative factors important to the make-or-buy decision. First, they should compare the cost of making the part with the cost (or price) of buying it. For example, assume the following costs are reported:

Costs of Making Part No. 1200

	Total Costs for 1,000 Units	Cost per Unit
Direct Materials	$ 2,000	$ 2
Direct Labor	7,000	7
Variable Overhead	3,000	3
Fixed Overhead	7,000	7
Total Costs	$19,000	$19

Assume also that another manufacturer offers to sell the company that same part for $15. What should the company decide? It needs more information on the nature of the costs involved.

As a second step, management can determine whether some of the costs are unavoidable (that is, whether they will continue to be incurred regardless of the decision). Assume in this case that $3,000 of the fixed overhead is unavoidable. The comparison of the cost of making the part with the cost (or price) of buying it is as follows:

Per-Unit Costs

	Make	Buy
Direct Material	$ 2	
Direct Labor	7	
Variable Overhead	3	
Fixed Overhead ($4,000 ÷ 1,000 Units)	4	
Total Relevant Costs	$16	$15

Management should choose to buy the part, assuming that the capacity used to make the part will become idle.

Thus, as a third step in evaluating quantitative factors in make-or-buy decisions, management must investigate how to best use the idle capacity if they decide to buy the part. Essentially, the decision to buy or make becomes a decision of how to use the available facilities. More explicitly, management must determine the opportunity cost of resources that will be expended as a result of the decision to buy rather than make the product.

Assume the following courses of action are available:

	Make	Buy and Leave Facilities Idle	Buy and Lease the Facilities	Buy and Use Facilities for Other Products
Lease Revenue			$ 10,000	
Net Revenue from Other Products				$ 13,000
Cost of Making the Part	$(16,000)			
Cost of Purchasing the Part		$(15,000)	(15,000)	(15,000)
Net Relevant Costs	$(16,000)	$(15,000)	$ (5,000)	$ (2,000)

Management should decide to buy the part and to use the facilities to make other products.

It is important to insure that the costs used to compare make-versus-buy situations are future costs that take into account fully what costs "should be" under all existing conditions.[4]

16.3 PRODUCT PRICING

Pricing decisions in most firms are preceded by and depend on pricing policies, which indicate the main factors to be considered in pricing decisions. Pricing policies must be congruent with the overall goals of the organization, such as profit maximization, achieving a target rate of return on investment, or reaching a target market share. When these goals and the corresponding pricing policies are determined, management can proceed with pricing decisions. It is useful to make a distinction between the economist's and the accountant's approaches.

16.3.1 Economist's Approach

The economist reasons on the basis of a nonlinear total revenue and cost function and assumes the existence of a profit-maximizing sales volume where marginal costs equal marginal revenues. Hence the optimal selling price for the economist would be the price necessary to reach the optimal sales volume. To illustrate the computation of such a price, assume the following example:

$$\text{Demand function: } x = 22 - 10p.$$
$$\text{Total cost function: } y = 3.2 + 0.2x + 0.1x^2.$$

1. Solving the demand function for p yields the price function as follows:

$$\text{Price function: } p = 2.2 - 0.1x.$$

2. The total revenue, marginal cost, and marginal revenue can be computed as follows:

$$\text{Total revenue function: } R = 2.2x - 0.1x^2.$$

$$\text{Marginal cost} = MC = \frac{dy}{dx} = 0.2 + 0.2x.$$

$$\text{Marginal revenue} = MR = \frac{dR}{dX} = 2.2 - 0.2x.$$

3. Setting the marginal cost equal to the marginal revenue and solving for x yields the optimal sales volume:

$$MR = MC = 0.2 + 0.2x = 2.2 - 0.2x \text{ where } x = 5.$$

4. Finally, solving the price function on the basis of the optimal sales volume yields the optimal sales price, as follows:

$$p = \$2.2 - 0.1(5)$$
$$= \$1.7.$$

16.3.2 Accountant's Approaches

The accountant's approaches can be based on either a target rate of return on investment or a cost-plus approach.

Target Rate of Return on Investment

Firms generally set a target rate of return on investment computed as follows:

$$\text{Return on investment (ROI)} = \frac{\text{Income}}{\text{Total investment}}.$$

Assuming p = price, Q = sales volume, v = variable cost, F = total fixed cost, t = tax rate, and C = investment, then the rate of return on investment can be computed as follows:

$$\text{ROI} = \frac{[Q(p - v) - F](1 - t)}{C}.$$

Solving for p yields

$$p = \frac{\dfrac{\text{ROI} \times C}{(1 - t)} + F}{Q} + v.$$

For example, assume that Fabiani Ltd. has a target rate of return on investment of 20 percent, a capital investment of $300,000, a tax rate of 40 percent, a total fixed cost of $300,000, and expected sales volume of 40,000 units, and a unit variable cost of $100. The selling price can be determined as follows:

$$p = \frac{\dfrac{20\% \times \$300,000}{(1 - 0.4)} + \$300,000}{40,000} + \$100 = \$110.$$

Cost-Plus Approach

The cost-plus pricing methods can be determined on the basis of either the full cost or the incremental cost. The markup will vary between the two methods as follows:

$$\text{Full cost markup} = \frac{\text{Target profit}}{\text{Estimated full costs}}.$$

$$\text{Incremental cost markup} = \frac{\text{Target profit} + \text{Estimated unallocated fixed costs}}{\text{Estimated incremental costs}}.$$

For example, assume that Fabiani Ltd. is instead using an accounting product pricing method. The target profit before tax is estimated to be $500,000, the variable costs to be $5,000,000, and the fixed cost to be $15,000,000. The markup for Fabiani Ltd. will be either

$$\text{Full cost markup} = \frac{\$500,000}{\$5,000,000 + \$15,000,000} = \$0.025.$$

or

$$\text{Incremental cost markup} = \frac{\$500,000 + \$15,000,000}{\$5,000,000} = \$3.1.$$

If we also assume that Fabiani Ltd. has an incremental cost per unit of $5 and a fixed cost per unit of $15, then the selling price would be as follows:

Full cost markup method: $(1 + 0.025)(\$15 + \$5) = \$20.5$.

Incremental cost markup method: $(1 + 3.1)(\$5) = \$20.5$.

The cost-plus pricing methods are generally favored by corporations because they provide a practical benchmark in pricing decisions.

The cost-based approaches to pricing are useful if the firm is to remain in operation in the long run given that the approach allows a recovery of all costs and secures an adequate return on investments in the form of the markup. There are, however, some limitations to the use of cost-based pricing.

First, the cost-based approaches ignore the type of market demand facing the firm. Given a downward-sloping demand curve for the product, the company will be able to sell only a quantity Q_1 at the cost-based price p. A higher quantity than Q_1 requires a lower price than p_1.

Second, the cost-based approaches compute the markup for a given target volume and the target profit. Different target volumes and target profits require a different markup.

Third, the cost-based approaches to pricing rely on unit costs (unit variable cost and unit fixed cost) in the determination of the price, by adding a markup to the per-unit cost of the product. The unit fixed cost is affected by the choice of volume of production. It is high when the volume is low and low when the volume is high. Therefore, if prices are based on per-unit cost of the product, they will be set higher when the volume is low and lower when the volume is high. It is equivalent to management's slashing prices when the demand is high and skyrocketing them when the demand is low: an unwise situation.

Fourth, as seen earlier in the analysis of special contracts, the use of a cost-based pricing can lead to incorrect decisions.

16.3.3 Time and Material Pricing

Small service-oriented firms use an alternative approach to the cost-plus formula: *time* and *material pricing*. The approach consists of deriving two pricing rates: one based on direct-labor time and one based on the direct material used. The price includes an allowance for other indirect costs, selling and administrative costs, and costs for a desired profit.

The time rate is computed as the sum of (1) the direct-labor cost of the worker, including salaries and fringe benefits, (2) a pro rata allowance for the indirect costs and selling and administrative expenses of the unit, and (3) a provision for a desired profit per hour of the worker's time.

The material loading charge to be added to the invoice price of the materials used on the job includes the costs of ordering, handling, and carrying the materials in stock and provides for a desired profit on the materials.

16.3.4 Illustration of Time and Material Pricing

To illustrate the use of time and material pricing, let us assume a television repair shop incurred the following expenses: For the employees involved in repairs:

Shop supervision	$10,000
Supplies	3,000
Depreciation	2,000
Selling and administrative expenses	5,000
Total	$20,000

The employees worked 20,000 hours per year. The owner planned a profit of $6 per hour of each employee's time. The employee is paid an average of $10 an hour including fringe benefits. For the employees involved in handling materials:

Wages and fringe benefits	$10,000
Property taxes	2,000
Utilities	5,000
Insurance	2,000
Miscellaneous	8,000
Total	$30,000

The invoice cost of materials for the year was $100,000. The owner planned for a profit of 6 percent of the invoice cost of material used. The time rate and the material loading charge are computed as follows:

Time rate

Direct labor cost per hour	$ 6
Pro-rata allowance of indirect costs	
($200,000/20,000 hours)	1
Provision for profit per hour	10
Total time rate per hour of service	$17

Material loading charge

Material servicing costs ($25,000/$75,000)	30% of invoice
Provision for profit on materials	10% of invoice
Material loading charge	40% of invoice

Therefore, if our employee completed a repair job in three hours using $30 in materials, the price would be as follows:

Labor cost: 3 hours × 17		$51
Material used		
Invoice cost	$30	
Materials loading charge		
(40% × $30)	12	42
Total price of the repair job		$93

16.3.5 Pricing under the Robinson-Patman Act

The Robinson-Patman Act of 1936 prohibits certain kinds of price discrimination. Its purpose is

To make it unlawful for any person engaged in commerce to discriminate in price or terms of sale between purchasers of commodities of like grade and quality; to prohibit the payment of brokerage or commission under certain conditions, to suppress pseudo advertising allowances; to provide a presumptive measure of damages in certain cases; and to protect the independent merchant, the public whom he serves; and the manufacturer from whom he buys, from exploitation by unfair competitors.[5]

The legislation, however, does not prohibit price discrimination when it is justified by differences in costs of manufacturing, sales, or delivery. The act states:

That nothing herein contained shall prevent differentials which make only due allowances for differences in cost of manufacture, sale, or delivery resulting from the differing methods or quantities in which such commodities are to such purchasers sold or delivered.[6]

Because the act rests on the interpretation of cost, Patman defined cost as including all costs of manufacture and sale, excluding the return on invested capital by including a prorated share of all overhead costs. The courts and the Federal Trade Commission base their decisions accordingly—on the full cost rather than on the direct or differential cost.

16.4 CONCLUSION

This chapter elaborated the use of differential analysis to resolve short-term, operational and tactical, and product-pricing decisions. Relevance of the information chosen in the decision process is shown to be the key for making decisions that are correct and beneficial to the firm.

NOTES

1. Ordinarily, income tax considerations and the effect of the interest value of money should be considered in analyzing whether to buy new equipment or keep the old equip-

ment. In any case, the book value will still be considered as a sunk cost, and only the tax cash flow will be the basis of analysis.

2. Gordon Shillinglaw, "The Concept of Attributable Cost." *Journal of Accounting Research* (Spring 1963): 77.

3. National Association of Accountants, *Research Series No. 23,* "Direct Costing." (New York: NAA, 1953), 55.

4. National Association of Accountants Committee on Management Practice, *Statement No. 5,* "Criteria for Make-or-Buy Decisions." (New York: NAA, 1965), 8.

5. Wright Patman, *The Robinson-Patman Act* (New York: Ronald Press, 1938), 3.

6. Ibid., 7.

SELECTED READINGS

Abel, Ryan. "The Role of Costs and Cost Accounting in Price Determination." *Management Accounting* (April 1978).

Bruegelmann, G., Wolfangel C. Haessly, and M. Schiff. "How Variable Cost Is Used in Pricing Decisions." *Management Accounting* (April 1985): 58–65, 65.

Corr, Arthur V. "The Role of Cost in Pricing." *Management Accounting* (November 1974): 15–18, 32.

Dillon, Ray D., and John F. Nash. "The True Relevance of Relevant Costs." *Accounting Review* (January 1978).

Patman, Wright. *The Robinson-Patman Act.* New York: Ronald Press, 1938.

Shillinglaw, Gordon. "The Concept of Attributable Cost," *Journal of Accounting Research* (Spring 1963): 73–85.

Cost Allocation: Part I

> Cost allocation at best is loaded with assumptions and in many cases highly arbitrary methods of apportionment are employed in practice. Certainly it is wise not to take the results of the usual process of internal cost consumption too seriously.[1]

The nature of cost allocation has not changed significantly since this statement was made in the 1940s. The methods used are still arbitrary, and their utility is still open to question. In fact, in two American Accounting Association studies, A. L. Thomas has argued against allocations in general because they are not only arbitrary, but also "incorrigible" or incapable of verification.[2]

In spite of these criticisms and limitations, in practice costs continue to be allocated to serve a variety of needs, such as inventory value determination, income determination, price and production determination, and meeting regulatory requirements. Various reports filed with the Securities and Exchange Commission require that joint costs be allocated. Similarly, when manufacturing firms deal with the government for contracts, they must adhere to a set of standards in arriving at a cost-plus contract figure. The United States has established the Cost Accounting Standards Board to establish cost accounting procedures for such firms. In addition, to avoid price discrimination among classes of customers, a firm must justify its actions based on cost data. Joint cost allocation is also required to facilitate the approval of bids on commercial contracts and contract negotiations. It is also useful in labor negotiations.

Cost allocation involves tracing and assigning costs to specific cost objects for internal reporting and for aiding in decision making within the firm. In general, a cause-and-effect relationship between cost and variations in activity level is the criterion for allocation. Direct costs such as material and labor are good examples of cause-and-effect relationships. However, this direct relationship between cost and cost object is not always apparent due to the joint nature of costs.

The joint cost problem of allocation is observable in accounting for overhead and for common product costs. This chapter and chapter 18 discuss these two problems and emphasize the different cost allocation methods used in practice and in the related literature.

17.1 ACCOUNTING FOR OVERHEAD

As discussed in chapter 2, *overhead* refers to the operating costs other than direct labor and direct material. It includes all costs with an indirect relationship to the cost object. Thus, overhead can be associated with the cost object only through a process of allocation. Before being allocated, overhead is distributed to the various departments; after being allocated, it is applied to the products. In other words, three steps are required for recording overhead: *cost distribution, cost allocation,* and *cost absorption* or *application.* Costs are first distributed to the corresponding departments, hence establishing responsibility. The service departments' costs then are allocated to various operating departments, thereby insuring proper matching of costs and cost objects. Finally, the costs are applied to the product, which insures product costing, inventory valuation, and income determination. For the sake of clarity in this discussion, cost distribution will be examined first, then cost application, and, finally, cost allocation.

17.1.1 Overhead Distribution

Any transaction can be recorded using both the general and subsidiary ledgers, as discussed in chapter 8. Accordingly, overhead distribution takes place using, first, the subsidiary ledger accounts and, second, the general ledger accounts.

In the subsidiary ledger accounts, the overhead distribution takes place in the departmental cost ledgers. These ledgers, set up for each department, include as many columns as the number of detailed accounts required. For example, assume the indirect labor incurred was as follows:

$$
\begin{array}{lr}
\text{Service Department I} & \$100 \\
\text{Operating Department I} & 200 \\
\text{Operating Department II} & 200 \\
\end{array}
$$

Indirect material issued was used as follows:

$$
\begin{array}{lr}
\text{Service Department I} & \$200 \\
\text{Operating Department I} & 300 \\
\text{Operating Department II} & 300 \\
\end{array}
$$

These transactions will be recorded in both the Indirect Labor and Indirect Material columns of each of the three departments, as illustrated in Table 17.1. Notice that each departmental cost ledger includes a column for allocation from other departments, whether producing or service departments, and other columns for the other possible overhead items such as depreciation, cost, repairs, and so forth.

In the general ledger, a summary entry is made in the corresponding accounts: a debit of $1,300 to the manufacturing overhead control accounts and a credit to the appropriate accounts (Cash, Accounts Payable, or Prepaid Expenses). Notice

Table 17.1
Subsidiary Cost Ledgers

Service Department			
Indirect Material	Indirect Labor	Allocation from Other Departments	(Other Columns for Other Overhead Items)
$200	$100		

Operating Department I			
Indirect Material	Indirect Labor	Allocation from Other Departments	(Other Columns for Other Overhead Items)
$300	$200		

Operating Department II			
Indirect Material	Indirect Labor	Allocation from Other Departments	(Other Columns for Other Overhead Items)
$300	$200		

that the information is "pooled" in the general ledger, while at least two classifications are provided in the subsidiary ledger: a natural classification and a departmental classification. Other refinements are possible in the subsidiary ledgers.

The example in this section covered only the indirect department charges that can be associated and charged directly to a given department. In most cases, however, indirect expenses incurred benefit more than one department and should be distributed in proportion to the services used. The selection of the distribution bases is important; however, it is also arbitrary, given the state of the art. Among the more likely choices for a distribution base are the following:

Type of Overhead	Distribution Bases
Power, Heat, and Cooling	Square Footage, Rated Horsepower Hours, Cubic Volume of Space Used
Factory Rent	Square Footage
Inspection	Number of Units Completed
Depreciation—Buildings	Square Footage
Superintendence	Number of Employees
Lighting	Kilowatt Hours or Number of Bulbs
Telephone and Telegraph	Number of Telephones or Number of Employees
Depreciation—Equipment	Number of Operating Hours
Property Tax	Square Footage
Worker's Compensation Insurance	Departmental Payroll
Freight In	Materials Used
Building Repairs	Square Footage

Other alternatives may exist and should be considered to insure equity and fairness through allocation. In general, firms can elect to distribute the pooled overhead over single basis.

17.1.2 Overhead Absorption (Application)

Assuming first that overhead has been distributed to the various departments and second that the service department overhead costs have been allocated to the various operating departments, the next step is to apply the overhead to the various Work-in-Process Inventories.

Overhead is applied to the products on the basis of a predetermined overhead rate computed as follows:

$$\text{Predetermined overhead rate} = \frac{\text{Estimated overhead for the cost period}}{\text{Estimated level of activity for the cost period}}.$$

The cost period for the determination of the predetermined overhead rate is generally one year, although it may be different. The application of overhead to the job-order cost sheets or the process summary reports in the subsidiary ledgers and to the Work-in-Process in the general ledger was illustrated in chapter 12. This chapter concentrates on the distribution base (capacity index) and the activity level (capacity level) to be used.

Capacity Index

Given that the cost object in overhead allocation is the product, the capacity index, or base that offers the best physical association with the product, could be the units of production, direct-labor dollars, machine hours, or direct-material dollars.

No specific rule exists for the choice of the optimal allocation base, but the actual situation can be used as a determinant. The following rules can be proposed:

1. Where only one product is manufactured, the units of production method of allocation is adequate. If the firm manufactures several products that are alike except for one characteristic, such as weight or volume, an allocation method based on the weights of the units is more satisfactory than the units of production method.

2. Where the departmental tasks are heavily automated, machine labor hours or machine labor dollars can be chosen.

3. Where the departmental tasks include a large proportion of human assembly work, direct-labor dollars can be chosen.

4. Where the allocation base information is readily available, it should be assigned first priority.

5. Where the direct material constitutes a major part of the input mix, direct-material dollars can be chosen.

These are not normative rules; each situation should dictate to the cost accountant the allocation base most easily traceable to the product according to such criteria as information availability, accuracy, and reliability. Note, however, that using the estimation techniques presented in chapter 3 (especially the least squares regression analysis), each capacity index could be regressed against overhead. The one providing the largest coefficient of determination would be selected as the best capacity index.

Capacity Level

The capacity size, or production capability of a firm, usually can be classified as practical (or attainable) capacity, normal (or average) capacity, expected annual capacity, or actual capacity.

The *theoretical* (or *ideal*) *capacity* represents the maximum level of production at which a firm can operate efficiently, assuming an absence of human or engineering inefficiencies. It represents 100 percent of the firm's capacity.

The *practical* (or *attainable*) *capacity* represents a firm's maximum level of production with sufficient allowances for normal human and engineering inefficiencies. Allowances for unavoidable work stoppage for repairs, strikes, unreliable material, vacations, and other factors reduce the theoretical capacity to a practical capacity. In general, a firm's practical capacity levels range from 75 to 85 percent of its theoretical capacity.

The *normal* (or *average*) *capacity* represents the production level necessary for a firm to satisfy average commercial demands or sales over a period long enough to cover cyclical, seasonal, and trend variations. It provides a trade-off between the technical capacity of a firm and the sales demand, and it usually spans several periods and encompasses past, present, and future ones. Thus, long-term management inefficiencies reduce the practical capacity to a normal capacity. In other words, management's failure to account for variations in sales demand reduces the practical capacity to a normal capacity.

The *expected annual capacity* represents an estimate of a firm's production level for the actual period as defined by the planning process. It can also be called the *master-budgeted capacity*. Thus, allowances for the factors that cause production to vary from one year to another change the normal capacity to an expected annual capacity.

Finally, the *actual capacity* represents the level of production attained in the actual period. Allowances for the forecast errors change the expected annual capacity to an actual capacity.

Given the differences in these measures of capacity level, one can expect wide differences in the overhead applied. Consequently, the choice of an allocation base may center on the nature of overapplied or underapplied overhead the accountant desires to obtain. For example, a choice of the expected annual capacity, based on the rationale that sales do not fluctuate considerably from year to year, would enable the association of the incurrence of an overapplied or underapplied overhead with short-term economic or managerial factors. Similarly, a choice of the normal capacity, based on the rationale that sales are affected by cyclical, seasonal, and trend variations, would associate the overapplied or underapplied overhead not only with short-term factors, but with medium-term factors as well.

In general, the normal capacity is considered a good trade-off between the rigidity imposed by the theoretical or practical capacity and the wide fluctuations that can be generated by the use of the expected annual capacity or actual capacity. When normal capacity is used, the predetermined overhead rate can be referred to as a *normalized overhead rate*.

The computation of the predetermined overhead rate under the various expressions of capacity is illustrated in the following table:

	Theoretical Capacity	Practical Capacity	Normal Capacity	Expected Annual Capacity	Actual Capacity
Percentage of Plant Use	100%	80%	70%	60%	50%
Direct-Labor Hours	10,000 Hrs.	8,000 Hrs.	7,000 Hrs.	6,000 Hrs.	5,000 Hrs.
Budgeted Manufacturing Overhead					
Fixed	$ 8,400	$ 8,400	$ 8,400	$ 8,400	$ 8,400
Variable	5,000	4,000	3,500	3,000	2,500
Total	$13,400	$12,400	$11,900	$11,400	$10,900
Variable Overhead Rate	$0.84	$1.05	$1.20	$1.40	$1.68
Fixed Overhead Rate	0.50	0.50	0.50	0.50	0.50
Total Overhead Rate	$1.34	$1.55	$1.70	$1.90	$2.18

Budget overhead formula = $8,400 + 0.5x$, where x is direct-labor hours.

From this schedule, the following observations can be made:

1. The overhead absorbed by Work-in-Process using a total overhead rate and based on actual activity is

Using theoretical capacity:	$1.34 × 5,000 hrs. = $ 6,700
Using practical capacity:	$1.55 × 5,000 hrs. = $ 7,750
Using normal capacity:	$1.70 × 5,000 hrs. = $ 8,500
Using expected annual capacity:	$1.90 × 5,000 hrs. = $ 9,500
Using actual capacity:	$2.18 × 5,000 hrs. = $10,900.

    The large difference in the applied overhead rate indicates the importance of the choice of a capacity level best suited to a specific situation and managerial expectations.

2. The total overhead rate can be separated into a variable overhead rate and a fixed overhead rate. While the variable overhead rate remains unchanged, the fixed overhead rate tends to change from one expression of capacity to another. The absorption

or application of the fixed overhead, therefore, should influence the selection of the capacity level. Two solutions, however, are possible. A budget formula can be used for the application of overhead. In this example, the formula is $8,400 + 0.5x, where x is direct-labor hours used. Another solution, advanced in chapter 16, is to treat the fixed manufacturing overhead as a period cost rather than a product cost.

3. Although this example uses a total factorywide overhead rate, for accuracy some firms elect to use departmental overhead rates. The procedures and problems of overhead application are the same, except they may differ from one department to another and thus may be more detailed.

17.2 OVERHEAD ALLOCATION

17.2.1 Principles of Overhead Allocation

Firms generally have service departments in addition to producing or operating departments. By definition, the producing or operating department is involved primarily in the actual manufacturing process. A service department is not involved directly in any manufacturing process but provides viable services or assistance to the manufacturing process. Overhead of service departments includes the cafeteria; the purchasing, payroll, cost accounting, personnel, medical, maintenance, power, heat, and water departments; the repair shop, the production planning and control, the toolroom, the stores, and so forth. Because these departments are not directly associated with a product, there is no way of applying their costs directly to a product through a predetermined overhead rule. Instead, the service departments' costs are allocated to other departments (service and/or producing) in proportion to the amount of service rendered to those departments before the application of total manufacturing overhead to the products. This allocation of service department costs to other departments and the application of manufacturing overhead to products are illustrated in Figure 17.1.

The allocation of service department costs to operating departments is as follows:

1. The budgeted service department costs are established for each service department.

2. A reallocation base is determined.

3. A reallocation rate is computed:

$$\text{Reallocation rate} = \frac{\text{Budgeted service department cost}}{\text{Reallocation base}}.$$

4. The service department costs are reallocated to each producing department on the basis of their proportional use of the services provided, as measured in terms of the reallocation base.

For example, suppose a firm's medical services are allocated to the two production departments on the basis of the number of their employees. The budget-

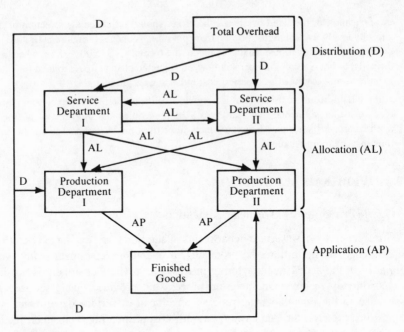

Figure 17.1
Allocating Service Department Costs

ed-cost behavior pattern of the service department is $20,000 plus $1 per employee operating in departments I and II. In January, the firm had 2,000 employees, three-fourths of whom were employed in department I and one-fourth in department II. When the allocation procedures are applied to service department costs,

1. The budgeted service department costs are equal to $22,000 [$20,000 + ($1 × $2,000)].
2. The reallocation base is equivalent to 2,000 employees.
3. The reallocation rate is equal to $22,000 / 2,000 = $11 per employee.
4. The service department costs are reallocated as follows:

$$\text{Department I: } \left(\frac{2,000 \times 3}{4} \right) \times \$11 = \$16,500$$

$$\text{Department II: } \left(\frac{2,000 \times 1}{4} \right) \times \$11 = \$5,500$$

Total service department costs = $22,000.

Although straightforward, this principle of allocating service department costs is subject to the improvements described in the following paragraphs.

Whenever possible, it is conceptually more appropriate to separate the cost allocation rate for variable and fixed costs and to allocate the costs by behavior. By definition, fixed costs are incurred to provide a service capacity based on the needs of the operating departments, while variable costs are a function of the actual activity base. Consequently, it is more appropriate to allocate the fixed costs on the basis of the "normal" capacity to serve and the variable costs on the basis of the actual services used. Accordingly, if, in the previous example, the service departments had provided a basic maximum capacity to serve other departments with the assumption that department I would employ 1,600 employees and department II, 400 employees, the fixed costs would have been allocated to the two departments on the basis of the capacity to serve, as follows:

$$\text{Department I: } \frac{\$20,000 \times 1,600}{2,000} = \$16,000.$$

$$\text{Department II: } \frac{\$20,000 \times 400}{2,000} = \$4,000.$$

The variable costs would have been allocated to the two departments on the basis of the services utilized:

$$\text{Department I: } \$1 \times 1,500 = \$1,500.$$

$$\text{Department II: } \$1 \times 500 = \$500.$$

The total costs allocated would have been

Department I: $16,000 + $1,500 = $17,500
Department II: $4,000 + $500   = $4,500
Total service department costs   = $22,000.

The above technique is called a *dual allocation rate* technique.

Whenever possible, it is advisable also to avoid a reallocation of actual costs rather than budgeted costs. Thus, reallocation of the actual costs may result in imputing the inefficiencies of the service department to the producing departments. Using the previous example, assume that the actual service department costs were $30,000 because of inefficiencies and uncontrollable price changes. Reallocating the actual costs on the basis of the actual hours would lead to the following results:

$$\text{Department I: } \frac{\$30,000 \times 1,500}{2,000} = \$22,500.$$

$$\text{Department II: } \frac{\$30,000 \times 500}{2,000} = \$7,500.$$

Actual service department costs   = $30,000.

The following arguments can be advanced against these allocation procedures:

1. They result in a reallocation of the inefficiencies of the service department costs to the operating departments.
2. One department may be heavily penalized for a greater use of the services. In this example, department I has a greater proportion of costs solely because it uses more employees.

Sometimes, the costs to be allocated depend on multiple factors. The dual basis method in the previous two examples include two factors. In the case of the presence of multiple factors, the company may elect to use a multiple factor formula that incorporates all the factors in the allocation base. For example, in a case where the cost to be allocated to two segments of the firm depends on the total payroll dollars in each segment, the volume of business in each segment and the gross book value of the tangible assets of each segment, the percentage of the costs to be allocated to each segment, is to be the arithmetic mean of each segment percentage of payroll dollar, volume of business and gross book value of tangible assets. For example, assume that a company needs to allocate $6,000 of administrative costs to two segments of the firm, and the following relevant information is provided.

	Payroll dollars		Value of Business		Gross Book Value of Tangible Assets	
Segment	Amount	Percent	Amount	Percent	Amount	Percent
1	$ 5,000	0.25	$12,000	0.3	$250,000	0.5
2	15,000	0.75	$28,000	0.7	$250,000	0.5
Total	$20,000	100	$40,000	100	$500,000	100

What follows are the percentages of costs to be allocated to each segment.

$$\text{Segment 1: } \$6,000 \left(\frac{.25 + .3 + .5}{3} \right) = \$6,000 \times .35 = \$2,100.$$

$$\text{Segment 2: } \$6,000 \left(\frac{.75 + .7 + .5}{3} \right) = \$6,000 \times .65 = \$3,900.$$

17.7.2 Allocation Bases

The choice of an appropriate allocation base facilitates the allocation of service department costs. A well-defined relationship between the activity of the operating departments and the services provided by the service department should guide the selection of the allocation base. In general, cause-and-effect relationships are preferred for cost allocation. The main criteria for determining such relationships used in practice and also advocated in the literature include the criterion of origin, the criterion of use, the criterion of facilities provided, the criterion of ability, and the criterion of fairness.

The *criterion of origin* favors the allocation of costs on the basis of their physical identification with the operating departments. This criterion is more applicable to overhead that does not tend to be organized in service centers.

The *criterion of use* or the *criterion of benefit received* allocates costs on the basis of the actual use or actual benefits received. This criterion implies that the cost of the services is related to the actual use, which may not necessarily be the case.

Using the *criterion of facilities provided,* costs are allocated on the basis of the estimated use of facilities rather than their actual use. This criterion of estimated use rather than actual use is more equitable in the sense that it emphasizes the capacity to serve rather than the actual performance.

The *criterion of ability* favors allocating costs on the basis of the ability of the operating departments to bear or to recover costs, such as allocation on the basis of sales or revenue. From a logical point of view, this criterion does not constitute an adequate criterion of a cause-and-effect relationship in spite of its popularity in practice.

Finally, the *criterion of fairness* or *equity* favors the allocation of costs on the basis of equitable relationships. In other words, the amount allocated to each operating department should be reasonable enough to be understood and accepted by the managers of each department.

Both the criterion of use or benefits received and the criterion of fairness or equity have been explicitly included in the regulations governing U.S. federal government procurement. In fact, the definition of "allocability" by the Federal Acquisition Regulation (FHR 31.201-4) states the following:

A cost is allocable if it is assignable or chargeable to one or more cost objectives on the basis of relative benefits received or other equitable relationships. Subject to the foregoing, a cost is allocable to a Government contract if it—

a) Is incurred specifically for the contract;

b) Benefits both the contract and other work, and can be distributed to them in reasonable proportion to the benefits received; or

c) Is necessary to the overall operation of the business, although a direct relationship to any particular cost objective cannot be shown.[3]

In the choice of allocation base, the following recommendations are important.

First, direct labor is not necessarily the only allocation base that can be used, now that labor is no longer the principal value-adding activity in the material conversion process. Shifting from labor hours to machine hours or to material dollars can cause some of the problems associated with using unrealistic bases for attributing costs to products. The use of multiple allocation bases can be suggested in most cases. As pointed out by Robin Cooper and Robert Kaplan:

In fact, some companies have been experimenting with using all three allocation bases simultaneously: labor hours for those costs that vary with the number of labor hours worked (e.g., supervisor—if the amount of labor in a product is high, the amount of supervision related to that product also is likely to be high), machine hours for those costs that vary with the number of hours the machine is running (e.g., power—the longer the machine is running the more power that is consumed by that product), and material dollars for those costs that vary with the value of material in the product (e.g., material handling—the higher the value of the material handling—the higher the value of the material in the product, the greater the material-handling costs associated with those products are likely to be.[4]

Second, for overhead costs that vary with the number of transactions performed, rather than the volume of product produced, the allocation bases should be other than the usual volume-related bases. In that case, a transaction of product costs is recommended. Cooper and Kaplan give the following illustration:

The volume products create more transactions per unit manufactured than their high volume counter parts. The per unit share of these costs should therefore be higher for the low-volume products. But when volume-related bases are used exclusively to allocate support-department costs, high-volume and low-volume products receive similar transaction-related costs. When any volume related bases are used for record stage allocations, high volume products receive an excessively high fraction of support-department costs and, therefore, subsidize the low-volume products.[5]

Third, some costs that have been traditionally classified as fixed may be in fact variable. One good example is the support department costs. They include such human activities as setups, inspections, material handling, and scheduling. Cooper and Kaplan suggest that the support-department costs do vary, not with the volume of product items manufactured, but with the range of items produced, in other words, in the complexity of the production process.

The traditional definition of variable costs, with its monthly or quarterly perspective, views such costs as fixed because complexity-related costs do not vary significantly in such a short time frame. Across an extended period of time, however, the increasing complexity of the production process places additional demands on support departments, and their costs eventually and initially use.[6]

Fourth, a distinction must be made between labor-paced manufacturing environments and machine-paced manufacturing environments. In the labor-paced manufacturing environment, the overhead costs are incurred to support the work force and therefore can be allocated on the basis of direct labor. Different allocation bases are however required in machine-paced environments.[7,8]

1. Units of production for factories producing homogeneous units
2. Investment for industrial engineering and other plant administrative costs
3. Standard direct conversion cost for most overhead costs
4. Standard material costs for materials management costs, such as purchasing, receiving, incoming inspection, and inventory control and material handling
5. Total standard direct costs
6. Machine hours with a clear distinction between idle time, setup time, and operating time for each machine.

Fifth, a problem with the classification of costs into fixed and variable is that what may be taken for fixed overhead may in some cases be variable. Various overhead items, thought to be fixed, have a tendency in fact to vary with attributes of the production process, such as the scheduling process, the extent of the product mix, and the organization of the logistic system.[9] The phenomenon, known as *overhead creep* indicates that a special investigation must be made before certain overhead items can be classified as fixed.

Although these criteria seem arbitrary, they provide possible choices for different actual situations. Their relative merit should be ascertained by the relative ease they provide in making an allocation.

The following general observations apply to everyday allocation procedures:

1. Criteria for overhead cost allocation that are capable of statistical verification have not yet been developed. The criteria that have been discussed have not been tested sufficiently to be considered objective.
2. The bases chosen for cost assignment are frequently imperfect expressions of the criteria. The choice of bases often consists of accepting or adapting available statistics to the problem. Expediency is the major factor that determines the choice of bases for cost assignment.

Allocation bases advocated in both practice and in the literature include the following:

Service Department	Allocation Base
Cafeteria	Number of Employees, Direct-Labor Hours Worked, Meals Served
Personnel	Number of Employees, Labor Turnover
Showroom	Weight, Units, Size
Maintenance	Number of Machines, Machine Hours
Material Handling	Tonnage, Units Carried
Toolroom	Requisitions
Medical	Number of Cases, Number of Employees
Cost Accounting	Labor Hours
Production Planning and Control	Machine Hours, Labor Hours

Various activity levels have been generally chosen as allocation bases. They are generally volume-related allocation bases used to allocate overhead from cost pools to products. Examples of volume-related allocation bases include machine hours, direct-labor hours, direct-labor cost, material costs, and units of production.

It is, however, evident that, in various activities, known as nonvolume-related activities, transactions drive the costs. Basically, the transactions are the cost devices, especially in the cases of inspection, set up, and scheduling. In those cases, the use of volume-related allocation bases would be erroneous.

17.2.3 Allocating Costs of Service Departments

The manufacturing firm includes both production and service departments. The costs of the service departments must be allocated to the production departments in order to generate the department factory overhead rate used for product-costing purposes. There are three basic procedures for allocating the service department costs: the direct allocation method, the step-down allocation method, and the reciprocal allocation method.

The following example will be used to illustrate the allocation procedures. Assume that the ZRIBI Manufacturing Company has three production departments (P_1, P_2, and P_3) and two service departments (S_1 and S_2). The January data are provided in Table 17.2. The use of single cost pool is assumed. The allocation bases to be used are as follows:

1. Personnel services are allocated on the basis of the number of employees.

2. Building and grounds are allocated on the basis of square footage.

17.2.4 Direct Allocation Method

The *direct allocation method,* or direct method, ignores the services provided by one service department to another and allocates each service department cost to the producing departments. In other words, it ignores the reciprocal services. The results of this procedure using the ZRIBI Manufacturing Company example are presented in Table 17.3. The following steps are taken.

Step 1. The building and grounds costs are allocated on the basis of square footage in the processing, assembly, and finishing departments. Given that the total square footage in departments P_1, P_2, and P_3 is 8,100 square feet, the allocation will be as follows:

$$\$266.67 = \left(\$600 \times \frac{3,600}{8,100} \right) \text{ is allocated to the processing department.}$$

$$\$133.36 = \left(\$600 \times \frac{1,800}{8,100} \right) \text{ is allocated to the assembly department.}$$

Table 17.2
Data for Service Department Cost Allocation Example

	Service Department		Production Department Costs			Total
	Building and Grounds	Personnel	Proc- essing	Assem- bly	Finish- ing	
	S	S	P	P	P	
	1	2	1	2	3	
Direct Department Expense Before any interdepart- ment Allocation	$600	$4,650	$1,200	$2,800	$3,000	$12,250
Proportion of Services Provided:						
a. By Building and Grounds Square Footage Served	–	900	3,600	1,800	2,700	9,000
Proportion	–	0.1	0.4	0.2	0.3	100%
b. By Personnel Number of Employees Served	800	–	3,200	2,400	1,600	8,000
Proportion	0.1	–	0.4	0.3	0.2	100%

$$\$199.99 = \left(\$600 \times \frac{2,700}{8,100} \right) \text{ is allocated to the finishing department.}$$

Step 2. The personnel service costs are allocated on the basis of the number of employees in the processing, assembly, and finishing departments. Given that the total number of employees in these departments is 7,200, the allocation will be as follows:

$$\$2,066.67 = \left(\$4,650 \times \frac{3,200}{7,200} \right) \text{ is allocated to the processing department.}$$

$$\$1,549.99 = \left(\$4,650 \times \frac{2,400}{7,200} \right) \text{ is allocated to the assembly department.}$$

Table 17.3
Direct Method of Allocation

	Building and Grounds	Personnel Services	Processing	Assembly	Finishing	Total
				Departments		
Direct Costs Before Allocation	$600	$4,650	$1,200	$2,800	$3,000	$12,250
Allocation						
1. Building and Grounds	($600)	–	$ 266.67	$133.34	$ 199.99	
2. Personnel Services	–	($4,650)	$2,066.67	$1,549.99	$1,033.34	
Total	0	0	$3,533.34	$4,483.33	$4,233.33	$12,250
Allocation Base to Apply to Production:						
Direct Labor Hours			1,000	–	–	
Machine Hours				2,000		
Units of Production					2,000	6,000
Factory Overhead Rate			$3.53334	$2.24166	$2.1166	$2.0416

$1,033.34 = \left(\$4,650 \times \frac{1,600}{7,200} \right)$ is allocated to the finishing department.

Step 3. Assuming that the allocation base to apply to production is 1,000 direct-labor hours in the processing department, 2,000 machine hours in the assembly department, and 2,000 units of production in the finishing department, Table 17.3 shows the corresponding factory overhead rate obtained by dividing the total cost of each production department after allocation by the allocation base.

If the ZRIBI Manufacturing Company used a single cost pool rather than a multiple cost pool, an allocation base of 6,000 direct-labor hours is provided, resulting in a total factory overhead rate of $2.0416 per direct-labor hour ($12,250/6,000 DLH).

17.2.5 Step-Down Allocation Method

The *step-down allocation method*, also called the allocation method or the sequential method, recognizes partially the services rendered by one service department to another. The general rule is to proceed by a sequence of allocation. There are two possible sequences: to distribute the costs of the service department with the "highest" cost first and continue the sequence in a step-by-step fashion, or to distribute the costs of the service department that provides services to the greatest number of other departments first and continue the sequence in a step-by-step fashion.

Table 17.4 uses the ZRIBI Manufacturing Company example to illustrate this method. The steps taken are as follows.

Step 1. The personnel services are allocated on the basis of the number of employees in the building and grounds, processing, assembly, and finishing departments. Given that the total number of employees served in these departments is 8,000, the allocation will be as follows:

$465 = \left(\$4,650 \times \frac{800}{8,000} \right)$ is allocated to the building and grounds department.

$1,860 = \left(\$4,650 \times \frac{3,200}{8,000} \right)$ is allocated to the processing department.

$1,395 = \left(\$4,650 \times \frac{2,400}{8,000} \right)$ is allocated to the assembly department.

$930 = \left(\$4,650 \times \frac{1,600}{8,000} \right)$ is allocated to the finishing department.

Step 2. The building and grounds costs are allocated on the basis of square footage in the processing, assembly, and finishing departments. Note that there is no further allocation made to the personnel services department. Given that the square footage of the processing, assembly, and finishing departments is 8,100

Table 17.4
Step-Down Reallocation Method

	Building and Grounds	Personnel Services	Processing	Assembly	Finishing	Total
					Departments	
Direct Costs Before Allocation	$600	$4,650	$1,200	$2,800	$3,000	$12,250
Allocation						
1. Personnel Services	$465	($4,650)	$1,860	$1,395	$ 930	
2. Buildings and Grounds	($1,065)	–	$ 473.34	$ 236.67	$ 354.99	
Total	0	0	$3,533.34	$4,431.67	$4,284.99	$12,250
Allocation Base to Apply to Production:						
Direct labor hours			1,000	–	–	6,000
Machine hours			–	2,000	–	
Units of Production			–	–	2,000	–
Factory Overhead Rate			$3.5333	$2.2158	$2.1429	$2.0416

and that the costs of the buildings and grounds are now \$1,065 (\$600 + \$465), the allocation will be as follows:

$$\$473.34 = \left(\$1,065 \times \frac{3,600}{8,100}\right) \text{ is allocated to the processing department.}$$

$$\$236.67 = \left(\$1,065 \times \frac{1,800}{8,100}\right) \text{ is allocated to the assembly department.}$$

$$\$354.99 = \left(\$1,065 \times \frac{2,700}{8,100}\right) \text{ is allocated to the finishing department.}$$

Step 3. Assuming that the allocation base to apply to production is 1,000 direct-labor hours in the processing department, 2,000 machine hours in the assembly department, and 2,000 units of production in the finishing department, Table 17.4 shows the corresponding factory overhead rate obtained by dividing the total cost of each production department after allocation by the allocation base. If the firm uses a single cost pool rather than a multiple cost pool, an allocation base of 6,000 direct-labor hours is provided, resulting in a total factory overhead rate of \$2.0416 per direct-labor hour (\$12,250/6,000 DLH).

17.2.6 Reciprocal Allocation Method

The *reciprocal allocation method,* also called the linear algebra method and the double distribution method, recognizes all the mutual services rendered by the departments. The steps of the method applied to the ZRIBI Manufacturing Company example are as follows.

Step 1. A service distribution matrix summarizing all the relationships is established as shown in Table 17.5.

Step 2. The costs for the service departments, expressing service department reciprocal relationships in linear equation form, are as follows:

Total costs = Direct costs of the service department + Costs to be allocated to the service department.

$$S_1 = \$600 + 0.1S_2,$$

$$S_2 = \$4,650 + 0.1S_1,$$

where S_1 = completed reciprocated cost of building and grounds and S_2 = completed reciprocated cost of personnel services.

By completed reciprocated cost, it is meant the actual costs incurred plus the parts of the costs of the other service departments that provided service to it. It is also termed the *artificial cost* of the service department.

Table 17.5
Service Distribution Matrix

Costs	Producing Departments			Service Departments		Costs to be Allocated	Allocation Base
	Process-ing P 1	Assem-bly P 2	Finish-ing P 3	Build-ings and Grounds S 1	Person-nel Services S 2		
Buildings and Grounds (S_1)	0.4	0.2	0.3	—	0.1	$ 600	Square Footage
Personnel Services (S_2)	0.4	0.3	0.2	0.1	—	$4,650	Number of Employees

Step 3. Solving the system of linear equations will yield the results for S_1 and S_2 as follows:

$$S_2 = \$4,650 + 0.1\ (\$600 + 0.1\ S_2),$$
$$S_2 = \$4,650 + \$60 + 0.01\ S_2,$$
$$S_2 - 0.01S_2 = \$4,650 + \$60,$$
$$0.99\ S = \$4,710,$$

and

$$S_2 = \frac{\$4,710}{0.99} = \$4,757.57.$$

Therefore,

$$S_1 = \$600 + 0.1S_2 = \$600 + 0.1\ (\$4,757.57)$$

and

$$S_1 = \$1,075.757.$$

Step 4. Using the results obtained in steps 1, 2, and 3, the following normal equations, expressing the relationships between the service and producing departments, are established as follows:

$$P_1 = 0.4S_1 + 0.4S_2,$$
$$P_2 = 0.2S_1 + 0.3S_2,$$

and

$$P_3 = 0.3S_1 + 0.2S_2,$$

or

$$P_1 = 0.4(\$1,075.757) + 0.4(\$4,757.57) = \$2,333.33,$$
$$P_2 = 0.2(\$1,075.757) + 0.3(\$4,757.57) = \$1,642.4,$$

and

$$P_3 = 0.3(\$1,075.757) + 0.2(\$4,757.57) = \$1,274.3.$$

Table 17.6
Reciprocal Allocation Method

	Departments					
	Buildings and Grounds	Personnel Services	Processing	Assembly	Finishing	Total
Direct Costs Before Allocation	$ 600	$4,650	$1,200	$2,800	$3,000	$12,250
Allocation						
1. Buildings and Equipment	($1,075.57)	$ 107.55	$ 430.22	$ 215.11	$ 322.67	
2. Personnel Services	($ 475.75)	($4,757.57)	$1,903.02	$1,427.27	$ 951.51	
Total	0	0	$3,533.25	$4,442.38	$4,274.18	$12,250
Allocation Base to Apply to Production						
Direct Labor Hours			1,000	–	–	6,000
Machine Hours			–	2,000	–	
Units of Production			–	–	2,000	
Factory Overhead Rate			$3.5332	$2.2211	$2.1370	$2.0416

Step 5. The final results in the allocation of service department costs to producing departments appear in Table 17.6.

17.3 SEGMENT PERFORMANCE AND THE CONTRIBUTION APPROACH TO COST ALLOCATION

The determination of segment performance may require the allocation of the income statement items of a company as a whole to the various segments of the company. To facilitate such an allocation and emphasize cost behavioral patterns, a contribution approach can be used. Table 17.7 illustrates the contribution approach to segment performance. This approach differentiates between the allocation of items that vary with the activity level and those that do not.

First, the allocation of revenues, variable costs, and the contribution margin to the various segments is accomplished in a straightforward manner on the basis of the activity level of each segment. The contribution margin of each segment is a first performance evaluation measure that can be used to assess the impact of changes in the level of activity on the segments' income.

Second, the fixed costs can be divided into those controllable and those not controllable by the segments' managers, and the fixed costs considered controllable by the division can be easily traced to the segments. A second performance evaluation measure, the contribution controllable by the managers of the segments, can be obtained by deducting the fixed controllable costs from the contribution margin. This measure may be helpful in assessing the performance of the segment's managers by focusing only on the revenues and expenses items that are controllable by the managers.

Third, assuming that the fixed costs controllable by persons other than the segments' managers can be traced to the various segments, a third performance evaluation measure can be obtained by deducting the fixed costs controllable by others from the contribution controllable by the managers. This measure may be helpful in assessing the performance of the segments rather than of the segment's managers.

Finally, there may be some fixed costs, such as general company costs, that cannot be easily traced and allocated to the various segments. Allocating such costs may be difficult, arbitrary, and "incorrigible."

17.4 BEHAVIORAL CONSIDERATIONS IN COST ALLOCATION

Internal decisions, such as the decision to produce various joint products or the extent of their processing, are not dependent on any allocation method but on a comparison between the incremental revenues and the incremental costs. However, if accountants continue to allocate and base decisions on the results of the methods, it will merely lead to incorrect decision making. Thomas has constantly argued that most joint cost allocation approaches generate dysfunctional deci-

Table 17.7
The Contribution Approach to Segment Performance

| | Company as a Whole | Region | | Division | | | |
		Region A	Region B	Division I	Division II	Division III	Division IV
1. Net Sales	$100,000	$60,000	$40,000	$24,000	$36,000	$8,000	$32,000
2. Variable Manufacturing Cost of Sales	60,000	36,000	24,000	14,400	21,600	4,800	19,200
3. Manufacturing Contribution Margin	$ 40,000	$24,000	$16,000	$ 9,600	$14,400	$3,200	$12,800
4. Variable Selling and Administrative Costs	10,000	6,000	4,000	2,400	3,600	1,000	3,000
5. Contribution Margin	$ 30,000	$18,000	$12,000	$ 7,200	$10,800	$2,200	$ 9,800
6. Fixed Costs Controllable by Segment Managers	10,000	6,000	4,000	3,000	3,000	1,000	3,000
7. Contribution Controllable by Segment Managers	$ 20,000	$12,000	$ 8,000	$ 4,200	$ 7,800	$1,200	$ 6,800
8. Fixed Costs Controllable by Others	6,000	3,600	2,400	2,000	1,600	400	2,000
9. Contribution by Segments	$ 14,000	$ 8,400	$ 5,600	$ 2,200	$ 6,200	$ 800	$ 4,800
10. Unallocated Costs	4,000	—	—	—	—	—	—
11. Income before Income Taxes	$ 10,000						

sions, confuse decision makers, or are otherwise perverse.[10] As an alternative, he suggests devising allocation methods that are neutral or "sterilized" with respect to a particular decision:

Although a sterilized allocation is preferable to one that potentially generates poor decisions, it would be even better to make no allocation at all. Decision makers would be no worse off, accounting efforts would be slightly reduced, and the dangers of inappropriately employing the allocation in a context where it was not sterilized would be eliminated. Sterilized allocations, therefore, should be employed only in situations where decisions are better made from allocation-free data, but institutions compel allocations to be made or decision makers insist upon thinking in terms of allocated data. . . . Otherwise potentially obnoxious allocations can be rendered harmless if we know exactly what will be done with them. But the best that can be said of a sterilized allocation is that in some circumstances it will be entirely ineffectual.[11]

Thus, given that a joint cost allocation method cannot be sterilized for all kinds of decisions and that joint cost allocations will continue to be made to provide management control data and/or expense measurement, the cost accountant's main concern should be to determine how cost allocation can be used to motivate users. A. G. Hopwood states:

For however sophisticated the procedures of management accounting may be, and they are continually getting more sophisticated, their fundamental rationale always remains behavioral in nature. The accountant contributes to the success of an enterprise primarily by the way in which he influences the behavior of other people and, at least in theory, his procedures should be designed to stimulate managers and employees to behave in a manner which is likely to contribute to the effectiveness of the enterprise as a whole.[12]

Allocation methods should be chosen with concern for the motivational dimension present in any allocation that affects financial performance. In short, the allocation method should be behavior congruent with respect to a particular decision. If it is behavior congruent with respect to more than one decision, it is a welcome case of multiple congruence.

The problem of how a behavior-congruent allocation method should be chosen is in need of empirical evidence. Among the rare suggestions in the literature are those of G. Bodnar and E. J. Lusk.

We suggest that management would a priori specify a set of performance measures, a set of bases for cost allocation and an allocation criteria functional, such as fairness or ability to bear. During the period, data concerning performance and activity relative to the set of allocation bases would be accumulated. Alternative cost allocations then would be generated based on activity statistics. The specific allocation scheme would be selected ex post based on a review of subunit performance relative to the allocation criteria functional.[13]

In other words, they suggest that subunit activity be evaluated as it affects particular nonfinancial measures of performance. This evaluation then leads to the cost allocation scheme.

17.5 CONCLUSION

Accounting for overhead requires three steps: cost distribution, cost allocation, and cost application. This chapter examined the cost allocation problem, namely, the allocation of service department costs. It presented three basic procedures: the direct reallocation method, the step-down allocation method, and the reciprocal allocation method.

NOTES

1. W. J. Vatter, "Limitations of Overhead Allocation." *Accounting Review* (April 1945): 163–176.
2. A. L. Thomas, *Studies in Accounting Research No. 3,* "The Allocation Problem in Financial Accounting Theory." (Sarasota, Fla.: American Accounting Association, 1969); A. L. Thomas, *Studies in Accounting Research No. 9,* "The Allocation Problem: Part 2." (Sarasota, Fla: American Accounting Association, 1974).
3. See J. Bedingfield and L. Rosen, *Government Contract Accounting* (Washington, D.C.: Federal Publications, Inc., 1985), 7.13.
4. Robin Cooper and Robert S. Kaplan, "How Cost Accounting Distorts Product Costs," *Management Accounting* (April 1988): 21.
5. Ibid., 24.
6. Ibid., 23.
7. A. Seed, "Cost Accounting in the Age of Robotics." *Management Accounting* (October 1984): 39–43.
8. G. Hakala, "Measuring Costs with Machine Hours." *Management Accounting* (October 1985): 57–61.
9. Anthony A. Atkinson, "Diagnosing Costing Problems." *CMA Magazine* (April 1989): 20.
10. A. L. Thomas, *A Behavioral Analysis of Joint-Cost Allocation and Transfer Pricing* (Champaign, Ill.: Stipes, 1980), 9.
11. Thomas, *Studies in Accounting Research No. 9,* 46.
12. A. G. Hopwood, *Accounting and Human Behavior* (Englewood Cliffs, N.J.: Prentice-Hall, 1976), xiv.
13. G. Bodnar and E. J. Lusk, "Motivational Considerations in Cost Allocation Systems: A Conditioning Theory Approach." *Accounting Review* (October 1977): 860.

SELECTED READINGS

Baker, Kenneth R., and Robert E. Taylor. "A Linear Programming Framework for Cost Allocation and External Acquisition When Reciprocal Services Exist." *Accounting Review* (October 1979).

Bentz, William. "Computed Extended Reciprocal Allocation Methods." *Accounting Review* (July 1979).

Bodnar, G., and E. J. Lusk. "Motivational Considerations in Cost Allocation Systems: A Conditioning Theory Approach." *Accounting Review* (October 1977).

Bost, Patricia James. "Do Cost Accounting Standards Fill a Gap in Cost Allocation?" *Management Accounting* (November 1968): 34–36.

Capettini, Robert, and Gerald L. Salamon. "Internal Versus External Acquisition of Services When Reciprocal Services Exist." *Accounting Review* (July 1977).

Churchill, Neil. "Linear Algebra and Cost Allocations: Some Examples." *Accounting Review* (October 1964).

Wright, Michael A., and John W. Jones. "Material Burdening: Management Accounting Can Support Competitive Strategy." *Management Accounting* (August 1987): 27–31.

Zimmerman, Jerold L. "The Costs and Benefits of Cost Allocation." *Accounting Review* (July 1979): 501–521.

Cost Allocation: Part II

Chapter 17 examined the methods and issues connected with the allocation of service department costs to producing departments. This chapter continues the examination of cost allocation by considering the methods and issues associated with the allocation of joint costs to joint products and accounting for by-products.

18.1 ACCOUNTING FOR COMMON PRODUCT COSTS

In most of the cases, considered in chapter 17, the inputs were associated either directly or indirectly with a single output. In the other possible cases where the manufacturing process yields more than one particular output, the problem of the common product costs, or joint costs, arises: For financial accounting purposes, the joint costs are the costs of a single process that yields two or more products. They are basically *indivisible costs* and must be allocated to each of the outputs, usually called *joint products*. A classic example of common product costs is the cost of copper ore, which may contain gold, copper, zinc, and silver in different amounts. What cost should be allocated to each of these products? Figure 18.1 illustrates the common product costs, the joint products, and the *by-products*. The costs of copper ore are *common costs* (*joints costs*) up to a separation point (*split-off point*), where additional costs (*separable costs*) are incurred to generate the identifiable products (in this case gold, copper, zinc, and silver). These separable costs are sometimes referred to as *specific costs*.

Although both joint products and by-products are generated by the same process, for accounting purposes they are distinguished on the basis of their relative sales value. The joint product is used to identify products having significant sales values and quantities (in other words, products that are commercially viable). By-products are products that in a given, specific situation have low sales value in comparison to the other joint products. In the example illustrated in Figure 18.1, gold can be considered a by-product, while copper, silver, and zinc are joint products.

Industries where common product costs exist include the chemicals, tobacco manufacturing, petroleum, meat packing, copper mining, fruit and vegetable canning, lumber milling, dairy, coal mining, flour milling, coke manufacturing,

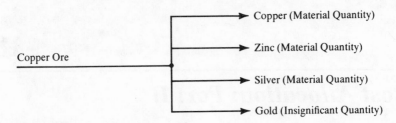

Figure 18.1
Example of Common Product Costs

and many other industries for which joint costs must be allocated to establish the unit cost of their products. In all these cases, the joint costs must be allocated on a justifiable and acceptable base given the impact of such allocation on inventory valuation and income determination. The reasons for allocating joint costs to individual products and services include the following:

1. The need to value inventory and compute the cost of goods sold for external reporting, tax reporting compliances, and internal reporting

2. The need for correct figures in cost reimbursement under contracts where only part of the jointly produced products are sold or delivered to a single customer

3. Compliance with rate regulation if only a subset of the jointly produced products is subject to price regulation.[1]

18.2 JOINT PRODUCT COSTING

Joint product costs are equal to the sum of the costs incurred in a single manufacturing process or in a series of processes that simultaneously yield two or more products of significant sales values and quantities. They include all costs incurred up to the point of separation of the joint products, or split-off point. For inventory valuation and income determination purposes, the question arises as to what amount of the joint product costs should be allocated to each of the individual joint products. Note again that the joint product costs cannot be physically identified or traced to any of the individual products, since the joint products were not separated before the split-off point. Nevertheless, the accountant is responsible for allocating the joint product costs to each of the joint products so ending inventories can be costed and income determined.

Several procedures exist in both the literature and in practice for the allocation of the joint costs to the individual products. The most popular are the following:

1. *Allocation by physical measure* (average unit cost method and weighted average method)

2. *Allocation by relative sales value*

3. *Allocation by relative net realizable value.*

Other approaches identified in the literature deserve consideration and will also be presented.

The following example will be used to illustrate the procedures for the allocation of the joint product costs:

King Kong Company, January 19X3

Joint Costs	$30,000
Joint Products: Unit Output (Sales)	
King	2,000 Units
Kong	4,000 Units
Selling Price at the Split-off Point	
King	$ 4.00
Kong	$ 0.50
Additional Processing Costs per Unit	
King	$ 2.00
Kong	$ 3.00
Selling Price	
King	$ 12.00
Kong	$ 7.00
Joint Products: Weights	
King	2 Pounds
Kong	4 Pounds

18.2.1 Allocation by Physical Measure

The method of *allocation by physical measure* consists of allocating the joint costs on the basis of some unit of measure. In the King Kong example, the joint costs can be allocated on the basis of the units of output or on the basis of the weight of output. The first method will be labeled the *average unit cost method* and the second, the *weighted average method*.

Under the average unit cost method, the $30,000 joint costs are allocated on the basis of the 6,000 units produced, or a unit cost of $5 per unit. The costs allocated are $10,000 to King and $20,000 to Kong, with the following results:

Products	Units of Output	Percentage of Quantity (Units of Output ÷ Total Output)	Cost Allocation (% × Joint Cost)	Unit Cost (Allocation ÷ Output)
King	2,000	33.33%	$10,000	$5
Kong	4,000	66.66	20,000	$5
	6,000	100%	$30,000	

The average unit cost method does not always provide adequate results in cases where the joint products cannot be measured by the same basic measurement unit or where the products differ in terms of other factors such as weight, size, and so forth. In the King Kong example, since the joint products differ in size, a weighted average method may be more acceptable. Using this method, the $30,000 joint costs are allocated on the basis of a weight of output to 20,000 pounds. The costs allocated are $6,000 to King and $24,000 to Kong. The results are obtained as follows:

Products	Units of Output	Weight (Weight × Output), in Pounds	Percentage of Weight	Cost Allocation	Unit Cost
King	2,000	4,000	20%	$ 6,000	$3
Kong	4,000	16,000	80	24,000	$6
	6,000	20,000	100%	$30,000	

18.2.2 Allocation by Relative Sales Value

The most popular allocation method in practice is the method that allocates the joint costs on the basis of the market value at the split-off point. The rationale is based on the choice of a revenue-generating power criteria. In the King Kong example, the $30,000 joint product costs are allocated on the basis of a $10,000 market value. The costs are allocated as $24,000 to King and $6,000 to Kong, with these results:

Products	Units of Output	Selling Price at Split-off Point	Market Value	Percentage of Market Value	Cost Allocation	Unit Cost
King	2,000	$4.00	$ 8,000	80%	·$24,000	$12.00
Kong	4,000	$0.50	2,000	20	6,000	$ 1.50
	6,000		$10,000	100%	$30,000	

18.2.3 Allocation by Net Realizable Value or Estimated Net Realizable Value Method

Assuming that the selling prices at the split-off point are not available and that additional processing costs beyond the split-off point are needed to bring the joint products into salable form, the acceptable alternative to the allocation by relative sales value method is allocation by net realizable value. This method consists of determining the approximate market values of the joint products at the split-off point. Take the sales price of the final products at the point of sale and deduct the additional processing costs to approximate the sales prices at the split-off point. In the King Kong example, the $30,000 joint product costs are allocated on the basis of a total net realizable value of $20,000. The costs are allocated as $16,667 to King and $13,333 to Kong, and the results obtained are as follows:

Products	Units of Output	Net Realizable Value per Unit	Total Net Realizable Value	Percentage of Net Realizable Value	Cost Allocation	Unit Cost
King	2,000	(12 − 2) = $10	$20,000	55.56%	$16,667	$8.33
Kong	4,000	(7 − 3) = $ 4	16,000	44.44	13,333	$3.33
	6,000		$36,000	100.00%	$30,000	

The following product line income statement results from the use of the net realizable value method of allocation:

	Total	King	Kong
Sales	$52,000	$24,000	$28,000
Cost of Goods Sold[a]			
Joint Cost	30,000	16,667	13,333
Separable Costs	16,000	4,000	12,000
Total Cost of Goods Sold	$46,000	$20,667	$25,333
Gross Margin	$ 6,000	$ 3,333	$ 2,667
Gross Margin Percentage	11.54%	13.88%	9.52%

[a]It is assumed that there are no inventories.

The unit cost of each of the joint products will differ from one allocation procedure to another, as shown in Table 18.1. These differences will ultimately

Table 18.1
Results of the Allocation Procedures for Products

	King	Kong
1st Weight		
Joint Cost	$ 3	$6.00
Add Separable Costs	2	3.00
	$ 5	$9.00
2nd Units		
Joint Cost	$ 5	$5.00
Add Separable Costs	2	3.00
	$ 7	$8.00
3rd Selling Price at Split-off		
Joint Cost	$12	$1.50
Add Separable Costs	2	3.00
	$14	$4.50
4th Net Realizable Value		
Joint Costs	$ 9	$3.00
Add Separable Costs	2	3.00
	$11	$6.00

result in different product values for inventory valuation and income determination. However, these differences in unit costs are not important for decision making, namely, for cost planning and control problems.[2]

18.2.4 Net Allocation by Overall Margin

Allocation by net realizable value can be criticized on the basis of its implicit assumption that the profit margin can be attributed entirely to the joint products without considering the separable costs. *Allocation by overall margin* is sometimes advocated as a method that corrects for this suggested anomaly. This procedure, also known as the constant gross margin percentage net realizable value method, allocates joint costs so that the overall gross margin percentage is equal to each individual product. First, under this procedure, the gross margin percentage for the total firm is computed. Second, the total cost that corresponds to each individual product is computed by applying the overall gross margin percentage to the sales of the individual products. Third, the joint cost assigned to each individual product is computed by deducting the separable costs from the total costs obtained in the second step. The overall margin method is used with the King Kong example in Table 18.2. When there is more than one split-off point, the net realizable value method may not be sufficient to perform all required cost allocations.

Table 18.2
Overall Margin Method

	Total	King	Kong
Sales	$52,000	$24,000	$28,000
minus Overall Gross Margin Percentage (11.54%)	6,000	2,769	3,231
equals Total Cost	$46,000	$21,231	$24,769
minus Separable Costs	16,000	4,000	12,000
equals Joint Costs	$30,000	$17,231	$12,769

18.2.5 Allocation by Cost Savings

In some cases, the products or services obtained through the incurrence of a joint cost could also be directly obtained by the incurrence of a separable cost. In other words, joint costs can be incurred to effect cost savings. In such a case, Shane Moriarity suggests *allocation by cost savings*.[3] He proposes the following procedures:

1. The costs that would be incurred if the products or services were obtained independently are summed. Assume they are represented by Σy_i.

2. The costs that would be incurred if the products or services were obtained jointly are also summed. Assume they are represented by X.

3. The cost savings arising from the incurrence of a joint cost rather than the incurrence of separable costs are computed. Assume they are represented by $\Sigma y_i - X$.

4. The cost of each individual product or service will be equal to y_i less some allocation of the savings ($\Sigma y_i - X$).

Moriarity suggests that this allocation may be proportional to the costs incurred to produce the products independently rather than jointly (that is, $y_i / \Sigma y_i$). Accordingly, the joint costs allocated to each product or service will be

$$y_i - \frac{y_i}{\Sigma y_i} (\Sigma y_i - X).$$

As an example, consider a company employing a consulting firm that has been charging $10,000 per year to provide advice to the accounting department and $5,000 per year to provide advice to the marketing department. It has been suggested that an in-house consulting department could provide the same services for a total cost of $13,500. Using Moriarity's alternative, calculations yield the following results:

Cost of consulting services purchased separately = $\Sigma y_i = \$15,000$

Cost of consulting services purchased jointly = $X = \$13,500$

Cost savings from joint purchase = $\Sigma y_i - X = \$1,500$.

Allocation to the accounting department would be

$$y_i - \frac{y_i}{\Sigma y_i} (\Sigma y_i - X).$$

$$\$10,000 - \frac{10,000}{15,000} (\$1,500) = \$9,000.$$

Allocation to the marketing department would be

$$y_i - \frac{y_i}{\Sigma y_i} (\Sigma y_i - X).$$

$$\$5,000 - \frac{5,000}{15,000} (\$1,500) = \$4,500.$$

The approach suggested by Moriarity fails to distinguish internal incremental costs from internal joint costs. A method proposed by J. G. Louderback explicitly considers the existence of incremental costs involved in providing a good or service internally, as well as joint costs. Hence "the departments (or any other segments, products, etc.) are charged with the incremental costs to provide the service internally plus a portion of the joint costs based on the *differences* between the incremental costs of buying the service outside and providing it internally. The result is that the total cost charged to the department is always equal or greater than the incremental cost to provide it inside and less than the incremental cost to buy the service outside."[4]

The formula for joint cost allocation under Louderback's approach is

$$(O_i - I_i) \div (\Sigma O_i - \Sigma I_i) \times JC,$$

where

JC = total joint cost

O_i = incremental cost outside for segment i

I_i = incremental cost inside for segment i.

To illustrate Louderback's approach, assume the same facts used for Moriarity's approach, except that there are joint costs of $6,500 involved in creating an in-house consulting department and incremental costs of $5,000 and $2,000 for the accounting and marketing departments, respectively. This makes the total cost $13,500 to provide the consulting service internally, which is the same as in the earlier example.

Under Louderback's approach, the allocation would be as follows:

Department	O_i	I_i	$O_i - I_i$	$\dfrac{O_i - I_i}{\Sigma O_i - \Sigma I_i} \times$ Joint Cost	Joint Cost Allocation
Accounting	$10,000	$5,000	$5,000	⅝ × $6,500	$4,062.50 + $5,000 = $ 9,062.50
Marketing	5,000	2,000	3,000	⅜ × $6,500	$2,437.50 + $2,000 = $ 4,437.50
	$15,000	$7,000	$8,000		$6,500.00 + $7,000 = $13,500.00

18.3 BY-PRODUCT COSTING

As stated earlier, by-products are identifiable products that, in a given situation, have low sales value in comparison to the sales value of the joint products. In accounting for by-products, a common problem relates to timing the recognition of revenues and expenses. There are two principal methods of accounting for by-products: *a revenue method* (wherein no cost is generally assigned to the by-product with any by-product benefits deferred to the period of sale) and *an asset recognition method* (wherein by-products are recorded at their estimated net realizable value with a concomitant recognition of by-product benefits in the period of production).

The revenue methods include the following:

1. By-product revenue is recognized as other revenue.

2. By-product revenue is recognized as other income.
3. By-product revenue is recognized as a deduction from the cost of production.

The asset recognition methods include the following:

1. The net realizable value of the by-product sold at the separation point is recognized as a deduction from the cost of goods sold. The net realizable value of the by-product sold is equal to the by-product revenue less separable costs incurred.
2. The net realizable value of the by-product produced at the separation point is recognized as a deduction from the cost of production. The net realizable value of the by-products produced is equal to the by-product revenues less separable costs incurred and to be incurred.

These methods are illustrated in Table 18.3. The variations in the net profits arising from the use of these methods should not be considered an important problem. First, these results tend to disappear in the long run, assuming equality

Table 18.3
Accounting Methods for By-Products

Accounting Methods / Income Statement	By-product Revenue Recognized as				Net Realizable Value Recognized as	
	Other Revenue	Other Income	Deduction from Cost of Goods Sold	Deduction from Cost of Production	Deduction from Cost of Goods Sold	Deduction from Cost of Production
Sales from Major Products	$ 20,000	$ 20,000	$ 20,000	$ 20,000	$ 20,000	$ 20,000
Revenue from By-products	1,000					
Total Revenue	$ 21,000	$ 20,000	$ 20,000	$ 20,000	$ 20,000	$ 20,000
Cost of Goods Sold						
Beginning Inventory	—	—	—	—	—	—
Production Costs	10,000	10,000	10,000	10,000	10,000	10,000
Revenue from By-products				(1,000)		
Net Realizable Value Produced						(600)
Ending Inventory	(5,000)	(5,000)	(5,000)	(5,000)	(5,000)	(5,000)
Cost of Goods Sold	$ 5,000	$ 5,000	$ 5,000	$ 4,000	$ 5,000	$ 4,400
Revenue from By-product			(1,000)			
Net Realizable Value Sold					(500)	
Gross Margin	16,000	15,000	16,000	16,000	15,500	15,600
Other Income		1,000				
Net Income	$ 16,000	$ 16,000	$ 16,000	$ 16,000	$ 15,500	$ 15,600

Main Product	**By-product**
Production = 1,000 units	Production = 1,200 units
Sales = 500 units	Sales = 1,000 units
Unit Cost = $10	Sales Price = $1
Sales Price = $40	Separable Cost Incurred per Unit = $.5

between production and sales. Second, by definition, by-products are minor products with an immaterial impact on management decisions.

18.4 JOINT PRODUCTS AND DECISION MAKING

The preceding discussion centered on the problem of joint product allocation as it relates to the inventory valuation needed for income and balance sheet determinations. Information on joint products is also needed for making at least two types of internal decisions:

1. An output decision involves the impact that increases or decreases in the output of joint products have on total cost and profit. Examples are the decision to expand or discontinue total production and the determination of the most profitable mix of jointly produced products. Output decisions vary according to whether the joint products are produced in fixed or variable proportions.
2. A depth-of-processing decision involves whether to sell a joint product at the split-off point or to process it further.

18.4.1 Fixed Proportion Output Decisions

Where joint products are produced in fixed proportions,[5] increases or decreases in the volume of one product affect the volume of the other product. Product mix, therefore, is beyond management control, and the allocation of joint costs is irrelevant to internal decision making. In fact, output decisions should rest on a comparison between the total joint products revenue less the total joint costs and additional processing costs beyond the split-off point.

As an example, suppose a firm makes two products (X and Y) from a raw material that costs $4 per pound. Every 20 pounds of this raw material will yield 12 pounds of product X and 8 pounds of product Y after the incurrence of a joint cost of $14. Additional separable costs of $3 per pound of product X and $4 per pound of product Y are required after the split-off point.

Using these data, only the costs of making both products X and Y can be determined, rather than the individual cost of either product X or product Y. Hence, the costs of producing 12 pounds of product X and 8 pounds of product Y are as follows:

Raw Material Cost (20 Pounds at $4)	$80
Joint Cost	14
Separable Cost of Product X (12 Pounds at $3)	36
Separable Cost of Product Y (8 Pounds at $4)	32
Total	$162

On the basis of this information, the following results can be obtained:

1. If the revenues from the sale of both products X and Y are higher than $162, both products X and Y should be produced.

2. If the revenues from the sale of product X are higher than $130, product X should be produced. Product Y should be produced only if revenues from the sale of product Y exceed $32.

3. If the revenues from the sale of product Y are higher than $126, product Y should be produced. Product X should be produced if the revenues from the sale of product X exceed $36.

4. If the revenues from the sale of both products X and Y are less than $130 for each product and less than $162 for both products, neither product X nor product Y should be produced.

18.4.2 Variable Proportion Output Decisions

There are two cases in practice where the proportions in which joint products are produced could be variable: (1) when the proportion produced of each product is *materials determined* (depends on the quality or composition of the joint material input) and (2) when the proportion produced of each product is *process determined* (depends on the changes in the processing methods used).[6] In both cases, output decisions rest on a comparison between the total cost differentials and the total sales differentials for each alternative product mix considered.

To illustrate, suppose a firm produces two products (X and Y) from a single process. Products X and Y sell for $10 a pound and $6 a pound, respectively. The processing method used yields ratios of 20 percent product X and 80 percent product Y. Another processing method can also be used that yields 80 percent product X and 20 percent product Y. The new processing method results in a total cost of $80. The application of the new processing method is equivalent to exchanging 60 pounds of product Y plus $80 for 20 pounds of product X. To determine the desirability of the new processing method, proceed with the following comparison:

Revenues after Processing		
Product X (60 Pounds at $10)		$600
Product Y (20 Pounds at $ 6)		120
Total		$720
Less: Processing Cost	$80	
Market Value of Product Y Processing (80 Pounds times $6)	480	560
Incremental Profit		$160

Put another way, the new processing method results in an incremental cost of another 60 pounds of product X at a processing cost of $80 plus the $360 sales value of the 60 pounds of product Y lost by the application of the new process, or $440, which is lower than the $600 incremental revenues generated by the additional 60 pounds of product X.

As H. Nurnberg notes:

Thus, where increasing the production of one joint product has no effect on the production
of the others, the incremental revenues should exceed the incremental costs: and where
increasing the production of one joint product causes a reduction in the production of
others, the incremental revenues of the former should exceed the sum of the incremental
costs of the former and the net decremental revenues of the latter.[7]

18.4.3 Depth-of-Processing Decisions

The allocation of joint product costs is used for inventory valuation, which is
necessary for both balance sheet and income determination. However, the choice
of any allocation technique and the results obtained should not influence the
decision making process in any way. In decisions regarding whether a product
should be sold at the split-off point or processed further, joint costs are irrelevant.
They have already been incurred prior to the decision and, therefore, constitute
sunk costs. The only information relevant to the decisions are the incremental
revenues and the incremental costs (including the cost of capital) from the additional processing. In general, the decision should be to process further if the
incremental revenue exceeds the incremental costs.

To illustrate, return to the King Kong example and assume that the company is
faced with the decision of selling Kong at $7 per unit or processing it further into
a more refined product (Pong) selling at $10 per unit. In such a case, 44,000
units of Pong would be produced at an additional cost of $10,000. To solve this
problem, proceed in three stages.

Stage 1. Show that joint cost allocations are not only irrelevant but may lead to
inconsistent results. For example, while the weighted average method shows a
loss, the net realizable value method shows a profit:

By Weighted Average		By Net Realizable Value	
Sales (4,000 × $10)	$40,000		$40,000
Joint Cost ($12,000 + $24,000)	$36,000	($12,000 + $13,333)	$25,333
Incremental Cost	10,000		10,000
Total Cost	$46,000		$35,333
Profit (Loss)	$(6,000)		$ 4,667

Stage 2. The incremental analysis is as follows:

Incremental Revenue (4,000 × $3)	$12,000
Incremental Cost	10,000
Incremental Profit	$ 2,000

As long as the incremental revenue exceeds the incremental cost by $2,000,
Kong should be processed further into Pong.

Stage 3. Opportunity costs can be introduced into the analysis as follows:

Product Pong Revenues (4,000 × $10)	$40,000
Incremental Cost	$10,000
Opportunity Cost Resulting from	
Not Selling Kong (4,000 × $7)	28,000
Total Cost	$38,000
Difference	$ 2,000

The positive difference between Pong revenues and the total cost (including the opportunity costs) again shows that Kong should be processed further.

18.5 JOINT PRODUCTS AND FEDERAL INCOME TAX LAWS AND REGULATIONS

The federal income tax laws and regulations are rather broad in attempting to resolve the joint cost problem. The most relevant statement is section 1,471-7 of the Internal Revenue Code, which states the following:

Inventories of miners and manufacturers. A taxpayer engaged in mining or manufacturing who by a single process or uniform series of processes derives a product of two or more kinds, sizes, or grades the unit cost of which is substantially alike, and who in conformity to a recognized trade practice allocates an amount of cost to each kind, size, or grade of product, which in the aggregate will absorb the total cost of production, may, with the consent of the Commissioner use such allocated cost as a basis for pricing inventories, provided such allocation bears a reasonable relation to the respective selling values of the different kinds, sizes, or grades of a product.

Although this regulation implies the required use of only the relative sales value method, the weighted average cost method has been used effectively under some circumstances. The regulations say that (1) the relative sales value is the suggested method "in conformity to a recognized trade practice . . . with the consent of the Commissioner" and (2) other methods can be proposed to the commissioner to decide whether they will be allowed.

18.6 CONCLUSION

Joint cost allocation is used to allocate the joint or common costs to the joint products produced from a common process and using a common input. Various methods are presented in this book. They are to be used for producing "numbers" useful or needed for external reporting. Their use for decision making is not recommended as cell costs allocations are arbitrary and incorrigible.

NOTES

1. J. Crespi and J. Harris, "Joint Cost Allocation under the Natural Gas Act: An Historical Review." *Journal of Extractive Industries Accounting* (Summer 1983): 133–142.

2. Franklin Laventhol, "Multiple Splitoff Points." *Issues in Accounting Education* (Fall 1986): 302–308.

3. Shane Moriarity, "Another Approach to Allocating Joint Costs: A Comment." *Accounting Review* (October 1975): 791–795.

4. J. G. Louderback, "Another Approach to Allocating Joint Costs: A Comment," *Accounting Review* (July 1976): 683–685.

5. H. Bierman, Jr., and T. R. Dyckman, *Managerial Cost Accounting,* 2d ed. (New York: Macmillan, 1976), 173–174.

6. G. Shillinglaw, *Cost Accounting: Analysis and Control* (Homewood, Ill.: Irwin, 1972), 243–244.

7. H. Nurnberg, "Joint and By-Product Costs," in *Handbook of Cost Accounting,* ed. S. Davidson and R. L. Weil (New York: McGraw-Hill, 1978), chap. 18.

SELECTED READINGS

Ayres, Frances L. "Models of Coalition Formation, Reward Allocation and Accounting Cost Allocations: A Review and Synthesis." *Journal of Accounting Literature* (Spring 1985): 1.

Balachandran, Bala V., and Ram T. S. Ramakrishnan. "Joint Cost Allocation: A Unified Approach." *Accounting Review* 56 no. 1 (January 1981): 85–96.

Barton, M. Frank, and J. David Spiceland. "Joint Cost Allocation as a Principal Cost Control Strategy." *Production and Inventory Management* (Second Quarter 1987): 117–122.

Biddle, Gary C., and Richard Steinberg. "Allocations of Joint and Common Costs." *Journal of Accounting Literature* 3 (Spring 1984): 185–196.

Cats-Baril, William L., James F. Gatti, and D. Jacques Grinnell. "Joint Product Costing in the Semiconductor Industry." *Management Accounting* (February 1986): 28–35.

Cohen, Susan I., and Martin Loeb. "Public Goods, Common Inputs, and the Efficiency of Full Cost Allocations." *Accounting Review* (April 1982): 336.

Crespi, J., and J. Harris. "Joint Cost Allocation under the Natural Gas Act: A Historical Review." *Journal of Extractive Industries Accounting* (Summer 1983): 133–142.

Dudick, Thomas S. "How to Avoid Some Common Pitfalls in Accounting Inventory." *Practical Accountant* (November 1982): 67–73.

Fertakis, John P. "Responsibility Accounting for By-Products and Industrial Wastes." *Journal of Accountancy* (May 1986): 138–147.

Louderback, J. G. "Another Approach to Allocating Joint Costs: A Comment." *Accounting Review* (July 1976): 683–685.

Moriarity, Shane. "Another Approach to Allocating Joint Costs." *Accounting Review* (October 1975): 791–795.

Nurnberg, H. "Joint and By-Product Costs," in *Handbook of Cost Accounting,* eds. S. Davidson and R. L. Weil (New York: McGraw-Hill, 1978), chap. 18.

Thomas, A. L. *A Behavioral Analysis of Joint-Cost Allocation and Transfer Pricing.* (Champaign, Ill.: Stipes, 1980).

Thomas, A. L. *Studies in Accounting Research No. 9,* "The Allocation Problem: Part Two" (Sarasota, Fla.: American Accounting Association, 1974).

Weil, R. L. Jr. "Allocating Joint Costs," *American Economic Review* (December 1968): 1342–1345.

Index

About the Author

AHMED BELKAOUI is Professor of Accounting at the University of Illinois at Chicago. His 13 previous books with Quorum include *Judgement in International Accounting* (1990), *The Coming Crisis in Accounting* (1989), and *Behavioral Accounting* (1989).